THOMAS   H.   STONER   JR.

SMALL CHANGE,
BIG GAINS

• • •

REFLECTIONS OF AN ENERGY ENTREPRENEUR

GREENLEAF
BOOK GROUP PRESS

Published by Greenleaf Book Group Press
Austin, Texas
www.gbgpress.com

Distributed by Greenleaf Book Group LLC

For ordering information or special discounts for bulk purchases, please contact Greenleaf Book Group LLC at PO Box 91869, Austin, TX 78709, 512.891.6100.

Design and composition by Greenleaf Book Group LLC
Cover design by Greenleaf Book Group LLC
Cover credits: Marble: ©istockphoto.com/mwpenny; Butterfly: ©istockphoto.com/proxyminder

Cataloging-in-Publication data
(Prepared by The Donohue Group, Inc.)

Stoner, Thomas H.
    Small change, big gains : reflections of an energy entrepreneur / Thomas H. Stoner, Jr.—1st ed.
    p. ; cm.
    Issued also as an ebook.
    ISBN: 978-1-62634-002-2
    1. Renewable energy sources—Economic aspects. 2. Energy consumption—Economic aspects. 3. Climatic changes—Economic aspects. 4. Energy industries—Economic aspects. I. Title.

HD9502.A2 S76 2013
333.79   2013938055

Part of the Tree Neutral® program, which offsets the number of trees consumed in the production and printing of this book by taking proactive steps, such as planting trees in direct proportion to the number of trees used: www.treeneutral.com

TreeNeutral®

Printed in the United States of America on acid-free paper containing 30% post-consumer recycled waste

13 14 15 16 17 18   10 9 8 7 6 5 4 3 2 1

First Edition

I dedicate this book to my family.

CONTENTS

LIST OF FIGURES
AND TABLES

Figures

Tables

FOREWORD

BY D. WAYNE SILBY

People come around to environmentalism in different ways. My career in socially responsible investing exposed me early on to the complex and urgent issues surrounding our environment. It was in relation to these issues that I first met Tom Stoner, when the Social Venture Network was being formed. I was a cofounder and Tom was the first acting director. Some might argue that business and environmentalism make strange bedfellows. On the contrary, my devotion to socially responsible enterprises has shown me that good businessmen and -women make good environmental stewards.

Calvert has a long-standing practice of screening companies for environmental issues. As such, Calvert is a formative investor in the China Environment Fund, a pioneer in the pure play of environmental venture-capital investment in China. We have also been part of the proxy process in getting more carbon disclosure from the large public companies in which we invest. At Calvert, we know that renewables and energy efficiency not only are part of the solution to achieving global energy sustainability, but also hold tremendous business opportunities. Tom has written a highly informative book on exactly how these approaches can work to address climate change.

In *Small Change, Big Gains*, Tom uses his extensive experience as an entrepreneur in the energy sector to provide a comprehensive description of the current state of affairs and the need for immediate action. He likewise provides an overview of the necessary business and regulatory actions that must be taken in order to address the pressing climate change issues affecting the world in the twenty-first century. He considers the imperative of taking action now so that the world does not fall off the precipice as a result of climate change. Described is a set of small changes that can be made, which in turn could have a huge impact.

This work challenges the audience to ask questions that many people consider too controversial. It further argues that the debate regarding climate change is over; now the discussion must instead focus on what constructive actions can be taken. The book also considers the role that innovative technologies will play in combating the negative impact of climate change. The reader is pulled into Tom's reflections on how his personal experiences have shaped his perspective and made him realize the imperative of immediate action. Tom questions just how bad things have to become before people begin to take seriously the challenges confronting the world.

The work that Tom is doing with Project Butterfly provides an opportunity for all the essential stakeholders—government, businesses, energy suppliers, and consumers—to come together to work on addressing the world's most pressing problems. All these stakeholders must be part of the brainstorming process and solution in order to create systemic change. Critically, the book does not merely reiterate the problems that exist but rather presents a tangible set of solutions that different stakeholders can begin to consider.

Tom has written a compelling narrative on creating a new business case and why it is important to consider all the stakes and the stakeholders in our allocation of valuable and finite resources. His approach considers how the whole ecosystem needs to be engaged in order to ensure that resources are transferred effectively. Upon reading this book, it becomes clear that Tom Stoner understands business and energy and that unless we begin to see the world as one community, it will be very difficult to create solutions that benefit all. Tom's new business case shows how to orchestrate the small changes that can transform our global energy system. I am heartened to see this innovative and thorough analysis of both the problem and the solution.

D. Wayne Silby, Esq.
Founding Chairman, Calvert Funds
Cofounder, Social Venture Network
Spring 2013

FOREWORD

BY DAVID SCHIMEL

Tom Stoner and I met as fellow alumni of Hampshire College. While we didn't attend Hampshire the same years, we were there in the same era and had many of the same professors. A few years ago I attended the retirement symposium for one such professor, Ray Coppinger, and gave a presentation on my research. For many years, I have studied the global carbon cycle—the science of how fossil fuel emissions of carbon dioxide affect the atmosphere and climate—because it's a research area I find exciting, challenging, and rewarding. I thought Ray would be excited to see what I'd been up to in science, but as I'd learned to expect several decades earlier, his response totally surprised me. "Your talk depressed the hell out of me," he said. "We're doomed."

I had spoken about how we've learned to study processes over enormous areas using advanced technology; about the drama of making measurements in research aircraft; and about how the lessons I'd learned as an undergraduate at a small liberal arts college prepared me to work in big science. While I had been focused on the excitement of scientific research, Ray went to the heart of the matter and understood (correctly) that what we're finding scientifically is that the impacts of climate change are going to be serious, probably even more serious than earlier studies had suggested.

Motivated by the challenge of global change, scientists have done an amazing job of understanding how our complex and wondrous planet functions. We have identified big threats to our environment and to our planet's life support systems. Accomplishing this has engaged some of the best minds of the century, but scientists are not as good at taking the next step. Now that we know fossil fuel use is a threat to life on earth as we know it, what are we going to do about it? Climate change is a serious problem, and the grand challenge for the next generation of scientists and citizens is to find solutions.

Small Change, Big Gains reflects Tom's passion for solutions, his need to do what he can to ensure a safe and beautiful planet for his kids to live on, and his incredible insights about mobilizing creativity around solutions. Negotiating a better energy future requires negotiating a solution that satisfies Tom's four different philosophical and practical worldviews, and he shows a path forward for accomplishing just that. This book is written for the creative entrepreneurs of this and the next generation whose challenge it is—knowing the fossil-fuel-powered planet will soon be history—to guarantee that the energy system of the future enables a better and more abundant world.

David Schimel, PhD
Research scientist, Jet Propulsion Laboratory, California Institute of Technology
2007 Nobel Peace Prize recipient (IPCC convening lead author)
Spring 2013

PREFACE

In 2002 I traveled to the Philippines to participate in a training program cosponsored by Manila's largest electric utility company, the US Agency for International Development, and the Institute of International Education. My friend and longtime associate Peter Oatman was facilitating the energy efficiency training with me. We had the weekend to rest, and rather than stay in our hotel room we decided to take a boat ride to the island of Corregidor. The island lies at the mouth of Manila Bay and houses the remains of a US military base dating back to the Spanish-American War. During World War II the Japanese had extensively bombed Corregidor and later occupied the island. The ruined buildings on the island still stand today. They serve as a tourist attraction as well as a memorial and a testament to this tragic history.

After spending the day exploring the island, Peter and I were sitting on a dock, looking out at the sun as it fell onto the horizon. It was a beautiful place to watch the sun set while we waited for our boat ride back to Manila—that was, until we looked down the stretch of beach to the west and saw miles of shoreline teeming with garbage. In fact, as far as my eyes could see, the beach was full of old grocery bags and brightly colored plastic containers. Suddenly, the sea air carried an acrid odor that stung my nose. I was stunned and saddened by the notion that I could no longer look out to sea and witness the water in the same way. It was painfully clear that the vast oceans that separated nations and created barriers of safety were now under attack by a flotilla of garbage, their indomitable nature now vulnerable and their health delicate.

Since that experience more than a decade ago, the extent of the threat facing island nations like the Philippines has grown dramatically. The pollution of the oceans, and even of the very air we breathe and depend upon to keep our climate in balance, has placed Manila Bay's health in peril. Threatened are not only the Philippines' ninety million inhabitants but also its unique ecosystem that comprises miles upon miles of mangroves and more than 10,500 square miles of coral reefs.

These reefs are critical to the fisheries, and these fisheries are critical to the diet of the Philippine people. The increased levels of moisture during the rainy season and heat during the dry season are projected to worsen as the climate heats up—a result of the buildup of greenhouse gases (GHGs) in our atmosphere. These trends will likely cause severe consequences, such as imperiling the country's other sources of food supply.[1] In addition, because of their geographic location near the equator, the Philippine Islands are particularly susceptible to climate change impacts, including increases in the number of tropical cyclones.

The Philippines are already experiencing larger economic and human costs from the flooding of its major metropolitan areas as a result of typhoons. On December 16, 2011, for example, Tropical Storm Washi struck the Southern Philippines and caused rivers to rise by more than ten feet in less than an hour, sweeping away entire villages and killing 1,268 people.[2] More recently, on December 4, 2012, Typhoon Bopha also tore through the Southern Philippines, with wind gusts as high as 138 mph, killing more than one thousand inhabitants.[3]

As the seas rise, fifteen of the Philippines' sixteen coastal provinces are predicted to suffer from the erosion of their shorelines. The stakes are getting higher. And Manila Bay is but one example.

This is just the beginning.

• • •

As Peter and I sat there on the dock, looking out at the sea I reflected on what I had witnessed by visiting the ruins of lost battles. I thought about the men and woman who had died and the heroes who led and tried to protect them.

One such hero, General Douglas MacArthur, served as the chief of staff of the United States Army at the beginning of World War II in the Pacific. He was stationed on the island of Corregidor. On March 11, 1942, he left the Philippines on President Franklin D. Roosevelt's orders: *Get out of harm's way. Escape to Australia.* The dock faced the beach where the general reluctantly departed Corregidor. On that beach there is a statue of him standing at salute, his back to the sea. The sign next to his statue quotes his parting words: "I shall return." The statue has special meaning to any American tourist visiting the island because General MacArthur and US forces did make good on his promise: MacArthur returned to the Philippines and Corregidor in 1944. The Japanese invasion was eventually repelled after years of occupation.

But as I looked up at the statue of the legendary general during my visit in 2002, I could still see the garbage lapping up against the shore and I had a different thought: *The climate change story will need its heroes, just as US forces in the Pacific theater in the 1940s needed General Douglas MacArthur. But who will appear in the twenty-first century to take on this threat?*

• • •

As I think back on my visit to the island of Corregidor when I was looking out at the flotilla of garbage that had invaded that historically sacred place, I am reminded of another story from history. I am reminded of the Greeks when they landed en masse on the beach before they took the city of Troy. The daughter of the Trojan king, Cassandra, had predicted their arrival, but the people cursed her gift of prophecy and no one heeded her warnings. *We certainly have our modern-day Cassandras, issuing warnings of catastrophe and cataclysmic change while the rest of us pay no heed.* Among them are our climate scientists and environmental activists. They suffer the same gift and curse as Cassandra did. And just as the Trojans needed the help of their gods and heroes to defend their city against seafaring Greek marauders, so, too, do our scientists and environmental activists need what amounts to divine intervention.

The Trojans failed in their eleventh-hour attempt to protect their home against Greeks bearing false gifts. Must we fail, too? Or can we acknowledge the severity of the problem and conjure the strength of conviction required to build and create a world that is environmentally and economically sustainable?

My experience in Manila was one factor among many that eventually led me to write this book. Other life experiences have led me not only to appreciate the severity of the environmental crisis but also to firmly support both the climate scientists who say we have a problem and the renewable energy engineers—many in the energy industry who have been my coworkers—who say there is a solution. Yet I have also come to realize that my simple acknowledgment of the gravity of the problem of drastic climate change—a problem we all face—often places me at odds with others and at a peculiar point on the political spectrum. In fact, as more and more of my conversations with climate scientists and energy engineers have revealed what is happening to our environment and how industry is failing to adequately respond, I have realized that I need to take up my own environmental sword rather than let this simple acknowledgment define my worldview. I have come to the conclusion that we can no longer afford to ignore the issues of global pollution. We need an immediate and dramatic solution to the crisis. It isn't enough to realize the problem. It is time to act.

The result is Project Butterfly (www.projbutterfly.com) and this book. I started the project and the writing of this book by assembling a board of directors—pulling together a team of climate scientists and former business colleagues—to conduct a feasibility study on how we could transform our global energy system in order to mitigate climate change. I also formed a small staff, and we have spent nearly two years researching and compiling data as we have searched for practical, realistic solutions to climate change. Early on, we decided to take the same financial modeling approach I had used throughout my career as an energy developer when looking at individual projects or individual technologies. But this time we wanted to look at the big picture—that is, to look at our global energy mix as if it were a single portfolio of energy assets in need of a retrofit. During the process, we developed tools, made discoveries, and fostered relationships that we believe can fundamentally change the debate over energy, the economy, and our environment.

In fact, I think it is fair to say, on behalf of everyone who has worked on Project Butterfly, it is our hope that the findings from our research will provide the human race (the global community) and the thousands of leaders who make up the energy industry with a new way of looking at the world and its global energy mix. This new way of looking at the world is not meant to scare the reader into some kind of political action. Instead it is meant to inspire young and old leaders to think radically about what is possible by making small changes to our global energy mix that can transform and improve the human condition.

The purpose of Project Butterfly, therefore, is to share a methodology that can be applied in looking for simple solutions that would simultaneously revitalize the economy and restore the environment. We at Project Butterfly felt that by identifying the diverse and inherent interests of our global stakeholders, and by working to create an alignment of these interests, we might be able to radically shift the debate about energy and climate, and to eliminate the notion that some kind of permanent sacrifice would be necessary to sustain human existence. Rather, the Project Butterfly team came to believe that what is missing is the necessary investment to ensure the availability of future energy supplies. By applying this methodology, we could see that it is possible for energy planners—regardless of whether they work for businesses supplying, using, or financing energy services—to add to the energy system without further burdening the underlying ecosystem. In fact, the methodology we developed was intended to help build a better world by creating a new alignment of interests.

I started working on Project Butterfly and *Small Change, Big Gains* during the summer of 2011. It was my wife, Laurie Larsen, who, after supporting me through three businesses and raising a family together, suggested that the time was ripe for me to research and write a book on energy and the environment. This book is dedicated to my entire family, but I must also acknowledge that you would not be holding it in your hands without her inspiration.

Over the course of writing this book, many other individuals worked with me in creating our own chrysalis, a think-tank cocoon where we would develop the ideas and research methodology that would emerge as Project Butterfly. The collaboration that has evolved along with this project has fulfilled my desire to bring together a dynamic team to tackle our toughest energy issues and open the possibility of transforming the global perspective on climate change.

Four individuals joined the collaboration in the beginning and have held the standard of rigor for the model results that are hosted on www.projbutterfly.com and summarized in this book. Three of these individuals serve along with me as founders on Project Butterfly's board of directors. The fourth individual has served as the technical adviser for the overall project.

David Schimel is the chair of the board for Project Butterfly. At his day job, David leads research focused on carbon-cycle climate interactions, combining models and observations at NASA's Jet Propulsion Laboratory. David is one of the recipients of the 2007 Nobel Peace Prize for his work on the United Nations' Intergovernmental Panel on Climate Change. He is also a fellow alumnus of Hampshire College in Amherst, Massachusetts. David contributed much to Project Butterfly in the way of support, advice, expertise, and knowledge of environmental research, all of which were invaluable in guiding the team.

Peter Backlund is another member of the Project Butterfly board and is director of the Integrated Science Program and director of External Relations at the National Center for Atmospheric Research (NCAR). Peter works at the intersection of scientific research and public policy, with a focus on studying how the scientific community can advise policy makers on issues related to climate change. Peter let us know where information and research was misleading, confusing, or missing completely and helped steer the ship away from the rocks.

James White, PhD, the third member of Project Butterfly's board, is a professor of geological sciences and the director of the Environmental Studies Program at the University of Colorado (CU) at Boulder. Jim's input on the issues, grounded by his years of research, has been enormously valuable to me. I am so grateful for his friendship and support.

Finally, Evan Evans, PE, has been a colleague of mine for more than twenty years and spanning three businesses, including his ten-year stint with me at Econergy International as the lead engineer. Evan, along with his team at WSP (www.wspgroup.com), serves as the technical consultant to Project Butterfly. Evan is vice president and director of the Sustainability and Energy Division for WSP, stationed in Boulder, Colorado.

Evan's team, including Josh Whitney, senior project director, and research assistant Becky Johns, fully owned this project from soup to nuts. The conceptualization of the analysis in this book started with a simple statement I made to Evan: "I want to look at the whole thing as if it is one." The WSP team managed to take this vision and translate it into a unique innovation to climate and energy modeling that we hope will forever transform the conversation about climate change.

These four individuals and the consultants and staff of Project Butterfly have served as the founding conveners for this project. As such, they have helped it evolve from the fundamental idea of looking at the world's global energy system as a single portfolio of energy assets into a rich feasibility study for our fellow stewards of the planet to consider and interact with. During the course of developing the model and writing the book, conversations with a number of interested people have added depth and multiple perspectives to these efforts. The circles of involvement continue to expand, and I am greatly heartened by the enthusiasm and support we have received from so many. Our hope is that the publication of this book will not be the conclusion of this project. We hope that, just as the butterfly progresses through its stages of growth, we have begun an evolution in the human condition.

In March 2011, before I began writing this book, I had the opportunity to interview Will Baker, president of the Chesapeake Bay Foundation (CBF). Right away I felt that CBF would be a good example of the "environmental steward," a concept explored at length via the project and in this book. After interviewing Will, I became certain that CBF set the standard for a global steward and that the global community must consider our atmosphere and oceans in the same way that Will has looked after the Chesapeake Bay—as our most precious natural resource.

Brian O'Neill and Bas van Ruijven, from the Integrated Assessment Modeling (IAM) group within the Climate Change Research section at NCAR, provided advice and steered the team to some of the best and most credible resources and data necessary for the feasibility study. Their collective depth of knowledge and understanding of the vast issues related to modeling climate change has been invaluable.

I wish to thank my friends at the Rocky Mountain Institute, including Robert "Hutch" Hutchinson, managing director for the research and consulting activities; Michael Potts, former CEO and president; and James Newcomb, program director. They provided much of the initial direction for the Butterfly Project and this book, along with support, encouragement, and constructive feedback.

Paul Jerde, former executive director of the Deming Center for Entrepreneurship, has been a constant supporter of this project from the very beginning, bringing talent and connections from both the Deming Center and the Leeds School of Business at CU-Boulder.

CU Cleantech's former director, Trent Yang, and intern program manager, Candace Mitchell, supported our project through their internship program, providing young talent able to research the varied subjects critical to a comprehensive analysis of the many issues surrounding energy, the economy, and our environment.

Stephen Lawrence is an associate professor of operations management in the Leeds School of Business at the University of Colorado and is a fellow of CU's Renewable and Sustainable Energy Institute. I am grateful to Steve for his participation in a review of the Project Butterfly methodology and model and for his consistent encouragement.

Climate Interactive creates interactive, accessible computer simulations that help users visualize the long-term climate impacts of decisions being undertaken today. I am grateful for the work of the brilliant team led by Andrew (Drew) Jones, including Beth Sawin, Travis Franck, Phil Rice, Lori Siegel, Stephanie McCauley, John Sterman (MIT), Tom Fiddaman (Ventana), and Ellie Johnston. In partnership with WSP, they have developed a unique and interactive simulation model (known as the Project Butterfly Financial Model) that illustrates the environmental impact of changes in energy use, consumption, and policies on global greenhouse gases and that serves as the backbone to the analysis presented in this book.

I enlisted the support of my friend Alan Poole to help on Project Butterfly. Between 1999 and 2002, I had the pleasure of working with Alan for the World Bank and the US Agency for International Development to advance how energy-services companies pursuing energy efficiency could thrive in an economy such as Brazil's. Such a task was much more difficult than he and I could have imagined, and yet he is still at it today. Alan is an expert consultant specializing in the analysis and development of programs and policies to promote energy efficiency and renewable energy resources. Some of my happiest days of working on this project have been working with Alan.

I had the pleasure of working with Heidi Sieverding, who was the environmental operations manager at Evergreen Energy while I was CEO. I always admired her diligence and the passion she brought to her work. She has managed to do the same in her research and editing assistance throughout this book.

Also at Evergreen Energy, I was pleased to work alongside Patrick Kozak, the quintessential Renaissance man. Pat, a key contributor in the climate-change-sciences community, provided editorial assistance and confirmation of key data during the development of Project Butterfly. To say that his talents and expertise are diverse would be an understatement.

Over the years, I have had the good fortune to meet and befriend some genuine heroes of the planet. Steve Rothstein, now president of the Perkins School for the Blind, is one such fellow. He is a shining example of the faith, tenacity, and will that it will take to change our energy system and save the planet.

Artemis Joukowsky is another one of my heroes—a serial entrepreneur, venture capitalist, and social activist committed to making the world a better place. I have had the pleasure of working with Artemis for more than thirty years and am pleased to have his support and participation again on Project Butterfly as a board member and colleague.

Brian Doubleday is first and foremost my friend. He is also a professional video producer/director with nearly forty years of experience producing and directing award-winning television and film projects. Brian helped Project Butterfly refine its message and gave us a voice on our website, using his expertise and knowledge of a medium of which I have a limited understanding.

Lori DeBoer, my writing coach, helped me polish and fine-tune my manuscript. She coaxed and cajoled personal stories out of my head and onto the page and reminded me that my voice needed to enliven the rich and sometimes dense subject matter in this book.

Research assistant Brandon Shenfield came to the project as an intern fresh from the Leeds School of Business at the University of Colorado, with a passion for the environment and a desire to put his new skills to work. I am grateful for his willingness to research areas and provide me with his analyses and interpretations. Of special note is Brandon's willingness to do whatever it takes, including his exceptional ability at playing devil's advocate during heated debates. I have no doubt that Brandon will make the world a better place.

Caroline Alden, a PhD candidate at CU, also served as a research assistant for Project Butterfly. I am grateful for her incredibly deep knowledge and understanding of the science behind climate change and her help in grounding much of the narrative on the subject.

Jessie Stoner is my daughter and an exceptional artist and magnificent healer in her own right. I am proud that both our logo and the visuals that helped guide us in our early days are her work.

It is a necessary understatement to say that I have enjoyed the support and friendship of Laurie Greenwood for more than ten years. I am grateful for her competence and leadership as director and project manager for Project Butterfly, and for her dedication and attention to all of the details. It was only with Laurie's help that we've been able to complete this ambitious project. She is truly the midwife to the Butterfly!

Sustainable development is development that meets the needs of the present without compromising the ability of future generations to meet their own needs.
—World Commission on Environment and Development, 1987

INTRODUCTION

In the fall of 2008 Senator Barack Obama campaigned against Senator John McCain on a pledge to address the looming economic crisis by promoting green jobs. He was a presidential candidate willing to talk about climate change, positioning himself in deep contrast to the policies of the previous administration. He was also a candidate who wanted to use his commitment to the environment as a way to regain US leadership on the world stage after two very unpopular wars.

Four years later, the world had changed. President Obama didn't even mention climate change in any of three presidential debates. His green energy policies were under attack. He certainly talked about the need for new energy, and especially clean energy, but he never used the issue of climate change as a way to differentiate himself from his Republican opponent.

After winning his second term in 2012, President Obama used his newly accumulated political capital and again started talking about climate change. Three weeks after his second inauguration, in his 2013 State of the Union address, Obama reaffirmed his commitment to combat climate change by declaring that if Congress won't go along with him, he will use his executive powers to ensure that action is taken.

Will his actions be enough? Probably not. My view is the political, economic, and ecological system that determines a global response to climate change will require a far more holistic approach.

For more than twenty-five years I have watched US presidents come and go. Over these years I have always considered myself to be an environmentalist, but never an activist by profession or avocation. Rather, I have spent my career as an energy industry entrepreneur, successfully raising hundreds of millions of dollars of early-stage project capital in the energy services and power industries. Along the way I have always followed and been curious about environmental issues, especially those relating to energy. In fact, I have often felt that because of my unique experience of working with early-stage companies, I've acquired a different way of looking at the development of new energy projects—a more holistic way that I believe could better shape the climate change debate.

Over the years, I have come to see the climate debate as an issue of finance as much as it is an issue of technology, physics, or economics. This financial perspective of the climate debate incorporates the views of the principle stakeholders in the energy industry, whose alignment, I believe, is so critical to the formation of any new energy project or program, including one to address climate change. These principle stakeholders represent the interests of energy suppliers, investors (both equity owners and financial lenders), and energy users. These stakeholders are all integral to the climate and energy debate because their households and businesses will be most immediately affected by any effort to mitigate the emissions of greenhouse gases (GHGs). In fact, the view I have come to is that failure to find a balance that aligns the interests of the key stakeholders will keep the global community in the status quo, whereas facilitating discussions to incentivize key stakeholders can open up vast opportunities for business and innovation.

DEBATE VERSUS RHETORIC

The current debate seems to center around whether or not climate change is caused by humans or is naturally occurring. If you dig down beneath the rhetoric, however, you'll find that the real debate is over the possible solutions to mitigate climate change and the impact any solution might have on the earth's natural resources as old and new industries vie for investors' attention.

In fact, even if you believe human-caused climate change is a hoax, once you leave the surface of the issue, you will find that a host of new questions emerge:

» Is cleaner natural gas the solution to our energy crisis?
» What role does nuclear energy play in our future?
» How can clean coal technologies be funded and incorporated into a national energy plan?
» Can energy efficiency and renewable energy scale up to replace aging infrastructure?
» Or can we simply drill our way to energy independence?

The answers to these questions and others like them therefore shape the real nature of the climate change debate. Different answers have different implications for our climate. Furthermore, industry players that have a stake in how we answer these questions definitely want to advance their position and worldview. There are entrenched interests within each solution set. What we must do is look behind the curtain of each issue and see who is pulling all the levers.

My aim is to be as transparent as possible and actually show the math behind the most critical calculations. The perspective I plan to share focuses instead on advancing the concept of the environmental steward as a key stakeholder and then crafting policy recommendations that will bring the other key stakeholder classes into alignment. However, before I share the findings of the Project Butterfly Financial Model, I will attempt to provide answers to the crucial questions facing decision makers and industry players, by evaluating many of the proposed solution sets through the eyes of the different stakeholders and by characterizing the social and economic history that form the status quo. This status quo is what we at Project Butterfly call "the business-as-usual scenario." I will explore these issues in order to see whether it is possible to create alignment among the stakeholders while satisfying the demands of the environmental steward. Let me tell you in advance, however, that throughout the story I am about to tell you, the quest is to identify the key ingredients of a sound energy policy—a policy that, in turn, will let the market efficiently allocate these different solutions to form a new business case.

OUR GLOBAL HABITAT

Traditionally the serious challenge that climate change poses both to our global habitat and to the viability of continued economic growth is expressed as a physics problem: You have too many GHGs in the atmosphere, and you have to find a way to reduce not only their growth rate but also their total concentration. Moreover, we as a global society also have a history of applying engineering solutions to physics problems: We have built dams to control the flow of rivers, created cisterns to capture water for storage, installed aqueducts for transporting water to dense populations or arid areas, and designed irrigation systems to make farming more productive. More recently, we have addressed ozone-depleting toxins, cleaned up polluted bays and rivers, and reduced pollutants and other emissions from our power plants. The application of these engineering solutions has, in turn, required financing. To finance the necessary projects, we have raised money through either direct tax levies or regulatory structures that tap capital market forces.

By contrast, at Project Butterfly, we started our investigation into the climate and energy debate with the proposition that the way one defines the problem dictates the solution set. Rather than providing an answer to a physics problem, our underlying conclusion (and that of this book) is that the global society must define climate change as more than an environmental challenge. Climate change is also an existential challenge similar to the rise of Nazism or the threat of nuclear war. Addressing climate change as a problem relating to the destiny of the human race means we will have to look beyond a single scientific breakthrough or a new technological solution set. Instead we must work to create sufficient resolve to change how we regulate or don't regulate our use of energy in order to improve our overall planetary condition—indeed, to ensure our very existence—even at the cost of pushing certain industries out of business while we create the conditions for new industries to thrive.

Addressing an existential problem requires first acknowledging that such a problem exists. Creating consciousness around an existential threat can either take time or awareness can emerge in an instant. The rise of Hitler's Germany was not widely recognized as a threat against the United States until after the Japanese bombed Pearl Harbor, demonstrating that the world's oceans no longer provided safe harbors. Similar to the war machine that had to be built during World War II, engineering solutions to address climate change will certainly need to be applied. But the global society will also need to reject and even shut down certain activities, and we will have to muster the resolve to do so. Tackling a threat to our lives on this planet—a threat brought about by our own making—means saying *yes* to things that serve a new outcome and *no* to things that do not. And finally, we must create a system that allows us to make public investments as opportunities arise. The system must be simple in design but still capable of addressing complexity, with rules of engagement that are clear and fairly imposed. Only then can industry proactively interact with the system to solve such an existential threat.

At Project Butterfly we have used our methodology in creating a "new business case." We propose that addressing climate change requires identifying market inefficiencies and then characterizing the efforts to address these inefficiencies as market opportunities. These efforts must generate value for multiple stakeholders, where the costs are not necessarily allocated to the suppliers or to the investors but passed on to the beneficiaries, the energy users. By proceeding down this untried path, we can avoid framing the issue as a new societal cost that only governments can cover. Rather, this new business case focuses on using government to alleviate a cost that already exists, for the benefit of other stakeholders. These other stakeholders, such as the energy supplier or investor, are then better equipped to take risks and to enjoy the rewards we reap when we reaffirm life and reject the causes of existential threats.

POINT OF NO RETURN

Picture yourself in a canoe on the Niagara River being swept toward the falls. You cannot see over the edge just yet, but the danger is imminent. In fact, there is a point of no return at which you can no longer get to the shore and avoid going over. As Jim White, my collaborator and the director of the University of Colorado Environmental Studies Program, puts it, "Exactly when the threshold is crossed is very hard to pinpoint but is nonetheless very real. Well before going over the falls, you're just as dead as when you do go over."

According to White and other scientists, there is a similar point of no return for our current environmental crisis. Carbon dioxide (CO_2) is the most prevalent GHG in our atmosphere, with the longest life cycle. Therefore, if you were to look at the world's ability to sustain a vast diversity of rich life, then an atmospheric CO_2 concentration level totaling about 550 parts per million (ppm) is approximately our threshold—our "point of no return."[4] Although it is somewhat arbitrary, not a hard-and-fast number, it's the number we chose to build our Project Butterfly Financial Model on and to use in performing our analysis. Many island nations, in order to preserve their shores, would like to see 350 ppm as an international target. Some European countries have targeted 450 ppm as the number that will limit crop failure by reducing the increase in average global temperatures. The concentration of CO_2 prior to the Industrial Revolution hovered at approximately 290 ppm. Scientists warn that the buildup of CO_2 in our atmosphere beyond 450 ppm will correlate to an increase of approximately 3.6 degrees Fahrenheit (or 2 degrees Celsius) from preindustrial times and will begin to threaten our very existence.

As a result of Project Butterfly's study, we believe that a 450-ppm target is no longer a feasible goal and that to try to achieve a 350-ppm target by the end of the twenty-first century would be grossly unrealistic because it would likely require *immediately* turning off every piece of energy-consuming equipment on the planet. Our judgment is based on our review of the technical, social, and political feasibility of such a target and on the fact that the concentration level in 2013 had already reached 400 ppm. Furthermore, it is clear that highlighting the level of threat to our existence will not change consumption patterns, and thus the behavior of our global economy will remain unchanged. Governments around the world, including that of United States, have already delayed efforts to develop new forms of clean energy that could have been implemented to address climate change back in the 1990s, when nations began negotiating international agreements to reduce GHGs. For example, the targets originally set in 1992 are now revealing themselves to be wholly unrealistic. Our canoe is a little bit closer to the falls than we realized.

However, if we can keep atmospheric CO_2 concentration below 550 ppm, the Project Butterfly Financial Model forecasts that the increase in average global temperatures will slightly exceed 3.6 degrees Fahrenheit (2 degrees Celsius), a situation to which humans may still be able to adapt. Our model shows that to keep emissions from exceeding 550 ppm will require continued diligence for the rest of the century and a significant shift in our global approach to energy use. Moreover, this target can be achieved only if we as a global society implement some facsimile approximating Project Butterfly's recommendations, starting now. Keeping CO_2 concentration below even the higher target of 550 ppm is not going to be easy, in spite of how simple the required changes might actually be.

In order to make the necessary changes to shift our global energy mix, the global society—constituted by governments, businesses, and policy makers—urgently needs to acknowledge the threat posed by rapidly increasing GHG emissions. The global society must then immediately make new and significant investments to soften the inevitable blow of a catastrophic change to our climate. A global agreement such as the Kyoto Protocol that sets targets and dates can be a helpful guide, but we absolutely need to take decisive action to shift the global energy mix. Rather than continue to subsidize the fossil fuel industries, we must redirect subsidies to unleash market forces and promote competition and energy efficiency. Aggressive mitigation must commence now—within this decade—if we are to address the threat of climate change before it's too late.

In fact, climate scientists warn that if we keep to "business as usual" in spite of current policies to develop alternatives, the global community will experience much higher GHG concentrations and corresponding temperatures will rise to devastating levels. The Project Butterfly Financial Model shows that under our business-as-usual scenario, by the end of the century CO_2 atmospheric concentrations will exceed 800 ppm, equivalent to an increase of about 7.5 degrees Fahrenheit (or more than 4 degrees Celsius) in average global temperatures. While this might not seem significant to some, science tells us that it will produce cataclysmic changes in climate, translating to ever more frequent extreme weather events. The increase in temperature will be more radical in the polar regions than at the equator, accelerating the melting of ice caps and ice sheets in Greenland and Antarctica. It will prolong the dry, hot days of summer in many locations while creating monster thunderstorms and hurricanes in others. Before we even reach such a level of CO_2 concentration, large population centers along the planet's coastal regions will be threatened with increasingly more devastating catastrophes derived from higher sea levels. The conditions will be ripe for global disease, war, and famine.

Imagine Bangladesh, for example, one of the poorest and most populated countries in the world, and the potential catastrophe it would face: A modest sea level rise of between 1.5 feet and 3 feet would displace between 3.4 million and 17 million people, respectively.[5] Similarly, if the sea level rose between 3 feet and 5 feet in California, approximately 480,000 people would be displaced and $100 billion worth of property would be lost.[6] Extrapolate these examples: On a global scale, either scenario would be horrifying.

PROJECT BUTTERFLY

When I first conceived of Project Butterfly, I just wanted to figure out a simple way to reverse the trend of the buildup of GHGs without disrupting economic development. My original goal was to discover how to reduce the growth rate of GHG emissions to a level that would allow natural sinks, such as oceans and forests, to drain the buildup of GHGs. I wanted a solution, or a set of solutions, that would financially incentivize the world's stakeholders to accomplish this end goal. Only through a financial incentive, I felt, could we change from an economy run by fossil fuel to one built on sustainable resource use. This simple solution might have been fixing a price on carbon, for example. Over the course of my research, however, I discovered that a comprehensive solution requires a more elegant set of financial remedies, one that is grounded in the principles of sustainability and that deconstructs old patterns and integrates new practices into how we actually conduct our day-to-day business here on the earth.

What the Project Butterfly team came up with was a solution set that is threefold, and it presents our global community with a new and unprecedented opportunity to alter its destiny. I believe this approach presents the best way forward because these actions are within our collective reach, allowing us to create a new sense of alignment between the requirements of the environmental steward and the needs of commerce. The solution offers actions that fall into three general, interrelated categories:

» The first category involves creating national policies and international agreements that will stimulate the vast powers of our global capital markets by internalizing pollution costs, promoting trade between nations, and encouraging investment in new technology.
» The second category involves investing in and employing technologies that lower GHG emissions through reducing the carbon intensity of the energy we consume.
» The third category involves changing domestic regulatory environments to allow greater capital to flow from banks and equity investors into renewable energy and energy efficiency investments.

As you will see, all three interconnected categories provide the basis for bringing sustainability to our global society and the energy system that underlies it. Following the description in part I of where we stand and life as we know it, part II will provide some of the history and reasons behind why we find ourselves trapped in the business-as-usual scenario. Part III then articulates a new sustainability model and the basis for why the threefold solution is the only strategy that can meet the challenges posed by catastrophic climate change. By the time you finish reading part IV, you should have a clear vision of what is possible through innovation and through a dramatic acceleration of technologies that promote renewable resources and drive energy efficiency to new levels. These categories, if implemented as a unified solution, also have the potential to create global wealth and prosperity rather than to limit our own economic and social development.

In other words, Project Butterfly's claim is that the act of internalizing the costs of emissions and implementing proactive regulatory initiatives will drive new private and public investment into low-carbon technologies and will tip the scales in favor of renewable energy and energy efficiency for all classes of stakeholders in the energy industry. When we incentivize all stakeholders to reduce their carbon footprint, we can reverse the buildup of GHG emissions by letting nature do its job.

A NEW SET OF LENSES

To examine the feasibility of mitigating climate change, the Project Butterfly team has applied a new set of lenses to the discussion of climate change and energy, by stipulating that the four global stakeholders (the energy user, the energy supplier, the investor/lender, and the environmental steward) must all be in alignment for any proposed solution to make sense. The team has borrowed several principles from traditional energy finance practices, one of which is to say that if we are unable to bring the perspectives of all four stakeholders into alignment, then a proposed project—whether it's energy from an alternative or a conventional source—is unlikely to move forward. Conversely, if all four perspectives do come into alignment, with clear benefits in excess of costs, then capitalization and a pathway forward become much more likely. Helping a CEO of an energy company, an energy manager of a Fortune 500 company, or a banker underwriting an energy project understand the interplay among the four stakeholder perspectives will raise awareness of the key barriers ahead of us.

By engaging in a deeply collaborative effort and by leveraging existing data sets, we have produced a feasibility study that is both a theoretical framework (in the form of our Project Butterfly Sustainability Model) and a series of financial pro forma documents that simulate the outcome of different policy measures as viewed from these four perspectives (the Project Butterfly Financial Model). This framework allows us to evaluate competing mitigation strategies that address the threat of climate change. The Project Butterfly Financial Model reveals that a significant investment in renewable energy is already gaining momentum, even in our business-as-usual scenario, over the period of 2012 to 2050. Our model also reveals, however, that the energy industry needs to dramatically speed up its adoption of alternative technologies and to better manage the mixture of conventional and renewable energy supplies through a rapid drive to market innovation. Finally, our modeling allows us to provide an analysis of the impact and feasibility of various simulations from each of the four perspectives as we work to minimize, and potentially reverse, the buildup of atmospheric GHGs.

Our modeling efforts have provided us with some encouraging and counterintuitive findings that challenge current paradigms and conventional thinking regarding the energy industry. One of the most remarkable findings provided by the new business case is that mitigating climate change can actually produce a *net increase* in value for all energy suppliers *as a class*, by converting our global energy mix to technologies that are experiencing higher energy outputs and higher yields for each dollar invested. In fact, it is possible under the new business case to create fiscal conditions in which all four of the stakeholders, *each as a class*, benefit. The key is fixing a global price on carbon, which would allow greater subsidies for renewable energy and would improve the condition of each stakeholder class while addressing the market's current failure to avoid catastrophic climate change or global resource depletion.

The second finding, perhaps not as surprising but nonetheless critical to recognize, is that the implementation of Project Butterfly's recommendations will cause corporate casualties. Conventional oil and coal companies, for example, will lose significant market share in the short term. The current climate debate is being shaped in part by those who realize that the survival of their industries hangs in the balance. But the potential exists for these industries themselves to adapt by converting their earnings engines to renewable energy supplies and by reducing the energy intensity and carbon content of their existing goods and services. If conventional energy suppliers fail to make the switch, they will eventually fade into the sunset until finally they cease to exist. This is a statement that can be made regardless of what scenario we chose to follow.

Furthermore, a third finding underscores the importance of acting immediately. Implementing new rules takes time. Capital markets will need time to adjust to new conditions. But once they do, the marketplace will respond and improve the conditions for all four of the stakeholder classes—the energy user, the energy supplier, the investor or lender, and the environmental steward—especially in providing long-term benefits to the energy user and increased profitability for the energy supplier.

Organizing the necessary capital is key to realizing our solution. Just as any company might consider making a change in strategy, widespread adoption of the new business case requires that the company match potential revenues with forecasted costs. We must look both internally, to our renewable and nonrenewable resources, and externally, to all the institutions at our disposal that will allow us, as the global community, to form the necessary capital. Part IV is dedicated to providing a list of recommendations for creating and allocating this necessary capital.

For instance, the new business case will require that energy suppliers and users have greater access to financial and risk capital to make new investments. It will also require cooperation and engagement among the myriad of institutions responsible for allocating all of the nonfinancial forms of capital, ranging from human resources to social networks. Such forms of capital are limited, but they can and would be enriched by pursuing the new business case as recommended by Project Butterfly.

The Project Butterfly team is pleased by its findings. We all share a sense of optimism about our future, born from the belief that if we can determine a way for these forms of capital to work together and achieve optimal levels of economic satisfaction at reduced levels of consumption, the capacity of the global community to build wealth and prosperity is enhanced. Our conclusion therefore is that the world may not be as insecure and limited as some suggest. Our concept calls for rewarding suppliers that produce greater user satisfaction while minimizing the consumption of nonrenewable energy and while maximizing the potential for new sources of renewable energy and energy efficiency. This financial strategy has the potential to not only produce a more efficient allocation of goods and services but also to address the current failure of the market to confront environmental impacts.

I am proposing a solution that requires a change in the energy game and a definite change in the dialogue that might provide the necessary answers. If we wait for government to provide funding for energy efficiency and renewable energy, we're not going to get anywhere in sufficient time to make a difference. We must empower the capital markets instead, regardless of whether such a statement seems crazy to skeptics of capitalism.

Our canoe is already in the danger zone. Going over the falls is imminent—that is, *if* nothing is done to stop us from going over. My intent is to show you how a small change in energy policy can create big gains—how the global society, by unleashing the power of capital markets, can implement the measures necessary to mitigate climate change starting now. As you will see, such a small change has the potential to enlist the support of everyone on earth.

TRANSFORMING THE WAY WE THINK

There's no mystery behind the title of the book you hold in your hands. A shift in our collective mind-set, a *small change* in our energy policy, can effect *big gains*. But why did I name the underlying work Project Butterfly? Because to me, the very concept of a butterfly represents transformation. My initial vision offered the potential to transform the way our global society thinks about energy use and climate change. I wanted to conduct a project to evaluate potential solutions to climate change, and I felt that a collaborative effort would be needed. As the impetus for this collaboration began to formulate, the image of a butterfly emerging from its chrysalis came to mind. I envisioned this butterfly struggling to break out of its cocoon, a daunting challenge that takes amazing perseverance. I felt that the project would require a similar level of commitment and perseverance.

The image of the butterfly continued to unfold in my mind. After emerging, the butterfly must marshal its strength and press onward to take its first flight almost immediately—there's no resting up for another day. I imagined the moist wings unfurling as this creature prepares to fulfill its transformation from earthbound caterpillar to airborne butterfly. It occurred to me that although the butterfly appears to be delicate and fragile, especially in those first moments, once its wings have dried, it is capable of long-distance travel and great aerial feats.

This amazing insect reflects beauty, functionality, and strength, but most important, it has a life cycle that embodies transformation and rebirth. The butterfly provides a metaphor for how a small repositioning in the existing conditions can lead to a major change throughout the system—a concept known as the Butterfly Effect. It seemed like the perfect name for a project that would constitute the work for the book *Small Change, Big Gains*—a symbol of how simple solutions could change the destiny of billions.

Since the beginning of the project, I have gained a further sense that the butterfly's journey is akin to the requirements of our own environmental stewardship. I believe that the majority of the world understands the gravity of the political challenges we face as we attempt to address the most serious environmental threat in human history. But I, and others, also believe that the general thinking around these issues has missed the vital connection among the various players in this critical game: the scientists who are studying and measuring the environmental changes; the industries and energy producers who want to keep their companies strong and financially viable; and the federal, state, and municipal policy makers who enforce regulations, protect natural resources, and foster sustainable economic well-being. Thus Project Butterfly came to be a unique collaboration of people from each of these sectors—people who are deeply committed to further building on the wealth we have created for our communities while fostering wise stewardship and promoting enduring transformation.

. . .

As a young man, I spent as much time as I could in nature. It was in part my love of nature that gave birth to my career as an entrepreneur and CEO who has focused most of his efforts on the concerns of both energy use and production. In the late 1980s, I created an energy services company by introducing venture capital to an energy consulting and engineering firm. As president of the company, I built energy efficiency projects for large energy users that stretched from coast to coast in the United States. We focused on generating energy savings by retrofitting and reengineering mechanical and electrical systems for school buildings, hospital complexes, and federal military bases.

My second business, which you'll read a little about in chapter 1, involved transforming an environmental advisory firm into an international renewable energy company that was traded on the London Stock Exchange's Alternative Investment Market (AIM). Raising capital in London enabled the management team to reposition this global advisory firm as a leading independent power producer building utility-scale wind farms, run-of-river hydro facilities, and landfill gas recovery projects throughout Latin America in the early 2000s. After the 2008 market collapse, I continued to expand my career by taking on the restructuring of a publicly traded coal and clean coal technology company.

In the course of my career, I have concentrated on building wealth for investors and shareholders, including many managers with whom I have had the privilege to work. While building and financing businesses, I have worked with friends and family, with venture capitalists, and amid the jungle of international capital markets. Because of these experiences and as an owner-operator of energy assets, as I mentioned earlier, I have long felt the need to speak up on the debate over climate change and energy policy. On a few occasions I have even sent letters to the editors of various newspapers—none of which were ever published. But before I felt fully prepared to speak out and share my perspective on the issues, I had questions that I wanted answered. In the process of writing this book I have addressed these questions through my collaboration with an amazing group of people who share both my concerns for the future of our world and my interest in being part of the solution.

The metaphor conjured up by Project Butterfly seemed appropriate given my interest in tackling certain questions about climate change and about our country's and the world's environmental circumstances—questions that center on the need for an economic and environmental transformation. Additionally, the metaphor seemed appropriate given the nature of our small initiative's ambitious objective: to model the world's energy mix and to publish a book on our findings.

To us, much of the argument over whether we can transform the world's global energy system from conventional power sources to renewable power seemed similar to this imaginary discussion: Envision a cluster of caterpillars sitting around, asking "Can caterpillars fly?" The notion would seem ridiculous to some. "Impossible," they would say. "We have lots of legs and no wings."

For humans, the equivalent of the caterpillars' conversation may be imagining a world without catastrophic environmental degradation, a world where violence and competition over natural resources is neither necessary nor tolerated by the global community and its institutions. Can't you hear the naysayers? "Impossible," they're saying. "We can't possibly make the necessary changes fast enough to reconfigure our global energy systems to be powered by renewable energy." Such skepticism keeps us paralyzed. We all know that transformation takes time. It takes vision. It takes capital investment. And it takes faith.

Happily, we are humans, not caterpillars. We are able to exercise creativity, insight, intellect, and judgment in the pursuit of meeting any challenge we face and transforming deadlock into opportunity. In order to transition, therefore, we must first define the problem, engineer a solution, and make the appropriate investments. We must let go of our collective fear of change, raise our level of consciousness, and adopt a good old-fashioned "get it done" attitude. Fortunately for all of us, these are uniquely human competencies.

This book and the Project Butterfly initiative are but a first step as we in the global community break out of our chrysalis, unfurl our wings, and take flight.

PART I

. . .

THE CASE FOR TRANSFORMATION

You may delay, but time will not,
and lost time is never found again.
—Benjamin Franklin

CHAPTER 1

On March 8, 2013, Capitol Hill heard the first public address in twenty years from George Shultz, secretary of state under President Ronald Reagan (1982–89) and a member of the Partnership for a Secure America. The topic he chose for this landmark occasion was the impact of energy and climate change on national security and economic sustainability. Secretary Schultz told Congress:

> I think it's essential that we apply the insurance policy, Ronald Reagan's insurance policy concept, to our present circumstances . . . We want all forms of energy to bear their full cost so they can compete in the marketplace properly . . . My proposal is to have a revenue-neutral carbon tax . . . I want this to be justified and thought of solely and only as a way of leveling the playing field.[7]

His words were carefully chosen. They conveyed the same wisdom that was always heard in the words spoken by another great statesman, Benjamin Franklin.

• • •

Five years earlier, and three years before the Great Recession of 2008, I was in London, looking for money. At the time, I was CEO of Econergy

International, a company that for ten years had provided technical assistance to international bankers and developers interested in clean energy. Econergy had assisted hundreds of projects throughout more than fifty countries worldwide. As a sideline business, the company had amassed a portfolio of carbon emissions credits in lieu of consulting fees, more so than any other company like it, which made Econergy a world leader in an uncertain and highly speculative carbon market.[8] Now I was in London to find a way to either monetize our portfolio or finance the company so we could survive long enough to transition from a consultancy into an owner of our own clean energy assets. I was traveling with two of my partners, J. P. Moscarella and Marcelo Junqueira, both senior vice presidents of Econergy. Ultimately we wanted to solidify our market position. Raising money, we thought, was the key.

Back in the United States the recent dot-com crash had made it difficult to raise money from the venture capitalist community. The dot-com bubble had driven portfolio values for these venture funds to the moon before the burst sent everything crashing down. The subsequent failure of Enron and the legislation that followed it (the Sarbanes-Oxley Act of 2002) had put a further damper on any attempts to gain new capital for small businesses. In 2004 and 2005, when I came knocking on doors repeatedly in New York, San Francisco, and Houston, venture capitalists and other private equity investors from coast to coast were still licking their wounds.

Moreover, raising money for international clean energy projects driven by the compliance requirements of new international agreements such as the Kyoto Protocol failed to capture the imagination of US investors. They were taking their cues from the sentiment forming in Washington, DC, that the United States should reject the Kyoto Protocol. In 2003 the Bush-Cheney White House had dismissed Kyoto out of hand in its communications to certain members of the US Senate. President George W. Bush thus reversed years of support for mitigating greenhouse gases and for the Kyoto process that dated back to his father's administration and the Reagan-Bush White House before it. In contrast, London-based investors were confidently funding clean energy companies, betting that the Kyoto Protocol would eventually take hold. Econergy's fiercest competitor, EcoSecurities, had recently completed a successful initial public offering (IPO) in London. Trading Emissions PLC, which had not even been on my radar screen, had just raised £135 million (the equivalent of $250 million).[9] The market in London seemed very promising indeed in that fall of 2005.

I was suddenly feeling bullish. The Kyoto Protocol had just gone into full force and effect. Russia had provided the final ratification required to give the agreement a sufficient level of support among its signatories. Kyoto had become a binding international treaty, negating the importance of US ratification. The trading of carbon emissions credits was already under way in Europe, and prices for carbon credits were only going up. Moreover, London was attracting business from the emerging markets for all kinds of natural resource plays, including renewable energy. The London Stock Exchange's Alternative Investment Market (AIM) was offering its investors early-stage opportunities with significant upside potential. London was creating a culture where emerging companies like ours could raise the capital they needed to build their clean energy businesses. Meanwhile, back home it was becoming increasingly difficult to raise money for any small company in the natural resource space.

The AIM looked as though it could be the opportunity Econergy had long been searching for. But I also knew that markets could be tricky and unpredictable. It seemed a little strange: We were an American company— headquartered in Colorado, registered in Delaware—developing renewable energy projects primarily in Latin America and looking for money in the United Kingdom. When I explained Econergy's current strategy to friends and shareholders, I was often confronted with a raised eyebrow. In spite of this response, my partners and I realized that not only had capital markets gone global, but so, too, had the marketplace for specialized services. Looking for money in London wasn't completely crazy—except when you considered the cost of airfare and the high price of a London hotel room. That we were a small and relatively unknown company asking for $100 million of fresh equity only added to the drama of our circumstances. We could only hope this wouldn't be held against us. We were running out of options. In spite of my bullish feelings about the world, I was uncertain as to whether we had the cash reserves to complete an IPO without going back to our shareholders, hats in hand.

Nevertheless, we felt that we were uniquely positioned to finally take advantage of a shifting tide. Our actions followed our worldview, and our view was that the Europeans had already set up their trading system for a carbon-constrained world. European investment bankers were placing their bets on international agreements and national programs that would constrain greenhouse gas (GHG) emissions and develop new, cleaner alternatives to conventional power generation. Meanwhile, the US government was overly preoccupied with its two-war strategy for combating terrorism, and American capitalism seemed confused and out of sync with the rest of the world's efforts. My partners and I saw a window of opportunity in London, and we knew that we needed to jump through it quickly—or risk missing the opportunity once and for all.

I realized that we were pinning our hopes on the fact that the trading of carbon credits could generate trillions of dollars in business transactions. The concept of trading carbon credits was appealing to European policy makers because it would enable countries to cap their GHG emissions and to reduce their carbon footprint through trading arrangements rather than force them to rely exclusively on mandatory investments in response to new regulations. Emissions trading provided the right kind of incentive to innovate technologies that would further reduce GHGs by encouraging the market to identify and build the most profitable clean energy projects first.

The European public media, including the *Financial Times* and the *Economist,* continued to quote scientists and environmental advocates who blamed the buildup of carbon emissions on coal-fired electric power generation and the burning of oil to fuel our global transportation system. Clean energy from renewable resources like solar and wind power was being promoted as the investment opportunity of a lifetime. Cap and trade systems offering new regulatory structures that promoted clean energy were seen as the preferred policy of nations to encourage private-sector investments in new clean energy, as aging conventional power-generation systems would eventually be taken off-line to meet global and national GHG reduction targets.

My team and I figured we had perhaps six months, and certainly no more than nine, to pull off an IPO—assuming our shareholders back home would support us. During that time period, we met with investment bankers in London, including ABN AMRO, Nomura Securities, and Numis Securities. We landed with a lead banker by the name of Amer Khan from Numis Securities. Khan had a reputation for taking on smaller but promising companies, and we felt the chemistry was right. We just needed the support of our board and shareholders.

As part of our engagement, Numis wanted Econergy to first create a London-based relationship that would provide third-party validation of our market position. Khan sent us to visit the CEO of Trading Emissions PLC, Simon Shaw, who had recently taken his own company public on the London AIM. Trading Emissions was in the business of "investing in environmental and emissions assets"—in other words, carbon.[10] Over the next thirty days, we jetted back and forth from Denver to London, often holding contentious board meetings on the fly. Asking for more money from friends and family is never a fun process, especially when you are on your third or fourth round of promising them future riches.

We were entering the final stretch, but nevertheless I was growing tired and uncertain of our ability to make this deal happen. I was living out of a suitcase, traveling between Latin America and London, and taking sink showers in the lavatory at Heathrow before meeting with investment bankers. Eventually, with longtime associate and Econergy board member Richard Perl at my side, our team pulled off a small miracle by entering into an $8 million financing agreement with Trading Emissions. The deal included $4 million of working capital and a commitment to participate in our IPO for an additional $4 million. The working capital was collateralized with carbon credits from Econergy's portfolio of renewable energy projects. Demonstrating the nascent power of the carbon market, it was the largest carbon futures contract of its kind and put us squarely on a path to launch our IPO. We had the full support of our board before the ink dried, and we started working with Numis Securities to prepare for the IPO just after 2006 arrived.

THE ELEPHANT IN THE ROOM

When scientists, physicists, or economists write their stories about global warming and how to address it, the solution they commonly propose goes something like this: "Shut down coal-fired power plants, close off oil pipelines, and build wind, solar, and nuclear power plants to replace them." It sounds simple. Unfortunately, it is not. The issue still outstanding—the elephant in the room—is this: Who will lead and fund this transformation? Do we get the government to fund it, or can we tap the capital markets? The amount of capital needed to fund this transformation is not trivial.

I believe that building small energy companies is a key part of any solution. My story about Econergy presents a microcosm of how to structure access to capital for the global energy market as a whole. For example, before any energy project can be launched, the company sponsoring a project or new technology needs to become a player in the industry and to develop alliances to attract institutional funding. The same is true if we are to make a big enough difference in our global energy mix to address the threat of climate change. Global alliances will need to be struck, and international funding sources will need to be made readily available. Once they are in place, the marketplace will do the rest.

In Econergy's case, in order for the company to be launched as an IPO, the board of directors had to be altered to include players known inside London's financial circles. So Econergy recruited Neil Eckert, the chairman of Trading Emissions (and later CEO of the freshly formed Climate Exchange PLC), to serve as its new chairman. Because of our focus on the carbon market, we asked Jed Jones, a consultant to the UK government on climate change, to join the board. In addition, we were required to have a resident from the Isle of Man (a small island that lies between the United Kingdom and Ireland, which was to be our new corporate domicile to avoid double taxation by the UK government), so we recruited a former public accountant, Peter Vanderpump. To finalize the makeup of the board and clinch the IPO, we recruited Wayne Keast, who represented the interests of investor Vincent Tchenguiz. Vincent, the owner of Consensus Business Group and one of London's more colorful elite investors, was trying to accumulate everything in energy that was "clean."

As part of the IPO process, Econergy also had to select securities counsel. We chose Giles Beale from Reed Smith, an international law firm headquartered in the United States but with a strong presence in London. His firm would provide the legal bridge between US shareholders and the London capital markets. Beale was an unusual lawyer by London standards. His boyish looks and frequent stammer disguised his penchant for negotiating the better end of a deal. When we ended our business tenure together, I called him "the only gentleman in London." How does the old saying go? *Keep your friends close and your enemies closer.* Well, I would now complete the sentence with: *and keep your lawyer even closer.*

The lessons I learned in the process were many, but the one that truly stands out is what raising real money actually looks like. In our early days in London, my Brazilian partner, Marcelo Junqueira, would say, "Never put your briefcase on the floor. It is a bad omen. You always put your briefcase on a chair. That way it can be easily opened in order to put the money in it."

FIRING UP THE IMAGINATION OF THE INVESTOR

When you are raising money, you are always in the presence of an investment banker carrying a PowerPoint presentation. Your only job as the CEO or as an executive on the management team is to fire up the imagination of the equity investor. Firing up the imagination of the investor requires having unique visibility into the big picture and ensuring that you share the essential background of your project with your audience. You also need a command of the details so that, if necessary, you can reshape and summarize them in headline-style sentences. With these three things in hand—an inspiring presentation, a sense of the big picture, and a command of the details—you'll increase the odds of money flowing into your briefcase.

Similarly, if the global society is to create a viable campaign to mitigate climate change, the energy industry needs to create a new investor presentation. This new presentation needs to show the big picture and establish a shared background. It needs to build the regional alliances. It needs to enlist the support of investment bankers. Then we need to fire up the world's imagination with a new worldview.

The boardroom provides a unique place where the senior executive is encouraged by the directors to look at the forest—the big picture—and not the trees. An executive's day-to-day management certainly involves looking beneath the bark of an individual tree as he or she interacts with other company managers. However, the navigation of any enterprise must start at the top by taking a broad view as a way to strategize and build consensus throughout the organization. The problem of addressing climate change is no different; we need to look at the forests before we examine the health of the individual trees.

In the introduction, I took this 30,000-foot perspective in summarizing the key findings of Project Butterfly: We need to stimulate capital markets to fund renewable energy. We need to invest in technologies that lower GHGs. And we need to create a regulatory environment that encourages the flow of new capital.

After more than two years of looking at the issues of climate change, the Project Butterfly team has assembled several executive-level questions and answers that helped us reach the above findings. They are the four fundamental principles that will help us form the new business case:

» **What will it take to fire the imagination of investors so that we can change our global energy system into one that can sufficiently address the threats of a changing climate?** Warnings of climate change have not fired up (and will not fire up) the imagination of our capital markets. Figuring out a way for suppliers and their bankers to make money will. And unless you can get investors fired up, they will be risk averse and capital will not flow.

» **What are the social, economic, and political changes necessary to engage the capital markets?** Our social, economic, and political institutions must evolve and respond to the bigger picture rather than negotiating exclusively from a place of self-interest. Incorporating elements of cooperation among stakeholders expands the game and can lead to mutual benefit and greater profitability.

» **Will change only come about when there is clear consensus within the global society that we face an existential threat?** Change is under way, but resistance to acknowledging the immediacy of the problem of climate change will persist until there is consensus on the solution, not just the problem.

» **Will governments have to declare war on climate change in order to condemn the burning of fossil fuels, or is it possible to simply change the rules that govern our energy assets and unleash the power of capital markets?** Sufficient precedent exists domestically and internationally to hold suppliers accountable for the transport of emissions, including CO_2, into the atmosphere. Simply implementing measures to tax what you burn and not what you earn would enforce these precedents and release market forces to counteract the largest threat that has ever faced humankind. That said, it will take a willful act by governments to align their energy policy with their economic interests.

The heart of the issue relating to all four of these principles is that energy is not just a commodity. Energy is a service, and this raises issues for certain stakeholders. Beyond working to create an efficient allocation of goods and services, the marketplace is affected by certain policy goals. Such policy goals can include working to enhance national security and to improve environmental safety. To achieve effective commerce, therefore, industry and regulators must work together to review policy goals and to establish the rules of the game. Such words may sound like heresy to market purists. But energy is a critical input to any economy. And policy makers often see markets as servants rather than as masters.

Allow me to illustrate. In any successful transition to a new transportation system using electric vehicles, "powering stations" for recharging must be available in adequate numbers and in appropriate locations so that a driver can rely on service no matter the route or the distance. Because initial demand will be very small, incentives may be required to prod existing gas stations to power up. This in turn will require a large capital investment and relative assurance that eventually there will be adequate demand for this service. Moreover, product delivery will need to be standardized; industry-standard smart plugs, for example, would allow different electric cars from different manufacturers to access the same power sources. A transformation to such an industry as automobile transportation is equivalent to building a large bridge over a river or bay. Only public ownership, or some sort of public-private partnership, can organize the necessary capital to construct such a bridge, because only government can either impose a community-wide toll or grant users the necessary relief.

So in order for industry to take an interest in and take advantage of a new opportunity, such as a technological innovation that is predicated on wide-scale use, public and private leadership must work together to shape the landscape of the energy market. It is a strange paradox that many may not be able or willing to see: The general public is by and large critical of corporate lobbyists and critical of public officials who engage with industry to form policy. But we are also forced to recognize that coordination is essential. To make it all work, we need to see that the difference between good and bad policy is as simple as knowing that there is transparency—that the social and economic innovation needed to address climate change will require federal, state, and city governments to coordinate with private industry—and that the process for setting this new landscape needs to be open to public view.

For example, the monopolies that were set up to electrify our nation at the beginning of the twentieth century will likely need to be deconstructed to allow free markets to innovate and bring in new capital. Tearing down these legal frameworks from the past to open up global energy markets to competition will need to take place in a public process and require a delicate balance. Without the proper assurances that past agreements will be honored, industry might simply wait on the sidelines for the dust to settle. Only if there is ample coordination by all market participants, including the government, will industry join in and make sure the public gets what it wants—a competitive, reliable, and safe supply of energy.

Furthermore, when both public and private leaders start using identical language, capital markets will get fired up. The system will work when both industry and the public see new regulation as reducing market uncertainty and creating price signals that stimulate investment without causing harm to the environment or creating an undue cost on any single class of stakeholders. Industry will move onto the playing field, and capital will form. Keep in mind that new regulations are not bad. They are just new regulations. The issue is whether they can be effective in meeting their policy goals.

These observations flow from the perspective that financial and risk capital can build new companies, even megacorporations, out of nothing more than an idea. Demand for the idea does not necessarily need to exist prior to the innovation itself. The potential may simply be ubiquitous. For example, no one demanded to hear music as they walked to school or work before the invention of the Sony Walkman. Now, listening to music as we traverse the subway system or walk through the park is considered essential, and this one-time "innovation" is a central feature of every smartphone. This observation has profound implications for capital markets: Although they can be characterized as fragile, fickle, or even ruthless, they have an astounding creative capacity to generate new possibilities.

To get capital to move, whether to build new empires or to rebuild old ones, requires only a new conversation that reignites the possibility of above-average returns. It all starts with a vision that is shared by the necessary community of participants, regulators, and industry leaders who are committed to making it happen.

INVOKING THE CAPITAL MARKETS

When the subject of climate change is discussed, a peculiar view often emerges. This view tends to accept the business-as-usual scenario as an inevitable outcome of the economic system or simply the human condition. According to this perspective, the power of greed shapes and drives our capital markets, and it is this greed that has caused the global society to industrialize and has allowed the buildup of excessive levels of GHGs. In other words, a merciless capitalist spirit is at the root of our climate change problem, and addressing climate change requires the elimination of the capitalist system that underlies it.

Oddly this point of view can emerge from both the far left and the far right of the political spectrum. In light of this view, it takes an almost aikido-like response to initiate a different world view. On the one hand, such a response requires agreeing that greed will work its way into our economic system and will have both positive and negative consequences. Furthermore, the response requires a counterintuitive and perhaps risky acknowledgment that the solution to climate change actually depends on capitalism to pull us out of the quagmire.

The only alternative to invoking the capital markets is relying on governments and public finance to rebuild our global energy system. Relying on governments has its own downsides, however. One of these is the uncertainty of whether governments and public finance can move quickly enough and at a scale large enough to make a difference. We know that governments have mounted wars in the past that have organized capital at unparalleled rates. For instance, during World War II the United States mobilized nearly every aspect of our industrial capacity to build enough ships and tanks to subdue the rise of Nazism in Europe and to overcome the Japanese in the Pacific. So we shouldn't dismiss public spending as a way to address climate change. The world spends about 4 percent of its global economic output on wars and military defense. But fighting wars is rarely sustainable, whereas efforts to spur the capital markets to address climate change can be.

The transition to a sustainable economy requires a different interpretation of what drives our capital markets. In spite of how greed may influence our capital markets, I don't believe that our global industry is the product of greed. Capital markets are the product of an intense human desire to build and create new possibilities. Capital markets exist as a creative source to address fundamental human concerns and needs and to organize the talents and capital necessary to manifest innovative solutions. Rather than avarice, our capital markets are an example of unprecedented human creativity. The creation of wealth is certainly a result of the process. But the maximization of wealth is more a measure of the capital markets' success rather than their raison d'être.

Regulatory policies play their role, too. Regulations exist to make sure that markets operate efficiently. Regulatory policy is therefore the principle vehicle for stimulating the necessary social innovations to obtain global sustainability and encourage us to live within a limited environmental footprint. Regulations are neither bad nor good, just as capital markets are neither bad nor good. But there is a difference between *effective* and *ineffective* regulations, just as there is a difference between efficient and inefficient markets.

Take, for example, the transformation from horses to cars in the United States, which occurred more than a hundred years ago. The government regulated safety and environmental standards in the automobile industry, and industry complied ingeniously at every intersection. For example, cars have evolved from having a simple tailpipe to being equipped with catalytic converters. Airbags, which are now standard in 100 percent of cars sold in the United States, hadn't even been invented when I was born. The system succeeds when regulations achieve their policy goals.

What makes capital markets work is that there seems to be no limit to the speed of money. Since the turn of this century, international capital markets have risen quickly and global equity markets, in particular, have become increasingly easy to access. Day traders in New York City, or even in Des Moines, are able to move their risk capital from the London market to Hong Kong and back to London practically in a single day. Twenty-five years ago, this would have been impossible. Flows of international capital were regulated and procedures were manual, whereas now all transactions are electronic and nearly instantaneous. Capital flows faster today, but not because of regulation or even deregulation. Capital flows faster because of technical *innovation*. Such innovation means that our regulatory bodies must respond even more quickly—because existing regulations become antiquated almost overnight and they must be regularly updated to remain effective. In order for capital markets to function efficiently, regulations need to keep pace.

Today trade magazines of nearly every industry acknowledge that global sustainability is the new condition we must strive for and design our regulatory environment to achieve. To keep pace, global regulations must be built upon an effective, shared sustainability model. Otherwise, the system risks the potential of a worldwide breakdown. Global markets are now linked with every regional market and can crash all at once, in one fell swoop. Oceans may separate nations, but they are certainly no longer a defining boundary for capital markets. So to achieve global sustainability, the global society must coordinate new regulations between and among nations to a degree never before imagined.

DRAWING FAULT LINES

What kind of regulations do we need? The crisis the environment faces, like any crisis financial markets might face, does not respect man-made borders. News of global environmental challenges—melting in the polar regions, crop failures, deadly hurricanes, and raging forest fires—regularly make front-page news. Left unaddressed—that is, if we fail to regulate our use of shared global resources—these events will intensify until the problem explodes. The consequences will likely show up in many ways, such as exorbitant prices at the gas pump, but will also be evident by the burst of a financial bubble as higher environmental costs work their way through the global economy. There are nearly infinite possibilities for global peace and trade, but the nature of our global resources is mostly finite, and fault lines reflecting this reality have formed all around the world. To create balance, our global society must first see the connection between these natural catastrophes and our resource use, and then we must set rules for competition to ensure that our use of resources allows the system to rejuvenate. When we are able to balance the use of our natural resources, we can then live within our limits while still preserving and creating greater value for all classes of stakeholders.

In fact, global sustainability is possible only when there is a strong ecosystem that is able to support the transfer of capital from our natural reservoirs into public and private ownership without jeopardizing their ability to replenish. Therefore, the regulations that will lead to global sustainability will result from governments setting rules that traffic our common resource use. To some market enthusiasts hoping for a technological solution, this is a depressing conclusion—but the alternative would be much worse. We don't need to look very far back in history to see examples of governments responding to similar crises. The events of World War II led to the rationing of both food and fuel in many countries. The same could happen again—or worse—unless we prove to be a little more farsighted.

FINDING THE CURE

Climate change skeptics have often claimed that "the cure is worse than the disease." Considering their ostrichlike perspective on the dangers of the climate change "disease," it comes as no surprise that this assessment includes a backward-looking view of what the "cure" might be. Indeed, since they appear to believe that any "cure" for drastic climate change is intolerable, one wonders how much serious thought these skeptics have given to the problem. Perhaps they, and all of us in different ways, need to be open to the possibility of surprise.

For example, when policies give clear and sustained economic signals to suppliers and investors, they can set off a process of market innovation. Sometimes the accumulated innovations can even change the definition of the goal. Among the many historical examples of this dynamic, the classic example for climate change policy is the regulation of sulfur oxide (SOx) emissions in the United States in the early 1980s, which resulted in the first large, practical application of a "cap and trade" approach to reducing pollution. Using econometric models that implicitly incorporated the parameters of existing technology at that time, industry lobbyists argued that the cost of compliance with the new SOx standards would be too expensive for industry. In the end, however, the cost proved to be very small and the benefits substantial. The policy was a huge success.

Today's climate change situation is similar. Some claim, based on calculations like those made in arguments against the SOx standards, that the economic costs of adequately mitigating GHG emissions will be devastatingly high. However, if policies to reduce GHG emissions can mobilize the forces of competition and enhance the capability of capital markets to support innovation just as with the SOx program, new solutions will appear that reduce the relative cost of the new paradigm. It has already begun with climate change: In spite of the controversy we may read about in the papers, the parameters of wind and solar energy have already proven their competitive power in the new millennium.

THE ULTIMATE DRIVING MACHINE

In looking around the globe for a market that has taken advantage of political and economic changes, including innovations in energy policies, the country of Germany immediately comes to mind. An industrial giant and a member of the G-7, Germany is one of the seven richest nations in the world. At the foundation of its economy is the manufacturing of high-end engineering goods and services. Its industrial base also has the reputation of having the highest standards for excellent design and workmanship. German name brands such as BMW ("the ultimate driving machine"), Volkswagen, and Mercedes-Benz attest to both.

With the largest national economy in Europe, Germany is the financial powerhouse within the eurozone. Globally, it is the third-largest exporter in the world, behind only the United States and China.[11] With a population of roughly eighty million inhabitants, Germany exports nearly $1.5 trillion of goods and services annually, which represents about one-third of the country's gross domestic product (GDP). The nation accomplishes this stunning achievement while still importing the majority of its raw materials, including the oil and natural gas it uses to run its industry.

Why Germany is a good example of social and technical innovation starts with the observation that it is a country capable of making bold moves. One such move was the 1990 reunification of East Germany and West Germany. The two countries quickly merged their economies by agreeing to replace East Germany's currency with the deutsche mark, transferring financial sovereignty to West Germany. In response, West Germany started granting subsidies to East Germany to diminish the large social gap between the two economic systems. Within a matter of months, the legislative bodies of both countries voted to apply the laws of West Germany and to unify the two countries after more than forty-five years of the Cold War.

Then in 1998 Germany made another bold move. This time it wanted to address its dependency on foreign energy imports in fueling its economy. The German Green Party joined the federal government in an initiative to redefine the country's power industry. The renewable energy sector immediately benefited from the passage of the Renewable Energy Sources Act,[12] which required electricity suppliers to pay tariffs for renewable energy to feed into the power grid. The German capital markets responded aggressively to this promotion of an alternative energy source by backing the emergence of existing and new suppliers that were offering technological solutions and taking advantage of available resources. Germany originally set a target of having 12 percent of its power come from renewable energy by 2010. By 2007 it had already exceeded its 2010 target and reached 14 percent. Three years later, more than 17 percent of Germany's electricity supply was produced from renewable energy.

On the heels of this success, in 2010 the German government announced an even more ambitious target of providing 35 percent of its electricity from renewable energy by 2020 and 80 percent by 2050.[13] With the nation's simultaneous phaseout of nuclear power, these new, higher targets are not just rhetorical. They are real.

Moreover, Germany has built new businesses on the back of its energy initiatives. Capitalizing on the country's reputation as a premier global supplier of engineered goods and services, Germany's leading banks have funded and developed an industry of wind and solar energy suppliers. Companies such as Nordex and Enercon (world innovators in wind energy) and Solar-World and Conergy (large solar energy companies with global interests) are headquartered in Germany.

The success of the Renewable Energy Sources Act was not unequivocal, but it was bold and innovative. The net metering approach implied a price set by the regulator, which was intentionally comfortable for renewable energy suppliers and reduced the pressures of competition. One unintended consequence was that the long-term fall in photovoltaic (PV) module prices was interrupted for a few years. In the future, greater attention must be paid to harnessing the power of competition to reduce subsidies per kilowatt-hour, especially with the European Union in the midst of its own economic crisis and with Germany engaged in a massive expansion of renewables in the wake of phasing out nuclear power. But given its industrial capacity and its penchant for innovation, something tells me that Germany will work out a solution.

SPARKING A FIRESTORM

The success of Germany can be contrasted with the disappointment over some of President Obama's first-term efforts to stimulate the economy in the aftermath of the 2008 financial crisis by promoting "green jobs." However, it is often said that we learn from failure more than we do from success. This is especially true in the world of business. The story of California-based solar company Solyndra (see text box on following pages) marks a black eye in the latest phase of public investment in clean technology in the United States. Solyndra secured a $535 million debt guarantee from the US Department of Energy in 2009. Just two years later the company filed for bankruptcy, sparking a firestorm against the Obama administration and its support of clean energy. This setback is an acknowledgment that "going green" is not necessarily a panacea to all problems, and yet it also provides us with some valuable lessons on how to move forward.

In the beginning Solyndra's technology seemed like a perfect example of technological innovation within the thriving solar business. In the end, however, global markets were ruthless. The ability to compete on price eluded the management team.

One of the many lessons to be learned from the story of Solyndra, however, is that as energy investors, we must separate investing in new technology from investing in new power generation. Technology investing is best suited to investors who can handle exposure to high levels of risk. You really do not know how well a technology will compete in the market until you have built it, sold it, and accounted for it. Moreover, *lending money* to a start-up company with an unproven technology rather than *investing equity* in that company is probably the best way to kill a technology. The general rule in business is that getting a new product to market always takes more time and money than anticipated. Strapping the company with high principle and interest payments and a maturity date will limit its flexibility for future equity financing.

In the 2012 presidential race the Republican Party used the failure of Solyndra as fuel for their argument against President Obama's green-jobs initiatives and economic stimulus plan. True, Solyndra was a failure. But it was only one failure in a long list of bold moves that stopped the economy from falling off the cliff. Taken from another perspective, the failure of Solyndra sparks a new conversation about energy policy. It is not an example of how green energy is wrong. Rather, Solyndra's failure provides insight on reshaping policy goals and an opportunity to learn about what worked and what didn't. It is an opportunity for us to examine how to reshape policy and make it more effective.

We can begin to see what is effective when we compare Germany's experience with the Solyndra experience. Investment-grade loans are geared to companies and projects that have either stable revenue streams or

ANATOMY OF A FAILURE

In 2008 Solyndra was a new company promising a new technology that would provide yet another breakthrough in the efficiency of solar energy. Solyndra's solar system provided an innovative design with rows of cylindrical cells rather than a single panel of flat cells. Throughout the day, as the sun tracked across a cylinder, it would always be shining directly on some part of the newly designed PV cell. The cylindrical design offered the added benefit of picking up indirect light, even sunlight bouncing off the rooftop on which it was mounted.[14] While Solyndra was developing its technology, however, prices for crystalline silicon were skyrocketing, and investors in the solar market were looking for alternatives to these materials. Solyndra promised a competitive advantage.

Solyndra wanted to quickly establish its technology by building a factory and producing its solar systems on a large commercial scale to compete for the booming international market. The company tapped a federal loan fund that had been created by the US Congress in 2005, initially to support the nuclear power industry. Public utilities had chosen not to develop nuclear power projects in spite of the availability of funds. In the absence of financing alternatives, companies in the solar, wind, and ethanol industries saw tapping these funds as an opportunity.

take-or-pay contracts that will immediately generate revenues upon a project going into operation. Power purchase agreements from a utility represent the kind of take-or-pay contract that can be backed by an investor or a lender. Alternatively, new technology start-ups require equity financing, not debt loads.

My observation is not just academic. I have a personal experience to share, having spent two years working a clean coal company out from under the remnants of a $100 million debt facility when the company was still

Meanwhile, the White House was looking for ways to support industry that would produce jobs. Solyndra, and other companies like it, sought to make use of government debt guarantees. After receiving its $535 million loan guarantee from the Department of Energy (DOE) in 2009, Solyndra immediately started construction on its second factory and expanded its workforce to more than a thousand employees.

One year later, the company was preparing for its IPO and executing on its business plan to raise an additional $300 million of new cash. It was also seeking a second loan under an expanded DOE program full of stimulus money, approved by Congress in the wake of the 2008 Great Recession. The new solar panels were working in accordance with their design, but some of the manufacturing machinery needed to be redesigned, which meant delays.

Suddenly the story about Solyndra began to change. Delays were only symbolic of the emerging problem. Pricing for their solar systems was well above Solyndra's original plans. Costs were being recalculated and coming in at more than 30 percent per watt above the price of traditional PV panels.

Coincidently, the Chinese solar industry was booming. Chinese manufacturers were producing panels at a price Solyndra could never compete against. As a result, Solyndra failed.

pre-revenue. The original purchasers of the debt facility hedged their positions by shorting the company's shares, creating what is commonly called a Wall Street "death spiral." All the company had was a breakthrough technology, which left it vulnerable to both positive and negative market speculation.

I suspect that the Solyndra technology will eventually reemerge once the company works its way through bankruptcy. My guess is that the next investor buying the technology out of bankruptcy will certainly use equity, not debt, to fund Solyndra's reemergence. Lending to Solyndra in the early stages of development was like throwing a big log on the campfire before there was a proper bed of coals. It snuffed out the potential by forcing the company, and its technology, into bankruptcy.

GUIDEPOSTS FOR UNITED STATES ECONOMIC AND ENERGY POLICY

The success of Germany's energy policy in setting targets and then exceeding them, and the bankruptcy of Solyndra, a promising technological solution, provide two guideposts for US economic and energy policy. Germany's energy policy called for feed-in tariffs that gave renewable energy suppliers (and their backers) confidence that when they built a new power plant, they would recover their capital. Conversely, the story of Solyndra suggests that capital using public debt sources should be made available only if a reliable revenue stream backs the underlying credit.

To validate our observations, let's look at how the capital markets seem to behave with respect to the financing of new power generation. New renewable power plant construction typically will be backed by a long-term power purchase agreement with a utility. Investors in the power plant can likely rely on payments from the utility given the monopolistic strength granted to the utility provider by state regulatory authorities. For example, independent power plant owners will raise money either internally through their own balance sheet or externally through tapping equity markets by issuing shares in their ownership. The equity invested in the project will then be used as collateral to secure a loan that covers the majority of the required financing—usually 60 to 70 percent of the total cost of construction. Often the power purchase agreement will provide take-or-pay provisions to give the lender and equity investor sufficient comfort that once the power plant is built, revenue will flow. The equity takes the risk that the plant will be built on time and within budget. The power plant owner ensures that sufficient recurring cash will be generated to cover not only operating costs but also debt service costs.

The feed-in tariff provided under Germany's Renewable Energy Sources

Act provided terms and conditions to renewable energy suppliers similar to those that a traditional power purchase agreement provides to any third-party generator. The energy policy that put in place the feed-in tariff simply set the rules for engagement and sent a clear signal into the power market. German industry was able to respond aggressively by providing innovative and competitive engineering solutions. Lenders were able to participate because they felt comfortable that once the project was built and performing, it would generate sufficient cash to satisfy customary debt covenants and thus achieve their requirements for funding.

The key to unlocking the potential of the capital markets, therefore, is to understand some of the principles that rule them. These general principles involve the advocacy of three of the four stakeholders discussed in the new business case for mitigating climate change. Equity, or risk capital, is typically advanced prior to any drawdown on the debt portion of the financing. Risk is greatest in the early stages of a project, when the project sponsor or supplier procures the right to the resource, conducts the appropriate resource measurement surveys and engineering studies, and secures equipment to build the project. All this groundwork solidifies the overall project budget and capitalization. Then, the drawdown on debt financing is dependent on certain thresholds being met while the project is under construction, when there is minimal risk relative to cost overruns and the possibility of creating a stranded asset.

Financial capital, or debt financing, is used to leverage equity returns, but only when revenues are secured through a contract with the energy user in the form of an electric utility and when construction costs are locked in through contracts with equipment suppliers. Such a structure provides a bankable transaction, unlike the construction of a new factory, as with Solyndra, whose product was still untested in the market.

The lender will then take a secured interest in the project that has superior rights to repayment over the interest of the equity holder. In exchange, the debt holder expects a lower return on invested capital and requires periodic interest payments, relying on the equity holder to ensure that the project is built and operated as efficiently as possible.

The challenge for the lender, particularly in the energy industry, is to make sure that the transaction is as risk free as possible. Any deviation in the market's demand for power can have disastrous effects. For this reason, lenders will look to federal energy policy for guidance and to the market for a signal that it is okay to proceed with their lending initiatives. The issue is not trivial. Typical repayment of a loan happens over a time span of fifteen to thirty years, so the lender is looking for as much assurance as possible that energy users will be around to buy the power for years and years to come and that the energy services generated from their investments remain competitive. That is why lenders look first to federal energy policy, then to the utility system, and finally to the relationship between the energy supplier and the energy user.

In contrast, the interest of the energy user is much different than that of the energy supplier or lender and is only part of the equation. Energy users want reliable energy services at the least possible cost, regardless of whether the power plant repays its debt or provides an equity return to the supplier. The interest of the energy user becomes aligned with that of the supplier only when the use of financing allows the supplier to charge rates at close to the levelized cost of energy.[15] Financing allows the minimization of out-of-pocket expenses and directly covers the cost of capital. Otherwise the energy user would have to incur the full brunt of the up-front costs.

The supplier, the lender, and the user are therefore all critical stakeholders in the development of any new power infrastructure. Although there is a symbiotic relationship between the stakeholders, each party has its own interests, which are unique but also interrelated. For the system to work, the lender requires assurances from the supplier. The supplier requires assurances from the energy user. What gives all of these assurances credibility is the federal, state, or municipal regulatory body that is responsible for the entire utility system. Taking on the climate change problem therefore requires looking at these relationships and designing effective policies that will change the global energy mix.

KEY OBSERVATIONS

A new business case is built on the following four key principles that I have shared with you in this chapter:

» Figuring out a way for energy suppliers and lenders to make money while mitigating climate change will fire up the imagination of investors. Germany did this by establishing aggressive renewable energy targets that gave investors the confidence they needed in order to invest. Because of these aggressive targets, investments in renewable energy in Germany reached €31.6 billion in 2010, up from €19.3 billion and €14.0 billion in 2009 and 2008, respectively.[16] The results of these investment decisions are beginning to show: In 2011 Germany experienced a 2.4 percent decrease in CO_2 emissions compared with its 2010 level.[17]

» Engaging institutions, including small businesses, to incorporate elements of cooperation that mitigate GHGs expands the game and leads to the mutual benefit of suppliers and users.

» Building consensus on solutions to climate change, in addition to acknowledging the existence of the problem, will lead to real and substantive action. The media and certain advocacy groups continue to argue over whether or not climate change is a real occurrence and whether or not humans are responsible. In reality, and within the scientific community, this debate has largely been finalized. To most of the global community, it has become painfully clear that the waterfall is just ahead and the safety of the shore is nearly beyond the reach of our canoe.

» Incorporating the true cost of burning fossil fuels by fixing a price on CO_2 offers the potential to unleash the capital markets and eventually lead to greater wealth for all stakeholder classes. It is the equivalent of a decision to portage around the falls well ahead of the tipping point.

We, the generation that faces the next century, can add the solemn injunction, "If we don't do the impossible, we shall be faced with the unthinkable."
—Petra Kelly

CHAPTER 2

Come. Enter into a different world. Consider a world that Petra Kelly—an influential politician and environmentalist, and founder of the German Green Party—warned would be "unthinkable." See what might unfold if the global society fails to act . . .

If I were to create a composite of all the predictions I've heard about climate change, an alarming portrait would emerge. The planet would heat up to intolerable levels, causing more and more of Greenland and Antarctica's land ice to melt, well before the end of this century. The seas would rise and devour shorelines and whole cities. Our fisheries would no longer produce fish. Our deserts would rapidly expand. Heat waves would create pockets of stagnation, trapping air pollution over landlocked cities, making it increasingly difficult for humans and animals to breathe. Fires would rip through our forests and countryside. Drought, erosion, and swarms of insects would cause worldwide food shortages and starvation. Disease would sweep through our communities. Businesses would falter as patronage drops and would be forced into short-term survival mode. Resource management would be a concept lost to the past. Long-term planning and investing would be moot. Democratically elected nations and their governments would struggle to hold on to power.

The Internet would give rise to interconnected crowds around the world. These crowds will demand that power centers take immediate steps to address climate change. The 2011 Arab Spring would have gone global, with protesters seeking greater democracy, but not from the monarchies overseeing oil empires. Those regimes will have already fallen. Rather, organizers would throw out elected officials put into office on the back of multimillion-dollar-funded campaigns. They would demand the broadcast of legislative decisions via Twitter in order to meet the need for rapid change. High on the agenda would be demands for corporations that have long hoarded cash to share their wealth and to cover the high costs resultant from climate change. The social outcry would make the Occupy Wall Street movement that started in 2011 seem like a picnic in the park.

And the response from commentators would be "It's just the way it is."

Does this sound like a science fiction movie?

The answer is "Yes, it does"—but also "No, not necessarily." It sounds like fiction because it's too horrible to imagine. It does not sound like science fiction because the warming of the planet actually is on a trajectory that is unlikely to change. This vision of a world gone mad parallels many of the projected outcomes from global warming—that is, if we fail to signal a change in course and try to stop it. Change usually occurs when there is a new signal, a request to vary the course. When the light turns from green to red at an intersection, the changing light demands that traffic stops. If the light stays green, traffic will just keep plowing forward.

You may have seen similar climate change outcomes depicted in such movies as *The Day After Tomorrow* (2004), starring Dennis Quaid as a climate scientist. The apocalyptic conditions set in the movie were fantasy-based, portraying a scenario where climate change didn't heat up the planet but froze it. Luckily, the predictions I am sharing will take years—perhaps to the end of the century—to be fully borne out, unlike this Hollywood film, in which conditions unfolded over a matter of days. However, the end of the century isn't really that far off. It is certainly within the reach of our grandchildren and, perhaps, even our own children.

Do you find this scenario—a world suffering from drastic climate change and the likelihood of ensuing chaos—alarming? The future I've described is not out of the realm of possibility. A Hollywood movie isn't a light signal that will cause individual consumers to change their behavior, nor is it meant to be. The movie is intended to entertain an audience, nothing more. And yet based on available data, the outcome described here is similar to what we should expect within the foreseeable future, especially if we stick to the status quo, with no one willing to flip the switch and demand a change in course.

THE FUTURE IS NOW

The scientific reports that suggest such a cataclysmic future are certainly much more measured in their tone than a Hollywood script is. The authors of these reports, such as assessments on climate change produced by the United Nations' Intergovernmental Panel on Climate Change (IPCC), almost always articulate the limitations of their predictive models. Moreover, they rarely try to quantify either the economic consequences of a warming planet or the practicalities of trying to mitigate those consequences. But you need to know that the future is now and that these scientists aren't joking. They are educated professionals who have devoted their lives to studies in the natural sciences. They are not giving you half-baked, handheld calculations. These experts are running computer simulations using the world's largest computers, taking in data that require weeks and months to generate probabilities. I have seen the computers running some of these simulations, and I have read many of the reports. Yet I don't need to look at their models to see what is happening. I only have to look at market conditions and to consider the year-over-year (compounding) growth in global energy consumption since the 1970s to know that the current situation is unsustainable.

There are certainly industry reports that show declining US energy consumption from higher efficiency standards. But these reports largely ignore the global trends. As an executive, I liken the reports from government-funded scientists on climate change to status reports from business managers that start out by saying "We might be slightly over budget" or "We are a little behind schedule." However, experience leads me to believe that if action is not taken immediately to address the problem of climate change, ultimately the scientific reports will show outcomes that are significantly over budget and substantially behind schedule. Based on observable data such as warmer ocean temperatures, melting ice sheets, and higher global temperatures, unless we devote executive attention and management to the climate change problem, we can expect outcomes to worsen, not to improve simply with the passage of time.

Moreover, I am alarmed by these reports not because of some potential, future danger. As I look at the global energy industry as it is today, I see self-protecting actions and a complex political debate keeping the United States, the world's most powerful country, from developing any kind of effective federal energy or international climate policy. Proposed energy policies throughout the 1990s and the early 2000s in the United States have represented nothing more than a bundle of benefits handed out like Christmas gifts to satisfy the lobbyists of each interest group. Even President Obama's "all of the above" energy strategy reflects this conformity to satisfy every energy lobbyist. Meanwhile, looking at the bigger global picture, I think about mass demonstrations in the summer of 2012 against austerity measures in Europe as a result of job losses and mounting national debts. I remember watching CNN report continuously on environmental disasters like Hurricane Sandy while natural gas and clean coal associations advertised the wonders of new technologies that enabled them to drill deeper and wider, freeing up vast energy supplies. These two themes have dominated the press, and I begin to see a link between them and climate change.

I acknowledge that the link between climate change and economic turmoil may not be clear to everyone. It can be a concept difficult to grasp. Even though most Americans focus on lost domestic jobs, internationally jobs have been both created and displaced because of globalization. From a global perspective, the number of jobs has actually increased in recent years as employment has shifted from high-cost regions to low-cost regions where there is a multiplier effect. For example, the loss of one job from a call center in the United States probably results in freeing up the money to hire two individuals in India. In the long run, however, jobs are lost because rising energy costs push up the cost of all goods. Rising prices kill economic value. As I listen to the political debates about the reasons for job loss and what actions are needed to create new jobs, I wonder: If rising energy costs are the result of our past actions, and if a changing climate will only push the direct and indirect costs of energy up further, what then?

Also, in spite of the significant advancement of new drilling technologies that can temporarily flood the market with new supplies and thus reinvigorate the myth of endless oil, scientists are seeing evidence of continued resource depletion. For example, the world's warming oceans have increased in acidity, which has reduced their capacity as a resource for food and, as a result, has increased the price of fish, a principal staple in nearly every coastal diet.[18] There are now more than seven billion inhabitants on the planet, and with nearly half of the world's population living near the sea, it doesn't take a giant computer to predict how those people will be affected.[19]

Moreover, the concern over climate change isn't just about warming oceans, rising sea levels, and the melting of the polar ice caps. It is about how changing environmental conditions can disturb the delicate balance that sustains the global ecosystem. For example, higher temperatures can tip the existing balance among insect populations that have relatively short life cycles and high reproductive rates, by leading to larger and more rapid effects on population dynamics. We can already see the consequences: Swarms of insects have weakened forests throughout western North America, creating stockpiles of fuel for superfires.[20] Meanwhile, the Midwest in 2012 experienced the worst drought since the 1930s Dust Bowl, reducing crop yields from the largest agricultural region in the world. And scientists in the Himalayas are watching mountain glaciers and land ice disappear in real time, raising the prospect of future water wars. Make no mistake: The depletion of our natural resources is upon us. The signs of climate change are here and now.

But even those who accept this reality don't necessarily know what to do about it. It is hard to rally behind a cause when there is no clear solution or progressive leadership. What is required is a shift in the debate. We need to visualize things from a new perspective, to unlock economic opportunities that can help us mitigate climate change and evolve the human condition. I say this not only as an executive but also as a father.

THE FALLING SKY

Shifting the debate may require asking a different question: Should we believe the scientists and environmentalists who are sounding the alarm? Or should we believe the largest energy companies, those that advertise and lobby for clean coal, cleaner natural gas, and increased oil drilling? Should we believe their scientists for hire, who claim there is still doubt about whether climate change is a real danger? Or should we transcend that discussion and look to others who might have a better perch that allows them to truly see the drastic changes ahead?

Consider a source whose continued public support is dependent almost exclusively upon its reputation. Take a mental step back, look at the big picture, and ask yourself: "Who in our society worries the most about the safety and security of our nation?" The answer: the military. Our armed forces have the sole duty and responsibility to protect US citizens and our way of life as a nation from external threats. For those who doubt scientists and activists, and for those who doubt the companies that profit from drilling oil, when it comes to examining climate change, it may be prudent to consider the views of the military.

So where does the military weigh in on this issue? A review of the evidence shows that the Pentagon has been concerned with climate change for several decades. Since before 1993, the US Department of Defense (DOD) has funded climate change research through university grants.[21] The most formal programs include the US Global Change Research Program (USGCRP) and the Climate Change Technology Initiative (CCTI). In 2003 the DOD commissioned a report to investigate abrupt climate change scenarios and implications for US national security. This report presented a startling potential scenario for 2023 if climate change were not gradual but, rather, accelerated.[22]

The DOD report presents regional abrupt climate change scenarios tied to potential geopolitical implications such as food shortages, water scarcity, destructive weather events, the spread of disease, human migration, and natural resource competition. Compared with the military's findings, the current studies by today's climate scientists look surprisingly conservative. The report considers nonlinear and cascading events, which includes most natural processes (such as the release of greater methane deposits from thawing tundra in the polar regions). It reveals the consequences of passing the tipping point and experiencing abrupt climate change that would quickly become severe:

> It is quite plausible that within a decade the evidence of an imminent abrupt climate shift may become clear and reliable . . . New forms of security agreements dealing specifically with energy, food, and water will also be needed . . . Disruption and conflict will be endemic features of life.

We are halfway to the DOD's imagined 2023 scenario. A decade later, we see rising evidence of the climate change that was highlighted in this report. Since the year 2000, the world has experienced nine of the ten warmest years in modern history.[23]

Other reports from the military support the scientific community's claims that climate change is clearly an emerging national and international threat. For example, the DOD is currently funding research at the University of Texas at Austin on the geopolitical relationship between climate change and regional instability. I encourage you to look at the austere map that demonstrates this frightening yet thought-provoking relationship.[24] This is unsecured data, publicly available, from a community noted for its classification of vital information. I ask myself, what might the DOD know that it is *not* making publicly available? This is not the beginning of a conspiracy theory but rather a dose of realism.

In May 2010 the United States Navy issued its road map to address climate change, acknowledging that the "preponderance of global observational evidence shows that the Arctic Ocean is losing sea ice, global temperatures are warming, sea levels are rising, large land-fast ice sheets in Greenland and the Antarctic are losing ice mass, and precipitation patterns are changing."[25] The report goes on to state that naval forces must prepare for climate change because it will influence "the type, scope, and location of future Navy missions through its effects on the distribution and availability of natural resources." If the US Navy is concerned about climate change, then I have to admit that I am concerned, too.

A region of the world in which the US Navy is already showing interest is the Arctic, where rising temperatures and melting ice are opening up long-dreamed-of sea-lanes and new resources for oil and gas drilling—while simultaneously creating the potential for new conflicts between nations. Already the United States, Russia, and other countries are conducting military training programs to address that challenge and to protect new claims.

Four-star admiral Samuel Locklear, chief of US operations in the Pacific, told the *Boston Globe* in March 2013 that unchecked global warming will "cripple the security environment, probably more likely than the other scenarios we all often talk about." He went on to say:

> While resilience in the security environment is traditionally understood as the ability to recover from a crisis, using the term in the context of national security expands its meaning to include crisis prevention. You have the real potential here in the not-too-distant future of nations displaced by rising sea levels.[26]

Has this insight into the military's concerns about climate change surprised you? The story should not cause you to be fatalistic, nor must you necessarily share my views (or the military's) on climate change in order to get on board with the solution I propose. As you will see, the mitigation of climate change is not dependent upon the military. The solution is far easier. It simply requires changing our global energy mix.

THE DISEASE AND THE CURE

The US military is not talking about mitigating or even avoiding climate change. The military is looking at ways to adapt to it. Actually slowing or eliminating the rate of climate change from human-caused (anthropogenic) sources, on the other hand, will require modifying our energy system—by changing the mix of investments in new energy systems, moving away from technologies that are responsible for much of anthropogenic GHG emissions. Trying to reduce the impact of climate change means making changes to how we manage our forests and oceans and to our energy mix. It means shifting from the use of conventional fuel sources to meet our existing energy requirements and toward the use of renewable energy and fuels with lower carbon intensity (such as nuclear power). It means increasing investments in greater energy efficiency to meet our future energy requirements.

On this score, some are reluctant to agree that climate change is upon us simply because they cannot comprehend what an alternative energy strategy might look like or they doubt the viability of such a strategy. One news item that went viral was when Rupert Murdoch, a longtime denier of climate change, finally acknowledged it via Twitter: "Climate change is very slow but real. So far all cures worse than the disease."[27] His timely tweet revealed an underlying concern many have about the climate debate. Changing energy suppliers is not an easy task, because financial relationships and industry infrastructure are well established, both institutionally and politically. Converting our energy system will require abandoning certain energy systems and creating new ones backed by financial and risk capital, causing an expense today and affording benefits that will be seen only in the future. For similar reasons, it is important to understand how conventional energy is being used and what expectations are built into our business-as-usual scenario to meet future energy use. Only then can we consider, by comparing and contrasting their magnitude, the actual changes required to adequately address climate change and to build a new business case.

THE INELASTICITY OF FOSSIL FUELS

Let's look at our global energy mix.

Oil totally dominates transportation energy use. Formerly, oil was widely used to generate electricity. Since the 1970s, however, the global use of oil for electricity generation has declined rapidly in the industrialized world. For example, in North America, Europe, and Asia, the abundance of coal-fired energy generation has allowed utility planners to dramatically diversify and move away from using heating oil to fire their boilers. Today electricity generation and heavy industry use mostly coal, and as we look to the end of this century, coal is still projected to increase globally not only in volume but also as a percentage of total energy supply. Among conventional fuel sources, the only competing alternative to coal is natural gas. Natural gas is a finite resource, similar to oil and coal, but due to its cleaner-burning characteristics, natural gas has historically been limited to heating buildings and industrial applications. Only recently has gas been finding its way into new markets—and only those where new drilling technologies are being deployed.

As we look at the energy market as a whole, it is this complexity and inelasticity of the fossil fuel distribution system that makes it incredibly challenging to find replacements or substitutes that use greater amounts of renewable energy. In fact, the complementary crisis that runs parallel to the climate change story is that we are depleting our higher-quality supplies of oil, coal, and natural gas without making the necessary investments to replace existing infrastructure with alternatives or to find reliable substitutes. This inconvenient truth is glossed over in the thousands of newspaper articles and industry announcements that flood our media outlets with reports of new reserves of shale oil and natural gas.

Indeed, the US natural gas industry is booming due to new drilling of unconventional shale resources. This boom has changed the public discourse over the need to find replacements. However, industry reports may also be overstating the case for natural gas and oil, as we will review in much more detail in chapters 4 and 12. By diverting the public's attention, the estimates of the amount of shale resources may dangerously offset valid national security and environmental concerns over future resource depletion.

SWITCHING TO RENEWABLE ENERGY

Project Butterfly's analysis of resource risk is not intended to be conclusive; rather, its goal is to raise sufficient questions regarding the sustainability of our current energy system. Our review seeks to improve our understanding of the status quo that defines "business as usual" and allows us then to look at alternatives. As some of us continue searching for more sustainable energy alternatives, I have wondered whether the authors of all those thousands of newspaper articles have it wrong. Shouldn't natural gas be characterized as a transitional fuel for industry rather than as a replacement for oil? When I overlay concerns about climate change, I am doubly perplexed. Why does it seem so important to characterize shale gas and oil, often called "unconventional resources," as a new source of energy? Doesn't climate change merely make the need for switching to renewable energy more urgent? And shouldn't innovations in new drilling technologies be looked at as a means to some other end?

Confirming my suspicions, new reports from the International Energy Agency (IEA) state that there is actually a surplus of fuels, including oil and natural gas, that can be used to power the world's economies. But the IEA also reveals that no more than one-third of those proven reserves can be burned by 2050 if the world is to prevent global warming from exceeding the controversial warming point of 3.6 degrees Fahrenheit (2 degrees Celsius).[28] So despite all those immediate benefits of new technologies allowing us to drill deeper and extract more, there are untold costs independent of the eventual depletion of carbon-based fuels.

The work we have done with Project Butterfly reveals this cost. Our projections of the business-as-usual scenario show that in spite of significant investments in renewable energy and energy efficiency and market-driven improvements in the diversity of the total energy mix, global carbon intensity as a percentage of final energy continues to climb. Our projections reveal that we are simply using more and more carbon to meet our energy needs. The consequence is continued growth in atmospheric GHG concentration levels.

Coal is usually the fuel most criticized for its contribution to global warming. It has the highest carbon intensity of any of the conventional fuels. From an economic perspective, however, coal is a tempting choice, and therein lies the challenge. Coal is both abundant and cheap, and it can be transported long distances by rail and sea. Coal is also the most difficult fuel to substitute with any other single source. Alternatives are hard to find because of both the quantity and energy density of the coal that suppliers burn.

There is a lot at stake, however. High-quality coal (which is low in moisture and ash) is becoming scarcer, and low-quality coal has to bear more of the total energy burden. The consequence is emitting more GHGs to produce the same level of energy, because low-quality coal burns less efficiently.

So climate change is not just an issue of economic growth. There are also more and more people consuming greater quantities of energy, coupled with a finite energy supply. Climate change, therefore, is also an issue of energy depletion, even when we look at the use of coal, the most abundant of our conventional energy sources. The story is not all gloom and doom, however. There is an alternative to burning finite resources: tapping renewable resources that have at least a theoretical potential to propel economic growth.

ENDING A CYCLE OF DEPENDENCY

For the reasons already outlined here we are in search of a new sustainability model or new business case to operate our global energy system. The precariousness of our current situation becomes even more dramatic when we look at the *global* dependence of our energy system on a few national suppliers. The simple fact is that a small group of countries that comprise the Organization of the Petroleum Exporting Countries (OPEC) controls more than half of the world's oil supply and trade conditions.[29] Additionally, OPEC members account for about 70 percent of the world's total oil reserves.[30] With a limited capacity to substitute conventional oil with alternatives, including natural gas, our global economy is dependent on the oil owned by just a few nations.

The large national oil consumers of North America, Europe, and Asia will need to find solutions to this predicament while avoiding such disruptions as price escalation or breaks in the supply chains (like those that occurred in the 1970s). However, these national consumers have a historic tendency to lock onto temporary fixes—seeking new sources of oil or new methods to extract more oil from known fields—rather than looking for fundamental solutions that will create more security and end the cycle of dependency. Simply finding greater domestic supplies or accessing new foreign resources will do little to offset the risky global politics of oil. This dependency is what links climate change to the status quo.

The United States, regardless of where its oil comes from, is one of these highly dependent national consumers. There is nothing new about the nation's energy policy. Ever since the 1970s, US energy policy has continued to focus on finding methods to extract greater supplies from existing resources. However, at the end of 2012 the IEA predicted that North America would finally be successful in drilling its way out of short-term pains and would become the world's largest producer of oil by around 2020.[31] This staggering forecast by the IEA can be viewed in one of two ways: either as a nation's last efforts to spur its domestic economy and separate itself from Middle Eastern oil or as a gift from nature to fuel a transition to a new economy. In the fullness of time, however, this increased level of production spurred by new drilling techniques will not last. Resource constraints will eventually reduce North America's ability to produce sufficient oil to meet the region's own needs. The United States is unlikely to ever become an exporter to other nations in need.[32] This eventual consequence means that we have been given nothing more than a gift.

Even if North America can find some way to maintain a high level of oil production, the United States will still be forced to import several million barrels a day due to the high demand for this fuel—all while remaining vulnerable to the volatility of the global oil market and without ever becoming a net supplier to other nations.

A MORAL IMPERATIVE

As we seek a solution to climate change in the present and future, perhaps the past may provide some guidance as to whether we can confront a global problem, like climate change, and how. In fact, we may need to look no further than the story of the movement to abolish slavery—one of history's greatest examples of a society making dramatic changes to improve the human condition. One of the lessons we can take from this era is that the end of slavery did not come about because of any economic change, although the movement did coincide with the beginnings of the Industrial Revolution. Rather, it was the result of a moral imperative—one that raised existential questions similar to climate change.

The abolition movement began as a claim by Quakers on both sides of the Atlantic that all men are equal in the eyes of God and that all men should be treated equally by society's legal systems. The Quaker message found a sympathetic ear in a young nation whose founders stated in their Declaration of Independence the "self-evident" truth that "all men are created equal." In spite of that bold affirmation of equality among men, however, slavery in the colonies was not abolished at the time of the signing of the Declaration of Independence in 1776, nor upon the writing of the US Constitution a decade later.

In fact, in 1776 the concept of abolishing slavery seemed to the vast majority of both Americans and Europeans as foolishly utopian as the idea of eliminating hydrocarbons from our economic system and the industrial machinery that runs it appears to many of us in contemporary times. The myths that held slavery in place for nearly another hundred years parallel many of the arguments that have kept us bound to our dependency on fossil fuels. Slavery was seen as a natural condition of man, suggesting that an elite class was deemed to have superior moral, intellectual, and technological prowess, making them the rightful masters. Slavery had always existed, and in nearly every society on earth. In the United States, slavery was built into our economic infrastructure and into the fabric of institutions we developed to create the national wealth that we so dearly needed to protect our independence. Ending slavery was unimaginable to most politicians of the time, who were more interested in stitching together a union of states. It kept our Southern state economies competitive with Europe and kept the peace at home between the newly formed states that relied on slave labor and the industrializing states of the North.

Imagine the discussion in the halls of government, between plantation owners and abolitionists, over slavery. It's not difficult to envision similarities to the discussion today between industry lobbyists and environmentalists, regarding the right to burn coal to generate electricity. The issues abolitionists faced regarding this contentious political, economic, and moral issue were akin to the opposition that a contemporary senator or congressperson who supports climate legislation would face, especially if that legislation led to shutting down the coal mining operations that employ thousands in other states.

And yet slavery *was* abolished. The Industrial Revolution laid the groundwork for a change in how the world viewed the importance of slavery to the health and competitiveness of a nation's economy. Industrial mechanization combined forces with a moral imperative to make the net benefit of slavery diminish in the eyes of American industry and its citizens. At the same time, mechanization—most notably, the innovation of the cotton gin—caused agriculture in the Southern states to flourish. The cotton gin increased labor productivity by nearly tenfold. As a result of this new, more efficient technology, cotton production in the United States grew from 750,000 bales in 1830 to nearly three million bales per year by 1850. While dramatically increasing production and profits, the cotton gin fostered a growing perception that the economics of slavery had become merely a social convenience rather than a fundamental condition to the health of the economic system of the time.

Ironically, instead of decreasing the use of slaves, the economic boon in the South brought about by the cotton gin initially resulted in slave owners purchasing even more slaves with their newfound wealth. The number of slaves in 1800 was approximately 700,000. That figure grew to more than three million by the outbreak of the Civil War in 1861. Growth in slavery incensed abolitionists and ignited a social revolution to end slavery that was eventually carried out by the industrial northern states.

Consider the similarities between what happened before the Civil War and today's climate change issue. The introduction of technological advancements and more efficient energy sources in our modern times is making our reliance on conventional fuels more of a social convenience than an economic necessity. Increased oil supplies and subsidized fuel costs at the pump allow us to buy larger SUVs when, for most of us, a smaller and more fuel-efficient car would satisfy the same needs. If you listen carefully, the faint and disparate voices of a new social revolution can be heard.

Consider the following: The act that truly initiated the end of slavery, however, was not outrage at the continuation of normal business advances or the Civil War. It was not a specific technological advancement such as the cotton gin. It was an international trade arrangement between Great Britain and the United States forbidding slave trading. Britain banned the importation of slaves to its colonies in 1807, and the young United States followed with a similar act in 1808. Both countries had the seafaring ability to monitor the other's activities and impose the antitrading law.

The new international agreements had a wide impact on the lives of existing slaves. Due to brutal living conditions in Brazil, for instance, slaves tending to the sugarcane fields lived only an average of seven years after being enslaved. The abolition of slave trading led to a much longer lifespan for Brazilian slaves as the price of slaves shot up and the easy supply went down. Plantation owners began to value the diminishing resource and improved the quality of slaves' living conditions in order to improve their declining economics. Increasing costs initiated the end of slavery.

The same principle applies to conventional energy. Today's climate debate crosses international boundaries in all directions. A similar approach that increases costs to conventional supplies and offers effective incentives to alternatives will be necessary if we wish to successfully avoid the catastrophic consequences of both resource depletion and climate change.

EMBRACING SUSTAINABILITY

The new business case I am proposing will tip the scales in favor of renewable energy and appropriately value conventional fuels through international trade agreements, similar to how the postslavery economy was launched. Project Butterfly illustrates this new scenario by employing a global model that reveals the impact of climate change and shows how we must alter our course regarding conventional fuels in much the same fashion as the world responded to slavery at the dawn of the Industrial Revolution. Abolitionists were calling for equality. Environmentalists are now calling for sustainability. The call is gaining traction, but in order to focus the global community's response to growing environmental concerns, we must broaden our definition of the word *sustainability*.

The words *green* and *clean* predate the use of the word *sustainability* in this context. The two earlier terms have been co-opted for political purposes, however, prompting the use of the new word. *Sustainability* has now proliferated in the marketplace, too, and is providing a platform for new corporate mission statements to rally around. Terms like *sustainable growth, sustainable living,* and *sustainable practices* echo in the marketing materials of our most progressive corporations. But failure to collectively define these terms will limit the effectiveness of the words to serve as a guiding force. To be effective, we must define *sustainability,* and especially *global sustainability*.

For example, old industries are adopting oxymorons like *clean coal* as a way to wash over the requirements for a new business case. The stakes for our world's leaders, including our politicians and especially our new CEOs, are high. While it might be possible to be "green" or "clean," ignoring global sustainability will lead to failure because it will keep their policies and businesses attached to the status quo. Alternatively, embracing and implementing a clear definition of *global sustainability* can lead only to success, because it will minimize the dependency of their operations on resource use.

The Project Butterfly team's view of global sustainability includes maintaining the quality of human life on our planet—a high-stakes component— by limiting the production of GHGs and thus mitigating catastrophic global warming. The act of defining *global sustainability* starts with an acknowledgment that human wealth and prosperity are created by taking resources out of nature. Sustainability is therefore a deliberate commitment on behalf of public and private owners to replenish our natural reservoirs with investments into renewable resources, allowing the ecosystem to regenerate and find a sustainable equilibrium.

In chapters 8 and 9, I will detail a theoretical model for sustainability that we can apply to any organization or business (the Project Butterfly Sustainability Model). Then, in chapters 10 and 11, I will explore the architecture behind the Project Butterfly Financial Model and the results from simulating our global energy system both with a business-as-usual scenario and with a new business case. To demonstrate the feasibility of global sustainability, the Project Butterfly team has worked to model the impact on the global energy system of redirecting capital toward greater renewable resources. The results are encouraging. We have discovered that by making small changes—by internalizing the cost of depleting nonrenewable resources and by redirecting incentives to the use of renewable resources—it is possible to find a sustainable equilibrium.

Furthermore, because it uses a financial approach with an eye toward creating new business opportunities, the Project Butterfly Financial Model builds initiatives into the energy system that serve to replace or substitute natural resources with renewable resources, all while diminishing reliance on resources that are otherwise finite in nature. The outcome is a more profitable and sustainable future—a very different vision from the future described at the opening of this chapter.

THE IMPORTANCE OF NEW LEADERSHIP

The Project Butterfly team has looked beyond just creating a financial spreadsheet, however, peering deeper into what is truly needed to address climate change. Implementing the new business case will take leadership, and *what kind* of leadership is an important consideration.

The kind of leadership that the Project Butterfly team is suggesting is illustrated in the aftermath of the 1929 stock market crash that led to the Great Depression. A very small change made back then has made a big difference ever since, and now it seems as normal and American as apple pie. None of us really recognizes the significance now, but this small change in the banking system may have seemed as "foolishly utopian" as taxing or fixing a price on GHG emissions might seem today. If the same principle applies, a simple but controversial policy to address climate change might be considered absolutely normal a generation after it is implemented.

As part of the sweeping New Deal economic package back in 1933, the US Congress and President Franklin D. Roosevelt approved and signed into law the Glass-Steagall Act, which established the Federal Deposit Insurance Corporation (FDIC) to guarantee the safety of bank deposits and to avoid future runs on the banking system. Roosevelt's economic reforms faced stiff opposition from those who feared increased government involvement in the banking system. However, this bold act bolstered the financial system for decades by providing the necessary assurances for money to reenter the economy. The hundreds of thousands, if not millions, of families and small businesses in the United States that had hidden their money under their mattresses during the Great Depression could finally feel comfortable putting their savings back into the banking system.

President Roosevelt buttressed his New Deal with other public and private initiatives. He reshaped the common interpretation of the role of government in managing a complex economic system. In fact, the New Deal was the game changer that preceded World War II and propelled the United States into its position as a global superpower. But the Glass-Steagall Act was the single action taken by the US legislature that changed everything. It gave every depositor good reason to trust the banking system, and this sensibility was key to rebuilding national growth and financial stability.

To respond to climate change, today's leaders will need to create a New Energy Deal rather than continue to advance the same strategies that might have worked in the past. These strategies have now proven to be ineffective and inefficient in addressing both resource depletion and climate change. Yes, the oil, coal, and natural gas industries have fueled possibly the greatest accumulation of wealth in history. Yes, the energy industry has powered a technological and industrial revolution that has improved communities and nations around the world. The leaders of these industries should be applauded for their accomplishments. However, we must acknowledge that the thousands of companies that constitute the energy industry and own the supply lines are dependent on the continued global consumption of their fuels. This wealth creation has come at a cost that has been largely unaccounted for. Burning these fuels is responsible for dramatic increases in GHG emissions and unacceptable levels of CO_2 concentration both in our atmosphere and in our oceans, limiting the ability of our planet to absorb more of this fuel-burning by-product.

Change is afoot. Large energy companies, ranging from oil companies to massive power suppliers, are scrambling to influence the direction in which we move. Some are taking a very sober look at the consequence of burning conventional fuels, the limitation of resource supply, and the possibilities inherent in a new energy mix. And they are responding by buying advertising space and shaping editorial views in the echo chamber we call our public media.

Meanwhile, the public is in search of clarity and leadership in addressing not only the cause of climate change but also solutions that fit our shared definition of *global sustainability*. We need leaders who will take up the sword knowing that conventional fuel suppliers are going to resist changes because renewable energy negatively affects demand for their existing products and services. We need leaders who understand that they will lose market share unless they can find a way to participate in the transformation of the energy industry. We need leaders who are willing to seek changes that improve the capacity of our businesses and governing bodies to integrate and adapt to new conditions.

We need leaders who will see opportunity in rejecting the notion that climate change is simply an environmental or an economic issue. We need leaders who see climate change as both a financial and an existential issue that classic economic fixes, such as stimulus spending to reboot our global economy, can no longer solve. These leaders need to see that the systemic problem is really the result of a polluted ecosystem limited in its capacity to rejuvenate and that rising prices do not necessarily signal rising demand but rather a scarcity of resource supply.

Such leaders will have solid ground to stand on. There is substantial market evidence that investments in renewable energy and energy efficiency are on the rise. Global investments in solar power jumped 52 percent to $147 billion in 2011.[33] In 2012 new wind turbines in the United States outpaced new natural gas plants. Yet these leaders must also know that current trends are not showing enough progress and are certainly not unfolding fast enough to offset rising greenhouse gas emissions and global temperatures.

According to the Project Butterfly calculations, a handful of adjustments in energy and climate policy can make all the difference to change our course. Institutions such as the IEA that gather and analyze data on the global energy system support these conclusions. Yet the global community keeps missing opportunities. We've had eighteen Conferences of the Parties (the organization that backed the Kyoto Protocol) since 1992, all with proposals that would have encouraged global capital markets to dramatically boost renewable energy to a much larger percentage of the global energy supply mix. The successes and failures of these proposals are prime examples of the inability of the energy industry and its sponsoring nations to escape the status quo. The necessity before the global community is to acknowledge the shortcomings of these international efforts and to use their failure as an opportunity to adopt new strategies. As a global community we need to assess what has worked and what has not. We need to determine what keeps us locked into the status quo and what levers can be pulled to transform our global energy mix into a truly sustainable model.

We therefore need leaders who see the current deadlock in international negotiations on climate change as an opportunity. Rather than setting targets and dates for international agreements to reduce GHGs, such as the

Kyoto Protocol, these leaders need to support a new business case for making meaningful progress through cooperative efforts to cut GHG emissions and to build alternatives to conventional energy supply. This new business case should be built upon replacing aging conventional fuel sources and meeting new demand with renewable energy and energy efficiency, and its backbone must be eliminating barriers to market competition and especially innovation. The result would be a dramatic transformation of our global energy mix toward a more diversified portfolio of energy assets. These new investments would decrease the energy intensity of new capital and improve the operational performance of our industry and of our economic system as a whole.

Finally, we need leaders who will help us move beyond our fear of change to meet the challenges in front of us. Denial of climate change has consumed much of our national consciousness, creating a fear-based dialogue by politicizing science and pitting economic interests against one another. When people are fearful, they don't act unless there is strong leadership. Much like the bankers before the Great Depression who feared that customers would run at the banks to withdraw their money (as indeed they did), today's government and corporate leaders are afraid of what might take place if the global community suddenly awakens to the harsh and rapidly impending reality of climate change. Our leaders must heed the advice of President Roosevelt, who had the courage to implement bold solutions during a previous period of national crisis, proclaiming, "The only thing we have to fear is fear itself."

Leadership starts with a declaration, which is usually followed by a request. To avoid the most dramatic effects of climate change, we need to acknowledge the severity of the crisis and then request a change in course.

PROTAGONISTS OF ALL KINDS

Every great story has a protagonist who risks it all—someone who is not willing to accept that "it's just the way it is." The story of climate change needs its protagonists, too—those who will stand up and demand that public and private owners of our global energy industries replenish the natural resources upon which they depend. This act starts in our homes and can take place in our schools, but it must end up in the halls of our governments and in every corporate boardroom.

What makes the climate change story unique is that it needs protagonists of all kinds, and these protagonists must come from every sector of our society. We need protagonists who are policy makers, business leaders, community organizers, scientists, and engineers—who warn us of the dangers we face and prompt us to find solutions to overcome them. Whatever their background or profession, these protagonists must simply be willing to follow a hero's journey, sacrificing short-term gains for long-term value. Our protagonists will call for change to a system that, at present, addresses only symptoms of problems, not root causes. Our protagonists will seek fundamental solutions in spite of possible political or personal cost, knowing that in the long run such fixes will produce more wealth and prosperity, not less.

Whenever there is a protagonist, there must also be an antagonist. The antagonist in this tale of climate change is the defender of energy solutions that lead to the same result—an increasing dependency on the same source of supply—no matter how the game is played. The antagonist backs a system that is self-serving and stifles competition rather than one that is open and supports competition between good ideas. The antagonists in our climate change story also are those who promote and protect a closed system—who are willing to accept that "it's just the way it is."

The climate story demands that the protagonist prevail. None of us can accept the alternative.

KEY OBSERVATIONS

The decision to reject the business-as-usual scenario and move forward with actions to mitigate climate change requires taking the following five steps:

» Recognize that the potential for cataclysmic climate change in the near future is very real and that climate change is not a problem that can and should be handed to future generations.

» Acknowledge that growing dependency on fossil fuels and resource depletion have been with us since the 1970s, and that recent advances in drilling techniques may give us only enough breathing room to address climate change.

» Accept that addressing climate change is driven by a moral imperative, not solely by an economic necessity nor by a technological breakthrough.

» Demand that leadership make the tough choices to address climate change.

» Rally around global sustainability. There are actions we can all take to lead our organizations into a new business case.

· · ·

*"Sustainable development" is a compelling
moral and humanitarian issue.*[34]
—*Colin Powell*

CHAPTER 3

FROM THE COLD WAR TO CLIMATE CHANGE:
CREATING A LEVEL PLAYING FIELD

For nearly forty years before the issue of climate change ever hit the front page of a major newspaper, the world's public media had been focused almost solely on relations between the United States and the Soviet Union. These two nations were the world's two nuclear superpowers and each competed for the world's resources.

For the Western world, the global expansion of communism was the *existential* issue of the times. The United States had dropped two atomic bombs on Japan in 1945 to end World War II in the Pacific. Four years later the Soviet Union developed its own atomic bomb, which meant the world was now divided between two spheres of influence. But the arms race didn't really get started until 1957 when the Soviet Union launched Sputnik, the first artificial satellite. The Industrial Revolution had finally reached the stars, and it was the Soviets who took us there. The possibility that the Soviet Union might put one of its atomic bombs in a rocket like Sputnik and deliver it within minutes to any city in the United States or anywhere else in the Western world sent a shiver down everyone's spine. The fear of such a possibility ushered in a technological arms race between the two industrial superpowers that would define the Cold War until the 1990s.

In fact, by 1991 the United States and the Soviet Union had each amassed huge stockpiles of nuclear weapons and developed the ability to deliver them to their intended targets by both air and sea. These superpowers aimed their weapons at each other, believing that the threat of total annihilation would keep both sides from launching a first strike. By 1991 both nations had gotten comfortable living under this shared policy of mutual assured destruction. This theory of deterrence made sense, but there were also weaknesses in the logic. For instance, what would happen if one of the two superpowers became unstable, for whatever reason?

In 1991 I was thirty-one years old. My wife, Laurie, and I had a three-year-old daughter named Jessie, and we were expecting our second child. I was president of Highland Energy, a start-up company that provided energy efficiency services to large-facility owners operating from coast to coast. The pressures of caring for a young family and a business weighed heavily on me and on most of my comanagers, who had their own growing families, too. But these pressures also made us focus deeply on the developments between the superpowers. There was a pervading sense that actions and events on the world stage might affect the safety of our families and certainly the health of our company.

To help me manage my duties, I had rented a beeper that I attached to my belt every morning so both my wife and my office could reach me at any time of day by simply dialing a number. I also had a car phone, but "mobile" phones at that time weighed as much as a hammer, and to make them work you also needed to tote a large battery. A beeper was lighter and far more convenient.

On the morning of August 27, 1991, I kissed my wife good-bye before leaving for the office. Our baby was due at any time, and as I reached the door, she called out, "Today might be the day." Indeed, a little after noon, my beeper sounded the alarm—it was time.

I hopped into my car and drove the short distance home to find two midwives already tending to my wife and preparing for a home birth. Laurie had been expecting a second girl. She had been having dreams for months about giving birth to a baby girl, and she had already named our second daughter Selena.

Rushing home from the office turned into hours and then more hours of waiting. Family members started to show up around dinnertime. Eventually I fell asleep as I waited. I awoke around midnight and made my way into the master bedroom, where my wife was in full-blown labor. A sleepy Jessie was nestled in her grandmother's lap. I took my place next to Laurie and held her hand as the midwives guided her through the birthing process. Within minutes the baby's head crowned to the outside world. A few seconds later, the next contraction surged and our baby was born. The midwife lifted our second child onto my wife's breast. Everyone in the room was smiling, with tears in their eyes at the same time. We were elated to have witnessed this precious new soul enter into our midst. After a few moments, Laurie lifted our child up to inspect her beautiful body—and discovered that "she" was in fact a boy.

Days went by after the birth of our son, and Laurie still couldn't decide on a name. I naturally felt that the solution would be easy. We could name our son Thomas. Why not? My name is Thomas. My father's (his grandfather's) name was Thomas. It made sense to me. In spite of my enthusiasm, however, my suggestion was met with my wife's pursed lips and a stink-eye.

When I returned to the office three days later, my son still didn't have a name. This deeply concerned my office mates. After all, our clients and partners wanted to send notes congratulating my wife and me. Eventually my colleagues at Highland Energy decided to take matters into their own hands. They made a list of names and took a vote. At the end of the day, they decided our new son should be named Boris. I rather liked the idea.

Why? In September 1991 the Soviet Union was in chaos. Shortly before my son's birth, in an iconic image broadcast around the globe, the Russian politician and reformer Boris Yeltsin had used only his body and sizable personal charisma to stop Soviet armed tanks from advancing on the newly formed government housed in Moscow. In the eyes of the world, Yeltsin was a hero who had single-handedly averted a military coup that could have led to a civil war in the nuclear-armed Soviet Union. Naming my son after such a great historical character would have marked both the time of his birth and the new hope for the world.

In the aftermath of the attempted coup, Yeltsin became the first freely elected president of the new Russian government. Nevertheless, my wife didn't particularly admire the name Boris. For me, it stood for the man who had stood down the Soviet military and freed the Russian populace from the grip of communism. But the name made Laurie think of Boris Karloff, the 1930s actor known for his role as Frankenstein's monster. You can imagine the headwind I was fighting on the home front in selecting Boris as a name for our son.

Finally, after two weeks of mulling it over, we named him Seann. I was glad to have the matter settled. To my former colleagues, though, my son would always be Boris.

• • •

As quickly as the Cold War was over, a new crisis loomed. By 1992 a new breed of concerned popular scientists was raising an alarm about the buildup of GHGs in the atmosphere as a result of more than two hundred years of rapid industrialization. In hindsight, the efforts to mitigate the threat of self-annihilation with nuclear weapons would seem like mere baby steps compared with the degree of international cooperation that would be required to avoid a global climate catastrophe. Agreements would have to be negotiated, but not just between two superpowers. To address the threat of catastrophic global warming, scientists and enlightened political leaders warned, the world would need a global agreement to be negotiated and ratified by all nations.

It has now been more than two decades since the emergence of climate change as an international issue, one that threatens not only the well-being of national interests but the entire international order. Back in 1992 the global community had a chance to do something different. It had the chance to extend the goodwill generated from the end of the Cold War. But this opportunity was eventually lost. Nevertheless, having made our way through two wars and the 2008 Great Recession, we may again be at a moment in time when the world can address climate change. But we cannot forget the past. Climate negotiations among countries have a certain history, and to move forward we need to know how we got to where we are.

THE DOOMSDAY CLOCK

Atomic scientists, who felt partly responsible for letting the nuclear genie out of the bottle, had been warning against the danger of nuclear war for decades. Year after year, each country increased its military spending and developed new, more advanced technology. The United States and the Soviet Union installed multiple reentry vehicles for their rockets, enhancing their respective abilities to hit their intended targets. These superior intercontinental missiles were loaded onto trains, nuclear-powered submarines, and stealth-flying jet bombers. In the face of all this stockpiling, scientists continuously expressed their concern that the military establishments within both the United States and the Soviet Union might have unique incentives to drive the world toward war. They warned that the buildup of "Star Wars" technologies might encourage one or the other country to develop a first-strike advantage that would undermine the shared policy of nuclear deterrence.

Atomic scientists had responded to the early signs of this nuclear madness by establishing the Doomsday Clock in 1947. The concept of the clock, which represented the scientists' countdown toward nuclear disaster, was first published in the *Bulletin of the Atomic Scientists* at the University of Chicago. Based on the unveiling of certain international events, scientists at the university would either set the clock forward (toward midnight) or move it away, to express their concerns or relief, respectively, over the possibility of war and the need for international agreements to control the use and proliferation of nuclear arms. For example, the clock advanced to three minutes before midnight in January 1984, at a point when US and Soviet diplomats had stopped communicating. If the minute hand reached midnight, nuclear weapons would be launched, either by accident or by intention, and it would be all over.

The buildup of atomic weapons continued for another forty years after the establishment of the Doomsday Clock. In 1982, three years after the Soviet invasion of Afghanistan, President Ronald Reagan announced an aggressive program to reduce the number of nuclear weapons held by the United States and the Soviet Union. Negotiations blew hot and cold for six years until 1988, when the two countries finally entered into the first treaty to ban intermediate-range nuclear forces in Europe. Three years after the initial breakthrough in arms negotiations, in July 1991, the United States and the Soviet Union signed a second arms control agreement—the Strategic Arms Reduction Treaty (known as START)—to reduce the total number of strategic nuclear weapons held by the two superpowers. The ice that had defined the Cold War had finally broken.

The signing of these two nuclear arms treaties, and the announcement of a new Soviet policy of glasnost (which granted greater freedom to the press) helped shape a commonly held view that the world was finally headed in a much safer and open direction. Walls would no longer stand to divide nations. New television and radio broadcasts were beamed through satellites and long-distance towers, bringing us all together. The world press reveled in the global revolution that was making it possible for families in Manhattan and Moscow to watch the same Western television shows. One of the more popular American TV shows in Russia was *Dynasty*, a prime-time soap opera about a self-made Denver millionaire in the oil business.

By late fall of 1991, the Doomsday Clock was at seventeen minutes to midnight, its lowest setting since its inception. Governments launched into new negotiations to secure the peace between these once-great adversaries. Even international oil companies jumped on the opportunity by making new agreements with the former Soviet Republic states, looking to exploit the energy resources that had languished under the Soviet regime. Leaders on both sides of the Iron Curtain declared that the Cold War was over.

THE ASCENDANCE OF
THE CLIMATE-CHANGE ISSUE

Back in 1992, with a vacancy created by the end of the Cold War standoff, climate change soon ascended to the position of the greatest threat facing our world. Perhaps the earliest concrete evidence of shared international concern over this issue was the United Nations–sponsored Earth Summit held in Rio de Janeiro, Brazil, in June 1992. More than one hundred heads of state from 173 governments were in attendance to discuss what commitments governments could make to reduce GHG emissions, both collectively and individually. The Earth Summit was the largest environmental gathering of its kind and marked the beginning of climate change as front-page news.

The result of the conference was the creation of the United Nations Framework Convention on Climate Change (UNFCCC), a treaty to establish national GHG inventories and voluntary commitments to reduce emissions below 1990 levels. As an Earth Summit attendee, President George H. W. Bush (Bush 41) formally backed the formation of the UNFCCC even though he remained cautious of its tenets. In spite of some minor dissension, the Earth Summit was hailed as a success, and the UNFCCC would eventually gain the support of 194 countries worldwide. The goals were ambitious: to eliminate the growth in the use of conventional energy sources from burning fossil fuels, alter our global energy mix toward greater renewable energy sources, and create a new business case for sustainable energy generation. But such a global achievement seemed possible only in light of previous achievements to reduce the threat of nuclear war.

Among its tenets, the UNFCCC committed many of the former Cold War first- and second-world nations to finding new and additional sources of financing to support new infrastructure in emerging economies, such as new power plants that would replace or eliminate GHG emissions. In order to meet convention goals, signatories anticipated the need to promote the transfer of technologies to nonindustrialized countries and to create trading "mechanisms" for climate change mitigation over the short, medium, and long terms. Those signatory nations representing the emerging economies of the world (many of which were formerly known as third-world countries) would commit to cooperate with these industrialized nations and to open up their markets to new investments and infrastructure projects that would reduce their GHG emissions.

In November 1992, shortly after the Rio Earth Summit, Bush 41 lost his campaign bid for a second presidential term to Governor Bill Clinton from Arkansas and his vice-presidential running mate, Senator Al Gore. Picking up on the advancements made at the Earth Summit, President Clinton and Vice President Gore continued working with their new counterparts in Europe and Japan to build on the success of the UNFCCC, which they both hoped would become a cornerstone of their legacy.

THE KYOTO PROTOCOL

Five years later, in December 1997, a US delegation attended a follow-up meeting to the Rio Earth Summit. The 1997 Conference of the Parties was held in Kyoto, Japan. There, the parties agreed to a critical amendment to the UNFCCC, called the Kyoto Protocol. The intent of the Kyoto Protocol was to promote new technologies that would mitigate GHG emissions and to impose *mandatory* caps on the industrialized countries that were signatories to it. Under the Clinton administration, the Department of Energy (DOE) had been engaged in numerous joint implementation projects in Latin America, Eastern Europe, and Africa to promote alternative forms of energy under the new rules of the UNFCCC. The Kyoto Protocol was one more step in that direction; it would usher in a set of rules for the international development of clean technology, and that would place the United States in a key leadership role. On behalf of the United States, Vice President Gore signed that amendment and submitted it to President Clinton, who in turn was to hand it over to the US Congress for ratification—a ratification that would never come.

At the time of the Conference of the Parties in Kyoto, I had recently sold Highland Energy to a utility holding company in Boston and was preparing to join a small advisory company: Econergy International, also headquartered in Boulder, Colorado. The Econergy management team was planning to take advantage of business opportunities created by the UNFCCC and enhanced by the Kyoto Protocol. As the company's new CEO, I was very hopeful that the meeting in Japan would usher in greater demand for alternative energy, an area of expertise I wanted to enhance within the company. I was ready to seize the new opportunities that such an agreement would present to companies looking to take advantage of national, market-based initiatives that would necessarily emerge to mitigate global warming.

As most journalists covering international relations saw it, the Kyoto Protocol would create new business opportunities from international trade by creating foreign demand for electric power technologies and project financing. As I saw it, the Kyoto Protocol was elegant in its design. It set the framework for an international "cap and trade" system that would encourage countries and their industries to reduce their GHG emissions. The approach required a two-step process. Each country would first quantify its inventory of GHG sinks and sources, and then it would create incentives to increase the size of its sinks and to reduce its sources of emissions. Regarding sinks, each country would be encouraged to reforest or to ensure the health of its natural tributaries. Regarding sources, each nation's electric sector would need to incorporate the cost of emitting GHGs into its electric generating systems and to improve the energy efficiency of its transportation systems. Incorporating the cost of GHG emissions into the electricity generation system would tip the scales in favor of clean energy and energy efficiency alternatives. Under Kyoto, conventional and business-as-usual power production might become more expensive, but new investment in alternatives would be brought into the country's electric sector at the lowest possible cost.

The Kyoto Protocol would reduce global GHG emissions by setting national caps. Individual countries would then reduce emissions either by investing domestically in new projects or by buying and selling credits through an international cap and trade system. The principle methodologies under the Kyoto Protocol that empowered the market to set a price on carbon were the clean development mechanism (CDM), formulated under Article 12 of the protocol, and the joint implementation provision of the agreement, which encouraged trade between countries seeking to reduce their collective emissions. Both of these methodologies permitted the trading of carbon-emission credits and offsets, which would spur investing in clean energy projects in nonindustrialized nations by allowing polluters in the industrialized nations to buy credits rather than to pay fines for exceeding their mandated caps.

The concept of the Kyoto Protocol was straightforward. If it is cheaper to reduce carbon emissions in country A than it is in country B, then allowing these two countries to trade emission allowances or credits offers the global benefit of a new investment to reduce GHGs at the lowest cost. In accordance with financial theory, but for the ability to trade, this new investment might not have otherwise occurred. Trading emissions credits provided a way for the marketplace to efficiently transition the global energy mix toward a sustainable rate of global GHG emissions.

Prior to the Kyoto Protocol, the concept of capping and trading emissions had been tested in the United States during the Bush 41 administration (1988 to 1992). President Bush had signed into law certain amendments that complemented previous amendments to the US Clean Air Act by President Jimmy Carter in the 1970s. The Bush 41 amendments installed a cap and trade system to regulate the electric power industry and to stimulate investments in technologies that would reduce nitrogen oxide (NOx) and sulfur oxide (SOx), emissions that caused acid rain. Many considered the US experience with this first cap and trade initiative an enormous success. For example, the Acid Rain Program, established under Title IV of the 1990 Clean Air Amendments, which set a cap for coal-fired generation facilities below 1980 levels, was a direct result of the Environmental Protection Agency's (EPA's) SOx and NOx program. In fact, thirteen years later, in 2003, a White House Office of Management and Budget study would report that the Acid Rain Program accounted for the largest quantified human health benefits of any major federal regulatory program implemented in the previous ten years, with benefits far exceeding costs (by a ratio of more than 40:1).[35] Such a success story in the United States—whose progress was already known to many back in 1997—boded well for a global mechanism to address global GHG emissions.

The Kyoto Protocol promised to put into place a market mechanism similar to the US SOx and NOx program, except this time on a global scale and focusing on GHG emissions. For the Kyoto Protocol to be successful, each nation would need to enact domestic legislation or regulation to reallocate the emission targets from a national-level commitment into the different sectors of their economy, such as electricity and manufacturing. Cap and trade was a market-based solution that had moved into the international arena. The Kyoto Protocol, unlike the broad agreement that formed the UNFCCC, would have "teeth" because it established mandatory requirements for industrialized nations, including (if not specifically targeted at) the United States, Russia, Canada, and the industrialized nations of Europe, as well as Australia and Japan. The nonindustrialized countries, or so-called Non-Annex I Parties, would have soft targets for reducing their GHG emissions but not mandatory requirements. Rather than meeting national targets, these countries could sell their carbon offsets to the industrialized countries, or Annex I Parties, which were subject to meeting emissions reductions based on their historical 1990 emissions levels.[36]

The intention of the Kyoto Protocol was to set up a system that would *eventually* place responsibility on both industrialized and nonindustrialized countries to meet the international goals set by the UNFCCC in 1992. The designers of the protocol believed that the targets were manageable for the industrialized countries so long as the nonindustrialized ones opened up their markets for new investments and the growth rate in the industrialized countries continued along their more steady and predictable paths. They also believed that Non-Annex I Parties would naturally support the goals of the protocol in order to access financing and new technology for their infrastructure needs, and that such technology would be more energy efficient and have a lower carbon intensity. Overall, the new game set up by the Kyoto Protocol would spawn even greater global coordination and stimulus for sustainable economic development through creating a level playing field for both industrialized and nonindustrialized nations. Moreover, the hope was that such cooperation could only lead to greater global trade of renewable energy technologies and less global competition over finite natural resources.

The Conference of the Parties—including the delegation from the United States—agreed to the Kyoto Protocol in December 1997. The agreement was, of course, subject to ratification by a satisfactory quorum of countries. It took more than seven years—until February 2005— before sufficient ratification was reached and the agreement could go into effect. Ratification came with a whimper rather than a bang, but the passage reflected a new fault line in the world: Of the 192 signatories to the Kyoto Protocol, 191 countries eventually ratified the agreement. The sole exception was the United States. The other United Nations members that never signed on to Kyoto were Afghanistan, Andorra, and South Sudan.

Nevertheless, the Kyoto Protocol was a success for two very important reasons. One, it created a legitimate global framework for measuring and reporting on global GHGs. Countries from every corner of the planet would gather at Earth Summits to set collective and individual targets for reducing global GHG emissions and then set up processes and procedures for measuring progress. The Kyoto Protocol also created financial mechanisms to incentivize trade between industrialized and nonindustrialized countries as both sought to reach their own domestic GHG targets. The result was greater trade and the opening of new markets. In fact, in the months leading up to and following ratification of the Kyoto Protocol, international banks and equity investors would finance thousands of Kyoto Protocol–related projects—from wind farms replacing conventional power sources to landfill gas recovery eliminating the release of methane, a powerful GHG.

Moreover, the Kyoto Protocol opened up opportunities for new companies such as Econergy International that were looking to find innovative solutions to meet demand for new energy and to meet the requirements placed on the market by the UNFCCC. New financing sources from the world's largest banks gave rise to a new breed of project developers. International banks wanted to build up their inventories of CO_2 credits from CDM projects. To accomplish this objective, these banks were willing to open up new dialogues with third parties to identify market opportunities. The Kyoto Protocol created a new gold rush, but this time the objective wasn't gold—it was carbon.

THE PROTOCOL RAISES EYEBROWS

The Kyoto Protocol was not without controversy, however. By 1997 Russia's economy had contracted sharply in the years following the collapse of the Soviet Union. The decline in the Russian economy from the 1990 baseline year set by the Kyoto Protocol meant that Russia was producing fewer GHG emissions. Russia's reduction in total economic activity had created a windfall of "hot air" credits under the Kyoto Protocol, and Russia wanted to sell them to Europe in addition to its natural gas. Russia found itself in possession of two coveted commodities, both carbon credits and natural gas. The ability to make such easy and profitable exchanges raised the eyebrows of those who were being asked to ratify the Kyoto Protocol and who did not have such an effortless way to meet their commitments. They claimed that Russia had it too easy and also had the ability to make it easy for the buyers of its leading foreign export, natural gas. Opposition to Kyoto started to build in response to the concerns posed by a reemerging Russia.

Accounting challenges also plagued the Kyoto Protocol at about the same time as it went into effect, in 2005. Third-party certifiers were criticized for approving credits that did not meet a rigorous standard and for recycling credits through their accounting methodologies. Two years later, in 2007, the carbon accounting scandal paralleled commentary in the press about how mortgage derivatives in the US housing industry were bringing the global banking system to its knees. This emerging criticism of the Kyoto Protocol on both sides of the Atlantic claimed that carbon trading schemes smelled as rotten as the Wall Street mortgage derivatives.

The situation was dynamic. The international carbon accounting system started to correct itself in 2008. The CDM Executive Board of the United Nations set new standards for third-party certifiers. Next, high-profile corporations began voluntarily reporting on their carbon footprint as part of a new wave that would facilitate a greening of the global economy. For example, Apple initiated a green certification of all of its products, requiring Apple to report to its shareholders about its carbon footprint. As a result, Apple's subcontractors in Asia, such as Taiwan's giant Foxconn, would then have to report on their footprint. The trade press wove stories of a chain reaction through Apple's entire supply line.[37]

Consumer- and investor-driven demand for carbon footprint reporting had the potential to affect public companies around the world. Companies that might have had a carbon debt on their books would now have to consider disclosing this liability in their quarterly and annual reports, whereas before, such a liability would have simply gone unrecorded. Resistance to change started to creep into businesses unsure of whether they wanted to expose their carbon liability.

Nevertheless, new requirements for carbon accounting, in conjunction with the establishment of an international and domestic cap and trade system, seemed like a great recipe for success in addressing climate change. In fact, trade journals were reporting on the convergence of proper accounting and expanded trading of carbon emissions credits, suggesting that modern-day capitalism was on the verge of creating a worldwide revolution. That is, until prices for carbon emissions credits in Europe started to fall in 2008—and negotiations to extend Kyoto beyond its sixteenth birthday started to unravel.

REMNANTS OF THE COLD WAR

Falling prices for emissions credits were not the first sign that the Kyoto Protocol was unraveling. The antecedents of Kyoto's decline can actually be traced to events prior to the September 11, 2001, terrorist attacks, when foreign policy between the United States and Europe rapidly shifted from efforts to reach an international agreement on climate change to efforts that would enhance security worldwide. The falling prices for carbon credits in late 2008 were simply the latest in a long string of incidents that threatened the first major international agreement on mitigating climate change.

Many of the security systems in place prior to 9/11, such as the operations of the North Atlantic Treaty Organization (NATO), were remnants of the Cold War and needed to be reorganized. After the fall of the Soviet Union, NATO had expanded its membership into Eastern Europe, and many of these new members were suddenly finding themselves committed to treating the attack from al-Qaeda on the United States as an attack on the entire NATO membership. Their tenure at NATO had begun with an emphasis on European nations working together to reduce global GHGs and improve trade; now they found themselves working with the United States to reduce the threat of terrorism and to prepare the world for a new war.

The front pages of US and international newspapers were full of stories about US efforts to get "boots on the ground" and build a NATO military presence in Afghanistan, which required coordination among nations that had formally been part of the Eastern Bloc. Television stations throughout the world showed image after image of the passenger airplanes crashing into the World Trade Center in New York. The debates surrounding climate change and the Kyoto Protocol were buried by more current events. Stories of rising temperatures were relegated to the back pages, if they were printed at all.

In the months after 9/11, President George W. Bush (Bush 43) began his call for a "Coalition of the Willing" as a way to mobilize US allies not only to bolster armed forces in Afghanistan but also to eventually invade Iraq and overthrow its dictator, Saddam Hussein. The ostensible purpose of his war against Iraq was to lead this hostile region of the world toward democracy, to eliminate its sponsorship of international terrorism, and to retain global access to its oil fields. Both critics and defenders of US policy pointed out that Iraq was also an actual nation that could be used to engage the world in a real war, while al-Qaeda was an untraditional network of organizations difficult to find, let alone fight.

In 2002, Johannesburg, South Africa, hosted the second Earth Summit. Ten years had passed since the initial Earth Summit gathering in Rio de Janeiro. Five years had passed since the signing of the Kyoto Protocol in Japan. The world was still nearly three years away from the Kyoto Protocol going into effect. My original optimism from 1997 was beginning to sour. I felt that the world had not made much progress in fighting climate change since the end of the Cold War and the formation of the UNFCCC. The promise of Kyoto was certainly falling short, and I was frustrated. I felt that the response to international terrorism should lead to greater coordination on energy issues, not less.

The culmination of the 2002 summit was the issuance of the Johannesburg Declaration, in which nations committed to addressing the conditions that could lead to sustainable development, such as ending chronic hunger, malnutrition, foreign occupation, and armed conflict, rather than marching down the path of another world war.[38] As evidenced by the declaration, climate change was taking a backseat to the war on terrorism. Interestingly, Bush 43 did not attend the meeting as his father had ten years earlier, signaling the new drumbeat for war. In the president's place was a former four-star general, Secretary of State Colin Powell.

At that time, Bush 43 also started to shift his rhetoric away from his original campaign promises, made just two years earlier, to address climate change. Instead he reached out to world leaders, including old Cold War allies such as Britain's prime minister Tony Blair, seeking friends who would support US efforts to take the battle against international terrorism into Iraq. A year and a half after 9/11, on March 19, 2003, President Bush declared war on Iraq. He signaled to the world the necessity of protecting global access to this oil-rich region and of ensuring that it was free of weapons of mass destruction (WMDs). The US Congress followed his lead and turned its focus to Iraq and also to Afghanistan, where troops were searching for Osama bin Laden. The changing conversation in Washington made it obvious to the followers of the Kyoto Protocol that, at least for the time being, the drumbeat for war would drown out the voices calling for action on climate change. The new voices on the airwaves and in print would be about setting a new imperative: reinforcing international access to foreign oil supplies while reducing dependency on foreign oil imports at home.

Inside Washington's power circles, if you listened carefully, you could also hear new voices that were defending the buildup to war in Iraq for reasons other than the threat of WMDs. The message they were calling out was clear: The Western world needs oil—and lots of it—to achieve energy security in a world order where no one is safe. Al-Qaeda was calling for jihad against the United States and the entire Western world, with threats of terrorism in Europe and Asia, too. In the same breath, these new voices expressed indirect opposition to the UNFCCC and the Kyoto Protocol. Specifically, the emerging criticism of the protocol was that it focused on expanding energy conservation and on preserving the natural environment at the expense of US energy security, which relied on the flow of international oil. These whispers started within the halls of Congress, in policy papers from the Department of Energy, and finally in memos to Bush 43 from the office of the vice president recommending a different policy path. For some, the added benefit of a new energy policy that stressed the importance of oil was that it would complement the Bush administration's concern about WMDs and thus reinforce support for the White House foreign policy of invading Iraq.

Keep in mind that publicly the United States had not withdrawn from its commitments to reduce GHG emissions under the UNFCCC. The Bush administration didn't stop promoting clean energy. Bush 43 never vetoed a bill that would ratify the Kyoto Protocol, nor did the US Congress ever vote to reject it. The White House simply shifted its priorities toward its war with Iraq—a shift that led to a lesser commitment on behalf of the United States to the Kyoto process and gave tacit permission to other signatory nations to reassess their own commitment.

In the wake of this shift, the commentaries that appeared in US trade journals and on television talk shows rationalized the reprioritization as a result of the despair the American people felt over the 9/11 terrorist attacks. These commentaries would express an awareness that the world had gotten much "smaller" and much more complicated. Terrorists had attacked our transportation system, our largest financial center, and the heart of our government by using four of our own commercial aircraft as weapons against us. The feeling of vulnerability ran deep in our collective consciousness, perhaps even more deeply than when the Soviets launched the Sputnik rocket nearly fifty years before. A change in policy from active foreign engagement on climate issues to an almost exclusive focus on retaliation against those nations that might be harboring terrorists seemed to be an appropriate response. Many people thought we could return to addressing climate change later.

Meanwhile, supporters of climate action had hoped that the drumbeat for war would eventually fade with the passing of time and after the formation of a new arrangement between old NATO allies to police terrorist organizations such as al-Qaeda. In 2003 and 2004 there was still hope that the United States would reengage in the Kyoto process, and possibly ratify the treaty, after reestablishing its national security system and modernizing outdated Cold War strategies. In fact, Kyoto supporters hoped that US leadership might come to see the benefits of an international agreement promoting trade in renewable energy as a means to reduce global dependency on Middle Eastern oil and as a way to unite the world against terrorism. The basis for such hope rested on the view that American leadership over the prior fifty years had been noted for its entrepreneurial spirit, its ability to mobilize capital to meet foreign and internal threats, and its tendency to take advantage of market opportunities. The Kyoto process would provide those opportunities, and supporters were still optimistic that US leadership would give everyone the chance to participate.

Those who believed the world would soon return to a more sensible order couldn't see the degree of sophistication of the opposing forces at play in the shadows of government and industry, however. The withdrawal of the United States from global energy and climate conversations had reverberating consequences on dozens of existing and impending agreements related to the Kyoto Protocol. The entrenched interests working against the Kyoto Protocol saw the undoing of these agreements as an opportunity to fight back. And they took it.

Ironically, the financial presses were slow to pick up on the implications of this policy reversal. Trade magazines continued to write stories about how, in spite of the world's new focus on combating international terrorism, business as usual was no longer an option. Some journals covering the renewable energy and cap and trade industries continued to run stories on how the simple accounting of carbon emissions would generate billions of dollars in new business. Climate change might have been relegated to the back pages of US newspapers, but the *Economist* and the *Financial Times* continued to cover new science findings on global warming and their potential impact on the energy industry and the international economy.

Trade publishers actually had reason to continue to be optimistic about the growing carbon market. For instance, total transaction values for carbon trading continued to *increase* despite the lack of progress in forming new international agreements or extending the Kyoto Protocol. Even as late as 2011, in spite of lower prices, the total transaction value for the carbon markets in Europe exceeded $170 billion. Moreover, increased volume had not been a result of European trading on an antiquated system. Total transactions for carbon credits under the Kyoto Protocol had been steadily rising as well.

Why did transaction values continue to grow? The political conversation and the market conversation of the time existed in parallel but opposite universes. Market commentators recognized the difficulties in the political landscape, but they speculated that the hedging, profit taking, and arbitrage behind the increased volume in carbon trading underscored a much harsher reality. Continued volume and market growth were all signs of an active and fertile carbon market, not signs of a market that had dried up.

Looking beyond Europe and the Kyoto Protocol, followers of the carbon trade industry have seen continued international efforts to develop cap and trade programs in support of other national programs to reduce GHG emissions. Australia has continued to work for years to put in place an ambitious bill that will create a nationwide cap and trade system by 2015 and that will cover more than 60 percent of the country's annual GHG emissions.[39] The state of California's cap and trade system has also kept moving forward, contrary to federal efforts. The province of Quebec in Canada adopted its own cap and trade system that is now working to link up with California's. In 2012 both Mexico and the Republic of Korea passed their own climate legislation. Even China is a frontrunner in the race toward reducing the energy and carbon intensity of its national economy; it has set up regional cap and trade systems that the government expects to build upon in order to provide a national foundation for the Chinese economy in the years ahead. These macro-trends suggest a very different reality from the one that dominates the publishing presses.

In fact, if you believed the trade magazines back in 2005, a new energy era was still emerging and seemingly couldn't be stopped—not by international terrorism and certainly not by lobbyists funded by Exxon Mobil.[40] In fact, some of the big oil companies seemed to be breaking rank, revealing the schism in the parallel universes. British oil giant British Petroleum (BP) began using the phrase Beyond Petroleum instead as a way to rebrand the company. John Brown, BP's chief executive at the time, had set out in 1997 to turn BP into a green energy company by fixing a target to reduce its GHG emissions by 10 percent through an aggressive investment strategy into clean energy assets. By 2005 BP's investments were having a measurable impact on the market, signaling that perhaps for the first time in history a large oil company was not simply spouting rhetoric about environmental responsibility: It was putting real money to work.

The market was telling a story that differed greatly from the daily reports in mainstream newspapers. The existing carbon market was functioning and growing, it said, and new cap and trade programs were being established. Yet anyone who read the headlines of popular newspapers knew that on the political front, Kyoto was dead.

KYOTO TAKES A BULLET OR TWO

So what is happening to Kyoto? Who (or what) has been trying to kill the protocol? The battle that has been waged against the Kyoto Protocol has been taking place in print and on the airwaves since its inception. It is not possible to say that Kyoto was ever truly "killed," but the Kyoto process has certainly faced its enemies. Between the summit in Copenhagen in 2009 and the meeting in Doha, Qatar, in December 2012, the Kyoto Protocol was only limping forward with solid albeit limited support from the international community. Kyoto was scheduled to expire at the end of 2012, but at the Doha meeting, three weeks before the scheduled expiration, the Conference of the Parties voted to extend the agreement until 2015, setting a new date by which Kyoto nations must negotiate a follow-on trading system. The vote followed a prior failure in 2009, at a summit in Copenhagen, to form a replacement agreement for Kyoto. The move to extend the Kyoto Protocol to 2015 revealed the extreme tension that existed between the push to eliminate it from the international stage and the underlying commitment to keep the conversation going.

Still, I think it is fair to say that Kyoto has taken a few bullets—and the armed beneficiaries are easy to identify. They are a dedicated group of fossil-fuel-industry advocates who have attempted to torpedo the clean energy revolution by attacking the science of climate change, by working to undermine the potential of alternatives, and by putting the rest of us to sleep with a deliberate campaign—a message to the American people that there are plenty of conventional resources available to take care of our future energy needs. The message has helped both to define and to support the business-as-usual scenario, and it dates back to at least the original negotiations of the Kyoto Protocol.

There are dozens of well-researched books on the subject of who has funded anti-Kyoto sentiment. One of the most popular is *Merchants of Doubt* (2010), by Naomi Oreskes and Erik Conway. Other books have been written by prominent scientists such as Michael Mann, the lead author of the 2007 IPCC report, and James Hansen, a NASA-funded climate scientist dating back to the Ronald Reagan administration. These leading scientists have served on the front line of climate change discussions, and with pinpointing accuracy they have detailed the efforts of groups funded by the likes of Exxon Mobil and the Koch Industries to discredit what they believe would be a clear emerging consensus. The buildup toward war in Iraq gave such large entrenched interests cover for a counterattack that would reestablish their dominance over policy formation. Their goal was to raise their own voices above those calling for climate action by seeding doubt about the science of climate change and the viability of new technologies.

The funding of the Heartland Institute by a small number of individual donors between 2007 and 2011 is just one example of how deep the pockets of these naysayers are and how they have been diversifying their resources to challenge the science of climate change. According to the *Economist*, the Heartland Institute is "the world's most prominent think tank promoting skepticism about man-made climate change."[41] Reviewing the list of donors to the Heartland Institute begins to reveal who has been working to kill Kyoto. It also raises several other questions, however: How well coordinated is this effort? Who is behind it? And when did it actually start?

There are clear reasons why the fossil fuel industry has engaged scientists for hire to produce scientific research contrary to the emerging consensus. But the timeline of events is what is most interesting—exactly *when* media coverage around the Kyoto Protocol shifted away from innovation and support of the clean energy revolution and back to the support of conventional fuel sources: Such a timeline reveals more than it conceals. Criticism of the scientific consensus on climate change emerged after 9/11 and again after the beginning of the Iraq War. Republican Senator James Inhofe from Oklahoma, chairman of the Senate Committee on Environment and Public Works between 2003 and 2007, served as the new lightning rod for fresh skepticism about climate change science and the Kyoto Protocol process. Senator Inhofe's efforts to discredit the scientific consensus included publicly calling climate change a "hoax" and impossible because of God's presence in protecting our home, the planet. Furthermore, he compared the EPA to the gestapo and the alarm being raised by climate scientists to the rise of the Third Reich.[42]

Senator Inhofe's wild claims sounded crazy to most, allowing commentators to dismiss them out of hand. But other, more prominent and respected voices started to join the emerging chorus. The editorial board of the *Wall*

Street Journal, for example, has made an attempt to appear balanced by always declaring its support of cap and trade of SOx and NOx emissions when it denounces the regulation of CO_2 emissions, arguing that CO_2 is not a pollutant.[43] The editorial board of the newspaper focused its message like a laser beam on the business community by expressing its support of an outdated cap and trade system (inactive for almost a decade) and its opposition to calling anthropogenic GHG "pollution."

In these and other ways, national support for addressing climate change started to wane. The debate over energy shifted from making sure that it was clean from GHGs to making sure that it was "plentiful."

From the beginning, the opposition to the Kyoto Protocol was not voiced by any single group of businesspeople, academics, or scientists. The opposition arose from a variety of politically savvy opponents who knew that by simply preserving the marginal dominance of conventional fuels, they could railroad the entire effort. They didn't need to prove that renewable energy could never replace oil and conventional fuels. They simply needed to position wind and solar energy as technologies worthy of research and development (R&D) support as long as their competitiveness remained marginal. That position translated into making sure that there would be no subsidies for the deployment of renewable energy and that existing, favorable tax structures for fossil fuels remained in place. Direct subsidies to renewable energy or rising renewable portfolio standards (RPS), mandating utilities to invest in renewable energy, would be criticized as distorting market-based solutions. In contrast, eliminating existing subsidies to the oil and gas industry would be tantamount to creating additional costs for energy users at the pump— or worse, undermining US national security. Oil companies would position themselves in defense of buyers of gasoline, who were already stressed by the high price of fueling their cars.

And yet the voices addressing genuine climate and energy issues continued to compete for national attention. In fact, a new message emerged that was very persuasive to those who were predisposed toward the energy revolution: If there were ever an appropriate time to invest in clean energy, that time would be in a post-9/11 world. Thomas Friedman, a columnist for the *New York Times*, became a prominent spokesperson for this competing response to world affairs. His op-ed pieces consistently echoed the name of the World War II project to develop the nuclear bomb. Friedman called for a new energy "Manhattan Project" to develop technologies that would end our dependence on foreign oil once and for all. In 2005, in the wake of Hurricane Katrina, he wrote that President Bush should have immediately started to support government investment in new energy programs on the morning of September 12, 2001:

> Imagine . . . that the president announced tomorrow that he wanted an immediate 50-cent-a-gallon gasoline tax—the "American Renewal Tax," to be used to rebuild New Orleans, pay down the deficit, fund tax breaks for Americans to convert their cars to hybrid technology or biofuels, fund a Manhattan Project to develop energy independence.[44]

Friedman's call to develop alternatives to fossil fuels inspired many readers who believed that coming from a high-profile *New York Times* commentator, such an idea would certainly have to be considered by the Washington elite. In fact, I recall reading Friedman's *New York Times* column at the time and speculating that if there had been a new Manhattan Project–like program, I certainly would have wanted to be a part of it.

Today, you and I have the benefit of a historical perspective. Friedman's call largely fell on deaf ears and was only partially addressed (if at all) by the Washington elite and, in particular, the White House. Rather, the forces opposing the Kyoto process echoed the idea that while renewable energy might be a good idea in the long run, the current times required an energy policy that would stick to the tried and true. Instead of searching for innovation and new technology, the message inside Washington was: *Let's try to find a new way to keep the shipping lanes open and drill more at home.*

Certainly there was no direct response to Friedman's call. Such a response would have shed light on the quiet efforts already under way and behind closed doors in Washington to form a new energy policy that would in fact maintain the status quo. Evidence of such efforts dated back to the very beginning of the Bush 43 administration.

SETTING THE STAGE FOR KYOTO'S FALL

To dig deeper into what set the stage for the failure of the Kyoto Protocol, however, we need to look back in time even further, to the year before the Conference of the Parties first met in Kyoto, Japan. In 1996 I was in Texas, running Highland Energy and carefully watching the young George W. Bush—the newly elected governor—and how his administration approached energy issues. A few weeks prior to the gubernatorial runoff, my company had successfully won a competitive bid and had signed a contract for its demand-side management program with a Texas utility based in Dallas. Over the next year I found myself traveling frequently to Austin, the capital of Texas, hoping to push our contract through the state's regulatory approval. Now that Governor Bush was in office, he would be setting the tone in Austin by appointing the new chairman to run the Texas regulatory body.

I watched the new governor and his appointments carefully over the first two years of his administration. While he was governor, George W. Bush took an approach to energy issues that seemed balanced, business-minded, and practical. His new appointees promoted open markets for new energy investments, a fresh perspective that created some surprising results. New energy solutions for energy efficiency and wind power development were given the green light.[45] During Bush's term, the Railroad Commission of Texas approved several energy efficiency and wind energy programs that helped set the stage for a new energy economy in Texas. In fact, the possibility of sweeping deregulation of the Texas electricity system prompted several new energy suppliers to enter into the market. As a consequence, a decade later Texas would become the first state to install more than 10,000 megawatts of wind energy capacity and be home to five of the ten largest wind farms in the United States.[46] At the time I thought, *If an oil state like Texas can adopt renewable energy under a Bush administration, so, too, can the rest of the world.*

Four years later I was back in Boulder, Colorado, leading another company and once again watching George W. Bush settle into a newly elected position, this time as the president of the United States. Bush 43 had narrowly beaten former vice president and environmental spokesman Al Gore in the November 2000 election. I was three years into running Econergy International and was struggling to help the company find its market niche as an energy developer rather than simply acting as an adviser to international banks and development agencies. I still felt that Econergy was well positioned to benefit from enhanced international and domestic policies to limit GHG emissions. However, I was uneasy about how to assess the impact of the new presidency on my business.

I was somewhat comforted by my previous experience in Texas, but I had also listened carefully to Bush 43's campaign promises and watched the appointments to his cabinet. On the campaign trail and during the presidential debates, candidate George W. Bush had made promises to promote efforts to reduce GHGs. He acknowledged that global warming was real and, without specifically endorsing the Kyoto Protocol, pledged to work with other nations to address climate change. In fact, candidate Bush had pledged to commit $2 billion to fund research on clean coal technology and to work with Congress, environmental groups, and the energy industry to require emissions reductions, including CO_2.[47] I took his promises to heart.

Moreover, once elected, Bush 43 appointed members to his cabinet who looked promising for advancing international agreements to curb GHG emissions. For instance, Christine Todd Whitman, a former Republican governor of New Jersey, was a strong supporter of environmental initiatives. She spent much of her first few months as the new EPA secretary traveling to Europe and Japan to meet with her counterparts and other heads of state, confirming the promises that her new boss had made to work with other countries to reduce GHGs. Bush 43 also appointed Paul O'Neill, former chairman and chief executive of industrial giant Alcoa, to the Treasury Department. Alcoa, under O'Neill, had been a corporate leader in the mitigation of GHG emissions. Two years before accepting the job as secretary of the Treasury, O'Neill said in a speech to members of the aluminum industry that civilization would go "down the drain" if it did not take climate change seriously.[48] O'Neill represented the best of corporate America: a leader with passion, commitment, and a global view. Similar positive remarks could be made about Colin Powell, too, whom Bush 43 appointed to serve as secretary of state. Powell was an internationalist and a coalition builder committed to working with European allies on shared goals.

All three of these appointees had demonstrated a commitment to mitigating climate change by reducing anthropogenic carbon emissions.[49] The strength of these individuals' characters also indicated resolve that the United States would not sit on the sidelines as the Kyoto Protocol moved forward on the world stage.

Furthermore, climate change negotiations with Europe and Japan were seen as a way of keeping international cooperation stitched together. During these early days of the administration, Bush 43 and his cabinet continued to express support for the goals established under the UNFCCC without directly supporting or rejecting ratification of the Kyoto Protocol. It appeared that the Bush 43 administration wanted something more to be brought to the table. The body language suggested to some observers that they wanted tougher Kyoto commitments, that perhaps they wanted mandatory commitments by all signatories. In other words, rather than backing away from the Kyoto process, the Bush administration might want Kyoto to be more encompassing. The prevailing thought was that even if the United States did not ratify the Kyoto Protocol, it would work toward a new and more comprehensive agreement by approaching the issues of climate change from a business perspective. This emerging view went so far as to fantasize that while there might be problems with Kyoto's structure, it seemed that the Bush 43 administration would be even more progressive in its approach to climate change than had Clinton and Gore by placing greater emphasis on market-based solutions to address it.

Such an optimistic view started to come apart nearly as quickly as it had materialized, however. One of the first indicators that the new administration lacked cohesive policies on energy and the environment was the appointment of Spencer Abraham as the new secretary of energy. Secretary Abraham was a controversial choice because, as a former US senator from Michigan, he had cosponsored a bill in 1999 to abolish the US Department of Energy. His appointment to that very same department, therefore, seemed exceptionally political in nature. The appointment of Spencer Abraham stood as a huge contrast to the other, more internationalist members of the Bush cabinet.

To me it seemed something was amiss.

RESURRECTING THE DEBATE OVER ENERGY

Back at the White House, newly elected vice president Dick Cheney was beginning to lay the foundation for his own energy policy for the United States. Within days after settling into his office, Vice President Cheney began an internal campaign to reopen the debate over energy. He wanted to move the country away from policies that promoted renewable energy and energy efficiency and toward policies that would return federal support to more conventional forms of energy capable of reducing our dependence on foreign oil and strengthening the US electric system. The emerging California electricity crisis, which had just led to large brownouts throughout the state, provided Cheney and his supporters a rallying cry for a new energy policy. The narrative he began to weave in Washington was that the electricity shortfalls in California were a result of its "green" environmental policies.

I was following the situation closely and wasn't particularly surprised by Cheney's early public comments about renewable energy. The new vice president had visited my home state of Colorado shortly before taking office and told reporters that renewable energy could not be counted on to meet our country's needs.[50] I remember being somewhat stunned that he would make such a statement in a state that housed the National Renewable Energy Lab (NREL), a large employer of renewable energy engineers and scientists.

What's more, Vice President Cheney had no background to make such a claim. He was, after all, a career politician. Yes, he was a former executive of Halliburton, a Texas-based company that provided technical services for the exploration of petroleum and natural gas. Halliburton did construct refineries, oil fields, and pipelines, but Cheney and his company had virtually no experience constructing or operating power plants. He certainly had no experience in renewable energy or energy efficiency. I foolishly dismissed his comments at the time as banter from an old-world politician and oil executive.

The next moves by the White House and the Office of the Vice President, however, took my breath away. In January 2001, two weeks after being sworn into office, President Bush appointed Vice President Cheney as chairman of a special committee of energy advisers. This new task force was formally called the National Energy Policy Development Group, but inside Washington it was known as the Cheney Energy Task Force. The official mission of the task force was to take up the cause of reviewing US energy policy. According to Cheney, the purpose was to "bring together business, government, local communities, and citizens to promote dependable, affordable, and environmentally sound energy for the future."[51] The announcement certainly piqued my curiosity as well as the interest of several nongovernmental watchdogs. These watchdogs immediately raised a red flag.[52]

In 2001, as the CEO of a small international advisory firm on energy, I had looked to see if any of my competitors from the renewable energy industry might be serving on the Cheney Energy Task Force. The universe of renewable energy and energy efficiency experts at the time wasn't that large, frankly, and so I thought Vice President Cheney would certainly pick someone I knew. I searched for news on the Internet. I made phone calls to friends and colleagues who might know about the committee and who the advisers might be. As I continued my investigation, I learned that only the names of government officials serving on the task force would be made public. The names of private industry representatives would remain private. I also found no open door to insert myself into the process of developing the nation's energy policy, nor did I know anyone who had.

The other shoe dropped in March 2001. Senator Chuck Hagel of Nebraska sent a letter to President Bush, asking him to clarify his views on climate change. Bush responded by sending a letter not only to Hagel but also to Senator Jesse Helms of North Carolina, Senator Pat Roberts of Kansas, and Senator Larry E. Craig of Idaho. Bush's response included something he had never stated publicly. In this simple letter he reversed his previous policies on climate change by saying that his administration would no longer seek to regulate CO_2 emissions.[53] The letter, when made public, angered Democrats who had supported Bush's cabinet appointments, frustrated moderate Republicans who were preparing to introduce legislation to cut CO_2, and rendered other members of his cabinet (such as Whitman, O'Neill, and Powell) speechless.

The following month the National Resource Defense Counsel (NRDC), a leading environmental group in the United States, filed a suit to obtain records of the Cheney Energy Task Force meetings in order to understand Bush's recent policy reversal. The NRDC suit rested on the grounds that the White House was not in compliance with the Federal Advisory Commission Act, which mandated that any such meetings be open to the public. The case being pushed by the NRDC, and later the Sierra Club, was whether the White House had allowed private industry lobbyists and large campaign donors uneven access to and influence on governmental policy development.

At the heart of the NRDC and Sierra Club complaint was how the vice president and his energy committee members conducted their business. If the White House sought to interact with private industry, according to federal law, public officials must conduct their business in the public and not behind closed doors. The thrust of the NRDC and Sierra Club argument was that if lobbyists were deeply involved in committee work, then the process for how the committee derived its recommendations must be made public. The legal spotlight would be focused on how these meetings were conducted and with whom they were conducted, and concerned parties would continue to seek this information for several years. The White House defended its secrecy under the auspices of the right of the president to keep confidential his sources of information. Watchdogs rejected the White House claims and sought to defend their rights under the Freedom of Information Act that required public deliberations to remain public.

Specifically, the case being advanced by the NRDC and the Sierra Club was based on the grounds that this group of select industry executives and lobby groups was pushing an agenda to promote conventional energy sources and ambushing efforts to advance renewable energy and energy efficiency. The NRDC and the Sierra Club accused the secretive task force of creating a new energy agenda that included drilling for oil in the Arctic National Wildlife Refuge, weakening government's authority to regulate power plant pollution under the Clean Air Act, and giving Secretary Spencer Abraham's DOE responsibility for promoting technology to ease global warming. Bottom line: The Cheney Energy Task Force was accused of gearing up to keep climate action away from the EPA's jurisdiction and to turn the task force's other recommendations into a federal energy policy that had virtually no room for renewable energy.

The official recommendations of the Cheney Energy Task Force weren't made public until May 2001. The Cheney recommendations had already made their way to the surface through back channels, however, as a way to deliver maximum impact through direct communications with congressional leaders and to minimize public outcry by powerful advocacy groups. In fact, when the policy was finally made public, it was positioned with exceptional finesse. The first policy recommendation was to highlight the importance of energy efficiency and conservation. The second recommendation was to immediately repair and upgrade the existing network of refineries, pipelines, electric generators, and transmission lines throughout the country. The third policy recommendation was to fund R&D for renewable energy. Energy efficiency was characterized as the highest goal of any policy, and renewable energy was characterized as a technology whose time would arrive—but in the future, some years down the road.

Nevertheless, the message was simple: Urgent action was needed to meet *current* power requirements by using *available* resources. Energy efficiency and renewable energy were good ideas, nothing more. The task force delivered its message in the form of a sandwich that might be palatable to those who were looking for at least a nod to energy efficiency and renewable energy. Energy efficiency was the top bun; renewable energy was the bottom bun. But all the beef in between was the demand for repairing and upgrading our existing network that relied on conventional energy sources.

The Cheney Energy Task Force was a startlingly contrarian move by the White House, especially when juxtaposed with the international efforts to create greater accountability on energy policy. The solution proposed by the Kyoto process was to create carbon markets and to put a price on carbon emissions. The Kyoto Protocol seemed like a policy mechanism to let the marketplace work. Capital markets around the world, from London to Tokyo to Abu Dhabi, were already forming to take advantage of new investments in clean energy.[54] In spite of growing financial concerns over the global economy, rising international terrorism, and competing technologies, industry and capital markets appeared ready to rise to the occasion and spur a new clean-technology economy. For the new White House, however, energy policy backed by the Cheney Energy Task Force was an effort to divert the flow of public funds from renewable energy programs back to conventional sources of energy—regardless of the international momentum in the other direction.

The White House's new energy policy—developed in secrecy behind closed doors—stood in deep contrast to the policies of its European partners. Many of the recommendations made by the Cheney Energy Task Force slowly made their way into formal policy during the Bush 43 administration; others remained central tenets of the Republican platform through the election cycles of 2008 and 2012. In looking at the historical landscape, starting with the Earth Summit in 1992, the Cheney Energy Task Force was the opening act for a new narrative that would grow and would oppose the Kyoto Protocol process for years to come while still positioning stopgap alternatives to oil as some kind of lofty ideal. The task force started by operating in secret, and its workings have largely remained in the shadows ever since.

Even after his tenure as vice president, Dick Cheney has continued to advance his criticism of renewable energy and to question the economic viability of alternative energy sources. In his memoir, *In My Time,* regarding his tenure as vice president and his observations on the achievements of the Bush-Cheney years, he writes:

> Right now, none of the alternative sources of energy can compete economically with petroleum and coal and other conventional sources. It's also the case that time and again we have found that developing alternative sources has undesirable, unanticipated consequences.[55]

Cheney also writes briefly about the formation of the task force and his pride in not having to reveal the names of those he consulted while generating its policy report. He expresses his feeling that this confidentiality was an appropriate defense of the president's powers. But this simply sidesteps the nature of the complaint lodged against him and the entire Bush-Cheney White House. The litigation was about all those he *didn't talk to.* The difference might appear to be subtle, but if the recommendations made to the Cheney Energy Task Force were nothing more than a wish list from a handful of big oil lobbyists, the significance is profound. In the execution of his duties, the vice president lacked both care and candor in reviewing US energy policy, and his actions obstructed climate action on a worldwide level.

SURVIVING THE GREAT RECESSION—ALMOST

The Cheney efforts to dismiss the Kyoto Protocol continued until the end of the Bush-Cheney White House. Then the Great Recession of 2008 provided the second opportunity for opposing forces to strike a blow against the Kyoto process and to drive the nail deeper into the protocol's coffin. The 2008 financial crisis was blamed in part on complex financial derivatives, ranging from aggregating mortgages by the largest international banks to inadequate regulatory oversight to guarantee sufficient liquidity within the global banking sector. The 2008 crisis was also blamed on rising prices for oil, transportation, and food. The single most important factor in all three cases was the cost of energy. For the critics, carbon trading was just another financial derivative created by Wall Street that would lead to even higher energy prices and thus economic ruin. The critics in 2008 were using Cheney's playbook: Blame the environmentalists.

Furthermore, opponents who needed ammunition to fight cap and trade programs accused the banking system of wanting to profit off of Main Street by raising commodity prices through the trading of derivatives. This time, instead of mortgage derivatives, it would be carbon credits. By 2010 the Republican Party had whipped nearly every one of its members into a unified block against climate change legislation, even though many of its members, including 2008 presidential candidate Senator John McCain of Arizona, had previously supported it. The lack of bipartisan support meant that any effort to approve a climate or energy bill under way in the Senate would never reach the floor.

But after eight years of the Bush-Cheney policies in Iraq, politics in Washington changed in 2008. Senator Barack Obama, a Democrat from Illinois, beat Senator McCain in the presidential race. Candidate Obama had promised voters that he would make the United States relevant again on the world stage by supporting the growth of green jobs and rejoining international efforts to reduce GHG emissions. In fact, after the 2008 presidential election, most observers of US energy policy, but not all,[56] expected the nation's position on climate change to return to active engagement similar to the US stance in the Clinton-Gore years. Obama had campaigned on strengthening the economy and was looking to create green jobs through a stimulus bill. In the 2009 federal budget submitted to Congress, the new administration initially included a provision that would generate revenue from an auction granting carbon permits to the energy industry. The Obama administration expected annual revenue from the auction to generate a minimum of $130 billion and a maximum of $370 billion by 2015. President Obama tried to position himself as a pragmatist by suggesting that the proceeds from the auction would be used to offset the costs of his stimulus bill.[57] The 2009 budget sent a strong signal to Congress and to global energy markets that the new president was serious about pursuing climate legislation.

The headwind in Washington was strong, however, and there was great resistance to any initiative to place a tax on carbon or to set up a national cap and trade program on GHG emissions. The $838 billion stimulus bill in the Senate passed with a vote of 61 for and 36 against. The Democratic majority delivered President Obama the backing he said he needed to tackle the worst economic crisis since the Great Depression, but in spite of Senator McCain's promise of working with the new president, support on the Republican side of the aisle showed little willingness to take Obama's lead and run with it. The shift in tide was consequential. The Obama administration's commitment to introducing a climate bill started to wane, and the White House also shifted its role from advocate to spectator as a small group in the Senate struggled to consummate a climate deal that would satisfy the sixty-vote requirement. The ripple sent out by the Cheney Energy Task Force so many years before had become a wave, and it was impairing any new energy initiative. The energy industry decided it was better to wait and watch.

Nevertheless, in 2009 the Democratic House of Representatives eventually shaped and approved a climate bill spearheaded by Representative Henry Waxman of California. But by the time it was approved, the concept of a carbon auction to generate new federal revenues had been abandoned to rising Republican opposition. The White House shifted all focus onto the Senate, where Democratic margins were much thinner, to form a consensus if there was ever to be any hope of the United States regaining world leadership or even of meaningful cooperation on climate change.

In the summer of 2010, I felt that there was still a ray of hope for a climate bill in the Senate. As the CEO of my third venture in the energy business, I was aware that the spread was widening between those who were betting for one and those betting against one. Democratic Senator John Kerry from Massachusetts, Republican Senator Lindsey Graham from South Carolina, and Independent Senator Joseph Lieberman from Connecticut were leading a bipartisan effort to approve a comprehensive energy and climate bill. Meanwhile, the White House wanted a legislative victory, any kind of victory, before the 2010 November elections while the Democrats still controlled the Senate. Rahm Emanuel, the White House chief of staff, was carefully watching the legislative race between the backers of the climate and healthcare bills before he was willing to give full White House support for either one. In spite of the individual reputations of the three senators lobbying to find the necessary sixty votes to pass a climate bill, the so-called trio was coming up short.

In fact, it was not clear at the time if the trio had the full support of the White House, but the senators felt they did have the support of the president, who could use his muscle to garner most of the Democratic votes in the Senate with the exception of a few who were too entrenched in coal country. Senator Graham's job was to win over Republicans who had supported climate legislation in the past, including Senator McCain. Senator Kerry's job was to shore up Democrats who might waver because of support from the coal and natural gas industries. The trio was willing to give in on a number of concessions to address positions that had been upheld by the Cheney Energy Task Force only a few years before. These positions required several special provisions in any climate bill that would gain the necessary support in the Senate: support for the development of new nuclear power plants, increased approval of offshore drilling, and (last but not least) a change in the EPA charter that would limit its authority to regulate GHG emissions under the Clean Air Act. The three senators agreed to all of these concessions right out of the box. They worked to make sure that the concessions had the support of the president and the White House. As they saw it, all they needed were sixty votes.

Yet to broker a deal, the senators needed to do more. In February 2010, Senator Kerry met with T. Boone Pickens, the oil and gas magnate and financier. Pickens had been Senator Kerry's nemesis during his 2004 bid for the presidency—he had funded the Swift Boat ad campaign that had tried to discredit the senator's military service during the Vietnam War—so Kerry's willingness to meet with him revealed the extent of the climate trio's desperation.

But the support of Pickens and the natural gas industry would garner both Republican and Democratic support from states with booming gas exploration, so Graham and Lieberman encouraged Kerry to cut a deal with Pickens. Before he would agree to support their efforts, Pickens wanted the climate bill to include tax incentives for natural gas vehicles and for building natural gas fueling stations. Putting past animosities aside, Senator Kerry immediately agreed to Pickens's terms. Time was of the essence.

Gaining the support of Pickens gave the trio a new sense of confidence. The trio started to plan their end game. They realized that key to their final success was getting big oil to agree to at least hold back its army of lobbyists from killing a climate deal. The oil industry already had the support of the White House for offshore drilling. To clinch the deal, the oil industry wanted to avoid a direct cap on oil-drilling emissions and instead wanted to negotiate a fee—a fee that some might call a "tax." The trio worried that any mention of "new taxes" would not only raise the hackles of the conservative elite but also, potentially, send scared Democrats seeking reelection in 2010 into retreat.

The trio didn't like the idea of either a new tax or making such an exception for the oil industry. Instead, they wanted to see a market-based approach to climate change. But before all the issues could be worked out, the emerging climate bill would receive a deathblow from an unexpected event.

In April 2010, the Deepwater Horizon oil rig experienced an explosion that killed eleven workers and caused an oil gusher that released an estimated 53,000 barrels of oil per day into the waters of the Gulf of Mexico. The spill flowed unabated for nearly three months as a loose international consortium organized solutions to stop the flow. Every news hour covered detailed explanations on what BP, the oil company responsible for the oil rig, was doing and not doing to curtail an environmental disaster that would exceed that of the *Exxon Valdez* oil spill a few decades before. The spill would cause extensive damage to the marine and wildlife habitats of the Gulf of Mexico, creating an eighty-square-mile kill zone. Unfortunately, the oil spill also had an unexpected impact on a certain climate bill in the US Senate: It killed it, too.

The Deepwater Horizon oil rig disaster shattered the integrity of all of the compromises that the trio of senators had made in their efforts to usher in a comprehensive climate bill. Most people might think this event would have *helped* legislation designed to protect the environment. As I watched CNN and the coverage of the Gulf of Mexico disaster, even I thought that such a crisis should have created more pressure on Washington to approve a climate bill that would address an environmental threat recognized by the leadership of nearly every country in the world. Inside the Beltway, however, Deepwater Horizon did the opposite. Ironically, the White House could no longer defend a climate bill that would promote offshore oil drilling.

For Chief of Staff Emanuel, the horse race between the climate bill and the healthcare bill was over. The response of the White House was to put all its bets down on the healthcare bill that has since been nicknamed "Obama Care"—and to never look back.

By November 2010, the midterm election transferred power of the Democratic-controlled House back to the Republicans. The Senate was left with a thin Democratic majority. Not only did the sweep give the Republicans a large majority in the House, but it also ushered in a new generation of reactionaries: the Tea Party diehards, who brought to Washington a host of antigovernment rhetoric, including a specifically anti-climate action agenda.

As a result, and in spite of support by individual Republican senators for a climate bill in the past, the bill never moved to the floor for a vote.[58]

THE COST OF DELAY

The lack of any material change to our global energy mix in recent decades means that business as usual has prevailed in both politics and climate action. The efforts to make international agreements such as the Kyoto Protocol effective, however, reveal that the global political system is struggling to create a new business case. It is a mixed bag of results. Meanwhile, GHGs have continued to build in our atmosphere ever since the news of the danger hit the front pages of newspapers back in 1992. The average concentration of CO_2 in our atmosphere in 1992 was 356 ppm. The average concentration of CO_2 in 2013 reached 400. The cost of this delay is increasingly difficult to calculate, and yet it is not necessarily the cost of mitigation that is mounting. Rather, it is the increasing cost of adapting to a new, more hostile climate.

Global average temperatures have risen more than 1.3 degrees Fahrenheit (0.75 degrees Celsius) since 1850. Along with rising temperatures since preindustrial times has come an increase in severe weather. For example, Hurricane Sandy, which hit New York, New Jersey, and Connecticut in October 2012, was a reminder to many that climate change is upon us. Unlike Hurricane Katrina, which eliminated dozens of poor New Orleans neighborhoods and destroyed critical services that left the city dark and uninhabitable, Sandy was much more indiscriminate. The storm leveled services for New Jersey residents in historically blue-collar Hoboken and also washed away luxury seaside homes on the New Jersey and Connecticut shores. The hurricane hit the eastern United States less than two weeks before the 2012 presidential election. President Obama flew to New Jersey to meet with those responding to the crisis. Presidential candidate Mitt Romney abandoned his campaign trail to hold fundraisers for victims of the storm. It was a moment when many Americans realized the fragility of our cocoon.

Both Katrina and Sandy were superstorms that caused severe damage. Katrina was a much larger storm, still a category 3 hurricane, when it hit the shoreline. In total, Katrina left three million people in eight states without power, and more than 600,000 families were still homeless one month later. However, even though Sandy was categorized as a post-tropical cyclone by the time it came ashore, it resulted in a huge storm surge that knocked out power and destroyed buildings up and down the seaboard. Eight million people in sixteen states, from areas as far south as Washington, DC, to the shores of Connecticut, lost electricity. Sandy severely damaged 300,000 homes versus Katrina's 125,000.[59] The longer we delay climate action, the more we can expect to see costs to the global community like these.

KEY OBSERVATIONS

The key observations from this chapter set the context for defining *business as usual*. These observations also help us begin to shape what a new business case might actually look like.

» The beginning of international efforts to curb the buildup of GHGs came on the heels of successful international efforts to end the arms race between two superpowers. Just as with the arms treaties of the 1980s and 1990s, the venue for negotiations for climate change was the United Nations and the parties were countries with UN representation.

» Initial efforts to curb GHG emissions had the support of then-president George H. W. Bush, who had already supported a cap and trade system to mitigate power plant emissions by addressing acid rain, through his approval of certain amendments to the Clean Air Act. Bush 41's support of this market-based approach made him an intellectual owner of the very principles that international organizers later used to form the UNFCCC and eventually the Kyoto Protocol.

» Direct opposition to the Kyoto Protocol did not develop in the United States until the formation of the Cheney Energy Task Force. Newly elected President George W. Bush had previously supported the UNFCCC goals and the Kyoto process.

» Congressional opposition to any climate legislation in the United States—primarily from the Republican Party, whose resistance was deeply seated in the principles advanced by the Cheney task force—continued through the first term of the Obama administration. Senatorial backers of climate change legislation in 2010 agreed to concessions that revealed that the Cheney agenda was alive and well.

» Interest in promoting offshore drilling, nuclear power, natural gas development, and limited cap and trade on any oil interests, as well as in gutting the EPA's role in GHG mitigation, has been deeply embedded into the Republican platform, keeping the nation, if not the entire world, locked into the status quo.

PART II

. . .

BUSINESS AS USUAL

Problems cannot be solved at the same
level of awareness that created them.
—Albert Einstein

CHAPTER 4

We were just thirty miles south of Boulder, returning from a hiking trip in southern Colorado, when we crested a hill and saw something beyond comprehension. It was a giant plume of smoke that trailed to the east for as far as the eye could see. It looked as if a nuclear bomb had exploded over the city of Boulder and the winds from the west had blown the smoke all the way to Nebraska.

"Oh my God," said Seann, my nineteen-year-old son. "Mom must be going crazy."

I didn't respond. I just pushed on the accelerator knowing that my wife would, indeed, be at her wits' end. All I could think about was what might be happening to our home.

Seann and I had spent the 2010 Labor Day weekend above the tree line, well out of range of cell phone service. When I turned on my cell phone that morning, I saw that there were numerous messages from home. The first message from my wife said that she could smell smoke. The second message said that our neighborhood was being evacuated.

As I drove, my son searched for news of the fire on his iPhone. He quickly learned that a forest fire, pushed by forty-mile-per-hour winds, had ripped up Four Mile Canyon in the foothills above Boulder.

Boulder is known for its dry air and its more than three hundred sunny, blue-sky days per year. Because we live in the foothills up Sunshine Canyon, where it's even drier and sunnier, I had always cautioned the kids to be careful with candles and matches, schooling them that our home is a potential tinderbox. According to the visual map in my head, the fire was headed straight toward our home. I thought, *These fires move fast, especially uphill with a strong wind.*

Fires in the western United States are a fact of life, but they've gotten worse over the last one hundred years, falling into the category of "superfires." In fact, wildfires in the state of Colorado, on both public and private lands, have increased dramatically since the second half of the twentieth century. On average the total number of acres burned over this time period has grown by an astounding 143 percent. In the early 2000s, the average number of acres burned increased by over 340 percent from the previous decade.[60] The trend line is discouraging.

And climate change is one of the causes.

You will see more evidence of climate change if you visit any of the national parks or ski areas in northwest Colorado. As you hike or ski the trails, you will see the results of a pine beetle epidemic. The evergreen forests are stained with enormous patches of infected pines. You will know them by their needles, which turn a reddish brown as they dry out and die. The pine beetle has been killing forests in the Rocky Mountains in part because of higher levels of drought and heat. These beetles sweep through and leave nothing behind but dry timber—fuel to burn. Forests with lodge pole and ponderosa pines have been hardest hit.

These trees are under stress because of the shorter winters caused by climate change. Over the last two decades average winter temperatures have failed to reach levels low enough to kill the pine beetle before infestations reach epidemic levels. The pine beetle hibernates during winter, using an alcohol-like fuel to survive. Shorter winters mean it takes less fuel to survive until the next season. The result is a population of pine beetles that grows every year.

Climate change wasn't exactly on my mind, however, that Labor Day when my son and I drove into Boulder and watched the sun set behind that giant plume of smoke. I wouldn't make the connection that the gigantic plume of smoke was heralding climate change until much later.

When we reached Boulder, Seann and I decided that first we would see if we could make it up to our home. At the base of Sunshine Canyon, an unsympathetic officer standing guard at a wooden blockade turned us away. I felt outraged at being denied the right to access our home. But with Seann's encouragement, I kept my cool as we turned the car around and headed into town with all of the other refugees.

In Boulder, at my daughter's college apartment, we met up with my wife and daughter, along with the family dog and cat, whom they had managed to find and coax into the car before fleeing. We checked into the Hotel Boulderado and began the long process of waiting for news and permission to return to our home. We spent our days traversing the neighboring hills, hoping to catch a glimpse of our house with a new pair of binoculars, but the smoke was just too thick. All we could see was the red glow of the burning treetops.

It was a nerve-wracking five days before we could return to our home, which was in perfect condition other than being covered in ash. Others weren't as fortunate: 169 homes were destroyed in the Four Mile Canyon fire that started at about 10:00 a.m. on that windy Labor Day. The fire had spread out of control immediately as it moved upward and westward, with flames nearly fifty feet high. It caused the most economic damage of any fire in Colorado's history, even though the damage was relatively contained, affecting only 6,200 acres, or roughly ten square miles.[61]

We still feel the impact of the fire years later. Each spring, helicopters have lifted seed and mulch into the burnt area to promote revegetation. Until the fire zone fully recovers, each summer, city officials fear severe flooding of Boulder Creek. The scorched earth in the mountains limits the ability of the ground to absorb water. During a rainstorm, officials worry that Four Mile Canyon could act as a gigantic funnel, gathering water and shooting it down into Four Mile Creek at the base of the canyon. Four Mile Creek eventually converges with Boulder Creek and runs straight through the center of town.

The looming issue is that adding a large rainstorm in early summer to the annual melting snowpack could lead to massive flooding of Boulder, similar to the flood in 1894, commonly known as the "hundred-year flood," that destroyed hundreds of homes and businesses.[62]

Other parts of the West are burning up. Nearly every summer new forest fire records are being set in Arizona, New Mexico, and Colorado. These fires are being measured for their size in terms of acreage burned and homes destroyed. The year 2011 was a record year for fires in New Mexico, and 2012 broke the record again. Scientists in that state attribute the dry conditions to what they call a "sponge effect." Prolonged heat turns the atmosphere into a dry sponge that sucks the moisture right out of the ground and trees.[63] Dried-out piñon trees provide ready fuel, needing only a lightning strike to ignite a blaze.

The situation in the West has reached such a critical level that President Obama signed new legislation in the summer of 2012 to speed up federal contracting for big aerial tankers with which to fight wildfires. Faced with imminent danger to their constituents from wildfires, the US Congress apparently agrees that early action will limit the damage.

DROUGHTS, FIRES, AND FLOODING

The most obvious consequences of climate change are droughts, fires, and flooding. However, the threat of a new dust bowl, similar to the 1930s Dust Bowl I briefly described in chapter 2, would have the most immediate and severe economic consequences and in fact may be the most pressing threat resulting from climate change.[64] The Great Drought of 2012, which destroyed millions of acres of crops in the United States, is just another example of the results of a series of hot summers that have already befallen other regions in Europe and Russia. What makes the Great Drought different is that it carried the reality of a dry, parched, and arid surface to our own backyard, an area of our planet that has nearly always been considered the most fertile agricultural land in the world.

How bad will things get if we continue with business as usual? Climate projections clearly show a trend toward more extreme precipitation that will lead to both flooding and periods of prolonged drought. As I mentioned in the introduction, the general consensus is that if atmospheric CO_2 concentrations exceed 450 ppm, average global temperatures will rise by 3.6 degrees Fahrenheit (2 degrees Celsius) or more above temperatures in preindustrial times.[65] As radiation bounces off the surface of the planet, rising CO_2 levels cause greater energy levels to be trapped in the atmosphere.

Project Butterfly's business-as-usual forecast puts global CO_2 concentration at 450 ppm within twenty years and above 800 ppm by the end of the century, if nothing is done to change our course. These figures derive from current trends, including fairly optimistic scenarios regarding the continuation of current policies to promote renewable energy and global reforestation efforts. The result of exceeding 800 ppm is consistent with a likely increase in global temperature of 8 degrees Fahrenheit (4.5 degrees Celsius).[66] The consensus is that somewhere between 3.6 degrees Fahrenheit (2 degrees Celsius) and 8 degrees Fahrenheit (4.5 degrees Celsius), the deterioration of the global climate will begin to cascade into a series of catastrophic events that will make the planet much less hospitable to human survival.

As I have already mentioned, scientists are ringing the alarm bells. Rainfall patterns and the hydrologic cycles are changing, and many climate models predict that these alterations in climate conditions will get much worse, because evaporation and precipitation are controlled largely by temperature. Rising temperatures will create significant imbalances in the planet's ecosystems. Dry areas, such as in the southwestern United States, will become drier. Rainy areas, such as the northwestern United States, will experience more torrential, extreme rain. Therefore, changes in drought patterns and seasonality bring a greater risk of large fires and more erratic crop production rates, including the potential for formerly agriculture-rich regions to form new dust bowls that will change the social, economic, and physical landscape around the world for generations.[67]

To understand what has been causing the increasing severity of weather patterns and why these trends are alarming, let's take a look at the science of climate and climate change.

DETERMINING THE PLANET'S BASELINE

Understanding the climate cycle and how it works will help us further define the climate change problem and identify potential solutions to mitigate the human impact on earth's weather systems. It also sets the physical conditions for defining the Project Butterfly business-as-usual scenario.

The earth's baseline temperature is set by three easy-to-understand factors. First, the strength of the sun, combined with our planet's distance from and angle to it, governs the amount of incoming solar heat that the earth receives. Second, not all solar heat is absorbed by the earth's surface; much is reflected into space, and that amount depends on the arrangement of continents and land cover. Ice sheets, for example, reflect almost 90 percent of the sun's rays. Imagine our planet wearing a black shirt on a hot summer's day versus wearing a snow-white cape. The third key factor that determines our planet's baseline temperature is the presence of an atmosphere, a thin veil of gases and vapors that surrounds the earth. This tiny skin of air has dramatic effects on climate.

HOW GREENHOUSE GASES AFFECT OUR CLIMATE

As you may recall from your high school science classes, the earth's atmosphere is composed mostly of gases: nitrogen, oxygen, and argon. The remaining 1 percent is made up of trace constituents. These traces include a small group of greenhouse gases (GHGs), principle among them carbon dioxide (CO_2), methane (CH_4), nitrous oxide (N_2O), ozone (O_3), and halocarbons.[68] These gases are mostly invisible to incoming rays from the sun but not to outgoing heat from the earth. Because the sun is the hotter of the two, the heat energy that it emits has shorter wavelengths than the heat energy leaving the earth's surface. GHGs vibrate and heat up when the earth's "long-wave" radiation hits them. Then these small, excited molecules of gas rerelease that heat energy in all directions—some of it back toward our planet. Without GHGs, the earth would be much colder—about 50 degrees Fahrenheit (or 28 degrees Celsius)—because it would lose all outgoing heat.[69]

Perhaps the best known of the GHGs is CO_2. It is not the most powerful GHG, but it packs the greatest climatic punch because it has a higher concentration in our atmosphere than the others do. In order to understand why increased anthropogenic CO_2 in our atmosphere can change the climate conditions, it is necessary to first examine the nonhuman system of CO_2 reservoirs (where CO_2 resides) and CO_2 fluxes (exchanges of carbon between reservoirs) on our planet.

Carbon dioxide exists on the earth in four main reservoirs: (1) in the atmosphere, in gas form; (2) in the land biosphere, in vegetation and biomass; (3) dissolved in the oceans; and (4) incorporated into various types of rocks, including fossil fuel hydrocarbons.[70] The sizes of these reservoirs of CO_2 vary: The atmosphere contains 840 billion metric tons;[71] the land biosphere contains roughly 600 billion metric tons; the oceans contain roughly 39,000 billion metric tons; and the rocks beneath our feet contain about 66,000,000 billion metric tons.[72] Fossil fuel reserves in the forms of coal, oil, and natural gas make up some 5,000 billion metric tons of the rocks and sediment in the latter reservoir.

Each year, the planet "breathes" CO_2 into and out of the atmosphere. During the growing season, land plants draw down about 100 billion metric tons of CO_2, and with biomass death and leaf respiration, about 100 billion metric tons of CO_2 are released back into the atmosphere. Most land on the earth that contains the biodiversity of our forests is in the northern hemisphere, and in the spring, with the blossoming of plant life, the atmosphere experiences a decrease in CO_2 (the planet breathes the gas in). Come winter, the reverse effect takes place: The atmosphere experiences an increase in CO_2 (the planet breathes the gas out). The oceans also absorb and release roughly 100 billion metric tons of atmospheric CO_2 within each year. We therefore expect to—and do—see large seasonal oscillations in atmospheric

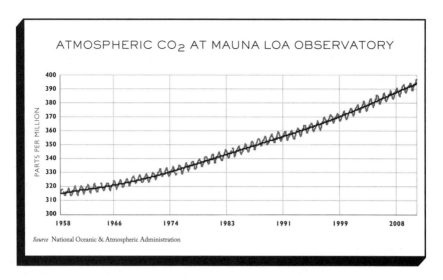

• *fig. 4.1:* Direct observations of atmospheric CO_2 made at Mauna Loa Observatory in Hawaii. Because of the site's remote location and minimal influences of vegetation and human activity, it serves as a good global mean estimate of atmospheric CO_2 concentrations.

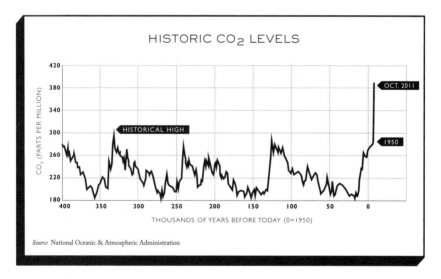

• *fig. 4.2:* These recordings from ice cores demonstrate that throughout the past 400,000 years, atmospheric CO_2 levels have not reached the levels at which they stand today.

CO_2. Figure 4.1 clearly shows CO_2 concentrations rising and falling each year, but it also shows that CO_2 concentrations in the atmosphere are currently on the rise. Figure 4.2 shows that we are reaching levels never previously attained within the past 400,000 years. This unprecedented increase is part of the evidence climate scientists provide to document the consequence of human activity on the concentration of CO_2 in the atmosphere.

HOW BURNING FOSSIL FUELS AFFECTS OUR CLIMATE

Fossil fuels—coal, oil, and natural gas—are all hydrocarbons, and they differ from one another because of varying ratios of hydrogen atoms to carbon atoms. The hydrocarbon molecules that comprise these energy sources are derived from geologically ancient (many millions of years old) organic material that has been fossilized. Like dinosaur bones, these fossils are just old, dead remains. These source materials (hydrocarbons) were formed only under specific geologic conditions that were rarely ubiquitous on the earth's surface. Large portions of available coal reserves, for example, formed during a particularly swampy period some 300 million years ago.[73] More important, fossil fuels took millions of years to form, hence their designation as a nonrenewable energy source. We extract and burn fossil fuels about 60,000 times faster than they were made.[74]

The reason we go to great lengths to uncover and extract hydrocarbons from deep in the earth is that they release large amounts of energy when they are burned. In a conventional power plant, the heat energy produced by burning ("combusting") hydrocarbons is converted to mechanical energy to drive turbines and generate electricity. Oxygen and hydrocarbons are the inputs to this reaction, and the outputs, CO_2 and water, are released into the atmosphere. In fact, each year, human activities are responsible for emitting roughly nine billion tons of fossil fuel carbon into the atmosphere.

Prior to industrialization, the atmosphere contained approximately 600 billion tons of carbon. Atmospheric burden of 600 billion tons of carbon might be considered "normal" for the earth to handle if we wish to continue human life within a healthy range. But the post–Industrial Revolution has given us millions of vehicles and thousands of power plants, releasing into the atmosphere CO_2 that was previously stored beneath the earth. Today the atmosphere holds 840 billion tons. A mixture of 840 billion tons of CO_2 with the rest of the air in the atmosphere results in a concentration of 394 parts CO_2 for every million parts dry air, or ppm. Lucky for us, land plants and the oceans currently absorb, in natural land and ocean "sinks," roughly half of the extra CO_2 that is emitted each year. However, these sinks are inadequate to absorb increased emissions and will soon become saturated. Consequently, the ever-increasing burden of human CO_2 added to the atmosphere each year will have an even greater impact on climate than it already does.[75]

The common climate change debate among regular citizens and in the media is about whether such high levels are part of any natural climate cycle and whether higher temperatures are sustainable or unsustainable. However, it should not be a matter of debate that the increase of CO_2 in our atmosphere since preindustrial times is from human burning of fossil fuels, the production of cement, and land-use changes such as deforestation.[76] It also should not be a matter of serious debate that more GHGs mean a warmer planet. As I've just described, GHG concentrations, solar input, and surface reflectivity are the dominant controls of the earth's climate. The variability of our climate is therefore a result not only of CO_2 concentrations but also of other complex and interconnected systems. The central point to understand is that the baseline characteristics of our climate—temperature included—are directly linked to changes in the concentrations of GHGs in our atmosphere.

The earlier we as a global community address climate change, the better, because it is a self-perpetuating phenomenon. In a climate "positive feedback loop," warming begets warming in much the same way as fire begets fire or a falling stock price feeds a falling stock price, because no one wants to catch a falling knife. For example, warming causes sea ice to melt and glaciers to retreat. The larger areas of blue sea and dark land, in turn, absorb more solar energy than the ice did, heating things up even faster. The less ice you have, the more quickly the remaining ice melts. Warming also increases evaporation and the amount of water vapor in the air. More water vapor means more warming, since water vapor acts as a GHG by trapping warmth on the earth's surface. Warming can also melt permafrost and frozen tundra, resulting in the release of high quantities of CO_2 and methane stored in the ground as dead plant matter.[77]

Clearly, this warming feedback can amplify even small perturbations and accelerate the crossing of the CO_2 threshold. In other words, we could arrive at the tipping point sooner than predicted. The feedback between different sinks and sources of carbon is potentially the largest threat to our current state of existence. Imagine how these positive feedback loops could tip us into a new set of projections that we might never have anticipated.

The conclusions of the Intergovernmental Panel on Climate Change (IPCC), the world's most authoritative assessment on the state of climate change, have been criticized as being too extreme. However, the IPCC's findings may in fact prove to be overly conservative, because the scientists who authored these studies included only linear events and ignored the potential impact of feedback that I have discussed here. The failure of the IPCC to seriously factor in worst-case scenarios may mean that our climate is even more fragile than we thought, and the economic, social, and physical consequences may be that much more severe.

HOW THE PLANET IS CHANGING

Signs of dramatic climate change are already in evidence: Surface temperatures have increased over the course of the twentieth century (see figure 4.3). Extreme weather events—evidence of more energy in the climate system—are increasing in frequency. Glaciers are melting in nearly every mountain range in the world. For example, evidence from photography in the Himalayas shows that glaciers have receded by up to four hundred vertical feet in just under one hundred years. Professor Lonnie Thompson, a paleoclimatologist from Ohio State University, has said, "I have always considered the glaciers

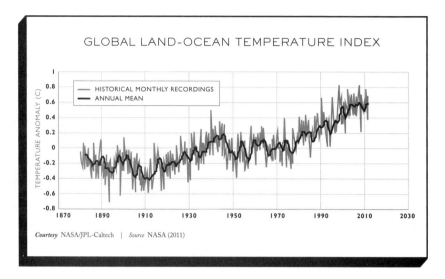

Courtesy NASA/JPL-Caltech | Source NASA (2011)

⬧ *fig. 4.3:* While temperatures have always fluxuated throughout history, the recent and continuous rise of the Global Land-Ocean Temperature Index is indicative that a new force, mainly man-made use of hydrocarbons, is affecting the balance.

on the mountain of the lower latitudes as the canary in the coal mine. They are in an area projected to warm twice as fast as the surface."[78] We are seeing the same signs elsewhere in the world. Even in Colorado I have seen the reduction of glaciers and snowpack in a collection of mountain peaks known as the Never Summer Range. Now, by July of every year, there is almost no snow, nor is there any visual sign of remaining glaciers.

Reinforcing the rapid retreat of our world's largest glaciers is the dramatic decrease of sea ice in the Arctic. The summer of 2012 saw the largest decrease (49 percent) in the Arctic ice cap in history.[79] So far, the Antarctic is experiencing degradation only at the edges. Climate scientists closely monitor sea ice extent in the Arctic and Antarctic, as well as the estimated mass of the land ice in the East and West Antarctic and Greenland. In all cases, declining ice mass is in evidence (see figure 4.4). Once land ice starts to slide off into the ocean, the sea level will rise dramatically. The second act of climate change will have begun, and all bets will be over regarding who was right on the climate debate.

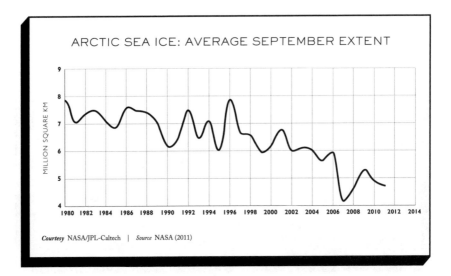

ARCTIC SEA ICE: AVERAGE SEPTEMBER EXTENT

MILLION SQUARE KM

1980 1982 1984 1986 1988 1990 1992 1994 1996 1998 2000 2002 2004 2006 2008 2010 2012 2014

Courtesy NASA/JPL-Caltech | *Source* NASA (2011)

• *fig. 4.4:* Acting as the "canary in the coal mine," the Arctic sea ice is more affected by the changing climate than other natural indicators. The recent loss of ice in this region is reason for alarm.

The changes are measurable. Between 1870 and 2000, sea levels rose 200 millimeters, or at a rate of 1.70 millimeters per year. Between 1990 and the present, sea levels have risen 60 millimeters, or at a rate of 3.2 millimeters per year.[80] Most of the rise that has occurred so far is due to thermal expansion from ocean warming. A small part of the rise in sea level to date is from the melting of ice caps and mountain glaciers, processes that are set to accelerate rapidly as the earth continues to warm. However, should the business-as-usual scenario continue without change, the projected temperature increase by the end of the century will result in ice loss and associated sea level rise of some 6.5 feet, or 2 meters.[81] Keep in mind sea level rise has staggering societal and economic implications; approximately 23 percent of the world's population lives within 60 miles (100 kilometers) of the coasts and less than 320 feet (100 meters) above sea level.[82]

The detailed graphs in figure 4.5 and figure 4.6 provide some interesting and relevant data illustrating the trend of melting land ice in Greenland and Antarctica since 2002. The melting of sea ice, such as the ice in the Arctic, causes a marginal displacement of water. But the melting of land ice, such as

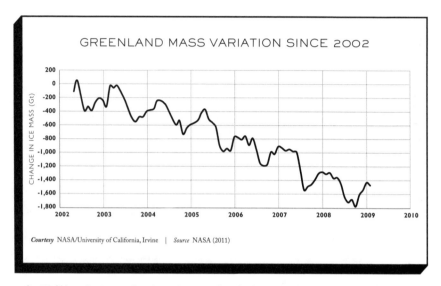

• *fig. 4.5:* Water that is introduced into the ocean from land ice is much more alarming than water from ice that already resides in the ocean. This is due to the fact that no new mass is added to the ocean when an iceberg melts, but mass does enter the ocean when it runs off a glacier from a land formation. The rapidly decreasing levels of ice in Greenland are causing scientists around the world to worry about the rise of the oceans.

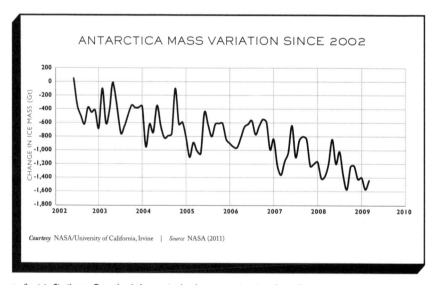

• *fig. 4.6:* Similar to Greenland, Antarctica has been experiencing a large decrease in its ice coverage.

the ice on Greenland and Antarctica, actually adds new water to the sea. If all the ice in Greenland were to melt, it would lead to a global sea level rise of nearly 24 feet (more than 7 meters). If all the ice in Antarctica were to melt, the seas would rise more than 200 feet (61 meters).

The impact of rising global temperatures on food sources and biodiversity is no small potatoes either. True, the effect of climate change in some regions may be favorable to agriculture: For example, rising precipitation and longer seasons will aid vegetation in high elevations or in the northern regions of the United States or Europe. But in other regions, rising temperatures will destroy biodiversity as a result of extended droughts where species are already under stress. There will be an asymmetrical change in food production, potentially affecting nonindustrialized countries the most. For example, rain-fed crop yields in parts of Africa that are already stricken with food shortages will likely be reduced by 50 percent by 2020 unless farmers manage to rapidly and significantly modernize their agricultural practices. Globally, the overwhelming conclusion is that the impact of climate change on the food supply will be negative. Models for fossil fuel emission scenarios suggest up to a 5 percent net decrease in global cereal production, which is critical to the maintenance of the human population's daily diet.[83] Remember, fire begets fire. As our global population grows and consumption increases, atmospheric CO_2 will rise even faster and more people will go hungry as a result.

The science behind climate change and the evidence that it is occurring—including the ice loss in the polar regions and Greenland, the rising ocean temperatures, and the rising CO_2 levels—are so clear in my mind that I often wonder when the world will wake up and realize the environmental threat we face. While I could never give up my Colorado home, I love to visit the ocean, where I can listen to the waves lap onto the shore. However, when I have visited the seashore in recent years and looked around at the ongoing development of luxury ocean-side condos, I am stunned. How can investors continue to fund construction at sea level when it is so very clear that the tide is rising? Low-lying areas like Key West will eventually be submerged even if such predictions come to pass as late as the end of the century. Is this business-as-usual activity an indication of widespread denial, a world gone mad, or simply an inability to find a safe way forward?

BASIC PRINCIPLES OF ENERGY

It can be difficult to accept the fact that we humans have done so much damage so quickly. But the evidence points clearly to electricity generation and fossil-fueled transportation as the largest sources of human-caused GHG emissions. What, then, is the link between the release of climate-changing gases into our atmosphere and the electricity and transportation sectors of our economy? That is, what exactly is "fossil fuel combustion"?

Different fuel types and combustion methods produce different amounts of energy and CO_2 emissions, but the basic principles of energy production from fossil fuel combustion are universal.[84] The global electric grid powers more than three-quarters of the world's population and is one of humanity's finest engineering accomplishments.[85] Electricity lights our communities and businesses, and powers much of our public transportation system. Our meals can be cooked on electric stoves or in microwave ovens. Our perishables can be refrigerated. Our children can study at night. Our timepieces run without winding. These accomplishments are no longer novel, but the electric grid and all of its related services continue to gradually and consistently expand and find their way into new markets.

And yet there is something very novel going on all around us. What is new is how the electric grid has allowed us to create a vast and instantaneous global communication system that nearly everyone can plug into. This system circles the globe in seconds, allowing us to share data, images, sounds, and knowledge almost instantaneously. The ability to Skype, tweet, and email allows for millions of communications within minutes, achieving a technological and social milestone we have yet to fully grasp. As recently as the early 2000s most of our stored information was kept in paper files. Today it is almost all electronic. There is now more information available online than is stored in all of the world's libraries by orders of magnitude, and it's growing rapidly. Electricity allows for a scale of information gathering, transfer, and storage that is unprecedented in human history.

Such a system is providing a new way of life for all of us and is now part of the status quo. Also part of the status quo is the expectation that we can all have access to it. Open access to information creates new markets and allows new economies to emerge. Although only a quarter of the earth's population is online so far, nonindustrialized nations can leapfrog the Industrial Revolution and compete aggressively in the Information Age. Social networking has given small companies the power to compete with big companies. Perhaps more significant, social networking has given the organizers of movements like the Arab Spring a new and powerful weapon against well-funded, entrenched political apparatuses.

The effect that the telecommunications industry has had on global electricity demand since the new millennium is already staggering. Data centers used to house telecommunications and storage systems accounted for 1.3 percent of global electricity consumption in 2010, a figure that grew by 56 percent since 2005. Continued growth is expected and an 11 percent rate of increase in energy use per year is likely to continue for the foreseeable future.[86] As a result, the information and communication technology sector of our economy has become responsible for the same amount of human-made CO_2 in our atmosphere as the entire airline industry, which is around 2 percent.[87] When we think of burning fossil fuels, many of us immediately blame our automotive culture, but to keep up with our increasing appetite for connectivity, the growth of the Internet is likely to far outpace the demand for more cars. In fact, as the number of people online continues to surge, we will see GHG emissions explode. This growth is now embedded into the business-as-usual scenario.

Addressing the problem of increasing greenhouse emissions due to electricity generation requires a full look at our electric power system. One perspective is that electricity generation is the chief contributor to human-caused GHGs. The more we use electricity, the more GHG emissions enter the atmosphere. The opposite perspective is that our increased connectivity can reduce GHG emissions by dematerializing the economy. Both arguments are valid. But they neglect to acknowledge the fact that electricity has provided humanity with great opportunities to build wealth, security, and prosperity, initially by powering our homes and industries and now by connecting the world in a single marketplace. Rethinking how we produce and use electricity may provide the ultimate answer and serve as a cornerstone to any new business case. The only other alternative is to stop using electricity altogether!

GHG emissions are a side effect of this explosion of electricity use, and the side effect—not electricity itself—is what needs to be examined. Simply put, electricity can come from either coal-fired power plants, which emit GHGs, or from renewable energy such as solar power systems, which are largely free of such gases. Moreover, energy efficiency can also reduce demand without diminishing the value of the energy service—known as producing "negawatts"—thus avoiding investments in new power production.[88] Making changes to our energy mix to eliminate the negative side effects requires understanding the dynamics of our current utility system. Understanding the drivers is the key to knowing whether we can afford global connectivity and how we need to adjust our global energy mix to accommodate the energy requirements such connectivity will demand in the future.

The unfortunate reality of the current global energy infrastructure is that demand for electricity translates into simultaneous drains on our natural resources and impacts on our climate. Making changes in our emissions requires changing the energy mix by eliminating fossil fuel use and increasing renewable energy resources. Such statements may be obvious by now. But these observations have been made before—in fact, for decades. A less obvious fact is that changing the energy mix requires changing the regulatory framework that sets the rules for how energy users buy their electricity, how suppliers provide electricity, and how banks and investors fund the massive infrastructure required to deliver a kilowatt to your light switch or toaster.

If we want to change the mix of our global energy infrastructure, it's instructive to look at how the vast electric grid that powers our homes and industries originally came into play. The regulatory rules that helped us install our present infrastructure are part of the existing network that, if we want to reject business as usual and adopt a new business case, are both a blessing and a curse.

THE ELECTRICITY SECTOR

The creation of the electricity sector occurred during the same time frame as the development of the oil industry. In the late 1800s, Thomas Edison and George Westinghouse pioneered the electricity industry in much the same way that Colonel Edwin Drake and John D. Rockefeller pioneered the oil industry. The oil industry would fuel our transportation system. The electricity industry would soon light up businesses and housing and would eventually provide cooling and heating for the global economy. Better lighting meant that homes and businesses could accommodate longer workdays and extended leisure hours. Cooling made it possible to transport agricultural products over long distances and to store them for seasonal use. Furthermore, higher and higher heating temperatures made it possible for industry to mold plastics and to bend steel.

One of the longest-standing debates in the power industry has been whether to build energy systems to meet the requirements of demand or to build them based on the availability and quantity of our resources. George Westinghouse promoted the idea of centralizing the power system and constructing power plants that maximized the available resource. Thomas Edison wanted a more decentralized system where the energy user's demand requirements dictated the delivery method. The debate centered on the type of current, either direct current (DC) or alternating current (AC), and on the necessary investment required for the transmission and distribution of electricity from a power plant to where it was being consumed. In the end Westinghouse's AC won out, and a system was installed that relied on a current that could carry electricity a long distance, making it possible to run power lines to more homes and businesses from a single resource.

The relevant issue being debated between Westinghouse and Edison was a matter of centralization versus decentralization. One's viewpoint almost always depended on which end of the extension cord you plug in first. Do you plug your cord into the socket first or into the appliance you are trying to power? The issue mattered because power plants that supply electricity to the grid under a centralized system are usually highly capital intensive and require multiple customers, over a long term. For example, new gas-fired power stations (perhaps the least costly kind of power plant to build today) cost about $1,000 per kilowatt, or $1 million per megawatt installed. Assuming that the plant runs every hour of the year, a single kilowatt installed produces 8,760 kilowatt-hours (kWh) of energy per year. For some perspective, the average American home uses approximately 11,500 kWh per year.[89] The average plant size is about 500 megawatts, which costs about $500 million to build.[90] The capital cost of an equivalent public project might be a new 80,000-seat football stadium. However, in the latter case, owners might fear they've bought a bad team with no fans. In the former case, power plant owners might fear the rise of a new technology that offers a lower cost and a more convenient service that entices their customers away.

Moreover, construction is not the only cost a power plant owner faces. Smaller-scale, decentralized generation, consistent with Edison's preferred approach, would have minimized transmission costs, whereas a grid of transmission lines, through which power from the plant is delivered to the thousands or tens of thousands of homes that a power plant might service, is a requirement for the centralized plants Westinghouse favored more. In 2006 nearly $7 billion was invested in the nation's grid from investor-owned electric utilities and stand-alone transmission companies. In order to handle the growing population of the United States, by 2015 nearly 13,000 miles of new transmission lines will need to be constructed and linked to the more than 200,000 miles of already existing lines.[91]

The financial implications of the debate over centralization versus decentralization does not stop there. Over the past one hundred years governments around the world have established electrification authorities, or public electric utilities, as the solution for funding the development of power-generating facilities and transmission and distribution systems. Utilities are given a license by the state or federal government that often grants an exclusive right to build and sell power in a given territory. The exclusive right to build and sell power provides investors with assurances and comfort, prompting them to capitalize these companies by buying up their bonds or by purchasing the capital stock (known as "shares" or "equity") of the company. The utility operates free of competition within its licensed territory, which allows it to guarantee both an investor and an independent supplier that a lower-cost source of power will never displace their power generation investments. Such licensing effectively gives power companies a "monopoly," making them the classic utility that must then be regulated by the state or federal government that issued the license. The benefit of this monopolistic authority is that it serves as an incentive for investors to become owners and for owners to build new power plants.

As electric power authorities and enterprises formed throughout the twentieth century, new laws became necessary. Thus important procedural and legal precedents were created for others to follow. Regarding the TVA (see text box), the strength of the electrification model was that investors could rely on the rules set by the regulators. The weakness of the electrification model has been that when new conditions arise, it is difficult to change the rules that govern the system. Indeed, changing a rule can be a substantial challenge. For instance, if changing a prior rule or precedent leads to the abandonment or impairment of an energy asset, the consequence is that ratepayers may still have to compensate the supplier. Cost recovery assurances are standard requirements for investors prior to construction. Otherwise, changing the rules of the game subsequent to approval of a new power plant can lead to either abandoned capital or litigation. So, forcing a plant to close down in order to eliminate GHGs may require state commissions to alter tariffs or to directly provide investors with adequate compensation for their stranded capital. Eventually, unless new rules are written, ratepayers will have to pay these costs. The challenge for regulators is therefore to find a simple and elegant solution that is lasting.

TVA: A CASE STUDY

Let's look at one of the first electrification authorities. President Franklin D. Roosevelt and the US Congress established the Tennessee Valley Authority (TVA) in 1933 to serve one of the least developed regions in the United States. Much of the Tennessee Valley lacked any power service. Because of its unique relationship to the federal government, the TVA set many of the early requirements for both regulated and nonregulated power generators.

The federally owned TVA was tasked with providing river navigation, flood control, electricity generation, and economic development to a region that included Tennessee, Alabama, Mississippi, Kentucky, and parts of Georgia, North Carolina, and Virginia. The corporation was given the authority to enter into long-term contracts for the sale of power. Moreover, the TVA was instructed to build electric power transmission lines in areas not otherwise serviced. The TVA also had the authority to establish rules and regulations for electricity retailing and distribution within the region, making it both a supplier of electricity as well as its own regulator.

As an early pioneer of large-scale electricity distribution, the TVA

The consequence is fairly straightforward. The rules and regulations that the global society has created to support the global electrification of the earth have allowed us to achieve one of the greatest engineering accomplishments in human history. However, the same system suffers from inertia and is so massive that making any changes to it is a cumbersome and daunting task. Trying to change the national electrification system (let alone the international electrification system through a Kyoto Protocol–like process)—or at least reform it to address new concerns—will definitely require a significant consensus and possibly require declarations of eminent domain. These are actions that only Congress can take and that only nations can ratify.

The solution therefore needs to be much more simple and elegant.

became a model for other efforts to provide electricity to rural areas. Prior to 1933, urban areas operated quite differently: Private contractors ran power lines off of trolley operations to serve local industry and large private homes. Eventually, to expand the level of service to underserved customers in urban and rural areas, regulated utility companies were formed with a mandate to provide equal and open access to electricity. In exchange, these utilities were given exclusivity over the generation, transmission, and distribution of electricity.

The TVA has matured from its early days and now acts as a wholesaler of power services to more than nine million customers. Its portfolio of power-generating assets includes hydroelectric dams, fossil fuel plants, nuclear power plants, and renewable energy systems. It is but one of many rural electric authorities that form a chain of utility companies lighting up even the most remote regions of the United States and supplying affordable and reliable power to agriculture and industry. The TVA and the many other electric power authorities—privately, publicly, and municipally owned—have created a successful model for establishing and financing a fully integrated power generation and distribution system.

A LONG STRETCH . . . OR IS IT?

It may require a long stretch in thinking to relate the consequences of choices about building the global electricity sector to the superfires in the American West and the drought conditions in the Midwest. But the long stretch does not mean that the consequence of these disasters is any less real. As I have previously mentioned, some still question whether anthropogenic GHG emissions are truly the cause of the recent rising temperatures that have led to the conditions highlighted in this chapter. And yet it is easy to trace the parallel paths of these rising temperatures and the increased use of fossil fuel combustion to power the transportation and electricity sectors of our global economy. Reducing GHG emissions therefore requires changing our energy mix, which in turn requires working with our electric utilities. So, addressing the climate change problem will require not only the presence of engineering solutions but also the introduction of regulatory changes that will allow these solutions to emerge.

Opening up the power system to allow greater competition may be that simple and elegant solution that will encourage an energy mix that includes renewable and alternative energy sources. However, the consequences of this innovation to the system itself are far-reaching: *Invested capital* will seek to preserve the status quo. *New capital* will want to back new entrants into the market that will attempt to disrupt the existing rules and regulations. Legislators or the courts will have to balance the competing interests in order to relieve tensions, but if both industry and regulators are mindful of the need to reduce GHG emissions, it might be possible to radically adjust the global energy mix and to address the human-caused sources of climate change.

KEY OBSERVATIONS

The key observations in this chapter are critical to the analysis performed by the Project Butterfly team. Prior to our research, the original question we had was whether it would be critical to shut down all energy-related human activity in order to mitigate climate change. Had the growth in population simply overwhelmed the earth's capacity to absorb so much energy activity? Would it be necessary to just shut everything down?

Instead we have come to understand that a balance needs to be reached between what the atmosphere and oceans can absorb and how much carbon we humans can release from what lies in the rocks beneath us. If this balance is maintained, then we have a sustainable system. If it is not, we have an unmistakable problem. Here is a summary of the key observations we can make about our global energy mix and how it affects the science of climate change:

» Projections for the buildup of GHGs are trending up as scientists and researchers fold nonlinear events into their calculations. The world will break through the 450 ppm or 3.6 degrees Fahrenheit (2 degrees Celsius) threshold within the next twenty years, perhaps regardless of whether we maintain business as usual or immediately adopt a new business case.

» Industrialized nations use hydrocarbons from deep within the earth (the "conventional fuel supply") as their primary energy sources. When these energy sources, previously stored beneath the earth's surface, are converted to mechanical energy to drive turbines, the output is CO_2 released directly into the atmosphere.

» Natural sinks absorbing CO_2 are insufficient to keep up with the pace of industrial activity. The result is a trend of increasing temperatures, which cause glacier and polar ice melting and other natural phenomena—signs of impending tragedy.

» To reduce CO_2 from industrial activity, the global community must make changes to the electric power grid. The urgency is particularly poignant as we evaluate the impact of greater connectivity and worldwide communications on the demand for power production.

» Changing the global power grid will require rethinking how we approach the development of new power and energy sources. Until now, large, centralized power systems have required extensive transmissions and distribution systems. To lower GHG emissions, the next generation must build decentralized power systems that allow greater openness and competition from renewable and more energy-efficient technologies.

In less than one hundred years this oil business will be finished. The need for oil increases daily, existing fields are becoming exhausted, and you'll soon have to seek some other source of energy. Atomic, solar, or whatnot. You'll have to resort to several solutions; one won't be enough. For instance, you'll have to exploit the power of the ocean tides with turbines. Or else you'll have to dig deeper, seek oil 10,000 meters below the sea-bed or at the North Pole . . . I don't know. All I know is that the time has already arrived to take measures, not to waste oil as we always have. It's a crime to use it as we do nowadays.[92]
—The Shah of Iran, 1973

CHAPTER 5

The danger signs of resource depletion have been with us for some time. As the foregoing quote reveals, it is truly remarkable that forty years ago the Shah of Iran would have been able to see so clearly into the future. His predictions—that the world would have to find replacements to oil that would involve drilling thousands of feet below the seabed and using such technologies as wave and solar power—were extraordinarily farsighted. He criticized the Western world not for its use of oil, which he gladly delivered. He criticized the West for wasting oil reserves, for failing to manage its oil addiction, and for being in denial about the limited supply. Now the global community finds itself facing the additional threat of climate change.

The situation is so grave, in fact, sometimes I feel that we are all just standing by witnessing humanity engage in a slow and deliberate form of geocide (environmental suicide). Indeed, comparing today's situation to suicide may not seem so far-fetched. Victims often fail to see other options for escaping from their current predicament. Therefore, they do nothing to change their circumstances. To close friends and family (the survivors), these victims are behind the wheel of a car that is careening toward a cement wall without anyone raising a yellow flag. Suicide victims have the option to turn safely right or left, even up to the very last moment, but still they shoot forward mindlessly.

This phenomenon, if you will, is part of the business-as-usual paradigm. Allow me to share with you my personal experience as a survivor of suicide.

My mother committed suicide when I was a young man. I was away at college when it happened. In fact, none of her children were in town. However, all these years later I still feel that I share some of the responsibility for her death even though I wasn't there. When I think back to the weeks leading up to her death, I cannot help wondering if there was something I could have done to make a difference.

I was twenty-one years old when my mother died. I had just returned to college after spending winter break with my family. I had said good-bye to my mother, who had checked herself into a local health clinic before my sister, brother, and I arrived for the holidays. At the time, I suspected that she wanted to minimize the time she spent with her family and to visit with us in a controlled environment. After the holidays were over, without any of us knowing, she checked herself out of the clinic.

The next day, I learned later, she drove down to the local gun shop and firing range. She asked one of the store managers if she could test-fire a gun from the glass case at the front of the shop. My mother then took the gun back to the firing range, loaded it with ammunition, placed the barrel under her chin, and fired.

In the years that led up to her death, there were times when I would find myself standing outside the bathroom where my mother lingered for hours, the door locked to the outside world. I was even younger then, barely a teenager, but I was also the man of the house. My parents had been divorced for some years. My older sister had already left for college. My younger brother would usually find a place to hide. I could hear my mother sobbing quietly as I pressed my ear against the door. I clearly remember the feeling I had—a combination of anger and helplessness. I simply did not know what to do.

Fast-forward to the last time I ever saw my mother during that winter break. We were sitting together, and she kept telling me over and over again, "I can't get out of here." As I understood it, she was in the clinic on a voluntary basis, so I couldn't make sense of what she was saying. I didn't realize she was headed toward that cement wall.

I can remember my last moments with her as if they were yesterday. I wanted to prove to her that she could leave. I had the wild impulse to pick her up and throw her over my shoulder. I wanted to take her straight to the airport to catch a plane to the Caribbean. She always loved the sun and the warm water. She loved taking off her shoes to walk on the beach and letting the sand seep between her toes. I thought that if I could remove her from her current situation, from the clinic's dreary commons room, and take her somewhere completely foreign, she could then gain some perspective and develop a plan for pulling her life together.

Those wishful moments ended quickly. The urge to do what I was supposed to be doing—heading back to college—overcame me. I left that sudden impulse in the clinic's commons room. I hugged and kissed my mother and walked through the heavy security door. I remember wavering as I looked back at her through the tiny window in that door. But I was in the groove of doing business as usual, not making grandiose gestures. I was not thinking about saving the world, not even the small part of it that was my mother. All I could do was raise my hand and wave good-bye.

My mother's act was deliberate. It lacked no bravery, nor was it a sin. However, I have often felt that sin was present—not in her decision but in the system of care that surrounded her. The sin was in the failure of anyone to sound the alarm.

Please note that I am not saying suicide is the result of any one person or of a poor standard of care. My meaning is much more subtle. There are many reasons someone might choose to take his or her own life, so it is difficult to know what kind of care to provide a would-be victim of suicide. What I am saying, rather, is that the real sin of suicide is the resistance of the community surrounding the victim to try something different, perhaps even radically different, in the process of caring. This resistance may stem from fear, denial, or ignorance. No matter its cause, the lack of a clear social agreement is part of what defines business as usual.

As I think rationally about the events of my mother's suicide, I certainly couldn't have prevented what happened. I am not the one who pulled the trigger. My mother did. It is these facts and circumstances that have helped me reach a deep level of personal peace with and understanding about my mother's suicide. Nevertheless, I have never fully reconciled whether or not there were any actions I could have taken earlier that might have made a difference—perhaps not to save my mother, but at least to raise the alarm and avoid the painful feelings of responsibility that have followed me. The feeling persists that I might have done something differently. I know that I am not alone in this feeling. It tends to follow survivors of suicide.

Consider the following: The issues surrounding suicide are often similar to the helplessness survivors feel when acting according to business as usual and the empowerment that can happen by simply raising the alarm. The sin of climate change is not necessarily in the act of causing environmental degradation. The sin is in the lack of care and understanding that exists *before* and *after* the act. It is in the lack of any social agreement to raise the alarm. Just as I was unable to stop my mother's suicide, I realize that none of us alone can prevent what's happening to the earth and its global ecosystem. No one individual, not even the president of the United States, has that much influence. However, the question persists about what we could have done in the past to prevent environmental suicide—and what each of us can do now to raise the alarm regarding climate change.

ENVIRONMENTAL SUICIDE

I have come to the view that the circumstances facing the victims and survivors of suicide are very similar to the circumstances of climate change facing the global community. Humanity is engaged in a form of environmental suicide because we are failing to build a sustainable ecosystem. This global act of suicide—simply marching on toward that cement wall or canoeing toward the falls without demanding change—is so slow that most of us don't realize we are in the process of doing it. We don't notice the heightened pace of new crises that are arising all around us. We don't know that we are victims and survivors of these crises. The process of care is in breakdown because no one with sufficient authority is examining the sustainability of the earth's ecosystem. To continue going down our current path simply because we can't agree that different choices about energy use and the mix of energy assets can create different results—this is suicide.

The heart of the issue is therefore whether the human race has enough self-awareness not only to acknowledge the need for change but also to embrace it. The sin in environmental suicide is our failure to sound the alarm, to care for those who are already suffering the many consequences of resource depletion and climate change or for those who will lose their homes to rising seas or their crops to droughts. It continues with the denial that we have any collective responsibility for these consequences, or that it is possible or even desirable to avert or mitigate them. The sin is in denying that we have any option other than to turn up the air conditioners, build sea walls, and pray.

Similarly, the blame game surrounding climate change should not be focused on the *cause* of the buildup of GHGs in our atmosphere. For example, the suppliers of coal are not to blame. They are simply responding to a market need and are engaged in an activity that is not only *lawful* but is also responsible for massive, positive economic and social development. Moreover, those who burn the coal to generate electricity are also not to blame. Each utility company is providing a vital service to tens of thousands, hundreds of thousands, and even millions of customers who are using electricity to light and heat their homes, operate their businesses, and create a highly efficient, interconnected global community. Nor are the consumers to blame. These energy users are meeting their own needs and doing their best to care for their families. It is, rather, a failure of our communities as a whole to take care of the *conditions* that cause climate change. That means we all share the blame fairly and equally. Anyone who cares to be informed now knows what the full consequences of climate change will be. Yet we are failing to respond or to act on behalf of either the environment or humanity to stop it.

Moreover, we cannot feasibly avoid all the consequences of climate change. We can only reduce their severity and hope that we are lucky enough to stabilize atmospheric levels before some tipping point is reached. The consequences of failing to make this change as I have clearly indicated—of letting CO_2 emissions continue to increase—will be catastrophic. Perhaps not all of us, but enough of us will suffer in order to make clear the difference between what is right and what is wrong.

You might think I am stretching a point way too far. Even with all of the evidence available to us, some might think predicting a future filled with resource depletion and environmental disaster is an exaggeration, a stretch of the imagination. How can we really know that we are headed for self-destruction by continuing down our current path? In chapters 2 and 3, I walked you through some of the math of this complicated issue—math that suggests the human population would be much better off if we cleaned ourselves up, improved the efficiency of our energy use, and encouraged the development of renewable energy. Our experts have run the calculations. We know that we are emitting GHGs beyond the carrying capacity of our planet and beyond the earth's ability to sustain human life as we know it. We also know that oil, gas, and coal are finite resources. Eventually we must replace them with substitutes that are renewable if future generations are to continue to prosper.

But first we must admit to ourselves that on some level our continued attachment to the business-as-usual scenario is tantamount to an act of suicide.

TWENTY HORSES UNDER THE HOOD

To understand more about what I mean by the "business-as-usual scenario," let's take a look back in history to the introduction of one of the innovations that led us to that scenario: the internal combustion engine, perhaps the most significant technological development of the nineteenth century. Keep in mind that these innovations were not "bad." On the contrary, they were quite wonderful. The issue is our attachment to them and our unwillingness to continue innovating beyond them.

In 1858 Jean J. Lenoir, a Belgian engineer, developed and first commercialized an engine that was gas-fired rather than steam-driven (a method that had required burning large amounts of coal). The Lenoir engine used high-pressure gas produced by combustion that was used to apply direct force and move pistons, thereby transforming concentrated chemical energy into mechanical energy. A mere fifty years later, the internal combustion engine would be used to motor a car. The car then replaced the horse, using the equivalent power of twenty horses under its hood.

The introduction of the internal combustion engine was also a key landmark in the unfolding of the post–Industrial Revolution. By the end of the 1800s, the internal combustion engine gave new and unparalleled capacity to industry to produce and transport goods at levels of efficiency, distances, and speeds never previously imagined. Nearly continuously from 1860 to 1910, technological advances—ranging from reducing piston resistance to creating spark plugs—led to improvements in the speed and efficiency of combustion engines. These innovations led to new applications for the engine and to cost reductions, which ultimately drove the demand for and consumption of oil through the roof.

We have accomplished many things in our short history as human beings on a planet with vast but still limited resources, and over the past 150 years we have built an impressive global economy that would have been unimaginable even to the greatest science fiction writers of those earlier times. The recognition at the onset of any climate-related problem would have demanded even more from the world's brightest minds. Only in retrospect can we see the emerging problem. Thanks to our growing dependence on advanced technologies, the global energy system is now highly dependent on the use of oil and other natural resources like it to power these technologies and the corresponding services they enable. The adequacy of these resources' supply is now uncertain.

Moreover, the increasing rate at which humans use these resources leads any reasonable observer to question how long the global economy can sustain itself under its current configuration without further radical innovation. The impact of a continued rise in oil consumption is far-reaching, and there is no universal agreement regarding the urgency to find substitutes. Yet almost all of us would agree that the situation we face today is vastly different from the situation at the dawn of the Industrial Revolution and certainly different from the period in the 1970s when we experienced two oil shocks. In fact, the world's dependency on oil has gotten much more intense, not less.

OIL: A PRECIOUS COMMODITY

Just what is this substance we are so dependent on? In a nutshell, oil is solar energy that has been stored over millions of years in geological formations beneath the earth's surface. Due to its high-energy intensity, ease of transportation, and relative abundance, oil derived from conventional drilling techniques has been the world's most important energy resource for more than a hundred years. Globally, approximately 56 percent of crude oil is used for transportation in various forms, such as diesel, jet fuel, and gasoline or liquefied gas. There are important differences, however, in the quality of crude oil found in the ground. Lighter grades of crude oil produce the best yields for these rich fuels. As we build new airports and planes, and new highways and cars, demand for oil—especially the higher-grade rich fuels—grows.

Oil powers our cars, but it also is used in manufacturing the plastics so vital to the construction of the automobile itself. Manufacturers take basic materials, such as oil-based plastics and metal, and assemble them into functional end products. Oil's penetration into our global economy goes even deeper. Oil feeds the chemical fertilizers, or petrochemicals, that sustain agriculture and produce larger and larger crop yields. Oil has made the state where I grew up, Iowa, the breadbasket of the world by maximizing output and providing a global storage and transportation system for those goods. Petrochemicals are also used by industry in making synthetic rubber. All of these products—plastics, fertilizers, rubber—are essential to the functioning of modern-day commerce. In fact, the petrochemical industry has become the second-largest global consumer of oil.[93]

In the future, we may find adequate substitutes for fueling the cars, buses, planes, and trains of our global transportation system—by electrifying them, for example. But it may be difficult to imagine equivalent substitutes for the petrochemical industry. Seen in this light, oil is not some dirty substance that should be kept in the ground. It is the most precious commodity on earth. As the Shah of Iran advised energy users back in the 1970s, we must stop wasting this commodity. The question is, what should we do with it?

If there were plenty of substitutes for oil, the answer would be easy. Let the market determine the best use for oil. The user that assigns the greatest value for the existing oil supply would end up in possession of it, and then the rest of the market would begin to organize around developing substitutes. However, the challenge with any energy source is that energy is the only substitute for energy. Developing substitutes means developing alternative forms of energy. The challenge arises because it may be easier to substitute for some forms of energy than for others. In the case of oil, it may be easier to electrify transportation using wind energy than it is to substitute other organics in the sheer quantity required to replace oil-based fertilizers in the agricultural industry while still feeding a world headed toward eight billion people.

One of my favorite movies from childhood was *The Graduate*, starring a young Dustin Hoffman, whose character had recently graduated from college. While at a party, Hoffman's character is asked what he is going to do with his future. One of the guests, Mr. McGuire, escorts the young man outside. He says, "I just want to say one word to you—just one word . . . Plastics . . . There's a great future in plastics." This movie was made in 1967, and this prediction couldn't have been more accurate for the decades that would follow. Today, however, the world has changed again. The new word is *organics*—natural replacements that can be recycled or reused in order to end the use of plastics.

To address the increasing issues of depletion, the global society will need substitutes. We will also need to diversify our existing energy mix using more renewable resources. By making the necessary investments to achieve this goal, we will be showing a duty of care in the system and a willingness to try something different before we reach the final supplies of this precious commodity.

REACHING GLOBAL PEAK OIL

The theory of Peak Oil is the most popular approach to estimating how the final days of oil will play out and what will bring an end to the status quo. Marion King Hubbert, a geologist from Houston, Texas, developed the Peak Oil theory in the 1950s by studying the behavior of a single oil well and applying a mathematical calculation to known US oil reserves. He became famous in the 1970s when his calculation proved correct.

Hubbert based his theory on the notion that once oil production peaks, it will immediately begin to fall in a fashion that will appear similar to its rise to the top. According to the US Energy Information Administration (EIA), the United States hit its peak level of oil production in 1970.[94] Since that time, aside from a few minor discoveries, the amount of oil production has decreased as quickly as any reserve estimates have gone up. The innovation of shale oil drilling is giving oil production new life, but all estimates of future oil production still leave the year 1970 as the peak of US production.

So, when will the world hit global Peak Oil? Determining the global peak will be more difficult. It may be driven by supply constraints or by reductions in demand as prices escalate and alternatives emerge. One reason for this unpredictability is a lack of knowledge and transparency in the reporting of oil reserves between countries. Another reason is that the introduction of new technology—such as innovative drilling techniques—also affects the ability to make an accurate prediction. Initially the International Energy Agency reported that global production of conventional oil peaked in 2006, while new sources of unconventional supplies—shale oil and tar sands—were coming online. The IEA later reported that 2008 was the peak in conventional crude oil extraction, at 70.4 million barrels per day (mb/d). New discoveries and drilling initiatives will likely shift the numbers around for some time to come. Moreover, advancing technologies in both shale and offshore drilling increase extraction efficiency, further complicating any estimate of global Peak Oil. But regardless of when it happens and whether it is a result of waning supply or demand, global Peak Oil will likely still be depicted as a simple bell curve, with its eventual descent mirroring its ascent, if nothing is done to preserve the resource.

Oil production, including both conventional and nonconventional processes, is currently about 87 mb/d and is expected to rise to 96 mb/d by 2017.[95] Managing the tight market equilibrium between the demand for oil and the sources of supply is an agenda item for any country dependent on oil, whether it is a national consumer, a supplier, or both. The United States leads the pack in total consumption of oil, followed by the European Union and then China.[96] The leading producers in the Western Hemisphere are Canada and Venezuela, with the United States quickly regaining some of its lost ground due to new drilling technologies. However, the bulk of the world's largest producers lie within the Persian Gulf region, including Iran, Iraq, Kuwait, and Saudi Arabia.[97] The capacity of these Gulf nations to control energy prices may give them the ability to set the global peak in total oil production as they seek to maximize the value of their remaining reserves and as domestic demand within their own region begins to compete with their exports.

Oil is interwoven into today's society, so it is no surprise that increasing oil prices can damage the global economy. According to Dr. David Greene of Oak Ridge National Laboratory (ORNL), OPEC's ability to charge above-free-market prices over the past three decades has cost the United States more than a year's worth of its GDP and has depressed total cumulative real GDP by about 10 percent.[98] The issue of market pricing is serious, and it relates to our key economic measures. OPEC's role in managing world oil prices has given those exporters with excess production capacity the means to ensure that their interests are met first. Some argue that the world is seeing the largest transfer of wealth in history, with capital flowing from the industrial world to oil-exporting nations as a result of global dependency on oil.

A CAUTIONARY TALE OF TWO CITIES

Let's look at two cities, both dependent on oil, that lost access to their source of fuel because they either didn't have the ability to pay for oil on the open market or lacked the alliances necessary to continue open access to supply.

Between 1918 and 1939, Tokyo imported 90 percent of Japan's oil needs. The vast majority of these imports were being drilled in Texas and shipped from California. In 1939, partly due to US oil sanctions, Japan attacked southern China and Indochina in hopes of securing a new source of oil. By July 1941, the United States had entirely stopped supplying oil to Japan. For the next four years, Japan was fuel starved. It began an aggressive military campaign to secure new energy resources and to establish a self-sufficient economic bloc in East Asia. Japan's desperation was so great that it attacked and successfully occupied British-controlled Borneo, which was poorly guarded and contained a rich and nearly untapped petroleum reserve.

The Japanese government was uncertain whether the United Kingdom or the United States would mount a counteroffensive. To stymie such an effort, and in an attempt to defend its flank, Japan attacked the US Pacific naval fleet stationed at Pearl Harbor, in the Hawaiian Islands. Japan would try to use its success in Hawaii to create a geopolitical bloc in Southeast Asia.[99] Of course, Japan failed to form these alliances, and President

Why does the theory of Peak Oil matter? Falling levels of oil supplies, coupled with increasing levels of demand, equate to higher relative prices on all accounts. The consequences of reaching peak oil production are higher food prices, higher costs to transport people and things, and less money to spend on other items of value. These factors will promote an economic shift, one in which the economy will begin to be powered by other types of fuels, accelerating the reduced production of oil.

Franklin Roosevelt went on the offensive by declaring war against Japan. But the story illustrates the extreme measures a country is willing to take to guarantee a vital fuel source. It could happen again.

Oil shortages can also lead to starvation, as seen in Pyongyang, the capital of North Korea. Prior to the 1980s, North Korea's totalitarian regime had invested in coal mines and hydropower to satisfy the country's energy needs. This diversification didn't extend far enough, however. North Korea depended on oil from the Soviet Union for its modernized agricultural system. In 1990 the estimated per capita energy use for North Korea was twice as large as in China and over half that of Japan.[100] In 1991, after the collapse of the Soviet Union, Russia stopped subsidized exports of oil to North Korea. Two years later, total Russian exports to North Korea dropped 90 percent.[101] Lack of fuel for machinery and for the manufacturing of chemicals and pesticides significantly curtailed agricultural production. The production of rice and maize fell by almost 50 percent between 1991 and 1998. The resulting famine left an estimated one million Korean people dead from starvation, and North Korea was forced to ask for international aid.

The tales of Tokyo and Pyongyang reveal how important it is to monitor the level of global fuel supplies. If a country loses access to these vital resources, the consequences—to both domestic conditions and international affairs—can be far-reaching.

That said, the worst-case scenario involves waiting to act until we hit high prices due to Peak Oil from insufficient supply or the failure of reliable substitutes to emerge. If we wait until then, it's likely that energy inflation will flood the economy, making financing of and investment in new technologies or substitutes even more difficult. On the other hand, if we make the transition before oil prices peak, we stand a better chance of transitioning to substitutes without creating an economic disruption or possibly even a market collapse. Failing to plan for Peak Oil is like delaying capital expenditures to modernize your facility and finding yourself no longer competitive on the global market. If you had made the planned investments when you had the budget, you would be a market leader now, maintaining or gaining market share. After you have lost market share, however, next year's budget constraints will make the necessary upgrade a level-two priority.

The consequences of waiting for Peak Oil to occur can theoretically run two ways. While we wait, new technology might come along, creating easy access to substitutes. But the opposite—exposing yourself to a price squeeze when supplies are nearly depleted—is also possible. Don't forget, the only substitute for energy is energy. This is the essential challenge of Peak Oil, and it not only makes the situation unique (economically speaking) and demanding of greater attention, but also makes for a truly frightening worst-case scenario (see text box on previous page).

MORE THAN JUST A FUEL

Over the past century, the North American continent has provided the United States with a rich reservoir of drillable oil that the nation has successfully tapped while working its way through two world wars and the Great Depression. The supply of oil was limited only by the ability of the US energy industry to extract, distribute, and transport the oil. The size of the national oil reservoir was not a limiting factor until 1970, when the United States hit peak oil production. Figure 5.1 shows peak oil production during the 1970s in the United States, broken down by the Lower 48, Alaska, and the Gulf of Mexico. It was three years after the US peak in 1970, halfway around the world, when another event made hitting Peak Oil an actual global crisis.

On October 17, 1973, the first oil price crisis began as a result of the Yom Kippur War. Arab OPEC members announced a monthly 5 percent reduction in oil production and an oil ban on nations that supported Israel, establishing an oil embargo that lasted six months. The effect was immediately visible, with prices quadrupling from $2.59 for a barrel of oil in September

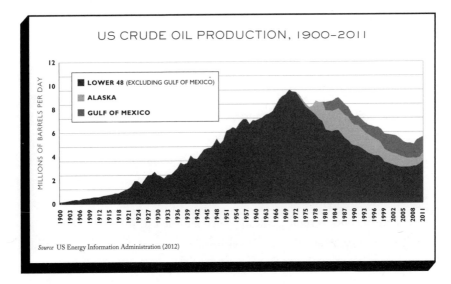

US CRUDE OIL PRODUCTION, 1900–2011

Source US Energy Information Administration (2012)

• *fig. 5.1:* The United States peaked in the production of crude oil back in 1970 and has been on a relatively steady decline since that time. Alaska and the Gulf of Mexico were very large discoveries that greatly aided the United States in its total level of production, but these two large fields were unable to bring the total production volume back up to the levels seen in 1970.

1973 to $11.65 in January 1974.[102] Oil was more than just a fuel. Oil had become a weapon.

The use of oil as a weapon was still an imprint on the world's psyche five years later when a second crisis flared up, this time caused by the fall of the Shah of Iran to Islamic revolutionary forces. Iran had been a major supplier of oil to the United States, and the Shah was a critical US ally against Soviet expansion into the Middle East. With the memory of 1973 still fresh, people panicked and began to hoard gasoline and oil supplies in 1979, leading to higher prices and a stalled domestic economy. The link between national security and energy would be forever connected in our collective consciousness.

The United States responded to the oil crises of the 1970s by building new alliances in the oil-producing regions of the world. In addition, we encouraged domestic oil companies to exploit foreign operations and encouraged power producers to convert from burning oil to burning coal in order to produce electricity. The US government also dabbled with renewable energy resources by promoting research and development of alternative energy supplies. Scientists and economists started to call for a new energy future. Scientist Amory Lovins published his book *Soft Energy Paths,* laying the foundation for a departure from subsidized fossil fuels toward distributed generation using renewable resources. Economist E. F. Schumacher wrote *Small Is Beautiful,* calling for a rejection of nuclear power as a potential solution to our energy crisis and promoting small-scale solutions that would generate income from renewable fuels such as solar energy and wind power.

These authors and their messages struck a chord with many in the United States and Europe. Several US leaders echoed the call for renewable energy. Newly elected President Jimmy Carter installed solar collectors on the White House, and in 1977 he launched a federal facility in Golden, Colorado—the Department of Energy's Solar Energy Research Institute (now known as the National Renewable Energy Laboratory)—dedicated to harnessing power from the sun.

The promotion of energy alternatives was a call to arms. It was a response countering the use of oil as a weapon.

COOKING THE BOOKS

Forty years later, there are some clear similarities between our current economic and geopolitical environment and that of the 1970s. Back then, the United States hit the point of peak oil production, making the largest economy in the free world dependent on a few oil producers in a somewhat remote region of the world. Today we face the prospect of hitting global Peak Oil. That makes the entire global community dependent.

The rhetoric we hear today also harkens back to the 1970s. There is a drive to reduce energy dependence in North America by working with Canada and Mexico to become a regional net energy exporter. The strategy is based on the idea that it is possible to become independent of foreign oil imports by increasing domestic oil production, reducing demand through improving fuel efficiency, exporting natural gas, and refining Canadian tar sands for export.

The Keystone XL pipeline is at the heart of this drive toward energy independence. But the energy issue is larger than just shuffling our energy sources or "cooking the books." True energy independence means having a reliable mix of energy goods to power the total needs of any economy.

Some industry analysts argue that the world has not reached global Peak Oil, basing their views on an analysis of resource availability not just in the United States but everywhere, including new supplies being discovered in the polar regions, where there are likely vast reserves. Others argue that global Peak Oil has already come and gone. Figure 5.2 shows global oil discoveries peaking as far back as 1960, which suggests that peak oil production at some point will inevitably come to pass. Furthermore, figure 5.3 shows the growth of global oil production since 1985, plotting when certain producers reached their domestic peaks in oil production. Because we can observe the peak experienced by individual producers, it is sensible to suspect that eventually the globe will reach its own peak.

From a financial perspective, simply estimating the amount of oil reserves misses the point and keeps us from acknowledging the current crisis, because

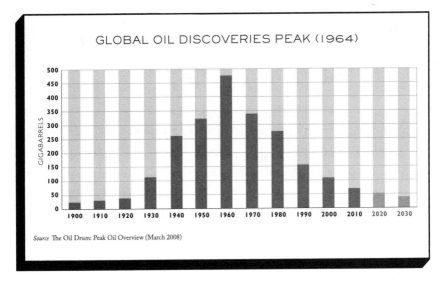

* *fig. 5.2:* Oil discoveries peaked in the mid-1960s. This means that the bulk of oil extracted today is coming from aging fields discovered decades ago.

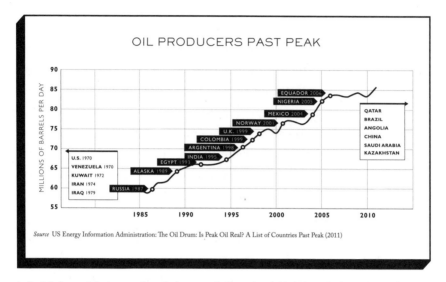

• *fig. 5.3:* Some of the largest oil-producing countries have already hit their peak oil output, including the United States, Venezuela, and Colombia. While the number of barrels of oil per day is still increasing, it is only a matter of time before countries like Saudi Arabia hit their peak.

any observer just looking at market conditions can see that global Peak Oil is upon us. It has been upon us for forty years, and the crises of the 1970s were simply the opening salvo in the competition over global oil supplies. Moreover, in order to mitigate climate change, the discussion of global Peak Oil needs to be enlarged. It is not simply about running out of oil. It's about supply and demand and the declining net energy from each dollar spent.

Let's first talk about some of the ways that Peak Oil plays out in our current economy. Then we'll turn to the issue of net energy and climate change.

One way to validate that global Peak Oil is upon us is to recognize that many nations grant their oil industry financial subsidies to keep that precious commodity flowing and to maintain business as usual. In the United States, direct subsidies to the oil and gas industry through tax breaks and development credits total approximately $40 billion a year.[103] The oil industry also benefits from tax support to the automobile industry, which in actuality doubles or triples the size of direct federal subsidies, effectively stimulating the demand for oil.[104] Imagine if federal subsidies were dissolved. Prices for oil at the pump would rise. Demand would certainly fall. If this occurred in the United States, the single largest consumer of the world's oil supply, we might reach global Peak Oil even more quickly. Peak Oil would occur not necessarily because of supply constraints but because of high-energy costs and lower demand as users scrambled to find efficiency improvements as viable substitutes.

Another indicator that global Peak Oil is upon us is oil's vulnerability to market manipulation. Thus far in the new millennium suppliers have been increasingly willing to let speculators drive up the cost of a barrel of oil. Prior to this, the leading suppliers of oil were focused on a particular price point that would limit the feasibility and development of oil alternatives. The goal of oil policies for exporting nations was maintaining a low enough price point that alternatives to oil, such as converting coal to gas, would be kept uneconomical. Oil suppliers saw this as an important self-limiting factor. From their perspective, while higher prices might improve short-term profits, higher prices would also reduce consumption and encourage development of other energy resources, whereas reasonable, stable prices would maintain a lucrative status quo. Simply put, the oil suppliers have never wanted competition in the oil supply chain from the gasification of coal to create a fuel that would compete for the transportation market.

Sometime in the early 2000s the attitude of oil producers toward potential competition changed. The energy industry is now investing millions to produce alternatives to oil, including ethanol, algae, and gasified coal. The fact that oil suppliers themselves, including the largest distribution companies, are now the largest funders of alternative fuels means they are no longer threatened by alternatives and are comfortable in letting prices vary. British oil company BP has spent more than $7 billion on alternative energy. Exxon Mobil has spent more than $600 million just to turn algae into an oil equivalent.[105]

The willingness of oil producers to tolerate price volatility is another red flag that signals that the business-as-usual scenario is under stress—and that rising levels of stress are now part of business as usual. In the 1970s and 1980s, OPEC reigned supreme in controlling oil production to influence prices. Sometimes OPEC members would even increase production to maintain global stability. Today OPEC members seem more concerned about limiting production than about capping prices. The attitude that appears to have evolved is that the traditional oil game is nearly over. OPEC countries appear to be making hay while the sun is shining, maximizing their current profits as a hedge against future disruption caused by declining reservoirs and the corresponding loss of revenues that keep their political systems intact.

For example, during the 1970s (especially during the Nixon administration), the White House worried about increases in oil prices and their impact on the global economy. The Nixon White House feared that a global economic recession and rising prices would lead to the spread of communism.[106] The threat of Soviet expansion into the Persian Gulf region created an alignment of interest between the oil-producing countries and the energy-consuming countries of Europe and the United States. The United States and other industrialized nations would use this shared concern as a negotiating tactic with oil producers, such as Iran and Saudi Arabia, to keep prices from rising too quickly. The monarchies that ruled these oil-producing countries feared for their own security and believed that having a strong Europe and United States would counteract Soviet interference and the rise of their own domestic opposition. That alignment of interests disappeared with the fall of the Soviet Union back in 1991. Today, with a market free of these aligned interests, we are seeing an imbalance of power that is unsettling to those on the wrong side of it.

Even though OPEC seems to be less concerned about competition and price stability and more concerned with the internal dissension brought about by the Arab Spring that started in 2011, that's not to say it's no longer a player on the world stage. Its control over the marginal supply of world oil markets is the primary source of OPEC's power, relying on huge proven oil reserves and export volume. Additionally, the Gulf states of OPEC have the lowest production costs ($40–$80 per barrel, compared with $70–$90 per barrel for the Canadian tar sands and heavy oil from Venezuela, or $70–$80 per barrel for deepwater oil), so in a pinch they can still spike prices up or down.[107] During the embargo of 1973, OPEC accounted for 53 percent of global production, and it was able to exercise its control of oil to dramatically raise the price for the rest of the world. While the power of OPEC appears to have waned, it continues to have a strong market presence (40 percent). For example, in 2008 it was the only provider with sufficient margin of spare capacity. In the midst of the Great Recession, OPEC was able to increase global production and stem further price escalation. However, this exercise in market muscle seemed strained.

The principle point regarding Peak Oil is that in spite of OPEC's capacity, oil prices have become highly volatile, which suggests a diminished capacity by oil producers to manage oil markets. Oil prices reached a record high of $147 a barrel prior to the 2008 Great Recession, before retreating to levels below $50 a barrel, a level at which the Gulf economies start to strain in managing their own public spending commitment.[108] To the market observer, it is clear that OPEC participants had tight control over pricing from the 1970s until the introduction of oil futures trading on the New York Mercantile Exchange in 1983. Based on more recent events, however, all pricing buffers appear to have been lost. This suggests that traders see Peak Oil as they speculate on supply constraints or interruptions in the supply chain due to terrorism and regional conflict. Increasing price volatility is therefore a critical characterization of business as usual and also evidence of Peak Oil.

Figure 5.4 shows the upward pricing and increased volatility of prices since the 1980s. Increased volatility suggests that traders of oil are speculating on the certainty, or rather the lack of certainty, of global oil supplies.

We are also seeing oil price volatility increase as we experience the "bull–bear" oscillations in the markets over predictions in market recovery. When combined with the cost of interest due to high national debt levels in industrialized countries, this spells uncertainty about how our economies can absorb price shocks, especially in essential commodities that are highly correlated with oil supply—such as food.

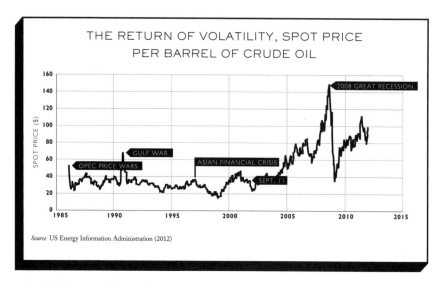

THE RETURN OF VOLATILITY, SPOT PRICE
PER BARREL OF CRUDE OIL

Source US Energy Information Administration (2012)

• *fig. 5.4:* Oil price volatility may be one of the best means of predicting whether or not we have arrived at a period of Peak Oil. Low volatility within the markets generally refers to investor confidence and a positive outlook, but high volatility generally means the opposite.

FUEL, FOOD, AND CLIMATE CHANGE

As is clear in the case of Pyongyang, North Korea (see text box earlier in this chapter), modern-day agriculture is particularly vulnerable to the availability of fuel. This creates a potentially dangerous link between the issues of fuel, food, and climate change. Oil is used for much of the production and distribution of agricultural goods and has been used increasingly in recent years to maximize agricultural yields. Currently, one billion people worldwide are undernourished, and even in the United States, nearly 15 percent of the population is considered "food insecure."[109] Rising fuel prices caused by dwindling supply and declining food production—thanks to climate interruptions—will only exacerbate the problem. In fact, food production will need to rise by 70 percent to feed the projected 9.1 billion humans on the earth in 2050, according to UN projections.[110] The World Bank estimates that food prices will continue to climb by as much as 35 percent by 2020, while the number of undernourished people in the world will rise by as many as eighty million.[111] As a result of this dependency, demand will rise for increased food production quantities but prices will almost certainly skyrocket, creating massive societal distortions.

In 2008, when oil prices hit $147 per barrel, up from $35 in January 2005, food prices were also at a peak.[112] Due to this rise in price, an estimated forty-two million additional people worldwide were pushed into the undernourished category. One of the important consequences to keep in mind is that high food prices have a much stronger negative impact on the poor, minorities, single-parent families, and children than the impact on families with even moderate disposable income. It's not just a matter of the middle class tightening their belts, but of the poor becoming the starving masses. A rapid increase in oil prices could catapult us into a short-term catastrophic food crisis.

Even within the United States, we can't ignore that the rising cost of oil is going to affect our food economy. In fact, in 2005 the United States imported 44 percent of its fruits and 16 percent of its vegetables.[113] Additionally, conventional produce travels on average 1,500 miles to institutional markets. Part of the reason we purchase produce from overseas is to get the best price. Production and processing of these foods generally occur where costs are lowest.[114, 115]

The dangers of relying on oil to transport our foods is compounded by the fact that we are consuming more, too. Between 1970 and 2000, the amount of calories that Americans were consuming increased by about 25 percent, or approximately 500 calories per day, requiring a corresponding increase in the US food supply.[116] Even though we are eating more, food costs relatively less for people living in industrialized nations—for now—thanks to processing and mechanization. In 2008 food purchases comprised about half the percentage of disposable income that they did in the early 1960s.[117] This combination of lower-cost foods and increased consumption has contributed to illnesses of overnutrition, such as obesity, cardiovascular disease, diabetes, and cancer.[118] These simultaneous countertrends are creating a rather perverse dynamic.

Not only are we importing, shipping, and eating more, but to increase our food supply, we are using more fuel to improve our domestic agricultural yields, making food more carbon intensive. US farm policy has heavily incentivized oil-dependent monocultures by providing direct fuel subsidies to agriculture in excess of $2 billion annually.[119] Currently, with fossil fuels as the main energy source to run large-scale food operations, it takes about 7.3 to 10 calories of energy inputs to produce, process, and transport each calorie of food energy.[120] It is estimated that feeding each American requires approximately 528 gallons of oil equivalents annually, including non-oil energy.[121]

Considering the fact that 528 gallons of hydrocarbons would fill your car's tank fifteen or twenty times, the phrase *watching your carbs* takes on a whole new meaning.

DIMINISHING PRODUCTION VALUES

All of this information has a ring of warning to it, but I am not trying to scare you. Plenty of other books out there will do a good job of that. The importance of the Peak Oil theory is related more to understanding climate change than to capturing an absolute point where production peaks. Despite its traditional definition as a maximum level of oil production, the critical component of Peak Oil is in fact the peak in the *net energy output* from oil production. The implication of this peak is that running our global economy increasingly requires more energy and a higher carbon intensity to produce the same level of economic output. Looking at Peak Oil from this perspective, it is likely that on a global scale, we have either reached or surpassed a peak in net energy output from oil production.

The reason it is important to expand this definition is that we aren't going to run out of oil in the ground anytime soon. The issue, rather, is the quality of the oil reservoirs and the cost of running our economy from them. Additional oil can be extracted to combat diminishing production values. For example, the tar sands in Alberta, Canada, contain huge reserves of unconventional oil—an estimated 173 billion recoverable barrels, which is equivalent to $15.7 trillion at today's price.[122] Additionally, the US Geological Survey estimates that ninety billion barrels of oil and 1,670 trillion cubic feet of natural gas are contained within the area north of the Arctic Circle.[123] These are extremely large resource basins that together have the potential to power the global economy for the better part of a century. The question, therefore, is one not of supply but of cost.

To determine the true value of these resources, and of all future conventional and unconventional oil discoveries, we must analyze the "net energy" that is realized and available for use after extraction. The metric is the energy return on investment (EROI). This simple equation shows how the EROI ratio is calculated:

EROI = Energy gained/Energy required for extraction

When the amount of energy gained from an endeavor is greater than the energy spent, the action is worthwhile. Conversely, if the energy gained is less than what is spent, the action is not worthwhile.

We can see this equation at work in the natural world. One of the earth's top predators, the great white shark, has evolved to the point where this equation has become hardwired into its brain. After a single bite, the great white is able to determine whether the calories from its meal will justify the calories it will expend on the kill. Therefore, the shark is not concerned with the overall size of its prey so much as with the quality of the meal. An adult shark has an extremely high metabolism and requires a food source that can keep it afloat and active in temperate waters. Because of this need for calorie-dense foods, great whites favor sea lions and seals, whose body weight can be nearly 50 percent fat, which is high in calories.[124] Like the great white shark, society needs to have a fuel source that can efficiently power its needs. The conventional fuels we currently consume are rich, but the unconventional fuels from drilling for tar sands and shale oil decrease in calories with every bite.

The oil industry's response is that new technology will continue to advance and overcome any depletion to the EROI ratio. Independent geologists, in contrast, maintain that our rate of consumption will overwhelm technology advancements. Perhaps it is hard to know for sure when it will happen, but time is definitely running out.

Let's look again at the market. The amount of energy the oil industry needs to invest in order to extract energy from unconventional oil is increasing. During the extraction process, energy is spent manufacturing drilling equipment, transporting it to the desired location, and then performing the actual drilling. In the 1930s, the United States was able to receive around one hundred barrels of oil for each barrel of oil it invested in the recovery of the resource. Then, in the 1970s, this ratio of 100:1 began to decline to about 25:1. In the 1990s it shrunk further, from about 18:1 to 11:1. Today the Alberta, Canada, tar sands—which require large amounts of natural gas, water, and other inputs to extract usable oil—are experiencing an EROI of around 4:1.[125]

The "Best First" principle explains why we are seeing this decline in net energy. Like the great white shark, humans prefer to extract their fuel from the easiest to access and highest-returning sources. For oil, these easy-access, high-return sources include Spindletop in Texas and the Ghawar field in Saudi Arabia. Both fields are only a little over 1,000 feet below the surface, are extremely large, and have exceptional EROIs. Think of them as the oil equivalent of high-fat seals. To extend our analogy further, the great white that runs out of seals must begin to feed on less optimal sources. We have seen that scenario play out in the Macondo field in the Gulf of Mexico, which was the site of the Deepwater Horizon oil spill in 2010. This oil field doesn't provide easy pickings; it is beneath about 5,000 feet of water, plus 13,000 feet of rock and sediment, and it holds only around 1/1,000th of the oil that Ghawar does.[126] Even with advancements in extraction technology, the oil withdrawn from the Macondo field had an EROI that was much smaller than the optimal 100:1 of the 1970s. This best-to-worst ordering of resource exploitation is the main reason the trend toward diminishing EROIs will continue into the future.

Evaluating the net energy balance reveals that the market is scrambling to meet demand because many of the incremental suppliers are providing suboptimal substitutes. Just as the great white would ideally like to feast on the rich fat of seals for the entirety of its life, the global economy would greatly benefit from superior fuel rather than being forced to diversify its fuel sources. Finding a satisfactory global minimum EROI is extremely difficult. Is a 4:1 ratio sufficient? This means that many oil development projects currently under way may provide an unsatisfactory EROI—one that does not allow the global economy to survive and thrive.

Now let's make the connection between declining net energy and climate change. The impact of lower EROIs is greater carbon intensity: We need to spend more energy to get more energy. The consequence is more carbon emissions produced, all while generating less energy.

Here is an example: Canada has announced its intention (by 2020) to cut output of GHGs by 17 percent from 2005 levels. Government data show that emissions from tar sands in northern Alberta will make this goal a major challenge, however, because emissions levels from this region will rise 226 percent by 2020. This increase in GHGs from Alberta will account for more than 17 percent of all projected GHG output in 2020, assuming Canada otherwise meets its GHG target. Extraction from the massive tar sands of Alberta, the world's third-largest proven oil reserves, requires large amounts of steam and water in using a method that produces more GHGs than are released when refining using conventional methods.[127]

The issue of net energy and climate change is global. While emerging economies are demanding more oil, the demand for oil in the United States is actually on the decline, allowing politicians to claim victory. In 2011 the United States had an oil demand of about 17.6 mb/d, and this figure is expected to decline to about 12.6 mb/d by 2035. Additionally, we imported about 9.5 mb/d in 2011, but this figure is expected to decrease to 3.4 mb/d in 2035 as large improvements are made in the fuel-efficiency of vehicles, as consumers transition to natural gas–powered vehicles, and as improved biofuels enter the market. The United States is expected to burn at least 20 percent less gasoline by 2030, even as the number of vehicles on the road continues to rise. Nevertheless, we still are (and likely will continue to be for some time) the world's largest oil-consuming nation.[128]

As we look globally at diminishing production values, the important message is that we're not the only players in this game. The rest of the world will still use whatever we cut back on. By 2035 the world demand for oil is predicted to increase by 15 percent, which translates to demand hitting 99.7 mb/d, up from today's 87 mb/d.[129] Add this growing demand for fuel to the diminishing returns on energy, and it's clear that globally we face a very large and serious problem.

AN INCREASING APPETITE FOR OIL

For all of the progress we as a global society have achieved during the Industrial Age and beyond, there has also been a cost. Today in the United States we are experiencing the consequences of reductions in net energy at the gas pump. Commutes to and from work that require fifty miles of travel a day are close to the average for employees nationwide. Over the course of a month, this adds up to 1,000 miles. At 20 miles per gallon, and at $4 a gallon, you are looking at a cost of $200 per month to pay for gas in order to commute to and from work. Wage earners with a salary of twice minimum wage are looking at a cost roughly equivalent to 10 percent of their take-home pay just to pay for their fuel. Mothers and fathers who support their families on such salaries are facing the difficult prospect of not being able to afford the expense of driving to work.

As a consequence of diminishing net energy, we now have a growing percentage of the population—globally and nationally—for whom the vital resource of oil is edging out of reach. We are facing a situation where hundreds of thousands of vital workers in the industrialized nations are being displaced. They are joining the hundreds of millions who already live out of reach of the wealth created by oil. The vast amount of wealth that has been created because of the oil industry may have reached its zenith. The supply is not endless, and yet the appetite for oil continues to rise. In 2012 the IEA stated that at current levels of consumption, the United States should expect proven oil reserves to last around forty more years.[130]

Will that be enough time for us to redirect our canoe and make it to shore?

KEY OBSERVATIONS

The key observations we can make about global oil consumption and Peak Oil are as follows:

» Industrialization sparked by the creation of the combustion engine has driven the demand for oil to levels that are unsustainable.

» Oil is concentrated solar energy stored over millions of years that is critical to the running of our modern economy, from transportation to agriculture. Oil can be substituted only with alternative forms of energy. Substituting conventional oil with unconventional oil does not create a sustainable model. It creates greater uncertainty and costs.

» Global Peak Oil is the tip of the bell curve measuring total oil production over time. The peak can be reached because of either constrained supply or reduced demand. The worst-case scenario is the failure to invest in alternative forms of energy prior to a peak brought on by supply constraints.

» Net energy is the concept that links Peak Oil to climate change. Measuring Peak Oil should not be limited to the measurement of the peak in total production, but should also measure the net energy output from oil production. From this perspective, the potential consequence of Peak Oil is a global economy that requires more and more energy and greater carbon intensity to produce the same level of economic activity.

The prosperity and security of one nation should not depend on the poverty and insecurity of other nations . . . Lasting peace and prosperity are only possible when nations join together in a common commitment to seek the welfare of all . . . Foreign and economic policies must follow the way of compassion for true peace to be possible.
—*Thich Nhat Hanh*

CHAPTER 6

FINDING A STRAIGHT LINE TO SAFE HARBOR:
NATIONAL SECURITY AND ENERGY SUPPLY

In my life I've found myself in the middle of several storms, both literal and metaphorical. Perhaps one of the most dangerous—and the most illustrative of the point I wish to make here—was in 2010, in the waters off Newport, Rhode Island.

My son and I had ignored the small-craft advisories, thinking we would stay close enough to the shoreline to avoid any real danger. We were twenty nautical miles out, heading back to Newport from Martha's Vineyard in a forty-foot sailboat, when the sky suddenly went from bright blue to dark gray. Within a matter of minutes, the wind went from fifteen to twenty-five knots. The boat began to pitch. The spray splashed against the dodger. Pretty soon the rain was coming down so hard, you couldn't see the bow of the boat. Then the winds hit forty knots. We were towing a dinghy and when I looked back, I saw it was flipping in the gales.

"Seann!" I shouted to my son, who was pulling the life preservers out from down below (standard procedure when the seas get rough). "We need to get the dinghy lashed down!"

He smiled, knowing that to do this he would need to lasso the stern of the dinghy, turn the little boat right side up, and get the engine out of its submerged position. I watched him carefully. He was hanging off the back of the boat and holding on to a rope he'd made into a lasso. He got it on the third try.

Meanwhile, I had to quickly reef the sails, which is what you do when there is too much wind in the sails, and I was starting to lose control of the boat. I was holding as tight a point of sail as possible, trying to make a straight line to safe harbor.

Sailing into the wind is very different from sailing downwind. The pressure on the sails keels the boat over. The helmsman has to remain steadfast on his heading to make sure that the boat doesn't suddenly come about or that no ground is lost by falling too far off the wind. Tacking to a destination takes additional, sometimes precious time.

The primary concern for the captain is how much sail to keep up in a storm. Changing the sails while under way, especially while moving into a headwind, is challenging. The captain at the helm will feel it when he finds himself oversteering to compensate for the force of the wind. The captain needs to remember the advice of his teacher: "Change the sails when you first think of it!" He must give the order to do so knowing that his crew will not like him very much, because to change the sails, they will have to get wet. The crew will have to reef in the mainsail and foresail to reduce the amount of sheet, stabilizing the boat and allowing the helmsman to retain command of the wheel. If the headwinds build further, failure to act promptly makes reducing the sail later all the more difficult and dangerous. If the headwinds calm, his crew might question his wisdom as they replace the sail they just reefed, but a good captain takes the criticism, knowing nothing was lost.

Regarding climate and energy issues, we are on a path equivalent to a sailboat at sea with a storm approaching. The mounting carbon debt is like the arrival of gale force winds. The climate change issue regarding mitigation isn't whether a storm is coming or not. It is an issue of how bad the storm will be and whether the captain and crew are ready for it. At sea, a responsible crew will reef the sail ahead of time in order to hold the boat's heading and make it to a safe harbor. The crew will come topside in order to navigate to safety. Coming topside is an act of commitment—an indication that the crew is ready to take action if necessary. It's a lesson that could teach much to our global society.

SURVIVAL OF THE FITTEST: THE UNITED STATES

The United States and other industrialized countries have failed to heed the advisories of climate change and seek safe harbor in a storm that threatens us with resource depletion and uninhabitable living conditions. Through the storm, the rally cry we often hear, since at least the 1970s, has been to enhance national security through increasing domestic energy production. Increased domestic production of oil and gas would decrease dependence on foreign suppliers. This call for "energy independence," regardless of any reference to global Peak Oil, truly reveals the business-as-usual mind-set regarding our energy mix. Energy independence, so the thinking goes, becomes the path to a safe harbor.

Let's take a look at the case of the United States.

To start, one commonly held belief that binds the United States to the status quo is the national tradition of, and historical commitment to, free trade. Back in the 1700s political economist Adam Smith's "invisible hand" created an almost mythological image of a greater power working its magic to find the optimal allocation of goods and services in any given market, including energy. Kings would no longer be needed. This system would be mirrored in Darwin's theory of the survival of the fittest nearly a century later, where those who have the ability to reach the valuable and necessary ingredients for life will thrive, and those who don't will be forced to alter their behaviors or risk the threat of extinction. So it should come as no surprise that US energy policy is defined by the conflict between, on the one hand, the necessity of having adequate and unfettered access to oil supplies, and on the other hand, equality (equal access) between the buyers and sellers that define the free market.

US leadership is also aware that equal access helps build international stability and national security. If any nation is restricted from having access to energy, it will likely strike out to gain that access. The conflict between necessity and equality sets up a fundamental paradox, however, for our status quo–oriented policies. You and I might like to think the world provides a free market that governs the energy industry, but it doesn't. This reality was discussed briefly in chapter 4 regarding the rules that govern the electricity sector of our global energy economy and the inequitable nature of energy deposits. Nevertheless, these limitations on a free market do not exist, because we lack commitment to a free market system. Either by omission or by intention, what we have is a global energy market full of distortions created by competing national and international security interests.

The United States' response to these distortions has not been to deny their existence and blindly wish for a free market to magically emerge. Rather, the US response has largely been to balance the need for international stability and national security while promoting healthy competition, innovation, and trade. Nor has the US response for at least the last sixty years been to try to clean up political interests that surround the oil-industrial complex, though there are some reasonable comparisons of today's circumstances to those of the past. (For example, at the turn of the twentieth century, it was necessary to impose antitrust efforts on large industrial interests that transcended national interests, such as limiting the power of John D. Rockefeller's Standard Oil.) Rather, the US response has been to acknowledge that it is natural for any country, as it looks at its national security concerns, to evaluate its energy needs and allow for government to intervene through regulation, taxation, and subsidy. This process is necessary to ensure a nation's access to its energy resources—and then to open up the market to competition.

For example, as we discussed in chapter 5, in the United States we have an energy system in which we are subsidizing carbon-based fuels to promote domestic production of oil- and petroleum-based goods. That approach creates market distortions. Such policies have intercepted the natural global peak in oil production that would occur but for the presence of oil-based subsidies. The concern over US policy has come when subsidies and market preferences continue beyond their original intent. In such an environment, it may become impossible for legitimate substitutes to compete or to rise up from within the marketplace.[131] The potential consequence is a situation where a single nation or region could become unduly vulnerable to the exports of another nation.

Let me be specific. In 1998 the United States subsidized its auto industry with $111 billion[132] through rebates and tax incentives that had the impact of making gas-guzzling cars like Humvees cheaper. The absence of higher fuel efficiency standards added to the country's dependence on foreign oil suppliers. In the United States, every time a barrel of oil is purchased from imports to make gasoline, roughly 50 percent of the money we spend goes overseas. In 2008, for instance, $388 billion of the United States' $0.9 trillion oil bill went abroad in spite of increased exports of energy-related products from the United States.[133] These kinds of policies have reverberating consequences for national security.

As the global community looks at alternatives to oil, US policy makers react. The issues of energy are not without political and legitimate economic interests. Almost every policy maker feels that he or she must review each alternative with an eye toward its impact on building national and international security. It is useful to recognize up front that the issue of energy with regard to national security has two sides to it. On the one hand, there is the geopolitical aspect of ensuring not only security over supply but also adequate supply to keep the economy moving. If a sovereign state denies another state access to a pipeline, then the result will likely be mounting international tension. If prices escalate rapidly, that, too, can have devastating effects on the global economy and capital markets. On the other hand, there is the more technical dimension of the reliability of supply in the event of natural disruptions, which requires that nations hold on to their reserves for domestic use before considering them for export.

This debate between national and international interests will go on for some time and will define much of each government's policy on energy. Whether taking the boat to safe harbor or simply sailing safely along the coast, the captain must adjust the sails from time to time. The same is true for US energy policy.

SECURING FOREIGN SUPPLY

It is no surprise that the United States consumes much more oil than it produces. Currently, the nation has 4.5 percent of the total global population, produces about 23 percent of global GDP, and uses 22 percent of the word's crude oil. Yet the United States supplies only 8.5 percent of the world's crude oil.[134] Because of the imbalance between the amount of oil consumed and the amount produced, the nation is increasingly locked into a position in which it has to adjust its foreign and domestic policy decisions to secure its supply to foreign sources of oil, even if such decisions compromise national security interests or environmental standards. This approach has become business as usual.

One of the barriers to moving away from business as usual and toward alternative energy supplies is that the global economy, and by implication the US economy, has a symbiotic relationship to the price and supply of oil and other conventional fuels. For example, the development of the US oil industry through both World War I and World War II propelled the United States into a position of world dominance economically, militarily, and politically. Maintaining this status in turn relies on an economic system that continues to be fueled by uneven access to energy—access that allows the United States to consume more resources than it produces.

As discussed in chapter 5, the United States hit its peak in oil production back in 1970 after a decade of import restrictions imposed by President Eisenhower. The Nixon administration lifted these restrictions and the United States started to import more and more oil to meet domestic consumption. The concern of many US policy makers back then, including those in the White House, was that we might become overly reliant on the Middle East's oil supplies. Considering this large exchange of resources, the question that arose then was: How should the United States best meet its financial obligations under a new balance in its energy mix, between declining domestic production and a growing reliance on foreign suppliers?

The concern of US policy makers back then was justified. The domestic energy mix and its reliance on foreign supplies has continued to grow and has defined much of US foreign policy ever since. The United States has worked itself into a position of being increasingly dependent on foreign suppliers. In 1973 these suppliers got together and exposed US vulnerability by imposing an oil embargo, and this history has helped shape much of the world's political and economic institutions ever since. In fact, the United States' continued military presence in the Persian Gulf region since the 1970s demonstrates the alternating defense and exploitation of this vulnerability. This dynamic illustrates what keeps the United States attached to the business-as-usual scenario driven by the necessity of making sure that the nation has enough oil to meet its domestic requirements and ensuring that the rest of the world does, too.

There are hundreds of books and articles in magazines such as *Foreign Affairs* that have analyzed the events that led up to the 1973 oil embargo. The realpolitik of the Nixon-Kissinger era, including shuttle diplomacy and the Nixon doctrine of selling guns for oil, worked to build the US economy into a superpower. The United States replaced the United Kingdom as the hegemonic power of the Persian Gulf, gaining commercial control over the supply lines of the largest oil-exporting countries. In 1971 the British pulled their last ships from the Strait of Hormuz after nearly a century of operations in the region. As the United States became more powerful, however, it became more dependent, strengthening its symbiotic relationship with oil. For example, throughout the 1970s the United States became both the largest consumer of Iranian and Saudi oil and the largest supplier of state-of-the-art fighter jets to the region. Today it is not just the United States but much of the world drinking from the tap of Middle Eastern oil while the US pays the freight in the region through continued military support. The US has been left holding the proverbial bag.

How did our public investment in the Middle East affect international stability? In the 1970s both the Shah of Iran and the royal family of Saudi Arabia were able to build a sizable military presence in the region by buying armaments directly from US contractors in order to carry out their competing visions of a reemerging Persian empire. When the Shah fell to Islamic forces in 1979, the balance of power shifted and the conflict between a revolutionary Iran and a militarized Iraq replaced the historic rift between Iran and Saudi Arabia. The strategy of selling guns for oil worked because it kept the balance of payments in check by creating a sufficient level of tension in the region.

To see how powerful this international relationship was in keeping US policy in check, we need only consider the outcome of the administration that followed the Nixon and Ford presidential terms and the 1973 oil embargo. President Jimmy Carter expressed his concern over how the game was being played in one of his 1976 presidential campaign pledges. He announced that he would immediately stop the exportation of armaments to Iran because (he claimed) the Shah had access to new weapons technology even before the US Armed Services did. In spite of his campaign pledge, however, Carter continued to play this game while he was president. It is likely that he changed his approach after experiencing the overwhelming power of entrenched interests at work and saw how those interests served the United States energy security.

The Shah eventually fell from power in 1979, precipitating a second oil crisis. The White House again had to scramble to build a new balance of power in the region. In 1980, four years after his election, the failure to keep the problems with Iran contained cost Carter the presidency.

The challenges that resulted from the 1973 oil embargo and the fall of Iran's government in 1979 were not limited to the region. US dependence on oil meant that the situation at home wasn't stable either. In *The Oil Kings*, Andrew Scott Cooper writes about the US response to the 1973 oil embargo:

> Americans were experiencing oil shock. It began over the New Year's weekend when motorists in New York City fought one another with fists and knives outside gasoline stations and a man in Albany walked into a gas station with what looked like a hand grenade and left with all the gas he could carry.[135]

In fact, the 1973 oil embargo could have provided the necessary impetus for the United States to shift its focus to alternative sources of energy.

However, the effort to develop renewable, efficient energy wasn't seen by industry as sufficiently viable, even though research and development was under way. So instead, policy makers became more determined, even desperate, to maintain a strong and viable domestic oil business. Oil prices rapidly increased after the formation of OPEC. In spite of higher prices, the United States kept losing ground to rising demand. Energy demand was outstripping domestic production, and the country was meeting its marginal demand with supply from an exclusive club thousands of miles away. Rising demand beyond internal production created a seller's market for OPEC countries. Consider the impact: After 1973 Iran's oil revenues grew from a few billion annually to more than $20 billion, giving the Shah and others in the Persian Gulf region new prestige in world affairs and excess cash to build up their own military machines. In terms of US foreign policy, the result was a strategy to do more of the same: Sell more arms to strengthen nations that were sympathetic to US interests. The strategy worked for a time, as long as the regional conflicts provided for a stable balance of power and created more global oil supply. But the side effects were mounting, and they created unintended consequences.

In spite of more military hardware being shipped into the Middle East region, global energy costs were rising because of the demand for more and more oil. This created inflationary pressures on the US dollar during the 1970s. In response to economic woes, popular movements that supported socialist agendas mounted throughout the world, including key ally nations in Europe. External pressure on Iran from the Soviet Union, tensions between Iran and Iraq's Saddam Hussein, and internal Islamic revolutionary pressures eventually forced Iran into becoming an oil-funded police state. In response the Shah struggled to modernize Iran's economy, including its political apparatuses. His efforts would all come crashing down in the spring of 1979 after a rapid rise of internal opposition from Islamic revolutionaries. The Shah fled his country, and the United States lost its major ally in the region.

The US had relied on Iran to provide the leadership and balance of power in the Persian Gulf that would permit the United States to meet its energy needs. But in the end such reliance was ill founded as a long-standing solution. Eventually the relationship failed to fulfill its raison d'être. There were consequences because of the nature of the system itself: As oil suppliers began to exercise their power by raising prices, the system broke down and proved to be unsustainable. The 1979 crisis was an example of how a negative consequence can follow a distorted market. By virtue of supplying military equipment for a vital natural resource overseas rather than investing in substitutes, the United States became overreliant on foreign suppliers. This threatened both national security and international stability. The more "codependent" the United States and its industrial allies became, the more unstable the system became.

Despite the lessons proffered by the two oil crises of 1973 and 1979, the United States continued to try to ensure international access to Middle Eastern oil through a realignment of interests. US military exports to the region continued throughout the 1980s, with the US government supporting Iraq in the Iran–Iraq War. The fall of Iran created an opportunity for a young military dictator, Iraq's Saddam Hussein, to invade his former rival and secure greater oil supplies. This made for strange bedfellows considering that the United States had been supporting Iraq's enemy for the past decade. The public rationale was that the United States had to prevent the Soviet Union from using its access to the Middle East via Afghanistan to further its own Cold War objectives by legitimately threatening to interrupt Western oil supplies. This prospect scared both US policy makers and the regimes that ran the oil-exporting countries.

The drama continued to play out in the Middle East. The United States maintained an interest in that region through its budding support of Iraq and by creating security relationships with Iraq's and Iran's other neighbors, such as Kuwait. After eight years and nearly a million lives lost, the fighting of the Iran–Iraq war ended in a stalemate and a cease-fire, with neither side gaining any real ground. The end to this brutal war in 1988 coincided with the final years of the Cold War. After 1991, Russia reluctantly withdrew from the region and quickly became more engaged in its own domestic politics and in preserving its historical relations with former satellite states.

President Ronald Reagan was ending his second term. The fall of the Soviet Union and the end of the Iran-Iraq War led to decreased tensions in the Persian Gulf for just a short while. The world had clearly changed. Warfare continued in the region, but without the Cold War implications, it was increasingly difficult for the United States to maintain its presence and keep a balance of payments in check. Then Iraq, still heavily armed from its war with Iran, invaded Kuwait in August 1990, claiming that Kuwait (with help from US energy suppliers) was using a brand-new technology to horizontally drill beyond its borders into Iraqi-owned oil reserves. I was glued to the television set, not sure how the declining Soviet Union would respond. Russia decided to condemn Baghdad rather than to complain about US attempts to establish exclusive hegemony in the region.

The global response was an international coalition that repelled Iraq from Kuwait and led to more than a decade of sanctions. It also left the region free of the old Cold War conflict.

Still, peace came with a price for many oil-dependent nations, including the United States. If the countries in the Middle East didn't need Western guns to repel the Soviet Union or balance power with Iraq, how would we buy the oil we needed? As it turned out, buying oil without selling guns would lead to greater dependency in the form of an imbalance of trade, because guns for oil had kept the system going. That is, until the 2001 terrorist attack on the United States created a new opportunity. Suddenly there was a groundswell of interest in making sure that a strong Western presence in the Middle East continued. No matter what your politics are, the fact is that the United States initiated a war with Iraq in 2003 that opened up significant commercial rationale to maintain its military presence in the region.

The changing landscape presented opportunities for a large US military operation in the Persian Gulf without being outgunned by a competitor such as the Soviet Union in the past. Moreover, the circumstances of 9/11 presented an opportunity for the United States to actively maintain the status quo and to expand on historic relationships while keeping tensions high but stable. For example, the US presence in the region would allow for a redistribution of oil rights from Iraq, giving international oil companies new access to drilling and distribution contracts. Furthermore, continued tension in the Middle East would also enable the United States to profit by reviving guns-for-oil as well as other business interests that could take advantage of the region's rich natural resources. As long as oil profits were up, with a balanced degree of insecurity, the United States could rebuild its economic interests in the region and meet its balance of payment obligations. Business as usual is making sure that nothing disrupts this delicate equilibrium of power and trade.

This history I've provided is not meant to be an exhaustive summary, nor is it a complete characterization of the dynamics underlying US energy policy. Rather, it is the perspective of a business operator in the energy industry, the results of my career-long efforts to be a keen and interested observer. I have simply attempted to provide an understanding behind how US foreign policy has emerged for much of the first decade of this new millennium. A realistic view of this precarious balance of trade that has so clearly relied on the global flow of oil is a critical feature of Project Butterfly's definition of *business as usual*. Admittedly, it is only part of a long history. There are likely very different views on the subject.

However, I do know this: President Obama ended the Iraq War. By the end of 2011, he had formally pulled US troops out of the country. What is rarely discussed is the clear US diplomatic and corporate presence that remains stationed in Iraq and throughout the Middle East. Few would deny that US influence and national interests are as strong as ever in the region. Now that I've outlined the connection between energy and national security, it should be clear how conflict can develop as the United States attempts to achieve both goals. This conflict is an intrinsic part of what I mean by "business as usual."

In this context, the business-as-usual game can be characterized as part of the US influence on globalization. Or one might make the equally valid point that the current US experience of globalization is merely a by-product of business as usual. Either way, business as usual has always been inherently unstable, which makes our commitment to it more of an obligation to national security than a willing choice.

When the debate about US energy policy turns to discussions of international security, I realize that we are not alone in seeking to navigate our ship to safer shores. At the heart of any nation's energy policy is the notion that a disruption to supplies could threaten national security. There are consequences to consuming more than you produce—and dangerous dependency is one of them.

DRILL, BABY, DRILL

How can a nation steer clear of energy dependency and make sure that the oil market keeps flowing? Within the business-as-usual scenario, an obvious answer is by including in its energy policy a strategy to reduce foreign imports. This approach has propagated another theme that is consistent with business as usual: "We should just drill at home." It certainly was the suggestion Republican candidate Mitt Romney made in his 2012 presidential bid. The same was true four years earlier, during the 2008 presidential election cycle. Who can forget the Republican National Convention that nominated presidential and vice-presidential candidates Senator John McCain and Alaska's Governor Sarah Palin, where supporters repeatedly chanted, "Drill, baby, drill"? On one level, in light of rising gas prices at the pump and the threat of international terrorists cutting off our supply, I had to agree. Moreover, I even caught myself thinking that if the United States dramatically increased domestic drilling, it might be possible to change the balance of power and improve our bargaining position with the Persian Gulf nations.

Surely a policy of drilling at home could be sold to the American public, because it held the promise (justified or not) of freeing the nation from high-priced gasoline while decreasing the risks intrinsic to foreign oil dependency. However, it took me only a moment to realize that this would be nothing more than a "quick fix."

The irony is that in spite of the fact that the US public rejected the Republican platform in both 2008 and 2012, since President Obama has been in the White House, the United States has significantly reduced its net imports of crude oil, which in turn has spurred a move toward greater domestic drilling. In 2012, the United States imported approximately 45 percent of its petroleum, down from 57 percent in 2008. Perhaps this merely shows the benefits of a well-functioning democracy. The elected official gets to blame his predecessors for what is not working and to take credit for what is. The 2012 presidential election highlighted the decline in oil imports, and both candidates claimed they would do more to expand US oil production. But progress toward solving the long-term problem of foreign oil dependency has been in the works since the 1970s. Reductions in oil imports can also be seen as a consequence of a global and US recession and not necessarily the result of genuine planning or execution of a long-term strategy to look inwardly for our fossil fuels.[136]

However, let's accept the political characterization of the issue based on its face value. The fundamental question is, is it really possible to drill at home to a level that will set us free from foreign oil supplies, as we have actually witnessed (to some degree) in recent years? If the answer to the US security dilemma is truly to drill to energy independence, then what is the cost of this strategy? Is drilling at home really a feasible option, or is it just part of the schizophrenic nature of business as usual, always presenting a kind of mythical solution to the current problem? Moreover, if indeed the objective is to reduce exposure to foreign oil dependence, is there a better alternative? And if there is an alternative to drilling, what is its cost? The answers to these seemingly complex questions are actually fairly simple once all of the facts are laid out in a clean and coherent manner. But the question remains, how do these alternatives play out in a way that is still consistent with a business-as-usual scenario? In fact, how do these alternatives actually *shape* business as usual?

BUSINESS AS USUAL: A DEEPER LOOK

The number of oil and natural gas drilling rigs in the United States has quadrupled between 2008 and 2012, which has led analysts to predict that oil independence may actually be possible within ten years if this trend continues.[137] Conversely, the United States can develop alternatives that would lead to a more permanent solution. Since 2009 renewable energy in the United States has actually outpaced growth rates for fossil fuels and nuclear energy.[138] These simple facts may appear to address the question of whether it is possible to drill our way to energy independence, but in reality they only confuse the situation. Let's measure the options in front of us and consider what the market itself is saying.

Figure 6.1 shows the total amount of oil consumed in the United States today compared with our current domestic production. Clearly, the rate of consumption has outpaced the rate of production for the past thirty years. Similarly, figure 6.2 shows historic reserve levels being depleted at the current rate of US consumption. While increased drilling at home is favorable compared with meeting domestic demand with foreign imports, the results of domestic drilling may be short-lived. The data in figure 6.1 and figure 6.2 support this assessment. The answer, therefore, is to shift toward alternatives as rapidly as possible in order to avoid completely depleting domestic oil resources once new drilling techniques have been exhausted. Even without the rising concerns related to GHG emissions and climate change catastrophes, it is obvious that we can't go on expecting business as usual to power this nation indefinitely.

Increased drilling at home is but one of three possible solutions to

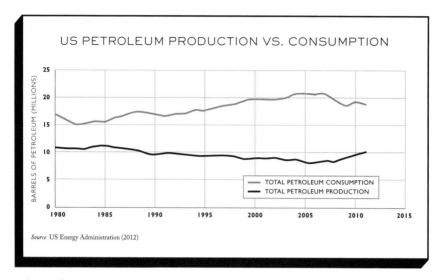

• *fig. 6.1:* Over the past thirty years, the United States' hunger for petroleum has outpaced the country's ability to produce the fuel.

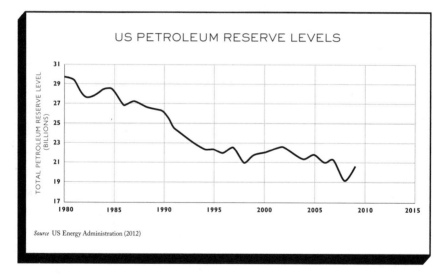

• *fig. 6.2:* Petroleum is a finite resource. The past thirty years have shown a steady decline in reserve levels, and at current rates of consumption, a similar downward-facing trend will continue unless dramatic new discoveries are found.

reducing US dependency on foreign oil that are under way in our markets—and each one reflects the business-as-usual model. These options have been generated by an energy system that lacks clarity and coherence, and yet all three are commonly heralded as part of a national energy policy.

One voice in the business-as-usual chorus is chanting that the potential solution is the continued rapid development of natural (shale) gas to replace conventional oil and coal until such time as other forms of energy emerge. A second voice croons that it is possible to reduce energy dependency by constructing a nuclear-powered economy where our transportation system is powered by hydrogen. (We'll take a closer look at this option in the next chapter.) Yet another voice chimes in that the rapid assimilation of a smart grid—greatly assisted by the mainstream adoption of electric vehicles, along with variable power from solar and wind, balanced by geothermal and hydro resources—is the answer to powering a renewable energy economy. (I discuss the smart grid further in chapter 14.) The business-as-usual choir is a medley of all three voices, each sung by its respective industry to present its case as an alternative to oil dependency.

Today, all of these options are components of business as usual, but as we will see, these options could be significant and fundamental parts of a new business case. In fact, all three solutions are benefiting from government assistance and regulation to spur them into the market. As I will explain, however, even though they are all gaining relative degrees of traction, we are not necessarily better off by pursuing all three measures without greater market coordination. As they are currently positioned in the marketplace, they lack harmony with one another. The business-as-usual choir is discordant and certainly less than inspiring. That said, each voice on its own *does* have a certain level of clarity.

Let's take the rest of this chapter to explore the first of these alternatives: natural gas.

INTRODUCING NATURAL GAS

There is a popular notion that natural gas is an alternative to drilling for more oil and that it has the potential to power the United States for many years to come. Natural gas may also present opportunities for powering the global economy as new discoveries emerge. In my home state of Colorado, the local utility, Xcel Energy, made a decision in 2010 to shut down, convert, and replace much of its fleet of coal-fired power plants with natural gas–fired generation. The move was fairly controversial at the time, but conversion of coal plants to natural gas has since happened elsewhere and is likely to continue. Conversion to gas is in part a response to both consumer concerns over rising GHGs and the low cost of conversion from coal- to gas-fired generation. In this light, natural gas becomes a cornerstone of potential solutions to reduce GHGs while still maintaining a fossil fuel economy.

In March 2013 Exxon Mobil issued an interesting statement. The oil corporation announced that in the coming decades, the United States will reduce its CO_2 emissions to levels not seen since the 1970s. Such a reduction, according to the report, will be a result of a "pronounced shift away from coal in favor of less-carbon-intensive fuels such as natural gas."[139] Some might question whether Exxon is a credible source of information on climate change and on estimates of US GHG emissions levels. Such a report might even seem self-serving. It clearly reveals an effort to position Exxon as being a continued part of the US energy mix, even if policies are launched to reduce GHGs. This move by Exxon preserves the notion that new, unconventional sources of energy are here to stay and are part of the answer going forward.

Natural gas exploration and production is certainly nothing new in the United States, but reports like Exxon Mobil's are efforts to smooth the road for a natural gas industry that is experiencing a dramatic resurgence. Since at least the 2008 presidential cycle, the natural gas option (like domestic oil drilling) has been promoted once again as a means to ensure national security and relieve US dependence on foreign sources of energy. A method that involves fracturing previously impermeable rock, which harbors much of the remaining gas, has been in a sort of testing phase for many decades. In fact, in September 1969, at a depth of 8,426 feet, a small atomic bomb was detonated near the city of Rifle, Colorado, as a means to fracture the surrounding rock bed. This experiment, called Project Rulison, under the Plowshare Program, was an attempt to extract shale gas using a large and relatively inexpensive detonation mechanism.[140] Needless to say, the site experienced high levels of contamination. The exploitation of shale gas has been waiting for a technological solution ever since.

The use of nuclear explosives to access gas and oil reserves has since proven to be not only obsolete but also a potentially grotesque use of nuclear power that would likely have propelled any community into revolt. However, new technologies, such as the advancement of horizontal drilling combined with modern hydraulic fracturing techniques (often referred to as "fracking") have created a renaissance for the unconventional gas industry since the early 2000s, raising questions of whether the United States may have indeed found yet another way back to energy abundance and independence through continued use of fossil fuels.

One of the key attributes of natural gas is that it has historically been considered a "cleaner burning" fuel source than its fossil fuel competitors. On average, natural gas emits about 29 percent less carbon than oil and 43 percent less than coal. As a potential transport fuel, natural gas emits about 20 to 30 percent less life-cycle carbon than oil does. Also, natural gas is essentially free of sulfur and metal emissions, and its combustion can be controlled to release lower amounts of nitrogen oxide (NOx)—a benefit that the natural gas industry has touted heavily over the past several years.[141] Taking this into account, it would appear that there are significant environmental benefits to moving toward an economy that is predominately run by natural gas. Seen in this light, business as usual is using fossil fuels to decarbonize the energy mix.

Economically, large benefits also appear to exist if the United States and the rest of the world were to begin exploiting the abundant natural gas reserves that naturally reside within many countries. President Obama noted in his 2012 State of the Union address that at current rates of consumption, nearly one hundred years of natural gas exists beneath our feet. Such a claim bodes well for those who value job growth and domestic sources of energy, especially in the aftermath of the 2008 Great Recession; it was also noted in the president's address that exploitation of this resource would support more than six hundred thousand jobs by the end of the decade.

On the surface, natural gas seems like a solution that would meet the Project Butterfly requirements of creating a condition that benefits all stakeholders in our energy industry and also reduces GHGs to acceptable levels. The pursuit of unconventional natural gas therefore has the ring of a new business case to it, while still promoting the idea that it is possible to drill our way out of both dependence on foreign energy supply and increasing GHG emissions. Underneath, however, we cannot be so sure. Representations made by the oil and gas industry require further analysis relating to natural gas being used as a *replacement fuel* for oil and coal.

As we address both a changing climate and a depletion of our fossil fuels, might natural gas actually be a Trojan horse? Is natural gas being oversold as a replacement for oil and coal, keeping us in business as usual rather than serving simply as a highly valuable *transition fuel* to a new business case? The answers to these questions clearly have serious national security implications. They also help further define *business as usual*. If natural gas is being oversold, it becomes clear that business as usual is a continuing mythology about conventional energy and its ability to carry on. Moreover, the gas industry is spinning the story that natural gas is a national-security solution. Some industry executives go so far as to suggest that exportation of natural gas is a pathway to energy independence—that the United States can use natural gas to become a net energy exporter. However, a review of the potential costs might reveal that these representations ring true only if natural gas is characterized and regulated as a transition fuel leading to a renewable energy economy. We can begin to see the importance of positioning as the global community addresses climate change.

There are at least four critical questions any investor needs to ask before accepting the business presentations being made by the natural gas industry:

1. Is this supply of natural gas as plentiful as everyone hopes, or is the American public being exposed to hype from industry?

2. Is natural gas as clean as the industry would like you to think?

3. If environmental externalities become internalized to the supplier, or if there is a price fixed to carbon, is natural gas from hydraulic fracturing ("fracking") still a cheap and abundant resource?

4. Can natural gas serve as a transition fuel toward an economy that emits less and less carbon, or will a growing dependence on this fuel trap the global economies into a system with dire environmental consequences?

Don't take these questions the wrong way. Undoubtedly, natural gas is a highly valuable resource with the capacity to burn with a high degree of precision. This extraordinary fuel has unique characteristics that differentiate it from coal and oil and that we can't ignore. But should we as the global community be asking ourselves whether we are truly maximizing the value of natural gas and meeting our national security concerns, as the natural gas industry suggests? As we find ourselves in increasingly choppy waters, is natural gas truly a straight line to a safe harbor?

CONSIDERING RESOURCE RISK

The one-hundred-year claim made by President Obama about natural gas originated in April 2011 by the Potential Gas Committee (PGC), an organization of petroleum engineers and one hundred volunteer geoscientists.

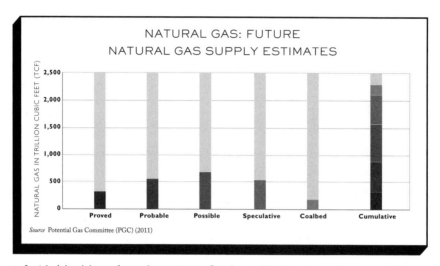

* *fig. 6.3:* A breakdown of natural gas estimates. Based upon this data, and assuming no growth in consumption levels, an eleven-year supply of gas is proven.

The Technically Recoverable US Natural Gas Endowment has engaged the PGC in biennial assessments since 1964. The committee generally combines its results with the US Energy Information Administration's (EIA's) proven reserves to arrive at the potential future supply. In 2012, the total US gas resources, as calculated by the PGC, amounted to 1,897.8 trillion cubic feet (Tcf). When this figure is combined with the EIA's estimate of proven reserves of 272.5 Tcf, we arrive at the future natural gas supply figure of 2,170.3 Tcf. Based on drilling data and current technological capabilities, and at the 2010 rate of US natural gas consumption, which was about 24 Tcf per year, this leaves the United States a ninety-year supply of gas. President Obama apparently rounded up his estimate of reserves by the natural gas industry to an even one hundred years.[142] This figure acted as the starting gunshot in a race to exploit shale gas.

The breakdown of the hundred-year natural gas prediction is largely made up of industry estimates, however, and can be better viewed by analyzing figure 6.3. Of the calculated 1,897.8 Tcf provided by the PGC, 536.6 Tcf are classified as "probable" from existing fields. This means that they are "*discovered but unconfirmed resources* associated with known fields and field extensions" as well as "*undiscovered resources* in new pools in both productive and nonproductive areas." The next level of increasing uncertainty contains 687.7 Tcf of "possible" reserves. Defined by the PGC, possible resources are "*undiscovered resources* associated with new field/pool discoveries in known productive formations in known productive areas." Finally, the most uncertain level contains 518.3 Tcf, and is labeled as "speculative." The PGC defines this as "*undiscovered resources* associated with new field/pool discoveries in *nonproductive areas*" (all emphases added).[143] On top of these figures are 176 Tcf of coal-bed methane calculated in a similar manner. Assuming the United States continues to use about 24 Tcf per year without any growth, then there is only an eleven-year supply of natural gas from the EIA's estimate of proven reserves of 272.5. This is the amount of gas that is certain; the remaining eighty-nine years are industry estimates. Moreover, don't overlook the notion of "without any growth," which seems unlikely if the United States shifts heavily toward natural gas.

Industry experts defend the hundred-year claim by stating that the accounting system for estimating natural gas supplies has been in place for years. The methodology has demonstrated a high degree of accuracy. Additionally, industry experts refer to the ever-increasing amount of natural gas reserves discovered over the past several decades. In 1996 the EIA estimated that US proven reserves amounted to 166.5 Tcf. Since then, the United States has consumed nearly twice that amount, showing some validity behind the "probable," "possible," and "speculative" reserve amounts.

However, the rising estimates are largely due to new advancements in horizontal drilling technology and hydraulic fracturing processes in order to extract oil and gas from shale deposits. This technology changes the dynamics of any calculation. Chesapeake Energy, the second-largest producer of natural gas in this country, defines *hydraulic fracturing* as

a process of creating fissures, or fractures, in underground formations to allow natural gas and oil to flow . . . Water, sand, and other additives are pumped under high pressure into the formation to create fractures. The fluid is approximately 98 percent water and sand, along with a small amount of special-purpose additives. The newly created fractures are "propped" open by the sand, which allows the natural gas and oil to flow into the wellbore and be collected at the surface.[144]

In recent years, fracking, combined with horizontal drilling, has allowed oil and gas companies to drill multiple wells on the same platform, for several miles, in multiple directions. These technologies have created a race to access the vast amount of shale oil and gas reserves underneath the earth. According to the EIA's *Annual Energy Outlook 2012*, shale gas made up 23 percent of the total US natural gas production. Shale gas is forecast to offset the decline of other sources of natural gas, to arrive at supplying 49 percent of total US natural gas production by 2035.[145]

But how reliable are these estimates? Estimates for shale gas reserves can be extremely volatile. Drilling history with new technology in these regions is very limited, which makes it difficult to predict reserve amounts. For example, the EIA's estimate of unproven technically recoverable resource (TRR) of shale gas decreased substantially from 2010's US estimate of 827 Tcf, to 482 Tcf. The Marcellus shale play, a large region of marine sedimentary rock that stretches from New York down to Tennessee, is a large reason for this decrease, as the play's own TRR estimate decreased from 410 to 141 TRR. This drop is attributed to the new recovery information about the Marcellus shale play (due to the doubling of production drilling in the Marcellus basin).[146] In essence, even if natural gas consumption were to remain flat, this adjustment effectively cuts eleven years of production right out of the mix.

It is difficult to be certain why the total reserve figure was overstated in the first place. But the figure remains largely unchallenged, because there is no real check-and-balance system. The industry has an incentive to provide strong projections to attract funding and to raise land values, whereas few others are incentivized to question industry representations and place downward pressure on reserve estimates.

One potential national security risk posed by unbridled development of natural gas is that if estimates prove unreliable, few other fuel sources can serve as an easy substitute in sufficient quantities to meet rising demand. Current projections rely on current rates of consumption, but reports of a one-hundred-year supply of fuel and low prices due to marginal excesses in the market are causing a run to natural gas. Government and industry are looking to find new markets, such as converting transportation fleets to natural gas and exporting the fuel overseas. The problem with this approach is that if natural gas becomes more widely adopted into the global economy, then the rate of consumption will certainly increase, quickly absorbing any perceived abundance of the resource.

In fact, recent events have been set in motion that will ultimately increase the consumption rate of natural gas. In 2012 Chrysler Group LLC initiated plans to build at least two thousand heavy-duty Ram bi-fuel trucks that run on a combination of gasoline and compressed natural gas.[147] The Natural Gas Act, which is pending before Congress as of this writing, will extend and increase tax credits for natural gas used for transportation. A key clause calls for the orderly replacement of the 8.5 million diesel-powered eighteen-wheeler semis and other heavy-duty vehicles with natural gas–powered vehicles over a five-to-seven-year period. This will amount to an estimated savings of 2.5 million barrels of oil a day.[148] All of these changes are spurred by the fact that, on average, it costs one-third less to fill a vehicle with natural gas than with traditional gasoline—and that 98 percent of the natural gas used by the United States is domestic.[149] It is tempting, as I suggested earlier, to accept a scenario in which outside political and economic pressures will no longer be a major concern.

However, with increasing consumption rates looking more and more likely, it is easy to see why it makes sense to calculate our national reserves using a higher rate of consumption instead of the current rate. Figure 6.4 represents the impact of varying levels of growth rates on the total lifetime amount of natural gas reserves. The consequences of rising consumption rates are profound, and the implications are serious. This obviously demonstrates the limitations of considering natural gas as a legitimate replacement for oil.

Of course, price will have an impact on consumption and supply. Unlike

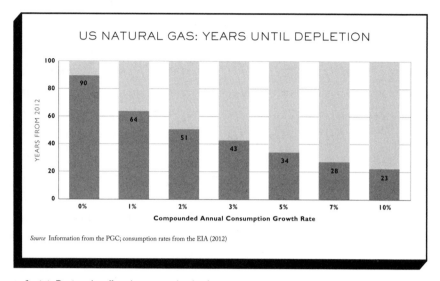

US NATURAL GAS: YEARS UNTIL DEPLETION

Source Information from the PGC; consumption rates from the EIA (2012)

• *fig. 6.4:* Depicts the effect that varying levels of consumption growth rates have upon the lifetime amount of natural gas reserves.

the base price of oil, set by the global oil market, natural gas prices vary through-out the world. Prices in Europe and Asia are three to seven times higher than in this country. This provides a large incentive to globalize the price of natural gas and entices US suppliers to take the competitive advantage. In the United States, gas production reached a historical high in November 2011, when 82.7 billion cubic feet of natural gas was being withdrawn from the land each day.[150] This expansion, largely due to the industry's new drilling techniques, has led to a reduction in domestic prices, while consumption levels have been increasing dramatically. As it currently stands, natural gas cannot be moved cheaply and in the volumes necessary to efficiently link the producing regions with the high-demand regions. But this situation may change.

The US Department of Energy is considering nine applications to export liquefied natural gas (LNG), natural gas converted into a usable liq-uid that can be transported in a manner similar to oil. In fact, the DOE has already approved a plan for one LNG export terminal, which is scheduled to be operational in 2016. If all nine export terminals are approved and their export capacity is fully utilized, then 20.6 percent of the current US annual consumption of natural gas will be exported to other countries.[151] This will undoubtedly raise the stakes for the US natural gas industry. It will certainly decrease the lifetime of the fuel's usefulness from the current hundred-year notion to something much, much less.

An EIA study released in January 2012 looked at the domestic consequences of this increasing amount of natural gas exports. The study concluded that if the DOE approves the pending applications, and if exports increase as expected, domestic natural gas prices could rise 24 to 54 percent.[152] The study also examined how these increasing prices would affect domestic demand for natural gas. The authors concluded that around 30 to 40 percent of the export demand would be met through reduced domestic consumption, not increased production. The study also projects that due to this rise in the cost of natural gas, coal-fired power generation will increase as a means to account for the expected decline in natural gas–fired electricity generation.

Exporting natural gas will decrease our net imports of energy. As I have pointed out already, this is an obvious benefit to national security. However, if US markets also become reliant on natural gas, exporting will leave the United States vulnerable to increased market volatility from rising global demand, reserve uncertainty, and a dependency on new technological discoveries to extract gas from shale. Failure to plan for depletion may create a situation where remaining reserves are inadequate to meet demand, causing a squeeze on natural gas prices to the detriment of both the economy and national security. We saw an example of such a squeeze between 2000 and 2008 when the price of natural gas rose by more than 400 percent before its dramatic decline trailing petroleum prices. If the current natural gas "rush" leads to capital projects dependent on the long-term supply of cheap and reliable gas, we may find ourselves experiencing another price shock—especially if these projects come at the expense of developing alternatives.

WHAT ABOUT THE ENVIRONMENT?

Because of the anticipated rapid increase in demand for and production of shale gas, new questions are being raised as to the environmental effects of this developing extraction process. Environmentalists are concerned with assessing damages caused by these new technologies as they extract gas from shale. One of the frustrating factors is having limited access to data considered by the gas industry as proprietary; also, the short history of operations leaves the environmental community frustrated in their efforts to independently assess impacts and determine credible results.

The most commonly discussed issue regarding shale gas, and one of the largest concerns, is the potential contamination of groundwater from the chemicals that are used in the fracking process. Because of intellectual property protection, many of these chemicals are unknown and kept secret from the public. Highlighting the issue is the so-called Halliburton loophole that protects gas drillers from disclosing the use of its chemicals. In 2005, at the direction of then vice president Dick Cheney, former CEO of natural gas exploration firm Halliburton, the Environmental Protection Agency exempted fracking from regulations under the 1974 Safe Drinking Water Act.

The process of hydraulic fracturing produces more than a million gallons per wellhead of wastewater that can be laced with highly corrosive salts, carcinogens like benzene, and radioactive elements like radium—all of which reside thousands of feet underground.[153] These harmful elements do not naturally mix with the groundwater that we extract to drink. But the concern raised by environmentalists is that the fracking process opens the gate and allows these chemicals to migrate into the water supply.

To make matters even more troubling, the oil and gas companies add chemicals during the fracturing process in an attempt to make the gas flow more freely. A report released in April 2011 confirmed that drillers often inject millions of gallons of fluids containing toxic or carcinogenic chemicals into a single well. The report lists 750 chemicals and compounds that were used by fourteen oil and gas companies between 2005 and 2009 through the hydraulic fracturing process. Twenty-nine of those chemicals are known, possible, or regulated carcinogens.[154] Environmentalists would not have much ground to stand on if these harmful chemicals were completely extracted from the well after the fuel is retrieved. However, the exact percentage of these chemicals that remains underground varies from site to site, and regulations may need to be imposed to ensure best practices. In areas like the Marcellus shale basin, it is estimated that up to three-quarters of the spent fluids are left underground, where it is practically impossible to monitor the movement and impact of these additives.[155]

As noted above, an exemption in the Energy Policy Act of 2005 protected hydraulic fracturing from oversight under the Safe Drinking Water Act.[156] This loophole exists thanks to a 2004 EPA study that cited the process as having "little or no threat" to drinking water, even though it was generally accepted that about 30 percent of the fracturing fluids remained in the ground.[157] Many oil and gas companies cite this EPA study as proof that the practice is safe, in spite of a growing concern within the environmentalist community that additional research is required to ensure the veracity of the science.[158] Moreover, the loophole hampers independent study, because gas producers are free from having to report the specific toxic chemicals used for fracturing, whereas other industries are forced to report their toxic emissions under the 1986 Emergency Planning and Community Right-to-Know Act.

As things currently stand, individual states are the ones responsible for requiring disclosures and for regulating the chemicals used in the fracturing process. New rules have been proposed that would require gas companies to disclose the chemicals they use; as these rules work their way into state capitals and onto the Hill in Washington, DC, oil and gas companies work to defend their right not to report their entire mixture of ingredients. Until then, oil and gas companies can refuse to disclose the use of certain chemicals if the information is deemed a "trade secret."[159] Full disclosure of all of the chemicals is a necessity if environmentalists and local communities are to determine the lasting impact of these chemicals on the environment and on the health of US citizens.

Another growing problem with the shale gas movement is the high probability that the fracturing process causes earthquakes that could bring underground radiation particulates to the surface. As I've mentioned, the majority of these radioactive elements, such as radium, reside thousands of feet underground; in the fracking process, they are unnaturally brought to the surface. The wastewater, which is a combination of natural particulates and the water and sand mixture used by fracking companies, is sometimes hauled to sewage plants that are not designed to treat water contaminated with radioactive chemicals. This water, once it passes through the treatment plants, is then discharged into the rivers that supply drinking water. The *New York Times* has uncovered thousands of documents that include alarmed EPA scientists' warnings that the drilling waste is a threat to drinking water and that there is no way to guarantee that the drinking water taken in by these treatment plants is safe.[160]

During 2011, within one mile of an injection well in Youngstown, Ohio, twelve separate earthquakes were reported, ranging from a magnitude of 2.1 to 4.0. These findings were published in a report that also discussed the fact that there had been no record of earthquakes in modern times from epicenters located in the Youngstown area. Only after D&L Energy began injecting drilling brine about 9,200 feet underground had quake detections been made.[161] Connections between fracking and earthquake activity are denied by industry experts, who say the complexity of causation makes it difficult to confirm the connection. However, environmentalists feel strongly that the method of extraction needs to be examined at a level beyond merely the potential economics of the technology.

Water contamination, radiation pollution, and earthquakes are all largely local impacts of natural gas drilling activities. The harmful incidences have predominately affected small groups of people who live in the areas where the oil and gas companies operate. However, the release of GHGs into the atmosphere as a related function of shale gas extraction raises the environmental debate to a global concern and one that is particularly germane to Project Butterfly. While natural gas is a cleaner fuel than coal, the emerging story is that the entire life cycle of the fuel causes just as much harm as, if not more harm than, that of its oil and coal counterparts. This claim dramatically changes the debate about natural gas and whether the global community can afford the environmental effects of using it as a replacement for oil and coal.

There are five points along the production line of shale gas where GHGs need to be counted as part of the accounting and reporting of its carbon intensity. These points are as follows:

1. Initial drilling and completion (which includes the repeated fracking of the rock)
2. Routine leaks and emissions at well sites (which include leaks from the 55 to 150 equipment connections, such as heaters, meters, dehydrators, compressors, and vapor-recovery apparatuses), and venting during liquid unloading (which occurs during attempts to mitigate water intrusion into the well)
3. Processing losses (which include the removal of impurities such as sulfur gas before being sent through the pipeline)
4. Transport, storage, and distribution losses (which include fugitive emissions that occur during each of these phases)
5. The actual burning of the natural gas at the end use

Based on a report written by several Cornell University professors, anywhere between 1.7 and 6 percent of the entire potential methane within the well for conventional gas (non-fractured) and between 3.6 and 7.9 percent for shale gas (fractured) is released into the atmosphere. These may not seem like large figures, but the potency of methane as a GHG is what makes these numbers so important to track. Based on a short time horizon (twenty years or less), methane is between seventy and one hundred times more potent than CO_2; on a longer time horizon (one hundred years), it is around twenty-five times more potent.[162] Most studies on the GHG impact of natural gas do not incorporate the leakage of methane into the atmosphere into their report, yet according to figure 6.5, it ultimately makes this fuel source worse for the entire environment in terms of global warming.[163]

The Cornell report has created significant controversy within the scientific community, and other reports have begun to emerge indicating very similar conclusions.[164] Not surprisingly, there are criticisms of the Cornell paper, stating that the work is incorrect in its findings and that natural gas, from both conventional and unconventional sources, is a cleaner alternative to coal.[165,166]

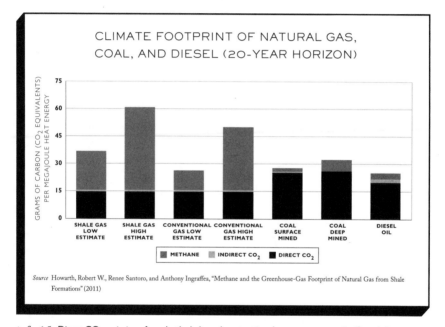

CLIMATE FOOTPRINT OF NATURAL GAS, COAL, AND DIESEL (20-YEAR HORIZON)

Source Howarth, Robert W., Renee Santoro, and Anthony Ingraffea, "Methane and the Greenhouse-Gas Footprint of Natural Gas from Shale Formations" (2011)

• *fig. 6.5:* Direct CO_2 emissions from both shale and conventional gas sources are significantly lower than both forms of coal mining and diesel oil. However, when methane is accounted for in the equation, the once beneficial attributes of gas seemingly dissipate.

Considering this ongoing debate, I think it is safe to say that we do not entirely know the role methane plays in determining the climate impact of natural gas. Regardless, this topic raises serious concerns about the claims made by the natural gas industry and its ability to supply a clean alternative to meet climate change requirements. Perhaps, in an effort to maintain business as usual, the idea of natural gas as a clean and abundant energy source is being oversold.

WEIGHING THE NATURAL GAS OPTION

In spite of the concerns raised by environmentalists, the fact is, domestic natural gas has become a tempting alternative to foreign oil; a large shift has occurred in the US domestic gas supply as technology has advanced and prices have fallen. Drilling for oil and natural gas in mostly shale formations, formerly considered too costly to develop, has begun to change the energy landscape. At the end of the day, however, drilling into these shale formations may prove to be less attractive than all the hype suggests. For one, shale drilling is expensive. If reserves amount to less than what is expected, if initial production rates fall faster than expected, and if environmental costs are incorporated into production cost, the short-term benefits may diminish quickly.[167] In fact, it may just take one of these three events to shatter current market expectations. Unfortunately, the cost of failure may prove to be more expensive than a simple spike in natural gas prices. Conversion of power plants from coal to gas, conversion of large vehicle fleets from diesel to natural gas, and construction of export facilities all cost money. These investments may run afoul if market participants suddenly call into question all the critical assumptions involved in increasing natural gas's share of the energy mix.

No doubt, natural gas provides a unique source of energy for industry and a source of heat for our homes and commercial buildings. Natural gas presents an undeniable advantage over other fuels when servicing these users. However, using natural gas to produce electricity and to replace oil as a transportation fuel presents a long-term challenge. Relying on natural gas supplies may create a national security risk at least equal to, if not greater than, relying on foreign imports. Those interested in the long-term health of our natural environment and in the security of our nation must remind those in charge that natural gas is simply part and parcel with business as usual, and not on its own a new business case.

FULFILLING THE MANTRA

Drill, baby, drill is the mantra within the conventional energy industry to address US energy needs, reduce the nation's dependence on limited suppliers of energy, and strengthen both domestic security and international stability. Since 2008 the United States has accomplished much to fulfill this mantra, by expanding domestic oil and gas production and reducing energy consumption. The unconventional energy industry has also responded to the call, by advancing alternatives that would not only provide new forms of energy supply but also address the demand for reduced GHG emissions. The industry has thrown out all the stops in trying to answer the call with natural gas. My response to these efforts is: Don't oversell yourself.

KEY OBSERVATIONS

The key observations about access to energy markets, national security, and how these considerations help shape business as usual are as follows:

» The development of energy reserves is key to any strategy to increase national security and preserve the peace. Yet national security goals can wreak havoc on energy policy and distort the market for energy. This is not an irreconcilable conclusion, however. Sound energy policy first meets the needs of national security and then supports greater market competition and innovation.

» Natural gas is experiencing a surge in approval from political and market forces as a result of exploiting new drilling techniques, such as hydraulic fracturing and horizontal drilling. However, natural gas from unconventional sources is still a finite fuel, and relying on it as a replacement for oil may be unrealistic.

» Extracting natural gas is part of business as usual. Unconventional natural gas can become part of a new business case only when it is viewed as a transition fuel.

· · ·

Before I came here I was confused about this subject. Having listened to your lecture I am still confused. But on a higher level.
—*Enrico Fermi*

CHAPTER 7

I was seventeen in 1977, and I had spent the summer flipping pancakes at the Lake Okoboji Pancake House in northwestern Iowa. One evening that summer I was hanging out on the dock with a few of my friends, looking at the stars and watching the boats troll by, when an older brother of one of my friends joined us. "Tom," he said, "you have *got* to go see this new movie." His excitement caught my attention. He described the movie as part of an epic saga about a young man with special powers who lives in a galaxy far, far away. "This kid," he said, "has unique mental and physical powers. He triumphs against all odds in a battle between good and evil."

I was immediately intrigued. "Where is it playing?" I asked.

"Oh, you have to go to Des Moines."

I thought about my friend's description of the movie all night. Des Moines was two hundred miles away, and I didn't have a car. But when I got up in the morning, I called my boss at the Pancake House and told him I needed to take a couple of days off. I dressed quickly and walked to the highway headed out of town. The first guy who picked me up was a farmer who took me only a few miles down the road. It took me all day to hitchhike to Des Moines.

As nearly everyone in this galaxy knows, the *Star Wars* trilogy was a huge commercial success. It struck a deep nerve and continues to resonate with stargazers everywhere, no matter their age. The movie is full of the kinds of heroes and villains that audiences love and hate. The story line completely captivated my imagination back in 1977. It also spoke directly to the culture of that time.

In the movie, the Rebel Alliance is fighting against the evil Empire to restore the Republic and peace throughout the galaxy. Meanwhile, the evil Empire is building a planet-size Death Star, an archetype representing the technological superiority of an evil force that the Rebel Alliance would have to overcome to survive. The movie follows the journey of a young man who finds the strength buried deep within his own being to fight this evil force. He is able to garner the necessary strength only by connecting to his past and his true self.

In the 1970s the Death Star could easily have symbolized either a Soviet-made doomsday machine or a nuclear power plant capable of a China Syndrome–level meltdown. The Red Scare was real back then, and so, too, was the Soviet Union's capability to launch a nuclear attack into the heartland of America. The other threat that ran through popular culture was the potential calamity that might arise from the proliferation of nuclear power plants, either by mad terrorists or from technology run amok. The 1970s were full of advancements in technology. However, new technologies such as supercomputers seemed to be disconnected from the more human concerns many felt in the 1970s. Building big bombs, big power plants, and big businesses created an existential issue for contemporary culture to ponder. *Star Wars'* Rebel Alliance represented the emerging counterculture that was built on questioning authority and on rejecting the idea that bigger is always better.[168]

In the 1970s the US energy industry was in the middle of building the world's largest fleet of nuclear power plants. In response to an escalating nuclear arms race with the Soviet Union, the United States was also engaged in building a new generation of delivery vehicles for its nuclear arsenal. Opposition was mounting against nuclear technology—both for energy and for weapons—because of its potential danger in the event of a national disaster, a terrorist attack, or a mechanical meltdown. In *Star Wars,* the band of rebels was fighting against an Empire that relied on a centralized power system: the Death Star, which was fueled by reactors running on "hypermatter." In contrast, the military fleet of the Rebel Alliance was limited to small- and medium-size cruisers, converted freighters, and outdated "starfighters."

I finally made it to Des Moines to watch *Star Wars* on that summer day in 1977. In fact, I returned the next day to watch it a second time. As I sat through the closing credits, I thought, *I want to be like Luke Skywalker.* I wanted to have the courage to take on the evil Empire. Millions of fans around the world would come to feel the same way.

• • •

Many of the themes in *Star Wars* are relevant today when we talk about how to mitigate climate change and the business-as-usual environment that limits innovation and any potential for a real solution to climate change. In the *Star Wars* series, a small group of rebels manages to overcome the efforts of a corrupt power system represented by mindless masses and power-hungry politicians wanting to dominate the universe. And the Imperial Death Star becomes more vulnerable because of its size, not less. A small and decentralized band of rebels defies those who seek to centralize power and are able to destroy the Death Star in spite of its technological prowess. The power flowing behind this small rebel force is the Force, "an energy field created by all living things, that surrounds and penetrates living beings and binds the galaxy together."[169] As I see it, this concept of the Force embodies the inner determination and willfulness that are required in order to make a change.

Business as usual, in contrast, is the endless pursuit of a technological innovation, as if all that matters is the innovation itself. It ignores the surrounding humanity, the existential issues that are so crucial to understanding why humans operate as we do. Perhaps the willfulness that flows from the Force is exactly what is necessary if we as a global community are to meet the need for a change from business as usual in order to save our planet.

THE STATUS QUO

Nuclear energy is part business as usual and part new business case. Conventional nuclear energy falls into the "business as usual" category because it is dependent on uranium for its fuel source. If nuclear fission could occur using alternative, renewable sources of fuel, nuclear energy would become part of the new business case. But this search for an alternative defines the limitations of nuclear energy.

At 2010 usage rates, the world has proven uranium reserves equal to approximately a seventy-year supply, making uranium clearly a finite resource.[170] This estimate is based on the efficiency of "once through" use—that is, the uranium goes *once through* the power-generation process, without reprocessing. Reprocessed fuel adds to the costs, increases the complexity of design, and involves some of the same technology that heightens concerns over the potential of nuclear weapons proliferation.

The world's installed nuclear power capacity of 393 gigawatts (GW) in 2010[171] may expand slightly due to growth of nuclear energy in Asia (especially China and South Korea), but without a specific breakthrough, electricity usage is likely to remain at existing levels. Nuclear energy's share of world electricity generation is currently 13 percent. Thus, proven uranium reserves may last a few years less than is currently being predicted for fossil fuels. Undoubtedly, more ore reserves of adequate quality will be discovered. Moreover, reprocessing of the spent fuel with current basic reactor types can extend the life of reserves. However, without the development and deployment of nuclear breeder reactors (discussed later in this chapter) to address the limited supply of fuel, there is probably less potential energy from extractable uranium than from conventional oil or gas resources.

Additionally, there is a large degree of uncertainty over the cost of constructing new nuclear power plants. For decades the nuclear industry has promised improved technology and construction techniques to reduce the cost of reactors (while also making them safer). These promises have been dashed largely due to the loss of R&D support. In Western countries, the estimated "overnight cost" per kilowatt (i.e., without the cost of borrowing, including the interest during construction) has risen steadily, in part thanks to rising commodity costs for steel and cement. In the United States, the estimated overnight cost of "third generation" reactors had increased to $4,000/kW by about 2008. Should a third generation reactor ever be built, the total cost will likely be substantially higher, given the long lead times for construction and the time to amortize the debt.[172]

As an example of the rising construction costs, one needs only to look at the two nuclear projects under construction at Flamanville (France) and Olkiluoto (Finland). Both plants are behind schedule and extraordinarily over budget, by as much as $5 billion each.[173] In addition to these explicit costs, there are security risks and a wide array of environmental and waste issues, which must also be incorporated into a cost-benefit analysis.

Coming in over budget and experiencing increased costs are negative market signals for any investor in nuclear energy. In fact, it's relevant to observe that the four US nuclear plants to be built in the near future are located in the southeastern United States. This is one of the few places left in the nation where regulators allow the full cost of increasing a utility's asset base to be passed on directly—indeed, preemptively—to its captive consumers through rate base guarantees.[174] As you can see, investors will only go where it's safe.

Not only does nuclear energy carry a high cost per megawatt to install, but a transmission and distribution system must also be built to take the energy produced from a centralized source out to where it is needed. The direct costs are further complicated when you consider the added indirect costs of (eventually) decommissioning the power plant. The life expectancy of a nuclear power plant is forty years, which is being stretched now to sixty years in the United States. Owners of aging nuclear power plants are uncertain about how to handle the costs of decommissioning and who will pay for it. Such costs, especially if they are at the end of the investment's asset life, might look small at the onset of a project. But when decommissioning is eminent, such costs can hit shareholder equity hard.

Another characteristic of nuclear energy that creates a red flag for those concerned about our global energy portfolio is that once you go nuclear, it's difficult to go back. Plant development and energy generation require power purchase agreements that extend beyond the norm for fossil fuel or renewable energy supply, with guaranteed rates sufficient to ensure that investors recover their costs. To develop nuclear power, utilities must make substantial capital investments that they cannot afford to abandon in the event that lower-cost alternatives, such as gas-fired power generation or renewable energy resources, enter the market. The consequence is that nuclear energy requires an even more heavily regulated utility industry, where investors can rely on projected revenues and returns through mandated cost recovery. Such regulations generally prevent utility markets from opening up to competitive energy services—a move that is critical to encouraging innovation in the energy industry generally.

When nuclear power is suggested as a possible clean source of power to meet energy needs and address environmental challenges, the common joke within the energy industry is, "Nuclear energy is a technology with substantial promise . . . and it always will be." Unfortunately, that joke tends to sum up the challenge that the nuclear industry faces in gaining acceptance, and it also defines the status quo. Still, the promise of nuclear power is so compelling that we cannot take the option off the table.

NUCLEAR WEAPONS AND NUCLEAR ENERGY

The prevailing thought within the energy industry in the 1970s was that nuclear energy would power the US economy to endless prosperity. It was a thought that competed with popular culture's desire for decentralized power systems and less mysterious technology. Nuclear power plants create electricity from the splitting of atoms (known as the "fission process"). The extraordinary heat released during the fission process produces steam, which then turns a turbine to generate electricity. Because of its unique atomic properties, uranium is the natural source of nuclear energy's fuel. However, the process that actually runs a nuclear power plant is similar to that of conventional power plants, which burn coal or oil to create heat that turns a turbine to generate electricity. The big difference between the fission process and conventional electricity is that nuclear energy is free from the pollution that results from burning coal and oil. Even in the 1970s, when climate change was not such an obvious problem, this was seen as a huge advantage of nuclear power over other viable resources.

In August 1977, around the time that I was hitchhiking to Des Moines to watch *Star Wars*, President Jimmy Carter signed some of the first amendments to the Clean Air Act. The Carter amendments mandated that coal-fired power plants install scrubbers to clean up their sulfur and mercury emissions. The combination of rising environmental costs to produce electricity from coal and the advancement of nuclear energy clearly supported using less power from conventional supplies and using more from nuclear energy. Those in charge of energy policy felt as though they were addressing all of the needs of the nation. Others who were a little more aware of history and concerned about runaway technology were less convinced.

History was part of the equation. In the 1940s the United States deployed "atomic" weapons to defeat the Japanese, and soon thereafter President Harry Truman presented the idea of using nuclear energy as a peaceful application of this incredible technology. The promotion of nuclear energy would be an important symbol in the aftermath of World War II and in setting up an initial détente between the United States and the Soviet Union. Creating a peaceful application of the technology might, in fact, provide the leverage needed to limit the expansion of the Soviet Union into Europe and Asia. On August 1, 1946, President Truman created the Atomic Energy Commission (AEC) to oversee the conversion of nuclear power into what President Dwight D. Eisenhower would later dub the "peaceful atom." Unfortunately, the nuclear era would soon be defined by the notion that whoever held access to nuclear technology now dominated the geopolitical playing field.

The Nuclear Non-Proliferation Treaty (NPT), negotiated in the late 1960s and made effective in May 1970, set the context for the ongoing power brokering between countries that possessed nuclear technology and those

INSTRUMENT OF WAR

To understand both the potential and the limitations for nuclear power, we need to go further back in history. The history of nuclear power and its acceptance as a viable energy source is complicated by the fact that this technology was first developed as an instrument of war. As such, nuclear energy and nuclear weaponry have always been bedfellows.

In fact, the genesis of the search for nuclear power was the race toward marginal improvements on the battlefield in Europe during World War II. Early in the war it was reported that Hitler was working on a super-bomb whose power derived from splitting atoms and creating a massive chain reaction. On August 2, 1939, Albert Einstein wrote a warning letter to President Roosevelt. In it, he stated that the German government might be constructing "extremely powerful bombs of a new type" and urged the president to respond in kind. Einstein later said that sending this letter might have been the "greatest mistake" of his life.[175]

Two years later, one of Europe's leading scientists, Niels Bohr, fled to the United States via Britain after a secret meeting in Copenhagen with German scientist Werner Heisenberg. Both scientists were German-born contemporaries of Albert Einstein. Bohr, a baptized Lutheran whose mother was Jewish, was a prized physicist specializing in atomic

that did not. At the time, the logic behind the agreement seemed compelling in spite of intense political conflict between the two superpowers, the United States and the Soviet Union, including a near fatal exchange in 1962 over the presence of Soviet nuclear weapons in Cuba. Countries that signed and ratified the treaty agreed to forgo control over their own nuclear technology to produce nuclear weapons.

To oversee these agreements, the nuclear powers created the International Atomic Energy Agency (IAEA) to employ scientists and field experts to inspect nuclear operations in member countries. Member countries structure and quantum mechanics. He had taken on Werner Heisenberg as an apprentice in 1924.[176] Almost twenty years later, these two scientists ended up on opposite sides of the table after Heisenberg began working for the Nazis. Bohr's impression upon their meeting in Denmark heightened concern within the US scientific community that efforts in Berlin to develop a nuclear bomb were accelerating.

The fear of such a weapon drove US policy makers to initiate a secret effort called the Manhattan Project. The world's top scientists were sent to centers in Los Alamos, New Mexico, and Oak Ridge, Tennessee, to make sure that the United States and its allies achieved nuclear capability first.

We all know the outcome. Neither the United States nor Germany prevailed in its race to develop a nuclear weapon prior to the end of World War II in Europe. The curtain had already closed on the European theater before the United States developed its first nuclear bomb. By the time the United States was ready to deploy a nuclear weapon, it did so in the Pacific theater, leading to Japan's surrender.

The dropping of "the bomb" changed the nature of war forever. The global community entered a new era in which our world institutions needed to be geared toward avoiding a potential outbreak of war, because now international aggression might lead to the use of nuclear weapons and the annihilation of entire nations—even of humankind.

developing nuclear energy would have to report to the IAEA and to the Security Council of the United Nations. The system would work if *all* countries agreed to the terms of the NPT. However, the IAEA's right to inspection had no teeth in countries that were not members or that eventually elected to withdraw from the agreement. For example, India, Pakistan, and Israel—all of which have developed nuclear weapons—never signed the NPT. The agreement also gave other nations substantial "wiggle room." Nations like Iran, which signed the NPT, are in technical compliance as long as they have not assembled weapons with nuclear capability.

Simply put, the NPT is an international agreement to limit the spread of nuclear weapons, not to eliminate them.[177] One hundred sixty-eight countries are party to the agreement. Five countries—the United States, Russia, the United Kingdom, France, and China—are officially recognized as legitimate nuclear weapons states. These are the same countries that make up the permanent members of the United Nations National Security Council. By setting up the "club" and locking themselves in, these countries have created significant market control over the technology for both nuclear weapons and nuclear energy, their fuel, and their waste. But they have also failed to get all countries to agree not to develop nuclear weapons. Unfortunately, it takes only one country possessing nuclear weapons to threaten the foundation of the entire agreement.

The terms and history of the NPT, like all of the institutional relationships that exist between allies and trade partners to develop nuclear energy, are one more critical feature of business as usual. Operating within this scenario is part of the reason nuclear energy has not developed to become a more significant percentage of the global energy mix, especially in emerging markets. Both the lack of uranium as a resource and a reluctance to locate reprocessing plants in politically remote regions of the world limit the willingness of capital to follow.

There are 196 countries in the world. Thirty countries produce nuclear energy for electricity. Ten of these countries are believed to possess nuclear weapons. Four countries possess nuclear weapons but do not produce electricity from nuclear energy.[178] International pressure on Iran and North Korea seems to be working to contain nuclear ambitions, although the idea that Iran and North Korea will adapt the technology to develop weapons capability continually threatens the precarious balance in their respective regions. Moreover, the system could quickly unwind. For example, it was perhaps not surprising to hear, during their third debate in 2012, presidential candidate Mitt Romney and President Obama emphatically agreeing that for US and global security to be ensured, a nuclear Pakistan would have to remain a US ally under nearly any circumstance. Such agreement between competing presidential candidates reveals the delicate nature of the balance that has been struck.

THE CONTEST OF NUCLEAR PROLIFERATION

In 2001 an international conference was convened by the IAEA to discuss whether or not the presence of a civilian nuclear power program naturally led to the development and the proliferation of nuclear weapons. The experts were divided in spite of the fact that the evidence suggested a strong correlation.

For example, India started construction on its first nuclear power plant in 1962. The 320 megawatt (MW) Tarapur Nuclear Power Station began operation in 1969. In mid-May 1998, India, a nonsignatory of the NPT, publicly detonated a nuclear device, showing the global community what it had already suspected—namely, that India possessed nuclear weapons capability. The Clinton administration quickly announced that in response to India's actions, the United States would cut off aid to India, even though India was not a signatory of the NPT. Within three years and without any fanfare, however, international aid from the United States resumed to previous levels of funding.[179] India had become a member of the nuclear club without signing on to any international agreement or incurring any real political or economic cost.

The development of nuclear weapons capability also created a mini–arms race between Pakistan and India. Pakistan began operations of its first nuclear power station in 1972, employing services from Canada to create a 137 MW reactor. Pakistan joined India as a rogue member of the nuclear club on May 28, 1998, demonstrating its own nuclear weapons capability by conducting five nuclear tests, including blowing an entire mountain into ashes. Sanctions that had already been in place since the 1990 discovery of Pakistan's nuclear program were tightened slightly. Otherwise, this time no one even threatened to punish the offending state. On the contrary, by 2003 the United States began using Pakistan as an ally in its war against the Taliban-controlled Afghanistan and began aggressively supplying Pakistan with new military aid.[180]

Since the signing of the NPT, five "illegal nuclear weapons states" have been documented, and there are likely to be more in the future. Many of these nations are located along some of the world's most vulnerable political fault lines. Both Pakistan and India are now nuclear powers with active power plant operations and nuclear weapons capability. China's dirty little secret was that it was aiding Pakistan[181] for many years while operating under the auspices of being compliant with the NPT. Likewise, in spite of an international call to boycott the apartheid government, South Africa was receiving international assistance in developing nuclear weapons in the mid-1980s. South Africa's nuclear program shut down with the end of the apartheid government in 1993, and all documentation was destroyed.[182]

In the Middle East, Israel has adamantly denied possession of nuclear weapons, even though the contrary has been common knowledge for at least the past twenty-five years. Israel was exposed as a member of the nuclear club in 1986 by former nuclear technician Mordechai Vanunu in a *London Sunday Times* article. It is also a commonly held view that Israel was perhaps spurred to develop nuclear weapons in response to the formation of OPEC, which was a retaliatory measure against the West for its support of Israeli foreign policy in the 1973 Yom Kippur War. Today Iran, soon to complete the 1,000-megawatt Bushehr nuclear power plant with Russian support,[183] is another major source of nuclear tension in the region. Thus far, Iran has not been shown to have nuclear weapons. However, given the historical relationship between nuclear energy and nuclear weapons, Iran is likely to develop them in the future.

Among the world's concerns over nuclear proliferation, North Korea presents perhaps the most troublesome case. The country first announced its intention to withdraw from the NPT in 1993. Then in 2006 it announced a successful test of a nuclear explosive device.[184] Of all of the "illegal nuclear weapons states," North Korea may be the most likely to act irrationally, given its isolation both geographically and ideologically. North Korea's ongoing efforts to develop nuclear weapons creates tension with its neighbors, results in sanctions from the international community, and does nothing to spur domestic economic progress.

It is easy to see what the drivers are with regard to the nuclear option. Emerging countries like Iran see the development of nuclear energy and nuclear weapons as a status play, and members of the UN Security Council are not willing to unify and truly condemn these actions since they are in fact the purveyors of this technology in emerging markets. Still, international perception is that support of the nuclear industry is "good" for the industrialized nations sitting on the National Security Counsel of the United Nations, but "bad" for countries whose policies and administration are counter to European and US interests. The domestic perception is mixed, without a compelling case one way or another. The cultural divide remains wide.

For all the attention being paid to nuclear energy by policy makers and utility executives, and despite all of these emerging countries trying to obtain some sort of nuclear power parity, it may be a lot of fuss for no value. Because in the end, most nations recognize the power of nuclear "doomsday machines" and the madness of mutual assured destruction. Nations are starting to recognize that the "peaceful atom" may not be the panacea that Harry Truman had hoped for back in the late 1940s—at least, not without some kind of social and technological innovation.

THE NEXT MILLION YEARS AND THE POTENTIAL FOR BREEDER REACTORS

Back in 1953, at the height of the Cold War, Charles Galton Darwin, grandson of the revolutionary theorist Charles Darwin, wrote a short, thoughtful, and rather pessimistic book about the next million years of existence on the earth.[185] The book is interesting reading and still remains relevant today, largely because humans face many of the same issues now as we did then. If nothing else, *The Next Million Years* demonstrates how little the world outlook on energy has evolved over the past sixty years.

One reason for the younger Darwin's pessimism was his outlook on energy. He observed that the world was living on natural capital—fossil fuels. He maintained that within a few hundred years, that capital would be exhausted. He could see no easy replacement. He was aware of nuclear energy but correctly observed that uranium was a relatively scarce material and that reserves were roughly equivalent to those for fossil fuels. Although thorium, another potential source of nuclear power, was more abundant, it would not qualitatively change the situation. Nor was there any other resource on the horizon capable of maintaining humankind's large-scale energy needs. Moreover, Darwin dismissed fusion power as a pipe dream. He emphasized the need for advances in energy storage technology and looked wistfully at direct conversion of solar energy via the photoelectric effect—what we call "photovoltaic solar energy" today.

Some in the emerging nuclear power research establishment were well aware of Charles Galton Darwin's book, which presented them with a kind of existential challenge. Then one day in the late 1950s researchers rushed excitedly into the office of Alvin Weinberg, the director of the Oak Ridge National Laboratory.[186] These researchers had just finished some momentous calculations. They had found an answer to the younger Darwin's challenge: a fast breeder reactor. This theoretical reactor would not only convert fissile uranium-235 into energy (which is what "burner" reactors do), but also convert (or "breed") considerable U-238 into fissile plutonium, or thorium into fissile U-233. Instead of recovering perhaps 2 to 3 percent of the energy in uranium ore,[187] this "breeder" reactor would be able to recover 70 percent or more. This meant that much more energy could be derived from the same amount of ore, and that much-lower-grade ores could be used.

The calculation that had excited the ORNL researchers, however, was that in the extreme case you had a positive energy yield even when using common granite. "We can burn rocks," one of the researchers claimed. Instead of a resource roughly equivalent to fossil fuels in terms of future availability, they had discovered an almost inexhaustible resource. Nuclear energy, it seemed, could be the needed revolution in long-term energy supply.[188]

The perception that energy could be taken from such a common source as rocks gave the nuclear enterprise an almost messianic quality. After all, this was true alchemy. From that point on, the real objective in the nuclear research community—the Holy Grail, if you will—was to get a reactor with a high-breeding ratio into operation. Technologists viewed with certain distaste the use of the natural capital, high-grade uranium ores in "burner" reactors. There was a sense of urgency to move on from the wasteful first-generation technology of burners to the new breeder reactors, which would generate more fissile material than they consumed, essentially creating a never-ending supply of fuel.

At the time, there were a few technologies being considered for creating the new reactors. The liquid metal fast breeder reactor (LMFBR) was chosen early on. Other types of breeders, such as molten salt reactors (MSR) using thorium, were possible to construct, were more difficult to turn into nuclear weapons, and would create less waste. But those issues were not prominent in the 1950s and 1960s. Out of the many possibilities, the LMFBR was soon chosen, and every other option was almost completely ignored.[189]

The early experimental days were exciting for those in the field of nuclear energy. There was a "cowboy" element of heedlessness that, in retrospect, is stunning. The mess made of military waste disposal at the Hanford and Rocky Mountain Flats facilities are examples. Incredibly, one utility started building an LMFBR in the middle of Detroit in the 1960s, even before a proper demo had been made. Not surprisingly, the reactor was shut down after a near miss.[190] More amusing, if only because they were never built, were efforts to build an "atomic airplane" and even a nuclear-powered rocket (using tactical bombs to provide the initial propulsion). In this heady atmosphere, unsexy issues like the fuel cycle and waste disposal had a low priority for most scientists and industry engineers in the field.

In those days, nuclear power had a special mystique, in part because of the link with superweapons and the complexity and newness of the technology. Those working on nuclear energy even developed some characteristics associated with those of a "priesthood," with competing visions of whether or not these trailblazers were operating on the "dark side" of the Force. The elitism and condescension this bred toward enquiring minds in the public paved the way for many fiascos when people began to question the safety and viability of nuclear energy.

One of the first issues to be raised by the public was long-term waste disposal. The AEC had given this question little priority back in the early 1970s. The ORNL had recently begun tests in an abandoned salt mine in Lyons,

Kansas, to evaluate possible solutions. Deep salt deposits were believed to be a promising geological repository for the safe disposal of nuclear waste, and these tests were devised to see how materials behaved in this context. When the question of waste disposal was raised in Congress in the mid-1970s, the head of the AEC said that the solution had been found in the Lyons site. The technical people back in Oak Ridge were appalled that an experiment had suddenly been turned into a definitive solution. Reporters and representatives from various nongovernmental organizations rushed out to Lyons and raised technical questions regarding the long-term sustainability of the site. To this day, there is no functioning site for the long-term storage of civilian nuclear waste in Kansas or anywhere else. It is a reminder that unresolved issues remain in spite of continued hope or promise of a new technology.

The next issue raised by critics of nuclear energy was that of proliferation, as discussed earlier. This concern dated back to 1946 and was voiced by many of the makers of the first atomic bombs, as documented in the Acheson-Lilienthal Report: "The development of atomic energy for peaceful purposes and the development of atomic energy for bombs are in much of their course interchangeable and interdependent."[191] Yet the United States remained unwilling to heed the proliferation warnings by the founders of nuclear energy, with the exception of negotiating the NPT. For example, the AEC repeatedly proclaimed that the spent fuel from civilian nuclear energy reactors was too "dirty" to be used to make bombs. Yet in 1962 the US government proved that theory wrong with a successful underground test of a bomb made from reactor-grade plutonium.[192] This fact only came to light more than a decade later, when one of the weapons designers decided it was time that the public should know the truth and frontally contradicted the AEC's self-serving myth.

In the 1960s and 1970s the United States made some hasty decisions with regard to nuclear power technology that had long-term consequences. In 1972 the Clinch River Breeder Reactor, the United States' prototype LMFBR, was fraught with controversy, budget troubles, and technical problems. The most serious of these was the fracturing of the pressure vessel alloys under neutron bombardment, making the reactor ripe for a meltdown. Upon learning of these test results, the first reaction of the US House and Senate's Joint Committee for Atomic Energy was to refuse to make them public, fearing that they could alter the chronogram of the program. But ORNL's Weinberg, who was responsible for the tests, refused to go along. For this he lost his job.[193] Nevertheless, the Clinch River Breeder Reactor soon collapsed. The commercialization of the LMFBR died in the United States. Other countries, such as France, the Soviet Union, and Japan, constructed their own prototype LMFBRs[194] that met with limited success and really never made it beyond the prototype phase. These countries simply didn't have the resources to further the technology.

With the death of the LMFBR, the nuclear dream began to unravel, and this was even before any serious accidents had occurred with civilian reactors. For twenty years, the US scientific and technological elite had generally believed that nuclear power was the ultimate energy solution. However, the hubris of the nuclear program's administrative elite and their propensity for "quick fixes" and hiding inconvenient facts destroyed this consensus. By the mid-1970s the United States had become divided on the subject, and the nation has largely remained so ever since.

Then came the accidents, such as the fire at the Brown's Ferry nuclear power plant on the Tennessee River, near Athens, Alabama, in 1975. No one mentions Brown's Ferry today because in the end there was no radioactive release. But this event was very important because it showed how things could go strangely wrong (the much-feared "common mode failure") due to a simple incident. In this case, a plant maintenance worker's candle ignited supposedly fireproof insulation and nearly caused a nuclear meltdown. It was a near-fatal miss, but the operators were superbly trained and extremely courageous. The control room was full of heavy smoke and many of the controls didn't work, but the operators stayed at their posts and were able to improvise and bring the temperatures down to manageable levels.[195] The Brown's Ferry incident was a nuclear Apollo 13. The most obvious contrasts, of course, are the operational lapses that caused Pennsylvania's Three Mile Island accident in 1979, the 1986 Chernobyl disaster in Ukraine, and the 2011 earthquake that led to the meltdown at Fukushima in Japan, all of which did get media publicity. For nuclear power plant operators, 99.9 percent of the time everything is boring and routine—and then you have a moment of pure panic. For much of the public, however, these disasters have created a view that the original concerns over the safety of nuclear power were well grounded.

Innovations such as the breeder reactor held promise for the nuclear energy industry, and they still do. Breeder reactors can mitigate much of the proliferation threat, but this is now largely a missed point. The question is, how can the global community return to testing this technology and reignite its potential? Is the way to do it through government support, guarantees, and financing—that is, through business as usual? Or is there a different way that will let the markets give their support?

THE ENDURING PROMISE OF NUCLEAR ENERGY

The promise of nuclear energy lives on in many who believe it still holds enormous potential to not only meet our energy requirements but also be the kind of energy the global community needs in order to address climate change. We at Project Butterfly say the issue isn't really dead—it's just "*Star Trek* dead." Fans of the cult series will recognize the trademark phrase of Dr. Leonard H. "Bones" McCoy: "He's dead, Jim." Yet inevitably, by the end of the episode, the "dead" individual in question returns to life.

One of the reasons nuclear energy continues to have a foothold today, even among leading environmentalists, is that it continues to offer the promise of reducing the global carbon footprint. The concern over reducing carbon did not become part of the common culture until the early 1990s, as we discussed in chapter 3. The idea of using nuclear energy to meet our energy needs arose most recently in 1997, at that year's Kyoto Conference of the Parties. In addition to setting carbon caps under the Kyoto Protocol, the parties to the UNFCCC agreed to undertake promotion, research, and development to increase "the use of new and renewable forms of energy, of carbon dioxide sequestration technologies, and of advanced and innovative environmentally sound technologies."[196] Note that nuclear energy was not specifically mentioned in the language of the agreement. Nor was it excluded. By and large, most climate negotiators agreed that nuclear energy was hamstrung because of its environmental and security risks. In fact, several NGOs and the Alliance of Small Island States (AOSIS) actively worked to ban nuclear energy from the agreement. But rather than deliberately disavowing nuclear energy, negotiators felt that it was politically correct to remain silent on the application of nuclear energy and to leave open the possibility for innovation. The threat of climate change was too great to leave any option off the table.

Proponents of nuclear energy, such as the IAEA, saw the passage of the Kyoto Protocol as a historic opportunity to advance nuclear energy.[197] The emerging position within the IAEA in the mid-1990s was that nuclear power plants would provide an abundant and viable clean resource, capable of meeting projected demand for new power. To meet the "viable" requirement, the clean development mechanism clause of the Kyoto Protocol called for alternatives to replace business-as-usual technology. The nuclear industry and the IAEA viewed the development of new coal power plants in China, at the rate of up to one per week, as the business-as-usual case, arguing that replacing coal with nuclear energy would mitigate massive quantities of GHG emissions and provide a new business case that supported cleaner nuclear power as an energy source.

Likewise, the marketplace started to respond to international and federal support for nuclear power beyond the clean aspects to meet the conditions of Kyoto, by proposing smaller and more manageable power plants, or "standard" plants, where safety is enhanced.[198] These proposals aimed for small-scale, distributed nuclear power plants that suppliers would fold into a set of clean energy solutions. Smaller-scale projects could shorten construction timetables, reduce capital outlays, and more reasonably be assembled by electric utilities. These plants, which would be called "small modular nuclear reactors" or "mini-nuclear reactors" to differentiate them from the nuclear fleet that was built in the 1970s, would make it easier for adequate govern-ment guarantees to underwrite the risk. Passive safety measures would also be installed, which would mean that even if all power for control were lost, the reactor would not experience a meltdown. Such conceptual designs have existed for some time, but the move toward clean energy has meant the pos-sibility of using a standard set of drawings to implement such technology.

Russia has been a leader in the early adoption of small-scale nuclear power plants. The state nuclear energy giant, Rosatom, is currently building a floating nuclear power station in the St. Petersburg shipyard. The approach builds upon the success of proven, existing submarine designs and large, nuclear-powered aircraft carriers. This power station is headed for the Arctic region, where currently there is little to no power infrastructure, and is the first of five such power plants scheduled.[199] By virtue of their ability to float, these plants are not nearly as vulnerable to earthquakes and other land-based disasters. These floating power plants could also be used to provide power to large coastal and river-based cities that are hungry for electricity.

Successful innovation for nuclear energy is possible, although certainly there are substantial obstacles to overcome. But that is the benefit of innova-tion: It is invention by necessity. The question is, what will spur the industry to make nuclear energy part of the new business case? What will revive it from "*Star Trek* dead" to "alive and well"?

A MILLION TIMES MORE

While far from perfect, nuclear energy can provide a supply of energy that meets any test or analysis an energy expert may wish to impose, except per-haps for its life-cycle cost. Nuclear energy is a million times more energy intensive than its nearest competitor. It is also a near-zero GHG emitter, with a carbon footprint roughly equivalent to that of wind power and as low as 0.005 percent of conventional coal.[200] Further, less than 1 percent of these carbon emissions occur during plant operation; instead they occur during the mining and enriching of uranium, the fabrication of the power plant, and the deconstruction required to decommission plants. These statements are clear and undeniable truths that make nuclear energy worthy of consideration as a technology to mitigate climate change. If reducing GHG emissions below current levels, or even just keeping CO_2 concentration levels below 550 ppm, is the only concern of the environmental steward, then nuclear power should be considered a viable technological solution. For now, nuclear energy remains a component of business as usual, but as we shall soon see, it could be a significant part of a new business case.

KEY OBSERVATIONS

The key observations we can make about nuclear energy and its role in defining business as usual are as follows:

» Nuclear energy exists in a business-as-usual scenario so long as its fuel source is dependent on uranium. Based on a once-through calculation, the world has proven uranium reserves to meet existing demand for only seventy years.

» Existing nuclear energy capacity will remain at roughly 400 GW under both the business-as-usual scenario and the new business case—unless the market can innovate a new solution that addresses critical issues such as the storage of waste, severe consequences from unexpected accidents, and the proliferation of nuclear weapons.

» The "small is beautiful" concept of energy practices may be true for nuclear energy, too. In order for nuclear energy to be innovative, it must address society's needs for safety and economic prosperity.

PART III

. . .

THE NEW BUSINESS CASE

Render unto Caesar the things
which are Caesar's, and unto God
the things that are God's.
—Matthew 22:21

CHAPTER 8

FISHING AT A NUCLEAR POWER PLANT:
CREATING A SUSTAINABILITY MODEL

In the spring of 2002 my ten-year-old son, Seann, and I had been looking forward for weeks to a fishing trip on the Chesapeake Bay in Maryland with my father and brother-in-law. It was still dark when we left on the morning of our trip, and it began to rain as we pushed the boat away from the dock. As we headed south, the sky began to lighten. I could see a large structure emerging directly ahead of us. My eyeglasses were covered in raindrops, so it was difficult to make out what it was. I looked over at Seann and saw the alarm on his face.

Our boat was headed straight for a power plant. A *nuclear* power plant.

What are we doing here? I thought. I could see the large cooling tower and wondered if I could trust my eyes. I looked back at our fishing guide. He had the engine at full throttle. His eyes were focused straight ahead as we advanced toward this huge fortress.

It had been just a matter of months since 9/11. I could see that this nuclear power plant was heavily guarded by armed security. I was worried about getting too close. I thought, *If I were the head of security at a nuclear power plant, I would be leery of a strange boat, disguised as a fishing expedition, headed full throttle toward me.*

Eventually, the water became calmer and the pounding of the waves beneath slipped into silence. Only a few hundred feet from shore, the guide slowed the boat to a full stop. Then, in a flurry of activity, he immediately pulled out our rods and reels in preparation for fishing. I decided to ask him if this was indeed our final destination.

"Yes," he said. "This is the best fishing spot on the bay. The fish are attracted to the hot water coming off the cooling tower."[201]

Seann and I hadn't spoken a word to each other, but I knew exactly what he was thinking by the look of horror on his face.

The Chesapeake Bay had always been a special place for both of us, full of nature and places to explore. Seann and I had sailed on the Chesapeake with his grandfather several times before, visiting tucked-away inlets full of flora and fauna and ports of call rich with history and local cuisine. More recently we had been fly-fishing in the clear mountain streams of Colorado, and we had shared a vision of fishing on the Chesapeake Bay, near some remote peninsula, watching geese land elegantly in the water surrounding us. Instead here we were fishing in front of a nuclear power plant!

Our expectations were based on the fact that the Chesapeake Bay— formed by glaciers more than 12,000 years ago—is one of the great natural treasures of the United States. The Chesapeake Bay is the largest estuary in North America and the third largest in the world, today serving as a drainage basin for six states. The tributaries for the bay stretch from the state of New York to Norfolk, Virginia, where they feed directly into the Atlantic Ocean. The land from which water drains into the bay measures 64,000 square miles, including 11,000 miles of tidal shoreline. There are hundreds of peninsulas in the Chesapeake, and geese fly up and down the bay at nearly all times of year.

Fishing in a boat in front of a nuclear power plant shattered our idyllic vision of this vast natural resource. The fishing guide's claim that the nuclear power plant's hot water runoff provided the best fishing in the Chesapeake made me wonder about the health of the bay. I was aware that the health of the Chesapeake Bay, which had been overfished in the past, rested delicately in the balance. I knew it wasn't thriving as it had a hundred years ago. But I had thought that just because of its sheer size, the Chesapeake would be able to endure higher levels of toxicity and still exhibit strong vital signs. *The bay isn't dying*, I thought. *Is it?*

Soon after that trip, I made an effort to learn more about the Chesapeake Bay. I discovered that forty years ago the health of the Chesapeake Bay looked much more dire, when more than seventeen million people were tapping its vital resources, creating severe consequences. Large areas of the Chesapeake Bay's waters had been depleted of sufficient oxygen to sustain marine life. Massive algae blooms had developed, caused by municipal discharges, agricultural runoff, and airborne toxins from Midwestern power plants. The algae blooms prevented sunlight from reaching the bottom of the bay. The lack of sunlight deoxygenated the water, making it difficult for the indigenous biodiversity to survive. Looking back, two hundred years ago the floor of the Chesapeake Bay had been teeming with clams and oysters that served as a natural cleaning mechanism for the waters. But by the 1970s, the Chesapeake Bay had turned into an environmental wasteland. The Chesapeake Bay had been one of the first places in the world to be identified as a marine dead zone.

Yet here we were fishing on that very same bay—in front of a nuclear power plant. The waters were still full of fish. The conditions of the bay had actually improved since the 1970s. I wanted to know why.

SAVING THE BAY

What I found out is that the Chesapeake Bay is a shining example of environmental stewardship. In the mid-1960s, a few farsighted individuals had gotten together to create the Chesapeake Bay Foundation (CBF) in response to growing concern over the health of the waters known as the Chesapeake Bay. These individuals wanted to provide what they felt had been missing for decades: a united defense of this natural treasure against an array of faceless forces that were killing it.[202] They positioned themselves to fight back and to wage a battle against strong antienvironmentalist sentiments embodied in nearly every conversation about the Chesapeake Bay. These sentiments had previously stymied any efforts to preserve the vast natural resources of the bay. The founders of CBF wanted to change this discourse. They wanted to put an end to the causal loop that had led to the bay's devastation, by exposing the dysfunctional relationship between the economic benefits of the bay and the environmental conditions critical to its health. They wanted to show that a different relationship was possible.

The original supporters of CBF saw the problem as having started many years before. They saw as the source of the problem a failure to anticipate and adequately plan for the impact of widespread urban sprawl. Specifically, few urban planners had realized the impact watershed deforestation would have on the health of the tributaries that served to oxygenate the waters and to keep critical vegetation alive. The primary culprits were excess nitrogen and phosphorus in the water caused by motor vehicles, municipal discharges coming from Midwestern power plants, overtaxed sewage treatment plants, and runoff from poor agricultural practices. All these causes were intensified by the increase in population that resulted from inadequate planning.

High levels of nitrogen and phosphorous were destroying the natural habitat of the bay's plant and fish life.[203] By addressing the initial cause of the problem, the original supporters of CBF saw a way of reversing the damage and restoring the Chesapeake Bay's health even after decades and decades of urban development and population growth. They began calling on their community and, in particular, on local businesses for greater sensitivity to the health of the Chesapeake Bay and for better urban planning.

As you can imagine, CBF quickly found itself surrounded in controversy. CBF supporters were criticized for interfering with many of the industries that depended on open access to the Chesapeake's rich resources. The organization responded to the criticism by launching an outreach program that would take the issue to the impacted citizenry, including local business leaders, rather than fighting the activated industries directly. Supporters of CBF printed and sold bumper stickers with the slogan *Save the Bay* as a way to build a movement and raise cash.

Opponents of CBF responded in kind by buying *Pave the Bay* bumper stickers that novelty stores were quick to provide. The opposition saw this as a way to push back on environmental efforts to use private or public funds for restoration work. The situation quickly became polarized, but CBF's leadership stayed focused on providing good science and making sure that the residents surrounding the Chesapeake were informed about the health and condition of the bay's waters and the consequences of increased pollution. CBF's leaders and spokespeople also reached out to build important alliances with those in management of the key industries that depended on the vitality of the bay for survival. Their focus was to show local businesses how efforts to protect the threatened bay would ultimately improve their bottom line. By asking businesses for support, the leaders of CBF were asking industry to participate in the solution.

Over the next four decades, CBF raised tens of millions of dollars for environmental cleanup and monitoring of the bay's ecological health. Interestingly, while most of the funding for CBF comes from its large membership base, financial support has also come from some of the wealthiest families in the United States and from some of the largest industrialists in the area. Stewardship of the Chesapeake Bay has been recast as a way to invest in the social capital of the very communities that the bay supports. Forty-odd years after its founding, CBF now has more than 200,000 members and supports more than 150 full-time employees. Its work has led to federal and state initiatives that in turn have strengthened fisheries management. Recreational fishing is now regulated (allowing the fishing industry to survive and, in some cases, thrive) by an agency that also restricts runoff by imposing fines for pollution.

Maryland governor Martin O'Malley spoke about the continued need for action at a November 2008 news conference:

> Historically, the bay has been one of the most productive estuaries on the earth that has provided a tremendous habitat for fish, wildlife, as well as unparalleled economic and recreational opportunity. However, our generation has also seen a big decline in the health of the bay, and of the rivers and streams that flow into it. Why? For many reasons, all of them having to do with human activity on the land around it . . . It is now our moral imperative to chart a new course for our bay.[204]

Saving the Chesapeake Bay has, in fact, become fashionable. Financial support of CBF is a way for industries to show support for the communities that are vital to their economic health. As a consequence, CBF is no longer surrounded in the same controversy. The Chesapeake Bay Foundation is now a respected community leader and has a seat at the table at nearly any substantive discussion that involves urban planning and the Chesapeake Bay.

CREATING A SUSTAINABILITY MODEL

The Project Butterfly team believes that the CBF story is one of the best examples of environmental stewardship in US (if not world) history. It is certainly not the world's only story of environmental stewardship. However, this particular story provides the basis for designing a workable "sustainability model"—a plan for what is needed if the global society is to address climate change.

The Project Butterfly team has reached this point of view because the approach of CBF over the course of its lifetime has been to foster better and more effective regulations by monitoring toxicity, species populations, diversity, and other indicators of health. These measurements are tangible and they have largely been successful in shaping the views of policy makers and other community leaders by building trust within their community and by opening and enriching the dialogue regarding the health of the waters of the bay. The trust CBF engendered was not only to educate the community but also to defend it when necessary by being its watchdog.

In December 2010, CBF was instrumental in reaching a landmark settlement with the Environmental Protection Agency to enforce limitations on nitrogen and phosphorous. The settlement called for specific pollution reductions that would allow for a cap and trade system of both nitrogen and phosphorus in the event reductions were not met by conventional mitigation efforts. The cap and trade system is similar in structure to the one proposed under the 1990 Clean Air Act amendments and the 1997 Kyoto Protocol (as discussed in chapter 3). As state and federal authorities issue new standards and regulations, CBF has acted as a watchdog by measuring the resulting improvements in accordance to the established indexes.

Specifically, the 2010 EPA settlement with CBF called for a total maximum daily load (TMDL) requirement that determines the pollution caps. Under the 1972 Clean Water Act the water quality standards for all waterways in the United States require that the water must be both fishable and swimmable. The TMDL is calculated based on meeting these minimum standards. Under the terms of the settlement, the EPA and CBF work together to evaluate whether or not states adjacent to the Chesapeake Bay are living up to their requirements under the Clean Water Act. The EPA is then responsible for enforcing the regulations, while CBF acts as the watchdog to preserve a national treasure. Although the arrangement is controversial, supporters of CBF in the past have put a value on the bay by valuing the local commerce. They have estimated that the Chesapeake Bay as a national treasure may be worth more than $1 trillion.[205]

In making such a claim about the value of the Chesapeake, supporters of CBF are suggesting that investments in upgrades to wastewater treatment, improvements in storm water infrastructure, and the implementation of agricultural conservation practices are not simply costs required to save a species of fish or to make it possible for us to swim in the bay. Rather, the supporters of CBF have made the radical argument that such investments directly create local jobs and contribute to urban and rural planning that is fundamental to the creation and preservation of financial value and wealth. This type of planning creates a multiplier effect throughout the regional economy, including preserving a natural reservoir that can regenerate and support the businesses and homes that rely on the resources of the Chesapeake Bay. The struggle between the health of the bay and the commerce that surrounds it are analogous to the seeming division between Caesar and God as quoted from Matthew 22:21 at the beginning of this chapter. The CBF successfully positioned this ecosystem as an arrangement that satisfies both in tandem. Industry gets the financial support it needs, while the environment secures its future.

One project under way that began in 2012 uses a $400 million thermal hydrolysis digester to clean up solid waste near the Washington, DC, waterways that feed into the Chesapeake Bay. The digester will take methane from waste and burn it to generate 13 megawatts of electricity.[206] The new waste-to-energy plant is an example of how such an investment can simultaneously restore waterway health and promote economic prosperity in the region. In other words, the investment in a waste-to-energy plant reverses the negative impact on water toxicity from increased urbanization, thus positively impacting the sustainability of the Chesapeake Bay.

By valuing the commerce sustained by the natural reservoir of the Chesapeake Bay, the supporters of CBF have ensured that the federal, state, and local parks along large swaths of pristine shorelines will be protected. They have also ensured the continuation of federal programs to preserve underwater sanctuaries that restrict oystering on certain critical bay bottoms. As a result, the businesses that drive the local economy have become much more sensitive to the need for urban planning and for minimizing the sources of pollution of the bay's waters. Moreover, businesses have developed a sense of ownership over the environmental efforts to preserve the Chesapeake as a national treasure and as a vital reservoir on which the community depends.

Looking at the big picture, this increased sensitivity and sense of ownership by businesses (both small and industrial-level) provides a sustainability model that can be exported to the climate change issue. The lesson is that while the initial reaction from industry may be a surge of denial and protest, over time it is possible for the environmental steward to engage business as part of the solution. Just like CBF, the steward that evolves to address climate change will have an equal and respected seat at the table as all the stakeholders review our shared natural resources and plan for their use.

Project Butterfly is making the case that CBF provides a replicable model that can serve global sustainability. CBF has accomplished an extraordinary task because of its fundamental approach of engaging business participation in a shared solution and of looking at the health of the Chesapeake Bay from a financial perspective. CBF makes the case for the preservation of the bay a pragmatic response rather than a nostalgic or ideological one. CBF supporters have been successful because they have positioned themselves not to be regulators but to be the watchdog of the regulators. They have sought to be a well-funded, nongovernmental steward in the form of a foundation that educates the public and takes legal action if necessary.

At the heart of the organization is a group of individuals concerned with both environmental preservation and asset valuation. CBF is not a research institute, even though it supports others that conduct research. It is not a political organization, even though its leaders are familiar with the workings of government and politics. CBF is an established and respected fixture as well as an effective watchdog for the preservation of the Chesapeake Bay— and an example to those of us who seek a new business case for addressing climate change and energy resource depletion.

THE TRAGEDY OF THE COMMONS

The global community needs a similar foundation or group of foundations to preserve the earth's atmosphere and oceans. Dozens upon dozens of organizations are working to address climate change, and some are our most effective nonprofit and environmental organizations in the world. These include large, well-funded nonprofits such as the Sierra Club Foundation and the World Resource Institute. However, CBF serves as an outstanding example because it has effectively navigated the full cycle of preserving a natural resource, from initial advocacy to environmental success. This accomplishment is a challenge to those organizations that have just started the journey to address climate change.

To scale up the CBF model and apply it to our global energy system, all we need to do is apply one of the oldest metaphors in environmental literature for looking at the preservation of any natural reservoir. It is the concept of a "commons." The term *commons* was historically used to define tracts of grazing land that were open to the public, but which were enclosed for regulated use to prevent overgrazing. In 1968 ecologist Garrett Hardin expanded on this concept when he defined the "tragedy of the commons" in an article in the influential journal *Science*.[207] By Hardin's definition, the tragedy arises when multiple individuals, each acting independently and in self-interest, inevitably deplete a limited shared resource. The tragedy of the commons occurs because the individual will continue to add cattle from his own herd to graze the commons, even knowing that the commons will be collectively overgrazed. The logic for such an outcome is based in game theory: that the individual will receive all the benefits from adding cattle but will share equally with others in the cost of overgrazing.

While Hardin's theory and the metaphor of the commons have some drawbacks as an effective model for the global energy system, the concept of a commons outlines three conditions that still suggest a present-day path that could help the world avoid catastrophic climate change.

First, more than one person or entity must own whatever is held in common for it to actually be a commons. When we look at a plot of land, it can be easy to define who the owner is by examination of a title. When we look at the atmosphere or the oceans, however, it becomes more difficult to define ownership. This is where agreements regarding the use of natural resources (such as the Kyoto Protocol or the settlement agreement between CBF and the EPA to establish maximum daily loads) become essential, because governments must coordinate and cooperate to define the boundaries of ownership.

Second, whatever is held in the commons must be enclosed. In the case of a town commons, building a fence creates the enclosure. Nevertheless, an enclosure is in effect nothing more than an agreement regarding the allocation of the use of the resource. A physical barrier, such as a fence, might need to be installed, but it is there only to enforce the underlying agreement that forms the enclosure. However, with harder-to-pinpoint elements such as the oceans or the atmosphere, enforceable agreements that are ratified by all parties to manage the allocation of use must take the place of fences.

Third, a potential for both tragedy and opportunity must exist. The tragedy for the traditional commons is the loss of suitable grazing land, which diminishes the ability to sustain a herd of cattle to provide meat or dairy for the community. The opportunity is that through enclosing the commons, it is possible to maximize the value of the shared property. Without the potential for tragedy—be it the depletion of the grazing land or of the natural resources of our entire planet—there will be little to no incentive to form agreements.

CBF saw the Chesapeake Bay as a shared commons. In essence the foundation took ownership of the waters of the bay on behalf of the greater community. The watersheds set the boundaries of the enclosure. The issue of municipal discharges and agricultural runoff were then cast as issues of encroachment. The twin potential of tragedy and opportunity was therefore embodied as the loss of—or the creation of value from—the commerce that is naturally supported by the resources of the Chesapeake Bay.

Can the energy industry follow CBF's example and view our shared resources—the atmosphere, oceans, and forests—as a commons that needs to be saved from depletion?

THE ROLE OF THE ENVIRONMENTAL STEWARD

If we apply the concept of the commons to climate change, the earth's oceans and atmosphere offer a tricky situation because they are not actually held *in common*. These natural resources are examples of that which is neither owned nor enclosed. They simply exist in nature. They are certainly subject to laws or claims that protect national rights—principles such as "US airspace," which sets restrictions regarding the flight paths of foreign and domestic air travel. However, if we are evaluating the extent to which the earth's oceans and shared atmosphere are subject to laws and claims regarding the right to pollute, we must acknowledge that they are neither held in commons nor privately held. They can be viewed instead as *potential real estate*.

The reason the atmosphere and oceans exist as only *potential real estate* is that they lack one or more of the three conditions inherent to the concept of the commons. These resources certainly face potential tragedy and opportunity (the third condition), a point that should be well established at this juncture of our discussion. The challenge lies in the first two conditions. No one owns the atmosphere or the oceans, nor are they adequately "enclosed" by any agreement to protest the pollution that is being stored in them. As a consequence, it is possible for nations—and even individual economists—to view these extremely vital resources as *free goods* that are practically limitless in their ability to regenerate. In the past, considering these resources as free goods may have been a safe assumption. But the global community is quickly finding out that such an assumption certainly isn't safe any longer. Especially if you are in need of clean air to breathe and clean water to drink.

As one looks at climate change from a financial perspective (as CBF has looked at the Chesapeake Bay), a useful assessment begins to form. The Project Butterfly team believes that the source of the challenge is the lack of clear ownership of the earth's *natural reservoirs* and the lack of anyone's willingness to serve as their watchdog. Because of this, I would like to introduce a new term that adapts the traditional meaning of the *tragedy of the commons* to our current circumstances regarding our atmosphere and oceans. The air and the sea are not part of a commons because they fail to meet the ownership condition. Therefore, their challenges should not be equated to a tragedy of a commons but rather to the "tragedy of the free resource."

Times have clearly changed. When I was a child, and even when I took my first college class in economics, the forests, oceans, and atmosphere were typically thought of as endless resources with no limit to their ability to provide for the needs of the human population. Even though we have evolved as a species in many ways, the human effect on these resources has intensified and our attitude has struggled to catch up. In preindustrial times it might have been acceptable for humanity to litter the oceans or chop down forests to provide fuel, because these resources could absorb such use. However, modern global society can no longer pretend that the size of the human footprint remains as small as it was. What once existed in nature and was considered free must now be "enclosed," because the earth's global resources produce value and are limited in their capacity to adequately rejuvenate. In fact, the Project Butterfly team has concluded that not only do we need to enclose our limited atmosphere, oceans, and forests into a commons, but we must consider them to be no longer free and instead, *inherently invaluable.*

The UNFCCC and the Kyoto Protocol were both efforts to, in effect, provide a social agreement about the use of our atmosphere and oceans to store the world's carbon emissions. Equally, the United Nations Convention on the Law of the Sea has sought to reach agreement over the use of the earth's oceans including the assignment of a cost for carbon emissions. The same principle applies if a carbon tax is imposed on industry by a city, state, or federal government. The imposition of a tax would necessarily constitute a social agreement.

Consider the following: The US Constitution is a social agreement of sorts between citizens and the nation. It authorizes government to impose taxes and to make expenditures in order to take care of the greater common good. For example, one of the first taxes imposed under the authority of the Constitution was an excise tax on the manufacturing and sale of whiskey. Other use taxes have been established to cover the cost of building or maintaining roads and bridges. National parks owned by the federal government often charge an entry fee so they can continue to preserve and protect public land. The same potential exists for a use tax on the extraction of carbon-based fuels. Such a tax makes sense if we consider the full fate and transport of these natural resources (following the chain of extraction, transport, and use) as they are transferred into the market. Such a tax would naturally fit into the national authority granted by the US Constitution and would likely fit into the constitutional makeup of most other nations.

Nations that have such constitutional authority also likely have the ability to form new social agreements between nations over global natural resource use. These are the kinds of social agreements that are necessary for us as humans to be good stewards over our shared atmosphere, oceans, and forests. It is the absence of such agreements that is the source of the problem and that makes climate change such a challenge, just as the source of the problem for the Chesapeake Bay was the failure to anticipate the impact of urban sprawl. Demanding stewardship and insisting that someone take ownership of our natural reservoirs is the pathway forward.

The radical innovation used by a small group of concerned citizens to protect the Chesapeake Bay was to place the bay—a natural reservoir—into a commons scenario, simply by declaring themselves stewards. They made a commitment to serve as its watchdog. In doing so, CBF *took ownership* over the reservoir (on behalf of the citizenry). It set the conditions for enclosing the bay by being willing to fight for it and by demanding a new agreement regarding the allocation of its use. It was a revolutionary act within the bounds of law. Over time, the strategy worked. As the watchdog responsible for the health of the bay, CBF has continued to ensure that the EPA's feet are held to the fire. Moreover, the relationship between the regulator and the watchdog is not necessarily contentious and can actually be welcomed by the enforcement agency. Politics can sometimes limit regulatory enforcement, and watchdogs can balance out entrenchment and inaction.

The success of CBF highlights the similarities and contrasts related to the use of our global natural resources. As a global community, we find ourselves in desperate need of an effective environmental steward with the credibility to change the global game of energy and resource use. As we look at our energy resources, the assumption of rights and ownership will be critical in any effort to shift the global energy mix.

THE LIMITS OF NATURAL CAPITAL

Natural capital is the other term, similar to the *commons*, that gets bandied about in relation to the use and management of our global resources. It is a useful term as we continue in search of a sustainability model that can be applied to the world's energy resources.

In the 1970s, German-born E. F. Schumacher (whom I mentioned in chapter 5) borrowed the concept of natural capital from Charles Galton Darwin (whom I discussed in chapter 7). Dalton had used the term to describe resource depletion in his book *The Next Million Years*. Schumacher argued that the global community must preserve its natural capital if we are to find a sustainable solution to our consumption of limited resources. He used the term *natural capital* to describe limited and valuable natural resources, such as coal and oil, that could not be replaced or substituted by other forms of energy. Schumacher felt that such a distinction was critical. He wanted to make a fundamental and crucial observation regarding the energy crisis facing the world at that time. In his argument, he emphasized the importance of the coal industry in the United Kingdom as a unique resource to that nation's economy. He argued that the liberal burning of this natural capital was equivalent to using your savings account to buy the staples for everyday life. Moreover, if you think you are deriving revenue from the burning of coal and oil, Schumacher said, you are grossly mistaken. You are confusing spending your savings account with generating an income!

Schumacher's work was revolutionary at the time. His use of the term *natural capital* created a movement to look for alternative energy supplies such as wind and solar energy. In fact, he referred to wind and solar as "income fuels" because they did not deplete the earth's natural capital as burning coal and oil did. His work also influenced the growth of organic farming, which minimizes the use of fertilizers and oil-based pesticides to preserve the regenerative qualities of the earth's limited supply of soil. Schumacher's revolutionary theories were embodied in the very title of his book, *Small Is Beautiful*.[208]

The concept of calling oil and coal "natural capital" and renewable energy sources such as solar power "income fuels," however, is difficult to extend into a workable sustainability model. The oil and gas industries have already incorporated the concept of depletion as a cost to the supplier in their use of resource management accounting. Amory Lovins (also mentioned in chapter 5), L. Hunter Lovins, and Paul Hawken attempted to extend the metaphor of natural capital into a sustainability model in their book *Natural Capitalism*, published in 2000, by criticizing industry practice. They used the term *natural capital* as a replacement for Garrett Hardin's term *commons*, defining it as containing both renewable and nonrenewable resources that needed to be preserved in order to maintain their economic value.[209] By going down this path, the Lovinses and Hawken discarded the benefit of Schumacher's definition of *natural capital,* because the use of renewable energy as an income fuel was now incorporated into their definition of *natural capital.* Nevertheless, the Lovinses and Hawken set the stage theoretically for working to preserve the earth's natural capital, which allows us to sustain our economic well-being.

Allow me to offer an alternative set of distinctions that, I believe, builds a bridge between the original work by Schumacher and the later work by the Lovinses and Hawken. These distinctions can help us as we build a workable model to create global sustainability—a theoretical model that will unfold throughout the rest of this book. This theoretical model will form what we call the Project Butterfly Sustainability Model. This model makes two distinctions: The first distinction is between *natural capital* and *natural reservoirs.* The second is between *renewable resources* and *finite resources.*

The basic concept of the Project Butterfly Sustainability Model is fairly straightforward. All things that come from nature spring from our "natural reservoirs"—sources that exist within nature. And yet some of these sources ("renewable resources") offer capital, while some ("finite resources") offer only the "savings account" from which we can withdraw only by paying the ultimate penalty of eventual depletion. The burning of finite resources to generate electricity or to fuel automobiles is essentially using a resource that can never be replaced or substituted once it is used up. Industry and government can tap both renewable resources (such as wind and solar rays) and finite resources (such as coal and oil) from within our natural reservoirs to create actual capital (things that are beyond nature and now exist in the human world).

These more specific terms allow us to see the phenomenon that Schumacher tried to illuminate in his discussion of natural capital—namely, that the burning of finite resources is depleting, while the use of renewable resources is wealth creating. Similarly, making the distinction that natural reservoirs are composed of both finite and renewable resources allows us to capture the plea made by the Lovinses and Hawken: to manage both finite and renewable resources efficiently in order to avoid permanent depletion and destruction of economic value.

It is perhaps an exaggeration to say that the burning of coal or oil is like a teenager spending his or her inheritance rather than investing it to produce income. But it is no exaggeration to say that once you burn a clump of coal, it cannot be burned again. Similarly, the analogy of the teenager allows us to see that using coal and oil to generate electricity or to fuel transportation today is an investment into the future that will eventually lead to the necessity for a replacement or a substitution.

To fully illustrate my point, let's consider another analogy: Burning oil to drive a car is like washing your socks in a single malt scotch. There are far better uses for both oil and scotch. Moreover, to make matters worse, oil is finite, so it can fuel your car only so far down the road. Good scotch is of limited supply, but the making of it is not limited, which (fortunately) renders it a renewable resource.

If you have followed the logic of my definition, you will begin to see the point: that by failing to establish ownership and to enclose shared natural reservoirs via an international agreement, we have created a market failure that looks a lot like the tragedy of the commons outlined by Hardin and his progeny. The tragedy is the failure of the global economic system both to eliminate the growth of CO_2 beyond tolerable limits and to create substitutes that will mitigate the finite natural resource depletion that is driving down net energy output.

If the global society is unwilling to impose a price on the suppliers of fossil fuels—a price that would force industry to internalize the cost of pollution or the cost of depletion—then conditions are ripe for market failure. In the world of economics, this is what is commonly referred to as *internalizing the externalities of production*. *Externalities* are real costs that are borne by society and are not shared between the supplier and user—costs that both nobody and everybody end up paying. In the tragedy of the commons scenario, this is represented by the herder who adds cows to the commons and gains all the benefit but shares in only a fraction of the cost. Simply put, the burning of carbon creates an externality because it depletes our natural resources beyond their regenerative powers and contributes to the buildup of GHGs, a result that has tangible costs that must be mitigated—costs that neither the supplier nor the user directly pays now but will inevitably pay in the future.

Moreover, because the global society has not placed responsibility for the cost of externalities on either the supplier or the user, the balance of our current energy mix is not optimized from either an environmental or an economic perspective. Thus, the value from optimization is lost. The energy mix has no impetus to change if the economics don't change. For example, if the energy mix fails to adjust prior to global Peak Oil, then the market is inadequately anticipating the rate and cause of depletion. In the case of climate change, the costs of depletion and pollution to the user are excluded from the global economic equation as nations compete over natural reservoirs, including the storage capacity of both oceans and atmosphere. The result is a global energy mix that is too reliant on the extraction of oil, coal, and natural gas, because there is no immediate incentive to establish a rental charge or incur a cost to create a sustainable equilibrium. For example, the US energy industry is not currently required to pay for environmental damages from GHG emissions, so why should it reinvest in replacements or create substitutes to address the environmental costs until such time as the storage capacity is fully allocated or the resource is fully depleted?

Keep in mind—and this point is essential if we are to keep the debate focused on the right parts and pieces—that suppliers and users are not acting inappropriately as long as they operate within the law. Rather, the behavior of suppliers and users can only be characterized as economical. They simply seek cheap, abundant, and reliable energy to fuel their economic activity. The inappropriate action (or the failure in the market) is the failure to enforce the internalization of the external cost. Without appropriate pricing to cover the real costs, the only logical tactic is for the market to continue to keep the energy mix in accordance with the business-as-usual scenario. We are not crazy. Therefore, what we have is neither a "tragedy of the commons" nor the depletion of our "natural capital." What we have is the overuse of *natural reservoirs* by the global community as if they were free. What we have is the *tragedy of the free resource,* which must be corrected if the global community is to stand a chance of adjusting our global energy mix in anticipation of further climate change.

The creation of a workable sustainability model, therefore, is relatively simple. There must be a social agreement regarding the allocation and use of our natural reservoirs when natural resources are transferred out of nature and into public or private ownership. The sequence is important because potential goods always flow from nature into public or private ownership; rarely do they flow from private or public ownership back into nature. If and when a resource is transferred back into nature, it would be considered a renewable resource. The sometimes hidden truth is that with the transfer of potential goods from nature into private and public ownership, wealth is created. In fact, the marketplace can perform its magic only once natural resources are transferred out of nature and into ownership. As long as these resources exist only in nature, they are neither enclosed nor in the hands of a steward. Under this condition, the market is free to extract them at no cost, without a tax or a toll. This leads to the depletion of the resource and, if the use or burning of the resource leads to the buildup of toxic levels of emissions, the potential for pollution. The extraction process starts a cycle where the full fate and transport of the resource wittingly leads to a social cost.

Therefore, only when natural resources have been transferred into common ownership and enclosed can the market perform and take the capital generated by the natural resource and impose a cost for their use. This is the Project Butterfly Sustainability Model. It requires an agreement that binds all parties to it. Without a social agreement, the market will fail and the global community risks both depletion of the resource and severe environmental damages.

Moreover, once natural resources have been transferred from nature into private or public ownership, they can begin to compete with one another in the marketplace. For example, timber competes with brick as a building supply. Industry can then put a value on the resource and establish a market price by allowing buyers to bid one source against the other. Conventional resource accounting accommodates this structure: Revenues are realized when the natural resources are sold and the supplier makes an adjustment on the balance sheet for the loss of inventory. The social agreement must be structured similarly. The tax or toll for burning carbon must be imposed as capital is extracted from nature and transferred into ownership. For example, once the price for storing carbon in the atmosphere is fixed, it creates the market signal and corrects the market failure. The marketplace will function, and the cost can be passed down the supply chain or can be transferred as the goods and services are delivered to the user, who is the ultimate beneficiary of those goods and services.

So that's where we stand: The burning of too much carbon (too many sources and not enough sinks) is the result of a failure to impose a regulatory or fiscal constraint at the time of the transference of a carbon-based resource from nature into private or public ownership. The situation is similar to a broken traffic light at a vital intersection. The problem is solved once the traffic light is fixed and traffic can flow. It doesn't really matter when or how the light broke. All that matters is that the traffic light is fixed, and the light is green. The relationship between nature and commerce can be restored.

REEXAMINING OUR NATURAL RESOURCES

My idea that climate change is the result of a market failure might seem to define my political views. It probably reveals that I am not a Marxist. It also shows that I am not a classical market theorist who believes that the market is all-knowing. I have always sought to find the middle ground. So, no matter where you are in the political spectrum, perhaps you can agree that the best approach for the environmental steward—the one at the table who is acting as a trustee for future generations—is to look at the earth's shared reservoirs of natural resources from a financial perspective and see if we can all share some common ground. That financial perspective is how we value the commerce that our shared natural reservoirs produce if we keep them renewable and rejuvenating. This is all that I am directly asking you to do. If you accept my proposition, then when we look at allocating resources, the priority should be on the earth's oceans, which is our largest shared natural reservoir.

Oceans cover 70 percent of the earth's surface and provide more than 90 percent of the space available for supporting living organisms and the biodiversity that exists. Needless to say, the oceans contain a rich supply of sea and plant life. Coral reefs, salt marshes, estuaries, mangroves, and sea grass beds are a few of the ocean environments that support the largest number of species and organisms. These smaller ecosystems interact with the whole by regulating our temperatures and managing the earth's climate and weather. For example, our oceans hold the energy to fuel storm systems critical to the making of wind. As air passes over warm water, it gains heat. Then, as the air cools, condensation of the absorbed water in the air creates rainfall. Without rainfall, our streams and rivers would no longer be fed and freshwater would no longer return to the oceans.

The valuing of our oceans creates a similar challenge to the valuing of our atmosphere or even of just the Chesapeake Bay. The only value we can give the oceans is some multiple of our global GDP that is reliant upon the preservation of this natural reservoir. For example, without vibrant oceans providing adequate and nontoxic rainfall, life as we know it would cease to exist. If we depend on the reservoir for our existence, we can value it as a resource by no other measure than to declare it *invaluable.*

Our atmosphere is the earth's second-largest natural reservoir. The atmosphere contains a blend of ingredients, including the air we breathe, that are essential to life. The atmosphere shields us from the sun's ultraviolet radiation while allowing other forms of extremely important light to pass through it. The atmosphere also serves as a blanket that holds the surface heat on the planet and prevents that heat from radiating out into space. This blanket is commonly known as the "greenhouse effect." Additionally, the atmosphere contains a small amount of CO_2 that, along with sunshine, allows plants and organisms in the oceans to carry out photosynthesis. This process converts sunshine, CO_2, and nutrients from the ground into the oxygen that all living organisms breathe. This is nature's causal loop, and it helps to sustain life. The atmosphere is the natural product of this interaction between sunshine, plant life, and CO_2. It creates a very thin and delicate shield that provides many beneficial attributes, including the retention of heat and oxygen on the planet that in turn allows us to live within a very narrow band of comfort.

Broadly speaking, the atmosphere is thirty miles thick, with 80 percent of its mass within ten miles of the earth's surface. During the summer, while I am riding my bicycle in Boulder, I can actually see this remarkable blanket. On any given day, the temperature might be a comfortable 70 to 80 degrees Fahrenheit (21 to 27 degrees Celsius) in town. As I look to the west, however, I can see snowcapped mountains. The temperature atop these mountains can be as much as 40 degrees Fahrenheit (22 degrees Celsius) lower than in Boulder. And yet the only difference is our elevation. I am riding my bike at roughly 5,500 feet above sea level, and the tops of these mountains range from 11,000 to 14,000 feet above sea level. In total, the vertical difference is less than two miles, and yet this is the difference between a comfortable afternoon and frostbite.

Now imagine you are orbiting the planet. You are standing back and looking at the earth's surface. The earth is approximately 25,000 miles in circumference. The thirty miles of atmosphere (in which there is only 10,000 feet of vertical comfort for humans) is nothing more than a thin, delicate membrane.

How do we quantify the value of the earth's atmosphere as a natural reservoir? For some guidance, let's look again at the Chesapeake Bay and its steward. CBF does not try to value the water or the fish in the waters of the Chesapeake Bay. Rather, the supporters of CBF place a value on the commerce the Chesapeake Bay, as a *natural reservoir,* supports. So, too, can the global community assign a value to our atmosphere. Perhaps the value would equal some multiple of global GDP, for without this natural reservoir, no commerce would be possible.

This larger definition of the earth's shared natural reservoirs allows us to see how CBF can serve as a workable sustainability model for this larger ecosystem and how a steward can garner the support of businesses. If people can unite to figure out how to serve as a steward for the Chesapeake Bay—an example of how would-be stewards intuitively treat a natural reservoir as a commons by enclosing it—then it may be possible to do the same for our largest and most vital natural reservoirs. Without recognizing it as such, we may already have a workable sustainability model that can be scaled to a global level.

LESSONS FROM THE PAST

The major innovation that Project Butterfly brings to the table is a new level of clarity regarding the role of the steward in the preservation of the earth's natural reservoirs. In effect, the stewards become the trustees for the social agreements that ultimately protect the resource. If the social agreements that govern the use of a natural reservoir are inadequate for the circumstances, the role of the steward is to demand revisions or tighter provisions in order to preserve the regenerative qualities of the natural reservoir. By so doing, the steward preserves value.

Regulators such as the EPA are therefore not the stewards. They are the enforcers. If the regulators are inadequate, or if they fail to uphold the social agreement, then the stewards must act as the watchdogs, as CBF has done. In this light, the concern of the stewards is neither solely for the health of the owl that nests in the trees nor for the fish that swims in the water. The concern of the stewards is the health of the ecosystem that supports wealth creation and prosperity for the community as a whole.

For example, the steward preserves the natural resource by measuring the value of commerce. The steward, therefore, should not be concerned with creating economic development and growth. The suppliers and users of the earth's natural resources will be the ones to seek opportunities for economic development and growth. In contrast, the environmental steward will seek to preserve wealth while encouraging the user and suppliers to create new value.

I need to clarify one last essential point before I can complete, for now, the definition of the Project Butterfly Sustainability Model. One of the barriers to mitigating climate change is that we tend to focus on what we *don't* have. Instead, we should focus on what we *do* have, such as the capital to fund an alternative fueling system and a transition plan to convert from finite resources to sustainable resource management. Recalling our sustainability model can help us adjust our focus. In addition, as I have often told my children, it is sometimes useful to look to the past. If something has worked before, perhaps the same principles can be applied going forward.

Greek and Roman written records allow us to peer into the inner workings of those two empires that spanned millennia and to reflect on our own approach to similar problems. I referred in the introduction to the Roman construction of aqueducts, some of them more than two thousand years ago, to address the environmental challenge of infertile and arid lands (see text box). Looking further back, the Greeks had their own idea about community property. Aristotle argued that property held in common is that which is least taken care of by man, because man has greater regard for what is his own than for what he may possess in common with others. Aristotle felt that communal property should be put into private hands so that a steward would invest in its value. Perhaps rightly, this logic formed the basis for taking communal property, or at least the resources held in common, and creating ownership rights for property that was either privately or publicly held.

Regardless of how long ago Aristotle lived, his teachings may still influence our conventional thinking or our business-as-usual mind-set. As we consider the Project Butterfly Sustainability Model, we fervently agree with Aristotle that we want to avoid a situation where there is a lack of ownership—where there is little regard for anything possessed in common. However, the difference between the perspective of this great teacher and the principles underlying the Project Butterfly Sustainability Model is that the resources held in common are not necessarily those we take care of least. The worst case, as we have discussed, is when there is no clear ownership or title to preserve a natural reservoir and when that resource is vital to all. I believe Aristotle would agree with the principles of the Project Butterfly Sustainability Model if he faced the circumstances we face today. Furthermore, I believe Aristotle would agree that rather than allowing unfettered access to a natural resource no one owns, it is better to place the resource into common owner-ship and to enclose it by agreeing to a social contract for the allocation of its use. Simply put, capital that is considered free may or may not be allocated efficiently in the future. In contrast, the taxing of such access in exchange for the environmental cost is an effective means to preserve and manage the resource to achieve sustainable levels.

It bears repeating that in our twenty-first century, with nearly eight bil-lion inhabitants on the earth, our shared atmosphere and oceans can no lon-ger be viewed as resources that provide free goods and services. The resources that flow from these natural reservoirs cannot be abandoned and left to fend for themselves. For example, we could never have imagined that bottled oxy-gen would be sold as a commodity in Mexico City because of poor air quality. How could we have imagined that there would be a need for it? Aristotle might have had a few more things to say about the value of natural resources if he had had to purchase one of those bottles in order to breathe.

The Greek and Roman distinctions between public and private owner-ship is important because both have distinct capacities to utilize finite and renewable natural resources in ways that, when combined, create greater total wealth for society. Private ownership is focused on the exchange of common goods and services that are critical to the maintenance and well-being of our homes or that are vital to the running of industry. Private ownership allows for the most efficient allocation of resources through direct exchanges between buyer and seller based on price. In contrast, public ownership provides critical infrastructure, such as bridges and roads, which has to be financed through public taxation. Each of us is an individual beneficiary of the publicly owned resource, but the ultimate beneficiary is the global society or the localized economy. Private capital, without public capital support, would not otherwise form to take full advantage of all the opportunities for trade. Commerce itself is often limited in its ability to find a pathway to exchange its goods and ser-vices. Bridges and roads facilitate commerce by creating the necessary byways to maximize the total potential transactions.

The issue can become political. Modern-day politics still focus on where

COMMUNAL PROPERTY

The Romans divided the ownership of goods and services into three categories to help them serve as stewards of their lands and act as creators
of wealth. These three categories, still commonly used today in various
forms and fashions, are as follows:

» Private property (*res privata*)—homes, cars, businesses, factories, industrial facilities

» Public property (*res publicae*)—land and buildings owned by
municipalities, councils, or governments, including city streets
and squares, schools, and libraries

» Communal property (*res communes*)—all things not publicly
or privately owned, including water, air, and other biological
resources

The Roman concept of communal property—in our model, the
natural reservoirs—required a social agreement that allowed for the

to draw the appropriate line between financing of public ownership and
the rights of private enterprise to act unfettered within the market. These
issues will probably never dissipate, but the discourse around them tends to
obscure the issue of what resources should reside within a commons and what
resources should be left exclusively in nature.

The essence of Aristotle's point was not that nothing should be held in
common. Rather, his deeper point was that all property needs a steward. For
vital, valuable resources to exist outside of any social agreement whatsoever
is an even worse predicament than the complete lack of regard for common
resources—the situation Aristotle was protesting against. Today our natural
reservoirs look and behave as if they have been orphaned rather than preserved
as they were in Roman times. But we cannot blame our parents or grandpar-
ents or even Aristotle for the lack of stewardship. Historically, resources that

efficient allocation of resources to maintain those reservoirs in perpetuity. For example, consider those extensive aqueducts that moved water from actual reservoirs into Roman cities and then to dispensaries where everyone had equal access. The Romans then used taxes to build their cities and to finance the infrastructure for this shared resource. In fact, many of these aqueducts and dispensaries still stand today as ruins throughout much of Europe and the Mediterranean region.

The creation of public and private property in Roman times was intended to transfer resources, such as water, out of nature and into a place where they could be used to create new wealth, such as in dry fields, irrigating for new agriculture. Finite and renewable resources left unharnessed and unharvested were not seen as wealth producing. The same is true today: Only by modifying natural resources to build housing and industry do we create wealth. Subsequent to its modification, the natural capital that has been used to build our housing and industry can be allocated or even reallocated in accordance with a market-based exchange.

have been considered free have not been owned or enclosed because they have been too inaccessible or difficult to manage in our business-as-usual manner. In the past, these resources were not placed into common ownership because they were too deep underground, too far offshore, or too high above us—and too ubiquitous by their very nature—to even consider claiming them as our own. Until now.

The conditions of our world have changed. Oil and gas rigs can drill down tens of thousands of feet below the earth's surface. Oil platforms can be placed miles offshore in deep waters. Smoke from our industrial plants can reach the heavens. Our predecessors even just a few decades ago couldn't have imagined that these enormous reservoirs, which teemed endlessly with finite and renewable resources, would ever become depleted or threatened by the pollution of our own making. Our predecessors likely valued our natural reservoirs, but they still saw the use of them as free. Now we must see them as invaluable and as our own.

OUR RICH CULTURAL HERITAGE

The residents who surround the Chesapeake Bay are aware of its rich cultural heritage as much as its rich natural resources. The Chesapeake has been home to some of the most famous battles in US history, from the Revolutionary War through the Civil War. In fact, one of these military engagements was during the Battle of 1812, when the British returned to fight after their humiliating defeat that ended the war of 1776. In what is now the Baltimore Harbor, young lawyer Francis Scott Key wrote "The Star-Spangled Banner" as he watched a British frigate bombard Fort McHenry. That song gave birth to a spirit of US pride and has served as the country's national anthem ever since. Preserving the Chesapeake Bay is therefore more than just about defending a natural resource. The Chesapeake Bay has served as a strategic stronghold for both the colonizing British and the early Americans, making its preservation a symbol of both our history and our national defense.

I have looked at the Chesapeake Bay as a microcosm of our global condition. I have evaluated our shared atmosphere and oceans in a manner similar to how the original supporters of CBF valued the bay. With this model in mind, I have begun to define the Project Butterfly Sustainability Model. Defending the Chesapeake Bay has required stewards of all kinds to protect and monitor its vitality ever since 1776. Defending our global natural resources will take a similar kind of strategy and the same kind of commitment.

Today, as my son and I can vouch after our fishing trip alongside a nuclear power plant, the shores of the Chesapeake Bay differ vastly from the shores settled by our collective ancestors. Over the years, population centers have grown in every direction. Pockets of commercial agriculture and heavy industry have caused extensive sewage and waste runoff that has degraded the vitality of the Chesapeake Bay's ecosystem. Regardless, the Chesapeake still supports more than 3,600 species of plant and animal life. Fishermen are still harvesting more than 500 million pounds of seafood from the bay every year. Locals and visitors alike know there is nothing like going to a Maryland restaurant that serves fresh crab from the Chesapeake Bay on a piece of butcher-block paper along with a hammer instead of a fork and knife. The annual output from this natural reservoir feeds hundreds of thousands of residents and visitors. The Chesapeake Bay can meet this demand while still combating the toxicity that threatens the waters.[210] These statistics demonstrate that the Chesapeake Bay is still a living organism and that its ecosystem is resilient.

Our entire planet can secure the same results.

KEY OBSERVATIONS

The key observations we can make about creating a Project Butterfly Sustainability Model for the successful stewardship of our natural resources are as follows:

» Our rich natural reservoirs, which contain both renewable and finite resources, represent the springs from which capital flows and from which the global community can build wealth and prosperity.

» The least desirable condition is when the use of the earth's natural reservoirs is falsely considered to be free, when their availability is actually vital, and when they must be maintained in perpetuity. In the past, the global community has not had to consider the size of humanity's footprint, as it was small enough not to jeopardize the regenerative capacity of the earth's shared natural resources. Today we need to reconsider the true state of our planet's condition and come up with a sustainability model.

» The best or ideal condition is when the global community works to preserve vital reservoirs and when we enter into social agreements regarding their use. Once nature's goods are pulled from our natural reservoirs and held in public or private ownership, the market can then efficiently allocate their use. This is the fundamental component of a workable sustainability model.

» The social agreements that best fit within the constitutional authority of sovereign governments are those that internalize the externalities of burning carbon. Suppliers and users act as economic agents. Neither can be arbiter of the use of our natural reservoirs. By taxing at the point that a resource is transferred from nature to either public or private ownership, the supplier can pass the cost down to the beneficiary, or user, until other suppliers emerge to provide suitable substitutes. This represents the application of free market principles to the successful functioning of the Project Butterfly Sustainability Model.

· · ·

Our country has met many great tests.
Some have imposed extreme hardship and
sacrifice. Others have demanded only
resolve, ingenuity, and clarity of purpose.
Such is the case with energy today.
—National Energy Policy
Development Group

CHAPTER 9

I wanted to build a bonfire.

The sun was going down, and I had just climbed an eleven-thousand-foot mountain in Wyoming. I wanted to build a bonfire that would be worthy of my achievement. I wanted to build a bonfire that could be seen for miles.

I was fourteen years old. I had previously built large bonfires when I had camped along the Raccoon River in Iowa. I would create a circle of riverbed rocks and make a pyre of branches. I would light them, and watch the flames flare. However, that was in a flat river valley, where the grass grew lush, the trees were tall, and nature would obligingly cover my tracks. Nature would renew the grasses within weeks, if not days, of my being there. As I would soon realize, standing atop the mountain, well above the tree line, with patches of snow still dotting the landscape, I was in a new environment. The task of building a bonfire would not be so simple.

The NOLS instructor broke away from the rest of the group and walked over to me. "Grab your shovel," he said. "We're going to make a fire."

When we had packed up a few days earlier for our monthlong journey, I had wondered what that small spade was for. I was about to find out.

The trick to making a fire on the tundra was finding adequate fuel for the fire. Wood is hard to find at eleven thousand feet. The air is thin, and small trees and bushes are scarce. That was the first clue that had started me wondering about the feasibility of my bonfire.

Next my instructor showed me how to cut a fire pit. He and I sliced small pieces of tundra from the surface and placed them neatly to the side of the pit, organized in the same configuration as they had been removed. As we worked, he told me that whatever we touched at eleven thousand feet would likely remain exactly as we would leave it: "If we burn a fire on top of the tundra," he explained, "we would leave a black mark on the ground." I realized that the fragile environment would reveal our footprint for the entire summer, if not longer. However, these cut squares of tundra presented a different option. I could return them to their former position, filling the hole as if the ground had never been disturbed in the first place.

I listened to my instructor carefully. Nevertheless, I was still thinking about a spectacular bonfire on the mountaintop. I figured the best option for maximum blaze would be to use my small supply of "Boy Scout fluid." I could give the new fire a little help. The wood was dry, but I was beginning to suspect my instructor wouldn't be too keen on me using lighter fluid. I decided to instead keep this idea to myself.

As it turned out, the fire we ended up building was small, but it was highly efficient. Here's what I learned: When you've dug a pit large enough to hold your fire, you stop. You gather closely around the fire to block the wind. You light the few twigs you have gathered in the center of the pit, and you slowly add the wood to create a bed of coal ash. Once this is accomplished, you can keep yourself warmed by your fire and cook using its glow.

The fire that we ended up with met our every need. When I think back on that trip, I realize it taught me the importance of using *only what you need*. In fact, that small fire was all we needed, and it was very, very satisfying. When it was time to call it a night, putting out the fire was easy. We simply ground the coal ash into the tundra.

In the morning, we gathered a few more pieces of wood to build a small flame sufficient to brew our coffee. Before we left, we took our spades and reinserted the squares of tundra that we had removed the night before. The coals were immediately extinguished, so there was no threat that a smoldering ash might catch fire. Once we spread a few remaining twigs and pieces of grass on top of the area that was once our fire pit, there was no longer any sign that we had been there. We left the space free of our footprint.

As a young man I had always thought I wanted to leave a legacy when I died. But I left a legacy right there, I realized. I left nothing. I had a choice, and I chose to leave nature the way I had found it.

VALUING OUR RESOURCES: THE FIRST STEP TOWARD SUSTAINABILITY

As I mentioned in chapter 8, part of creating the Project Butterfly Sustainability Model is putting a value on all critical shared natural reservoirs that feed into our global energy mix. The same must be done to set the context for a new business case for the energy industry in order to address climate change in the real world. However, it is important to be mindful that our archetypal steward, the Chesapeake Bay Foundation, didn't ascribe a value to the natural reservoir itself. For example, CBF didn't say what it would cost to replace the Chesapeake Bay (a *replacement cost*). Nor did the organization have comparables to measure relative values (*comps*). Instead the supporters of CBF valued the Chesapeake Bay in terms of the commerce it supports. Specifically, CBF called the bay a "national treasure" and recognized the commerce it is responsible for as a reflection of the value of the resource. I submit that *this* is the right approach for valuing all natural resources as long they reside inside the natural reservoirs. It is also the right approach for making the new business case. The new business case starts by asking how to maximize the commercial value of natural resources without diminishing the health of the resource itself.

As I mentioned previously, we should therefore consider our natural reservoirs as being inherently *invaluable* regardless of whether they are finite or renewable and whether it is even possible to value the commerce they support. For example, oxygen might sell as a commodity in Mexico City, but this trend is not sustainable. If you chop down a redwood tree, it will certainly fetch a market price, and you can apply this price to all the trees in the forest. But the tragedy of the free resource is that to ascribe a financial value to a natural resource itself ignores the constitutional nature of these vital reservoirs. The constitutional nature of these reservoirs is that they are inherently communal property, and the failure of society is not having a social agreement that governs their use. Rather, the value they possess is inherent in the commerce they enable.

Said another way, we each have an inalienable right to access the air we breathe or the water we drink. Individually, we have the inalienable right, and perhaps the obligation, to defend the preservation of these resources. Because these resources are now under attack, we must translate these inalienable rights into legal rights to enclose the natural reservoir or risk the natural and social consequences that will result. In developing Project Butterfly's new business case, the Project Butterfly team realized that by acknowledging that a natural resource is *inherently invaluable* we see the right the global community has to its preservation. Conversely, failure to acknowledge the inherent value of a natural resource can lead to resource depletion and the creation of a liability. For example, in the case of climate change, the buildup of CO_2 creates a carbon debt or a liability that must someday be paid down.

This observation has led the Project Butterfly team to reach some tentative conclusions about how to build a workable sustainability model. Since the earth's natural reservoirs are invaluable, it's not appropriate to apply basic accounting principles to them. That's where previous sustainability models have fallen short. Instead, in order for a sustainability model to work effectively, the environmental steward must measure the health of the natural reservoir by establishing health indexes. Similar to certain medical equipment that measures the vital signs of a human being, environmental indexes gauge the optimal prescriptions to maintain good health. In looking at the atmosphere, the measure of 350 ppm would be analogous to the "fighting weight" for an athlete. The benchmark 450 ppm of CO_2 concentration would be akin to a slight fever in a child. The child might feel kind of punk, but good enough to go to school. But a CO_2 concentration level above 550 ppm is comparable to the point at which you would consider taking your child to the emergency care center. (The other measure is whether the trend line is rising or falling. Compare this to weighing yourself on the scale to know if you are gaining or losing weight.)

Once resources are taken out of the natural reservoir and put into private or public ownership, it is okay to apply traditional accounting principles. At this point, the natural resources become *actual real estate* or *natural capital* once human labor and capital are applied to transform these resources into a good or service. The assets have been modified by labor or capital and are turned into tradable commodities, just as timber is turned into lumber or fish is turned into sushi. These assets become part of the marketplace and can then be priced and allocated efficiently in accordance with market demand and supply.

The measuring system I am suggesting for the Project Butterfly Sustainability Model takes its cue from comparable health indexes that call for remedies in the event of an imbalance that portends a health crisis. Without such an approach, the market fails to address our environmental challenges, just as the commons suffers a tragedy from overgrazing without the application of appropriate stewardship and oversight. For example, economists and even other countries have experimented with indexes that deviate from the use of GDP as the primary measure of economic progress and attempt to account for depletion and pollution costs. In environmental literature, one of the more popular experiments in creating an alternative accounting system is the "gross national happiness index" originally employed by the small country of Bhutan, located at the eastern end of the Himalayas.[211] The gross national happiness index is based on many psychological and social indicators, so it is difficult to break down into a mathematical calculation. However, the use of this alternative index does raise the issue that indicators other than purely economic ones (such as GDP) can have their place in measuring the true health of an economy.

CREATING A NEW ENERGY MIX

Let's bring our discussion back to the global energy mix and its connection to the Project Butterfly Sustainability Model.

The solution to climate change requires a workable model to achieve global sustainability through restricting the buildup of GHG emissions. Mitigating the tragedy of the free resource involves implementing international agreements to achieve the sustainability of the earth's atmosphere, oceans, and forests and to convert the global energy mix from its reliance on finite natural resources. For better or worse, social agreements such as the Kyoto Protocol to limit GHG emissions provide the global community with a foundation for putting a price on the use of finite natural resources and for helping finance the conversion to a more diversified global mix reliant on renewable resources. The question is, how do we do this given our definition of a global sustainability model?

On an international scale, the ideal solution would be to include agreements that not only encourage trade between nations but also are designed to reduce global GHG emissions through sharing carbon inventories and co-investing in new technologies and power generation that replace aging systems or meet new demand. On a national scale, the ideal solution would be to use fiscal policy (specifically, a government's tax collection authority or its ability to cap emissions) to, in effect, prime the pump by incentivizing renewable resources and by taxing the use of conventional fuel sources and redirecting subsidies to alternative sources of energy. As is, Kyoto has accomplished much of the above.

However, implementing the Project Butterfly Sustainability Model requires demanding that all the energy costs are internalized. The consequence of internalizing these costs is the rebalancing of choices being made by the energy supplier and the user. For example, the cost may be imposed on the supplier, but the user will have to pay the freight if the supplier cannot fully absorb the cost without adjusting the price of the goods and services offered to the energy user. The energy user then will have to reevaluate his or her choices in this sequence of events and, if necessary, search for a substitute resource (if there is one) or seek out an alternative supplier. If there are no substitutes, the final choice for the user is either to simply pay the price of use until a substitute eventually emerges or to forgo the use. Meanwhile, the supplier can change his or her inventory to meet the needs of the user.

For example, consider a buyer who wants to purchase a luxury hybrid automobile that gets a higher gas mileage rating versus a more classic, less fuel-efficient luxury car. The hybrid costs more because it is a new technology. The classic car costs less because it has little if any design or first-time production costs to amortize. But by demanding that the supplier (in this case, the car manufacturer) internalize the pollution costs from the use of the automobile, we change the pricing dynamic for the classic car. The manufacturer will now incur a cost on the classic vehicle for being less efficient. Innovation will receive its reward. The supplier of the new, more efficient technology will sell the luxury hybrid since the classic car is now less competitive. Increased sales will enable the new design to be amortized, so the manufacturer's price for the hybrid car will eventually fall. Thus, the first buyer will benefit from reduced fuel costs, and the second buyer will benefit further from reduced capital costs.

You might balk at my suggestion that the imposition of a social cost benefits the market. However, this point is essential, though at present we can review it only from a theoretical perspective (chapters 11 and 12 will take up the issue in much more detail from a financial perspective). Still, it is the likely outcome. The internalized cost demands innovation from necessity and thus forces a new direction, even if that new direction is a rejection of the use of fossil fuels.

As defined in chapter 8, the earth's energy resources flow from two different reservoirs: one that is finite and one that is renewable. In order to change the global energy mix, we need to prime the pump and create a positive feedback loop by increasing the flow and rate from our renewable resources through incentivizing capital markets to invest in them. Conversely, we need to restrict the rate and flow from our finite resources, through taxing or capping the burning of emissions, to create a negative feedback loop. These crosscurrents will eventually lead to a rebalancing of the natural reservoir until it reaches a sustainable equilibrium in the earth's energy mix.

The Project Butterfly Sustainability Model holds up in theory. It should keep the flow of renewable resources primed until the global energy mix is rebalanced and until the market value is maximized. For example, the mining of a coal seam or the drilling of an oil well to depletion leads to a finite level of profitability, whereas the profits from renewable energy can go on forever. There are certainly limitations to this statement that will undercut the potential for market values. Human-made equipment to generate renewable energy, such as a solar panel, has a limited life. Nevertheless, over an unlimited period of time, the exploitation of renewable natural resources leads to an unlimited profit potential—especially when compared with the exploitation of finite resources.

FINDING THE BALANCE

Our understanding of creating a new global energy mix is not complete without delving a little deeper into the gradations of what is *renewable* and what is *finite*. Certain forms of resources are clearly finite. For example, coal and oil take millions of years to form under heat and pressure from lying below the earth's surface. The same is true for the fuel that runs nuclear energy. Most of the uranium in the world formed more than two hundred million years ago. The rate of harvesting these finite natural resources far exceeds any conceivable capacity for renewal, and that is what defines these resources as *finite*. In contrast, other forms of resources are clearly renewable. For example, the amount of solar and wind energy far exceeds any potential demand for its use. It is unreasonable to conjecture that human use of renewable resources would ever reduce the solar energy produced by the sun or slow down the wind that propels the wind turbine.

However, the majority of our natural reservoirs can be easily reclassified as either finite or renewable, depending on how we use them and manage them. It is useful to think of these resources as sitting on the balance between renewable and finite resources, similar to the dark and light sides of the yin-yang symbol. For instance, the Chesapeake Bay is an example of a rich resource suspended in such a balance. If Chesapeake oysters are harvested responsibly, they can replenish themselves, which makes them a renewable resource. If the waters of the Chesapeake are polluted, and if overfishing permanently damages the ecosystem's ability to rejuvenate, the Chesapeake Bay and its oysters risk being reclassified as a finite resource that will disappear forever.

The Project Butterfly Sustainability Model defines *natural resources* in a way that allows us to manage their use. The model also demands that the extraction of these resources by public and private owners be governed by social agreement. It calls for the trading of goods and services that flow from such natural resources to be governed in accordance to the principles of the free market. The Sustainability Model is built on the idea that sustainability starts with a commitment to keep systems in balance and then lets the market maximize the value of their use.

MEASURING COST VERSUS BENEFIT: THE SECOND STEP TOWARD SUSTAINABILITY

Before we can explore in greater depth the Sustainability Model created by the Project Butterfly team, I need to cover one last subject: the concept of *maximum sustainable yield.*

We have already established (in chapter 8) that proper stewardship—the willingness to take ownership and to fight for preserving renewable resources—can lead to a workable sustainability model that ensures that our natural resources remain renewable. We have also established (in the previous section) that most renewable natural resources—such as productive topsoil, clean air, a stable climate, an intact ozone layer, fertile forests, abundant fish stocks, and biodiversity of both plants and animals—can be overexploited and depleted if overharvested. However, while I have argued that capital markets can be tapped to build renewable power systems that will replace nonrenewable fuels, it is critical to keep in mind that capital markets can just as quickly cause a breakdown in the balance of our ecosystems. This is the ugly twin of our free market system. The Project Butterfly Sustainability Model, therefore, must establish the baseline conditions for both business as usual and the new business case.

ESTABLISHING THE BASELINE CONDITIONS

Establishing a baseline condition is a challenge. If all you are looking for is short-term profitability, you not only harvest the fruit from the tree, but you also chop down the whole tree for its lumber. However, if you are the supplier, you've got a problem. You have created a conundrum, of sorts: You've maxed out your renewable resource, and there are no viable substitutes. Remember that only energy can substitute for energy.

Harvesting a renewable resource in this way is rarely a sustainable practice. Whether you are a single owner, a CEO of a public company, or director of a for-profit or nonprofit organization, maximizing your short-term profit should not be your only goal. Your duty is to get the most out of your resources in the long run. On the mountain with my NOLS instructor, I learned to use only what I needed. If I had burned all the firewood above the tree line to make my bonfire, I wouldn't have been able to rebuild the fire in the morning to brew my coffee.

In relating this conundrum to climate change, the global community has a carbon debt that needs to be paid down—an excess of harmful GHG emissions in the atmosphere that must be mitigated. We need a new business case that makes new investments into a system that either balances this debt with existing renewable resources or creates substitutes for our other uses of carbon. The Project Butterfly Sustainability Model calls for resource use that is perhaps nothing more than a balancing act. We have to find ways that optimize our investments in renewable resources without depleting or overharvesting them. That's the only way we can simultaneously pay down our carbon debt and create a sustainable system.

Back in chapter 2, I provided the Project Butterfly team's definition of *global sustainability*. I explained that global sustainability starts with an acknowledgment that human wealth and prosperity are created through a noninterchangeable transference of resources out of our natural reservoirs and into private and public ownership. Global sustainability is therefore a deliberate commitment on behalf of public and private owners to replenish their reservoirs with renewable resources, allowing the ecosystem to regenerate. What I didn't tell you in chapter 2 is exactly *how* we can manage this commitment to global sustainability. Effective management under an effective sustainability model requires employing another concept that is crucial to a new business case and similar to the use of the commons. That concept is *maximum sustainable yield.*

Put as simply as possible, the maximum sustainable yield is the amount that a venture can extract without depleting the capacity of the system to replenish itself. Back in 1976, in his book *Mathematical Bioeconomics: The Optimal Management of Renewable Resources,* Colin Clark laid out the conditions that set the maximum sustainable yield for any given ecosystem.[212] He set forth the claim that fully harvesting renewable resources is optimal for profit maximization *if alternative investments can be found as replacements or substitutes to keep the earnings engine going.* This parallels the business-as-usual scenario, in which it doesn't matter whether the energy resource can be replaced or substituted with an alternative. If you just let the earnings engine keep to its course, as long as there is another tree, it will keep chopping down trees. Even though such a strategy may be sustainable for the business, as Clark argues, it's not sustainable for the resource.

Clark's model is useful because to establish a new business case that is sustainable not only for the business but also for the resource, you have to look at the actual earnings engine. In many scenarios, the maximization of the resource value will ultimately translate into the maximization of the value of the engine, as we would hope. However, a challenge comes into play when we understand that there are no substitutes for resources such as breathable air, drinkable water, or coal and oil. These are examples of resources that are so precious we can't ever allow them to go beyond the maximum sustainable yield. For example, over the past century, humankind has developed methods to purify water and manufacture oxygen, but it has proven far more economical to preserve these global resources than to manufacture new ones. Imagine trying to rebuild and replace the Chesapeake Bay!

In contrast, some earnings engines can substitute one investment for another. An extraction company can move from extracting coal to mining gold, for example. The extraction company can also redefine its mission statement and even redevelop the land it has previously mined. In fact, if we monitor our earnings engines and balance the relationship between them and the resources they depend on, then we will be destined for a future with increasing returns and lower costs to humanity, reducing the potential for conflict between short- and long-term profit maximization.

Consequently, the concept of maximum sustainable yield is critical to the discourse of comparative values for different sources of energy. For example, renewable energy has historically been thought to cost much more than conventional energy sources. Often the focus is on initial costs rather than on a comparison of value. Proponents of the continued use of conventional sources of energy frequently employ the argument that energy supplies from wind, solar, and run-of-river hydropower cost more. However, the issue of cost is slightly more complex than the opponents of these kinds of technologies might like you to think.

There is a fundamental difference between something costing more and something being more economical. If you are looking at a situation that requires distributed energy, for example, it is often difficult to know what the best fit is. Diesel-fired power generation is likely to require the least initial cost, but the total cost of owning and operating a diesel generator includes the cost of running the generator (maintenance) and the perpetual cost of fuel. Compare owning and operating a diesel generator with owning a solar farm. The solar farm would likely cost much more up front, but the cost of running the solar farm would be comparatively minimal. Both systems require operating expenses and maintenance, but in substantially differing amounts. You need to factor in the relative operating costs before you really know which energy system is the most economical.

Comparing renewable energy to conventional power to determine the most economical choice requires a life-cycle cost analysis, which considers the total cost of ownership and operation from cradle to grave. Such costs include, for example, capital expenditures, financing costs, fuel, and maintenance. The life-cycle cost analysis of energy also always includes some environmental costs, such as removal of hazardous waste and any taxation or fines paid for the right to pollute. Energy assets that have a longer life will yield a higher value than an equivalent project with a shorter asset life will yield. As a consequence, assets that take longer periods to permit and build will also have a lower value than assets that can be assembled quickly and with less design, planning, and construction time.

Measuring the costs and benefits of energy is not as simple as comparing the price of like products. Because of energy's unique characteristics, it requires a life-cycle analysis. Investing in energy is similar to buying a house. There is the down payment, and then there are the ongoing costs of ownership, which include the eventual cost of replacing an aging asset. All of these ongoing costs of energy, including the environmental costs and the cost of depletion, need to be included in any buy or sell situation or in any policy that is designed to change the energy mix.

THE COST OF SUBSTITUTION AND REPLACEMENT

Conducting a life-cycle cost analysis thus becomes one of the principle ways of determining the maximum yield, because it considers the cost of substitution and replacement. Life-cycle cost analysis therefore allows decision makers to select the project that has the least amount of costs, or the maximum returns, throughout the life of the asset. It also allows the supplier or the user to compare alternatives and to calculate the present values of the long-term costs and benefits in a way that provides feedback for informing future decisions.

The challenge of transitioning from the business-as-usual scenario to a new business case appears when you are working with a limited capital budget. Your only choice may be to opt for the least-cost decision, where the up-front costs are minimized. This is often the case with diesel or backup generators. For example, cellular tower operators are required to have backup generation in the event of a power outage. Otherwise, in the event of a massive storm where power is lost, communications would be shut down as well. Nevertheless, cell tower operators will typically put the least expensive generator in place to meet code and compliance requirements and minimize capital expenditures. The alternative would be to build a secondary station where the cell tower sits, to generate its own power and store it. These kinds of investment decisions will add to the capital line of a balance sheet, but they have the capacity to diminish the operating line of a profit-and-loss statement later on. In a situation where the power outage is accompanied by fuel shortages, the cell tower operator might find that he or she has shot himself in the foot by having to absorb extraordinary fuel costs for the generator. The life-cycle cost analysis will at least allow you to weigh your options.

The issue for the energy user (in our example, the cell tower operator) is one of working within a capital budget versus the concern of limiting future operating costs. The constraint facing the cell tower operator will have consequences with respect to the deployment of energy efficiency and renewable energy. The situation might change if the necessary financing is made available to either the suppliers or the users so the cell tower operator can apply a life-cycle cost analysis. Available financing will allow the cell tower operator to implement the solution that creates the most value without depleting the asset—or to consider how to replace or substitute the resource if necessary. In other words, to create as dynamic an energy market as possible, the system needs to give the market access to the necessary financing so business operators can make the right decisions based on price signals that consider the full impact of the environmental costs.

Failure to do so will lead some people to build huge bonfires on mountaintops when a little fire might do much better.

KEY OBSERVATIONS

The key observations we can make about finding a path to sustainability, and defining the Project Butterfly Sustainability Model, are as follows:

» Renewable resources can be permanently exhausted if they are overharvested—just as cutting down a tree means it will bear no more fruit.

» The Project Butterfly new business case calls for a system that either balances existing renewable resources or creates substitutes.

» Effective resource management requires employing the concept of maximum sustainable yield that allows the resource to regenerate.

» Comparing renewable energy to conventional power to determine the most economic choice requires a life-cycle cost analysis that fairly accounts for the depletion of resources and the generation of substitutes in order to create sustainability.

There is nothing in a caterpillar that tells you it's going to be a butterfly.
—R. Buckminster Fuller

CHAPTER 10

In 1979 my friend Steve Rothstein had graduated from college and was working for Senator Paul Tsongas of Massachusetts when he received a call from his friend Joe Kennedy II. Joe had read news reports of people freezing to death in Massachusetts because they couldn't afford to heat their homes, while oil companies were making massive profits. "I don't think that's right," Joe told Steve. "Why don't we do something where we can make a little bit of money and give it back to people so they don't freeze to death?"

Joe's response to the situation in Massachusetts was to start a nonprofit oil company.

It was a pivotal time in our nation's energy history. The global economy had just started to fully absorb the shock of the 1973 oil embargo. Oil prices were beginning to stabilize. Then the country experienced another oil shock. This time it was the uprising of Islamic revolutionaries in Iran in 1979 and the overthrow of the Shah by revolutionary forces, televised for the whole world to see. President Jimmy Carter immediately placed a ban on Iranian goods to the United States. The response was dramatic and swift. Gas stations immediately started rationing their supplies, and fear of a new economic recession spread across the country. The impact of higher gas prices on job security and the inability of many to pay their bills weighed heavily on everyone's mind.

Does this sound familiar? It does if you have recently struggled through the Great Recession of 2008.

Telling me his story years later, Steve laughed. "I told Joe that I didn't think that it could be done," he said. "We couldn't possibly compete with Exxon. I told him I appreciated his enthusiasm, but we should focus on something that was real."

When I asked him how Joe responded, Steve paused and said, "He thought I was being too narrow in my thinking. So I told him that I would meet with him, and we discussed the idea several more times. It finally became clear to me that Joe couldn't be dissuaded."

Steve soon found himself with a group of like-minded individuals in the basement of Joe's home, sitting around a card table next to the boiler and the washing machine. They got a PO box as a front for their nonexistent office and started writing letters to oil ministers all over the world, asking the ministers to consider selling them oil. In spite of the Kennedy name, they didn't get any takers—until Venezuela agreed to meet with them. "I was completely terrified," Steve recalled.

Venezuela agreed to sell them a tanker of crude oil, and then the group encountered its next problem. "We didn't have any money. We didn't own anything. I didn't even own a bicycle," Steve confessed.

They decided to think outside the box. They knew that once the crude oil was refined, it would be worth much more, so they asked the seller to hold part of the oil as collateral. These young entrepreneurs planned to sell the by-products (gasoline and diesel) from refining the oil and use that revenue to cover their costs. This would allow them to sell the remaining fuel for heating to the citizens of Massachusetts at below-market rates.

Venezuela agreed.

Steve and Joe's start-up used the same tactic—using the asset to collateralize the sale—with the tanker company, and then the oil refinery, and so on. At several steps along the way, it was a logistical nightmare, but the group of young idealists kept going. Since there was not a centralized distribution system, they had to negotiate with hundreds of oil distribution companies to supply the list of individual homes in need of oil. Steve told me how exciting it was to finally see the tanker come in. He said it was even more exciting when he accompanied one of the first oil delivery truck drivers to a woman's home in Dorchester, on the outskirts of Boston. "This person didn't have a lot of resources," Steve explained to me. "She was literally choosing between eating or heating her home. People were making these horrific choices, ones that you shouldn't have to make in the wealthiest country in the world."

Thanks to the assistance of many people, it took the start-up just nine months from initial discussions to actual delivery of the oil. Their venture turned into Citizens Energy, a nonprofit that has since led the way into energy efficiency for affordable housing and expanded its oil trading business to take on the oil establishment by lowering costs and meeting unmet demand. It has taken on a host of other energy projects related to serving the needy in the state of Massachusetts.

This story is not just about entrepreneurialism. It is about a group of young heroes who stepped up to the plate and executed a game-changing end run. They exemplified the kind of thinking and courage that we need today to solve the current challenges of climate change.

Steve learned a lot of lessons from his experience that the Project Butterfly team felt could be applied to the pending energy crisis. "The fact that it hadn't been done had absolutely no connection to the idea that it *couldn't* be done," he declared. "We also thought about taking a negative—such as having no money—and turning it into a positive. We couldn't fight the economy. We couldn't fight the oil company. We could simply leverage the individuals who were going to be helped, such as the woman in Dorchester."

Listening to Steve recount his experience, I thought, *It's time once again to take on the unthinkable.* Only this time, instead of doing an end run around the large oil and gas companies, the Project Butterfly new business case needs to do a Hail Mary pass right up the middle of the field.

CREATING A FEASIBILITY STUDY

Research on climate change originally came from within academia. It gained government support because researchers made a strong case for the need to assess and address the complex issues surrounding the earth's climate. Probably few people realize that it was back in the mid-1800s that academics and scientists first started studying and correlating the impact of CO_2 and water vapor on surface temperatures. These early scientists originally discovered the greenhouse effect and made efforts to estimate atmospheric warming from a future doubling of CO_2. However, it was not until the 1980s and the use of computer modeling to verify previous calculations that climate scientists, such as NASA's Jim Hansen in his breakthrough 1988 testimony to Congress, began sounding the alarm. Since then climate scientists and, increasingly, economists have taken up the charge to build computer models that forecast possible impacts and costs.

The Project Butterfly team undertook the production of a feasibility study, built on much of the climate and energy modeling work since 1988, to establish a business-as-usual scenario and to evaluate the impact of a new business case on the key stakeholders related to the energy industry. It was our hope that this feasibility study could serve as the basis for a game plan that would work as the Project Butterfly new business case and that that new business case would provide a Hail Mary pass to address climate change.

In the view of the Project Butterfly team, the development of the new business case would start by incorporating the work of the many scientists and economists who had come before us to create a global climate and energy model.

Over the past few decades, computer modeling has enabled climate scientists to witness in real time how increasing levels of GHG emissions affect global temperatures. This modeling incorporates both historical data encased in ice cores taken from the polar regions and current meteorological data from weather anomalies such as hurricane-level storms and extended droughts. Moreover, these models are helping us understand the potential impact of rising temperatures on the shape of polar ice caps and on sea levels as we look decades into the future. Further, these climate scientists have broadly concluded that the additional GHG emissions caused by human activity are highly correlated with severe and abnormal occurrences in nature, as we reviewed in chapter 4. These same scientists, together with economists, have incorporated the cost of these environmental changes into their predictive models to run potential future scenarios with various levels of continuing GHG emissions. The result of decades of work is an industry of peer-reviewed and robust climate models that are used to simulate potential climate outcomes going as far out as the end of the twenty-first century.

The resulting dialogue has generally centered on pitting the cost of adapting to climate change against the cost of mitigation. The *Stern Review on the Economics of Climate Change*, published in 2006 and authored by Nicholas Stern—chair of the Grantham Research Institute on Climate Change and the Environment at the London School of Economics—sets the gold standard for evaluating the costs of both climate change and mitigation. The *Stern Review* was prepared at the request of then chancellor of the Exchequer Gordon Brown. The review analyzed both climate and energy models, including work performed by the IEA and the IPCC, to reach its results. The report stated that without policy action, the cost of climate change will be equal to 5 percent of the global gross domestic product (GDP) each year, with the potential to increase to as much as 20 percent. The *Stern Review* proposed an annual investment equal to 1 percent of annual global GDP to mitigate the full impact of climate change and avoid the worst effects. In June 2008, Stern revised his estimate to an investment rate of 2 percent of global GDP per annum as the required financial commitment needed to stabilize CO_2 concentration between 500 and 550 ppm.

Most independent climate scientists would likely encourage financial and government leaders to heed the *Stern Review*. Subsequent to the report's publication, the IEA announced that it largely concurred with the findings. The Project Butterfly team, too, would concur with the IEA analysis. However, it is critical to note that the purpose of the Project Butterfly study is considerably different from that which motivated the *Stern Review*.

Chairman Stern's purpose was to estimate the costs of climate change. Our purpose is to evaluate the feasibility, and the corresponding costs and financial benefits, of converting our global energy system to a sustainable mix of renewable energy assets and energy efficiency practices. The intent of the proposed conversion is to limit GHG emissions to a "satisfactory level"—that is to keep the concentration of CO_2 in the atmosphere below 550 ppm and to hopefully reverse the upward trend as future innovations take root. The focus of our inquiry is to reveal whether the global community should begin immediately to mitigate climate change with proven technologies, rather than wait a few decades for greater wealth accumulation and future technological innovation as many of the critics of Chairman Stern's review have suggested.

Figure 10.1, prepared by internationally renowned investment bank Lazard Capital, shows the levelized costs of the four primary renewable power sources in the market as recently as 2011—wind, geothermal, biomass, and solar energy—compared with those of conventional power alternatives

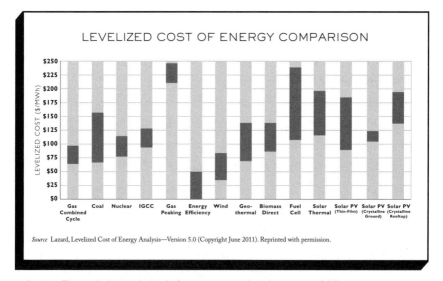

LEVELIZED COST OF ENERGY COMPARISON

Source Lazard, Levelized Cost of Energy Analysis—Version 5.0 (Copyright June 2011). Reprinted with permission.

• *fig. 10.1:* This graph depicts the level of competitiveness based upon cost of different energy generating technologies. While conventional generation technologies (coal and gas) are still significantly cheaper than other technologies, it appears that solar, geothermal, and wind are on their coattails.

gas, coal, and nuclear power. Lazard's estimate reveals that renewable energy sources are now nearly competitive with these conventional sources. This is a clear milestone in the maturation process of a new industry. However, the Lazard Capital data also reveal that we are still not to the point where renewable energy is the dominant winner without including the cost of depletion and pollution (as discussed in chapter 5). Twenty or even ten years ago, this would not have been the case. The Project Butterfly business-as-usual scenario would have shown a much more dire outcome regarding the buildup of GHG emissions. The competitive repositioning of these unconventional technologies today allows us to begin thinking about much smaller changes to energy policies that can dramatically adjust our global energy mix.

The Project Butterfly team has created a financial model of the global energy mix by building off the theoretical or technical perspective discussed in the previous chapters regarding the Project Butterfly Sustainability Model. As each nation takes measure of its own energy portfolio, small fiscal or regulatory interventions can have sizable results. For example, if renewable energy technologies were not cost competitive, adjusting each nation's energy mix might require more draconian efforts, making a market-based solution that much more difficult. However, new technologies have nearly reached parity even without the internalization of environmental costs. It is possible now, through tinkering with the inclusion of externalities in supplier prices (and the redirection of subsidies), to see substantial reductions in the carbon content of the global energy mix as we look into the future. It raises the prospect outlined in the story of Joe Kennedy and Steve Rothstein's nonprofit oil company: Just because it hasn't been done in the past doesn't mean that it cannot be done in the future.

The operating philosophy for the Project Butterfly team is that it would be very difficult for policy makers, economists, environmentalists, and the general public to ignore the results of a solution that shows the viability of an equivalent portfolio of energy assets that meets our global and bottom-line requirements. In fact, if staging such an important transformation begins to seem possible, the various global stakeholders might be encouraged to see new ways to boost it along a more aggressive developmental path. As the users, suppliers, financiers, and stewards of this critical industry (which includes nearly all of the global population), we may find ourselves in strong agreement for building a new global consensus.

The concept behind the Project Butterfly new business case is therefore to look at the entire global energy system as if it were a single portfolio of energy assets, with suppliers in search of lowering their carbon footprint. The desired outputs are defined as ones that would be required by any sophisticated project developer evaluating the consequence of changes in the energy mix upon each stakeholder.

The Project Butterfly team developed this financial model of the global energy mix as a single portfolio—our Hail Mary pass—by following a five-step methodology.

STEP 1: CHARACTERIZING
THE CURRENT ENERGY SUPPLY MIX

The first step was to ensure that the Project Butterfly Financial Model provided an accurate characterization of the current energy supply mix in order to set a baseline and determine the business-as-usual simulation. The breakdown of the current supply mix would allow the Project Butterfly team to calculate and forecast the buildup of CO_2 concentration, assuming there would be no change in either current policies or demand for the long-term growth of energy. The data underlying figure 10.2, prepared by the IEA, contrasts the most recent configuration of global energy production projections for 2035 with totals from 2009. The graphic also depicts what the IEA believes will be the likely impact on this configuration, assuming current policies (business as usual) and modest new international policies to curb carbon emissions. The IEA's "450 Scenario" shows what kind of changes in the global energy mix

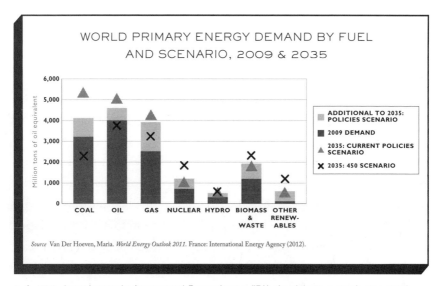

Source Van Der Hoeven, Maria. *World Energy Outlook 2011.* France: International Energy Agency (2012).

✦ *fig. 10.2:* According to the International Energy Agency (IEA), the globe is currently on a trend to further and further increase dependency on coal, oil, and gas. Renewables are set to also see an increase in use, but not nearly to the tune that the conventional fuels will realize. The IEA projects that in order to reach a limit of 450 ppm, the world must take a giant leap forward by decreasing its dependency on coal and oil, while renewables will need to drastically increase their share.

would be required to keep CO_2 concentration in the earth's atmosphere under 450 ppm. The IEA data gave us a benchmark against which to compare any model we might generate.

The Project Butterfly team wanted to simulate both energy demand and expected supplies in a manner similar to the IEA approach, and using available data sets based on public literature, which allowed us to meet expected global energy demand to the end of the century. By evaluating the carbon content of the final energy mix, the Project Butterfly team hoped to be able to create our own calculation for the impact on global GHG emissions.

Figure 10.2 represents a high-level executive summary of our current energy mix. Coal, oil, and gas dominate the supply mix, as you would expect. To meet the IEA demand forecast under its current policy scenario by 2035, the Project Butterfly team also noted that all forms of supply are expected to grow. We felt that this outcome was consistent with expectations based on the cost estimates of competing energy technologies as provided in the previous figure from Lazard Capital. The demand forecast suggests that each energy class would aggressively compete for market share.

The questions for our feasibility study, therefore, became much more refined. Is it possible for renewable energy to change its position relative to nonrenewable fuels, especially those with intensive carbon emissions, such as coal and oil, which currently dominate our portfolio? What kinds of price signals are needed for renewable energy to emerge and become the clear winner *in time* to make a difference—specifically, keeping CO_2 concentration levels below 450 ppm (in the case of the IEA) or under 550 ppm (in the case of Project Butterfly) until the end of the century?

Despite the fact that new policies are being implemented worldwide to promote renewable energy technologies by 2035, according to the IEA's own forecasts, we quickly realized that current measures would be insufficient. The Project Butterfly team would need to be able to model greater flexibility into policy. To change the global energy mix to achieve the IEA's 450 ppm scenario, the Project Butterfly team determined that it was necessary to more dramatically decrease conventional fuel sources from the business-as-usual scenario and to increase renewable energy from wind, solar, biomass, and other technologies.

We realized that we needed to dig down deeper into the costs for each energy type in order to evaluate its overnight costs.

STEP 2: MAKING OR BUYING NEW POWER

The second step toward viewing the global energy mix as a single portfolio of generating assets was to evaluate each energy supplier in the mix and its decision-making process for whether to make or to buy new power. By making new power, the utility can issue bonds and pass on the cost to its customer (the ratepayers), subject to regulatory approval. By buying power, the energy supplier often seeks to secure the least-cost solution yet still pass on the level-ized cost to its ratepayers. By taking either approach, the energy supplier can manage its conflicting responsibilities: to offer reliable and affordable energy services to its ratepayers and consumers, and to maximize shareholder value for its owners. The Project Butterfly team felt that this process would have to be at the very heart of the Project Butterfly Financial Model.

The business-as-usual scenario would need to incorporate current policies to promote diversification of the energy mix through renewable portfolio standards (RPS), a mandatory system used in more than half of the United States and throughout the eurozone to promote alternative energy. The RPS is usually a federal or state program that requires utilities or publicly owned or regulated power suppliers to meet a certain percentage of their individual energy mix using alternative forms of energy. The terms and conditions of an RPS policy can vary substantially and would have a material impact on any forecast generated by the Project Butterfly Finan-cial Model. For instance, the average RPS requirement in the United States mandates power suppliers to make or buy a certain percentage—between 4 and 30 percent—of their power production from renewable energy by a targeted date.[213]

However, the Project Butterfly team determined that the RPS system is not a cure-all from an environmental perspective, because such a mandatory program would bring the renewable power industry only up to the level speci-fied by the mandate. After the regulated energy suppliers meet the imposed standard, these energy suppliers would be free to return to purchasing (or making) the least-cost energy source. So, as long as cheap and abundant coal and natural gas supplies are available, it is unlikely the power supplier would continue to buy renewable energy. In fact, the power supplier would naturally pursue the lowest cost of supply to meet growing demand or to replace exist-ing and aging capacity because the RPS does not address cost.

The Project Butterfly business-as-usual scenario would therefore need to be modified to encompass both current RPS standards and the buying behavior of each energy supplier relative to the overnight cost of each energy type.

STEP 3: EVALUATING
THE EFFECTS OF SUBSIDIES

The third step for creating a financial model of the global energy system was to incorporate a capacity to evaluate the effects of eliminating certain built-in subsidies that foster the business-as-usual approach—such as continued favorable tax treatment for the extraction and transport of oil, coal, and natural gas. The model requires the capacity to simulate different outcomes based on potential changes to the direction of subsidies.

According to the IEA's 2012 *World Energy Outlook,* global subsidies to fossil fuel suppliers amounted to $523 billion in 2011, up almost 30 percent from 2010.[214] The level of subsidies to fossil fuel suppliers seems inconsistent with the articulation of most modern day energy policies to promote asset diversification. Subsidies to fossil fuels in 2011 were six times greater than subsidies to renewable energy. The Project Butterfly team quickly concluded that small changes to the levels of these subsidies could have significant impacts on future adjustments to the global energy mix.

We also adjusted our thinking about the future of the global energy mix to accommodate the turmoil in oil-producing countries in the Middle East and North Africa, coupled with the challenges of further nuclear energy development after the 2011 Fukushima Daiichi nuclear power plant disaster. Our assessment was that both of these circumstances cast doubts on the reliability of global energy supplies from new energy sources. In fact, the IEA's 2011 report said that "concerns about sovereign financial integrity have shifted the focus of government attention away from energy policy and limited their means of policy intervention, boding ill for agreed global climate change objectives."[215] The Project Butterfly team's view has been that nothing major in the global energy markets has changed since 2011 to alter this worldview.

STEP 4: ESTABLISHING GLOBAL
GDP AND POPULATION GROWTH

The Project Butterfly team's fourth step was to look at the broader economic environment and to determine the impact of global GDP and population growth on the energy market generally. Looking at these broader issues included reviewing how policy changes might affect innovation and improvements in the efficiency of new capital.

Demand for new energy is difficult to predict year to year and is heavily dependent on projections of economic activity. The headlines of nearly every major financial news agency continue to report an uneven recovery from the 2008 recession. Energy prices and volatility have been difficult to track, but in 2010 the IEA reported that energy demand rebounded a dramatic 5 percent over the previous year. The economic recovery has meant more energy consumption, and as a result CO_2 emissions from energy use have surged to a new high.[216]

The resounding message of the IEA's 2012 report is that policy makers are failing to address the financial and environmental crises facing our world. Alternatively, the IEA has expressed the view that if current policy initiatives along the lines of many domestic programs that have followed the Kyoto Protocol are enacted and enforced, significant differences in potential environmental impacts and scenarios are possible. Nevertheless, independently, individual authors of the IEA report have expressed concern over whether it will even be possible to limit atmospheric CO_2 concentration to a point where the global mean temperatures are limited to a rise of 3.6 degrees Fahrenheit (2 degrees Celsius). The IEA authors also confirm that, in their view, increasing temperatures above this target may be the maximum permissible increase before the climate catastrophically changes.[217]

STEP 5: ACCOUNTING FOR EXTERNALITIES

The fifth step in modeling the global energy mix as a single portfolio of energy assets was to develop policy mechanisms that boost the adoption of alternative energy supplies or that promote the use of energy efficiency by including environmental externalities in the price of supplying the energy. To internalize pollution costs, for example, utility-owned power suppliers and independent power producers can be assessed a fee in the form of a carbon tax or can have their carbon emissions capped to create a market price. If this fee or carbon tax represents the true cost of the externalities, this strategy would result in a comparative cost reduction for renewable energy supplies, making them much more competitive while decreasing the competitiveness of conventional sources of energy through the internalization of their environmental costs.

Consider the inclusion of environmental costs that would come into play under a cap and trade system (similar to that implemented by the Kyoto Protocol) or through a global tax or fee on GHG emissions: When nations set a cap on industrial emissions, the market creates a price on carbon emissions (if those nations are allowed to trade credits). At the domestic level, establishing a national fee or carbon tax can also fix a cost on carbon that indirectly sets the price. Suppliers and users can then adjust their buying behavior.

CALIBRATING THE MODEL

Upon completing steps 1 through 5, the next move for Project Butterfly was to work with our modeling team to calibrate the simulations so they would match up against the general expectations of the business-as-usual scenario. We wanted to make sure that the model reflected projections in energy demand and the carbon results from other energy and climate models. Our general expectation was that the demand for new energy would increase by one-third from 2010 to 2035, assuming an increase in global population of 1.7 billion people and a 3.5 percent average annual growth in the global economy.[218]

The other critical factor to consider was the actual dynamics of expected population growth. There are substantial differences in the energy and carbon impact of someone born in the United States versus China versus Africa, based on economic conditions and development forecasts for these regions. The population dynamics can be a mitigating factor that in our view must be included in the business-as-usual calculation.

We chose to accept the view of the Organization for Economic Co-operation and Development (OECD). According to the OECD, most of the assumed population growth will be in areas where energy use per capita is lower than in developed countries. For example, the IEA's presumption is that China will continue to be the world's largest energy user. By 2045, it is presumed that China will consume 70 percent more energy than the United States. This is in spite of the fact that China's per capita income will still be less than half that of the per capita income of the United States.

The other areas of concern for the IEA are the Middle East, Brazil, Indonesia, and India, where economic growth will exceed that in China over the same time frame. The IEA believes that rates of growth in these regions of the world will have a significant impact on global energy demand.

Accordingly, the IEA estimates that global investments in new energy supplies, under the agency's business-as-usual scenario, are estimated to grow to $38 trillion between 2011 and 2035. The majority of these investments will be outside of the United States and Europe, suggesting that efforts to reduce GHGs will need to be focused as much on new energy infrastructure in emerging markets as on replacing aging infrastructure in the United States and Europe.

The concern that immediately arose for Project Butterfly is that the vast majority of the infrastructure in our forward-looking calculations would already be built and operating. According to the IEA forecasts from 2010 to 2035 only one-fifth of global emissions are open to adjustments through 2035 in order to keep GHG emissions within the IEA 450 ppm scenario— that is, unless we start shutting down existing infrastructure. The IEA reports that nearly four-fifths of the total energy-related CO_2 emissions permissible by 2035 have already been locked in by our existing capital stock.

The Project Butterfly Financial Model would also need to reflect the IEA data for the business-as-usual simulation regarding oil supply and demand.

The business-as-usual simulation parallels the "bell curve" in our discussion of Peak Oil in chapter 5. The IEA forecasts that the cost of bringing oil to the market is rising as companies are forced to turn to more difficult and costly sources, such as shale and deepwater sources, to replace lost capacity. The IEA also predicts that the production of conventional crude oil will begin to fall prior to 2035. As a result, markets will turn to liquefied natural gas, coal, and renewable energy supplies as replacements.

The Project Butterfly team also wanted the business-as-usual simulation to reflect changes in oil imports to the United States even though we wanted to create a global energy model that would not make any regional distinctions. The IEA expects oil imports to drop as efficiency gains reduce demand (higher fuel efficiency requirements will be imposed on transportation, for example) and as new supplies are developed domestically. Nevertheless, we felt that we could accomplish our goal because international demand for oil would continue to rely heavily on a relatively small number of oil-producing countries, which ship their oil along vulnerable supply routes.

The Project Butterfly business-as-usual simulation also needed to reflect the recent advancements in renewable energy. In reviewing data from the IEA's 2012 *World Energy Outlook* we noted their enthusiasm for renewable energy generation. The IEA reported that in their forecast renewable energy power generation would nearly triple from 2010 to 2035, comprising almost 31 percent of total generation. Hydropower would provide half of this generation capacity, with wind accounting for almost 25 percent and solar photovoltaic accounting for 7.5 percent. Underpinning the development in renewable energy would be the necessary investment in renewables, to the tune of $6.4 trillion over the period 2012–2035, and the increase of $240 billion in subsidies by 2035.

One additional technology that we felt could have a meaningful impact, but is also highly dependent on carbon regulations or legislative measures, is the development of carbon capture and sequestration (CCS). Without a price on carbon emissions, the development of such technologies would be unlikely because of their initial investment cost. But if a price on carbon were to be put into place, it would be possible for existing coal deposits to continue to provide utilities and power producers with upgraded coal, even in a carbon-constrained and regulated market.

The business-as-usual simulation set the stage for making variations to determine the feasibility of a new business case, one that would meet our goal of reducing the rate of increasing CO_2 concentration levels. Calibrating our model to these other existing data sets gave the Project Butterfly team confidence in running other simulations.

UNDERSTANDING SYSTEM DYNAMICS

The desire of the Project Butterfly team was to provide a more detailed summary of the parameters of the underlying calculations of our modeling efforts and to make them available in full online. The intent of our exercise was to forecast energy demand under the business-as-usual scenario and then to forecast profitability, by energy type, under different simulations. The Project Butterfly team also wanted to view the different scenarios from each of the key global stakeholders' perspectives, including that of the energy user, who (we felt) would need to be in alignment with policy objectives. That is, the energy user would also need to see a direct financial benefit (even if it was in the long term) to any adjustment in the global energy mix. Our particular focus would be the impact on profitability and user cost from internalizing critical externalities and redirecting existing subsidies. The Project Butterfly team dubbed our approach the *Project Butterfly Methodology* and the result the *Project Butterfly Financial Model,* which would run two simulations: the business-as-usual scenario and the new business case.

The analysis underlying the Project Butterfly Financial Model has been designed to simulate changes to the energy mix from the present day all the way to the end of this century. To accomplish such a task, the Project Butterfly team selected "system dynamics" as its modeling approach, which was originally developed at MIT's Sloan School of Management in the early 1970s. System dynamics is a common, methodological approach used by business schools for creating simulations that help professionals in industry improve their understanding of complex situations and how they evolve over time. A system dynamics model is based on ordinary differential equations and the functional relationships that drive them. Notably, it has been applied to climate and energy modeling by the Climate Interactive team (whom I introduced in the preface).

To meet our modeling objective, the Project Butterfly team built a financial calculator on the back of the carbon and energy modeling platform, called En-ROADS, in order to evaluate the impact of changes in the global energy mix on an individual supplier's profitability. For example, we wanted to examine such impacts on renewable energy suppliers compared to those on coal or nuclear energy suppliers. The financial calculator was developed by one of the world's leading engineering and design consultancies, the WSP Group, in order to meet the specifications set by the Project Butterfly team. Climate Interactive, in turn, developed a sub-model within En-ROADS that performs the functions of this calculator. The reason the Project Butterfly team sought to incorporate a financial calculator into a state-of-the-art climate and energy simulation model was so that we could determine the financial impact on all classes of stakeholders and to see whether a new business case could be created to reduce the buildup of CO_2 emissions while simultaneously determining the optimal policies and technology applications to achieve this objective.

The purpose of the Project Butterfly Financial Model was to better understand the financial dynamics of various global energy investment scenarios. The Project Butterfly team felt that the broader approach of classifying energy assets, as reflected in other modeling work, is disadvantaged by the lack of such a financial calculator. The model allowed the Project Butterfly team to specify interest and discount rates and to calculate the net present value (NPV), the internal rate of return (IRR), and the return on investment (ROI) for each source of capital installed at a specified year. For each supplier, the model then calculated the total NPV and the weighted average of IRR and ROI of all sources.

Of course, we would have liked to create an actual crystal ball to help us determine precise profitability or quantitative predictions not only by each energy type but by individual technologies. If we had, I probably wouldn't have taken the time to write this book. I would be too busy making new investments or creating investment funds. In lieu of this crystal ball, the Project Butterfly team felt that incorporating a financial calculator would reveal results that would give us significant insights into the timing, feedback, and delays in the transformation of our global energy system.

Moreover, we did not optimize the Project Butterfly Financial Model to find the very best outcome. We wanted simply to find one or two outcomes that showed that it would be possible to reduce atmospheric CO_2 concentrations while still creating alignment between and among all stakeholders. Our hope is that others who are far more competent to run optimization scenarios will take up our work in the future.

The cost data also was limited in that it is based on reference costs of each energy path and is calculated based on its initial fractional share of each supplier's total energy capacity. Understanding and then manipulating this complicated set of equations in order to find optimal outcomes occupied a great deal of the Project Butterfly team's time. Nevertheless, system dynamics met the Project Butterfly specifications because the approach allowed us to forecast the behavior of complex systems, such as the energy market, under different circumstances over time. The system dynamics approach incorporates feedback loops and delays that realistically affect the behavior of the overall system. Our application of system dynamics also allowed us to look at stocks and flows and to analyze the rate of depletion of certain resources.

The results of the Project Butterfly modeling analysis have revealed what we believe is a perfect fit. The En-ROADS system dynamics model utilizes a simulation structure that is based on capital stocks on the demand and supply sides, on market clearing theory to balance the two, on emissions from the resulting energy mix, and then on applying the climate implications that result from those emissions.

Furthermore, we feel that the system dynamics approach is well suited to the analysis of the energy market, which is dominated by engineering innovation, technology adaptation, and economics. Our use of this theory in our model fits the global energy system perfectly, because we were looking to determine how our energy-supply mix might change over time based on different "what-if" scenarios, which would allow us to test certain policies and their impact on market conditions.

According to system dynamics methodology, a system or problem—such as the impact of certain energy-supply mixes on global GHG emissions—is represented by a simple map of all its components and their interactions. For example, as the demand for energy grows, more power plants are constructed. This in turn creates an abundance of supply, which lowers the price of electricity, which then further increases energy demand. Incorporating such feedback loops into a causal loop diagram reveals the structure of the system. By applying the principles of system dynamics to the design requirements set by Project Butterfly, it becomes possible to forecast the system's behavior over time.

The energy market is composed of supply and demand features from different sources of energy that form the evolving energy mix. By starting with the potential adoption of a certain technology, it is possible to establish the rate of adoption before a technology or supply source saturates a market. Saturation is a function of stock and flow. For example, the results of system dynamics simulations of a technology entering the market typically follow a classic S-shaped curve. The increase in adopters starts out slowly, followed first by exponential growth and, ultimately, by saturation.

The system dynamics model for the energy market is superior to traditional spreadsheet calculations because it allows modelers to account for the following considerations:

> **Adoption takes time.** Commercialization, permitting, financing, and construction proceed at a bureaucratic pace. For instance, nonelectrified end uses, such as cars and industrial applications, can be electrified, but not instantaneously.

» **Success builds success.** Costs of a new technology fall as cumulative experience is gained. Rising market share for a new technology builds familiarity. Familiarity broadens the reach of infrastructure so that success feeds on itself.

» **Constraints must be factored in.** Rising costs and scarcity of materials put limits on the pace of growth in a new or existing technology.

» **Demand and supply are linked.** Energy demand falls if energy prices rise. If energy prices fall, demand rises.

For these reasons, the Project Butterfly team adopted the system dynamics approach in order to calculate the impact of policy changes on the adoption of core technologies and to measure the consequential shifts in the total energy mix.

The goal of the Project Butterfly team, with respect to the Project Butterfly Financial Model, was to construct a new business case simulation in a way that deals with a very, if not the most, important aspect of project finance. In the business community, it is highly unlikely that any large-scale project will ever move forward unless it is accompanied by complete financial documentation so that all participants can view the impact on their unique concerns. All of the components must be laid out in as transparent a means as possible. The Project Butterfly methodology provides this transparency. It allows us to model the global energy supply and to see the financial effects of transitioning to a more sustainable energy mix.

In the subsequent chapters, I lay out some of the results of our simulations using the key financial formulas that the energy industry uses to compare different capital investments by showing NPV and IRR calculations, similar to how individual projects are analyzed. Both the total value of the project, demonstrated by an NPV function, and the overall return of the project, demonstrated by the IRR, must be immediately apparent. The limitation of other climate and energy models is that they show only the costs associated with their narrow area of specialization and in accordance to a single stakeholder perspective. For example, there are models on the costs to clean up after large natural disasters, models on the costs of a growing population, and models on the costs of rising sea levels. However, the comparison of costs alone will not dictate whether or not a shift in behavior will or should occur. What is needed is a clear and concise visualization of the value of new pricing and supply constraints in order to measure the shift in holistic and economic terms—a visualization that the Project Butterfly Financial Model (and the methodology behind it) does indeed provide.

Moreover, based on fundamental financial theories, the Project Butterfly Financial Model is able to represent the overall costs and benefits to the key stakeholders—the energy user, the energy services supplier, the investor/lender, and the environmental steward—as the global energy portfolio changes over time.

FIRING UP THE IMAGINATION OF THE WORLD

In the opening chapter, I said that in order to transform our energy economy, we must fire up the imagination of the investor—and of the world. The global society must find a way for our energy suppliers and bankers to not only see a different possibility for our environmental future but also find a way to make money. Otherwise, capital is risk averse. Without some expectation of financial return, bankers and energy suppliers that make up the energy industry will not invest.

To build a new model requires creating a feasibility plan for a different scenario. The energy industry must begin to attract new capital to create a new future, and this chapter has outlined the Project Butterfly approach for doing exactly that. The following chapter describes the Project Butterfly Financial Model in detail, as well as its results. It delivers our forecast of the business-as-usual scenario—and what is possible under a new business case.

KEY OBSERVATIONS

The key observations we can make about defining the Project Butterfly methodology are as follows:

» The IEA and IPCC are highly trusted sources of knowledge whose models and predictions were the starting point that allowed the Project Butterfly team to head off in the right direction.

» According to the IEA and the Project Butterfly business-as-usual scenario, all types of energy supply are expected to grow in the future. New types of energy from renewable resources are set to make a huge increase in global presence, but coal, oil, and natural gas will continue to dominate the stage for at least the next twenty-five years under the business-as-usual scenario.

» The Project Butterfly Financial Model is able to do something that other climate and energy models cannot: It adds the extremely important, and often omitted, component concerning financial drivers that illustrates how lead suppliers, financiers, and users change their buying behavior and adjust their tactics in a way that leaves the global community in the status quo. Calculating costs is a great first step in demonstrating the urgency of our current situation, but this alone is insufficient to get the point across and initiate real action. Profit and strong margins dictate the flow of capital; otherwise, capital is risk averse. It is our aim to show the necessary financial metrics to transition the global economy away from conventional sources of energy and toward a more energy-efficient and renewable economy— one that is sustainable and can limit CO_2 concentration levels to below 550 ppm by the end of the century.

» The consequences of catastrophic global climate change seem futuristic, and calculating their costs seems abstract. The key to change, therefore, is demonstrating that a concrete, measurable, and present value will be gained through global transformation—that is, through working to create a new business case.

Two roads diverged in a wood, and . . .
I took the one less traveled.
—*Robert Frost*

CHAPTER 11

It was about a week before graduation, and the 1982 annual meeting of Hampshire College's board of trustees was under way. As the student-elected trustee, I had spent my final year at Hampshire working on a student-led effort to diversify the college's recently accumulated endowment by withdrawing from some of its largest holdings. The students were working to document the "social injury" caused by weapons manufacturers and large US military contractors. These companies were publicly traded and common household names. They were held as investments in the college's endowment. Two years before, Hampshire had been a leader among other colleges and universities across the country by being one of the first to divest from companies that operated under South Africa's apartheid government.

In the 1970s and 1980s South Africa was known throughout the world for its abundant natural resources, including rich agricultural lands and significant deposits of unique minerals. Back then, South Africa was also known for its brutal and racial domestic policies under an apartheid regime. The student group I represented wanted to extend the line of thinking developed by the South Africa divestiture movement, by looking at other areas where socially responsible investing could be turned into social action. A subcommittee of the board had already approved the student proposal, but this meeting would be a make-or-break deal. Walking across campus toward the meeting place, I was a bit nervous.

As I turned the corner to the administrative building, I was surprised to see about one hundred students congregating in the hot sun. A few large loudspeakers were scattered about so the students would be able hear the deliberations going on inside. The conversation about divesting from military weapons contractors had obviously attracted a crowd.

Perhaps this shouldn't have been so surprising to me. After all, it was 1982 and the Cold War was in full swing. President Ronald Reagan was calling for public investments in "Star Wars" technologies. It seemed as though the warnings of a previous president, Dwight D. Eisenhower, who in his 1961 farewell speech to the nation coined the term *military-industrial complex*, were coming to bear. Specifically, President Eisenhower had warned of a triangular relationship between political contributions, political approval of defense spending, and lobbyist support of bureaucracies that fed the military machine. The concern that many students at Hampshire shared was that the US military establishment, set up to protect our nation but now on the brink of taking weapons into space, could ultimately drag us into war. Here was a small college in New England making a bold statement: "No more!"

One hour into the meeting, the chairman of the board, Colby Hewitt, asked for a report from the subcommittee that had previously passed the student proposal. I would learn later that two board members also served as officers of some of the companies that would be affected adversely by accepting the recommendations in the student proposal. These board members questioned me directly. We started by sharing differing views about US foreign policy, but the discussion quickly narrowed in on the delicate balance of deterrence required to keep the peace between two superpower nations. Was Star Wars technology simply needed to ensure peace, or was it the first step in a policy to develop first-strike capability? What was our responsibility as investors of a private college's endowment fund? I was pleased that all the board members were taking the student proposal seriously, but I could tell we were quickly reaching an impasse in the conversation.

Only years later did I realize that Colby Hewitt had been a master of boardroom politics that day. He pulled us out of a quagmire by asking the pivotal question: "Tom, if Hampshire College cannot invest in South Africa and if we cannot invest in weapons manufacturing, then what *can* we invest in?"

His question was deeply penetrating, but logical. I didn't have an immediate response. I realize today that it's the question we must constantly ask ourselves as we look at any existential issue: What kind of investments do we as concerned nations, or even colleges, need to be making to promote economic development, international stability, and a reliable energy supply?

On that early summer day, the board of trustees at Hampshire tabled the student proposal and instead voted to create a special committee that would further study how the college might implement a broader, socially responsible investment policy. The students were initially frustrated by the vote because they felt that immediate action was needed, but in subsequent meetings, the student body learned that what we had done was start a critical conversation not only inside the college, but also at similar institutions throughout the country.

As for me, I would continue to try to answer the question posed by the late Colby Hewitt, a businessman and devoted trustee to Hampshire College, long after I graduated and well into my career. In fact, the question *What do we invest in?* is at the very heart of why I gathered the Project Butterfly team, whose work underlies this book. I wanted to look at global warming through a lens of finance and investing to determine what we need to do if we are to avoid the cataclysmic consequences that are otherwise sure to come.

THE PROJECT BUTTERFLY FINANCIAL MODEL

The threat of climate change is an existential issue. The issue is every bit as important as the problem during the 1980s of directly or indirectly supporting the South Africa apartheid government through an investment portfolio. Climate change is also similar to the existential threat of an uncontrolled nuclear arms race. At the risk of repeating myself, I must start my summary of the results of the Project Butterfly Financial Model by saying that the Project Butterfly business-as-usual simulation is not the worst-case scenario. Rather, it is the expected case if the global society continues to follow the same trends exactly as we are now. That means the status quo preferred by energy suppliers and investors is far from being entirely negative.

Most countries that manufacture automobiles have raised their fuel efficiency standards over the last two decades. Most industrialized countries, to generate electricity, switched from burning oil to building nuclear power plants in the 1970s. Many of the same energy suppliers have developed natural gas–fired power plants over the past decade in order to comply with environmental regulations. From a market perspective, renewable energy is the fastest-growing form of new energy supply, as I discussed in the last chapter. However, meeting the energy challenge requires understanding something much deeper about how we will manage the energy requirements imposed by the growth of the global economy and specifically the world's gross domestic product (GDP). It is the underlying assumptions to the Project Butterfly Financial Model that makes our business-as-usual simulation the expected case. If these assumptions change for the worse—and they can—it is possible for climate change to become much, much more drastic. Of course, it is also possible to make small changes to the assumptions that can make the situation much better.

I will try to give you a flavor of these "underlying assumptions." GDP growth is the annual percentage growth rate in the total value of all goods and services at market prices based on local currencies, typically aggregated into constant US dollars. The actual GDP is the sum of the gross value added by all producers in the national economy, plus any product taxes and minus any subsidies. It is calculated without taking any deductions for depreciation, inflation, or depletion, or for degradation of natural resources. The challenge of managing the global energy mix, therefore, involves not only reconfiguring the mix of supply that feeds current energy demand but also mixing the kind of demand required to fuel economic growth.

The bad news is also the good news. Because energy is part of nearly every incremental component that allows producers to deliver their goods and services, it takes more energy to fuel a larger economy, or so the theory goes. However, every dollar spent in the global economy has had to incur some energy and carbon cost. That means that a slight alteration in the cost structure of energy and carbon changes everything. Consider that in 2012, global GDP was $71.2 trillion. The United States was (and continues to be) the single largest contributor to global GDP, providing approximately $15.6 trillion and making up approximately 22 percent of the total. To give a sense of this size, the entire G-7 (the United States, the UK, France, Germany, Italy, Canada, and Japan) accounted for $33.7 trillion or 47 percent of global GDP. Moreover, some regions have been experiencing meteoric rises in terms of global GDP—China and India, for example, which account for $8.25 trillion (11.6 percent) and $1.95 trillion (3 percent), respectively.[219] That means that when we agree to simply add a price to carbon, we change nearly everyone's relationship to energy use.

The implications are staggering. The simulations underlying both the business-as-usual scenario and Project Butterfly's new business case start with the assumption that the global capital growth rate will increase at 3 percent per annum over the short term before steadily declining toward a long-term growth rate of 1.5 percent by the end of the century. Such assumptions seem modest. But in spite of slower capital growth, according to our calculations, global GDP will more than quadruple by 2100, reaching $430 trillion, as figure 11.1 shows. Compounding obviously affects total economic activity over a relatively short period of time, for both the business-as-usual and the new business case scenarios, providing a baseline for comparison. That means that a small change in pricing to every unit of human-caused carbon emissions can have an enormous impact.

Looking ahead, our estimate for capital growth assumes a rate consistent with estimates of a declining population growth rate, based on the premise that the earth's population will reach nine billion people by 2045 and then begin to flatten out. According to the US Census Bureau, world population growth rates ranged from 1.5 to 2 percent between 1950 and 1991, toward

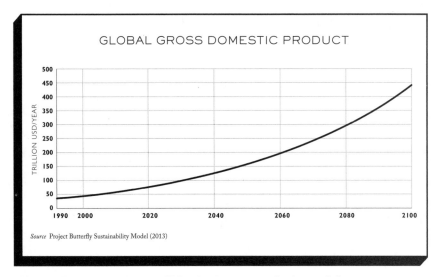

GLOBAL GROSS DOMESTIC PRODUCT

Source Project Butterfly Sustainability Model (2013)

• *fig. 11.1:* The connection between GDP and carbon emissions has historically been very strong. GDP estimates will continue to rise throughout the end of the century, and we can expect carbon levels to follow suit if left to current practices.

the end of the Cold War.[220] Growth rates have since dropped to a hair over 1 percent and are expected to drop by as much as 40 percent from there over the next fifty years.

Project Butterfly's business-as-usual and new business case simulations assume that population growth rates will fall as they have over the last few decades, because we expect continued economic and social development. The general explanation for the decline in growth rates is that when education is made available, especially when women have access to health care and when global per capita income rises, birth rates decline to more sustainable levels. If instead population growth rates held constant, the business-as-usual scenario would yield dramatically higher levels of GHG concentration into the earth's atmosphere than we expect, making the business-as-usual scenario a much worse case rather than simply our expected case today. Fortunately, population growth rates have fallen as global per capita income has risen, and they are expected to continue to do so. For example, our estimate of GDP growth rates corresponds with the UN's medium estimate of population through the end of the century. The implication is that part of containing climate change is promoting economic development in a way that encourages population growth to level off. It also means that there is room for improvement by continuing to promote economic and social development.

Based on available data, I agree with the view that the current population growth rate is indeed leveling off, and it seems reasonable that in fact the global population can stabilize. But again, it is important to remember that our simulation of "business as usual" is really only an expected case, not the worst-case scenario. It just means that now the global community, like Hampshire College's board of directors, needs to address *what we should invest in.*

Investing in the new business case builds upon the idea of working to create greater global wealth and prosperity through social and economic development by improving the condition of all classes of energy stakeholders, without overburdening resources. The answer to the question *What should we invest in?* is therefore straightforward. We need to invest in the kind of suppliers and technology that deliver a higher level of desired output while minimizing resource use. In this light, from the perspective of each stakeholder, global wealth generation and prosperity become the central features of any investment plan to mitigate climate change. This is the basis for the Project Butterfly Financial Model.

PERSPECTIVE OF THE ENERGY USER

Back in chapter 8, I defined the perspective of the environmental steward as looking at the intergenerational sustainability of our natural resources. The steward's role is to evaluate how the current system depletes natural resources and impairs the ecosystem underlying the health of the earth's life-sustaining reservoirs. The Project Butterfly Sustainability Model takes the steward's perspective on energy and the economy and forecasts energy demand. The model then estimates the expected supply, constrained by resource availability, and the cost trends as a result of depletion and learning curves. Finally, with the forecasts regarding the energy mix, the model projects GHG emissions and the likely impact on both atmospheric concentration of CO_2 and average global temperatures.

When looking at the global energy mix, the steward should consider the entire set of perspectives and integrate all stakeholders into a collective. Ultimately, however, the steward represents future generations. Thus the level of GHG concentration—the measure of the health and well-being of the ecosystem that will support those future generations—becomes the primary concern. In this way, the environmental steward acts as a check on authority, ensuring that the entire system functions properly. To illustrate the point, I'll refer again to the *Star Trek* character Dr. "Bones" McCoy, whom I introduced in chapter 7. Dr. McCoy acts as the steward on the bridge of the USS *Enterprise.* He is the only member of the crew with the authority to declare Captain James T. Kirk unfit for duty if his health is compromised. I often think of Dr. McCoy and wonder what the possibility for global sustainability might be if such authority were to be given to the environmental steward.

In this regard, the environmental steward will also need to be concerned with other indexes regarding the health of the earth and its inhabitants. These include gauges of literacy, the ratio of birth to death rates, and the risks of conflicts and war, among many others. A true global steward would also be concerned with the disparity between the rich and the poor, the living conditions of the global populous, and the ability of the earth's ecosystem to maintain the diversity of its species. The Project Butterfly Sustainability Model is limited in its capacity to measure the impact of these kinds of policies. The model focuses on minimizing CO_2 concentration and is thus a valuable tool for the steward, but mitigating GHG emissions also requires addressing these humanistic variables outside the direct purview of our model. Still, there is a single question underlying the policy settings that are required to achieve a successful sustainability model: How will the global community limit GHG growth to sustainable levels by shifting the energy mix and changing our relationship to energy?

The steward's main concern, therefore, is the impending threat of shorter winters and longer summers, including longer periods of melting and shorter periods of freezing. Project Butterfly's business-as-usual scenario forecasts that the concentration of CO_2 levels will surpass 500 ppm by the year 2046 and will reach more than 800 ppm by 2100, as shown in figure 11.2. The global energy mix is already changing rapidly toward energy sources from renewable energy, but with too many sources and insufficient sinks to absorb CO_2 growth, current fossil fuel emissions continue to grow. The estimated corresponding global temperature increase is expected to be 8 degrees Fahrenheit (4.5 degrees Celsius) by the end of the century. Keep in mind that temperatures at the equator will experience the least change. Temperatures in the polar regions will experience the most drastic change. Total energy in the atmosphere will increase because of the melting ice sheets and the greater water vapor in the atmosphere that complement the rising CO_2 concentration levels.

Figure 11.3 shows the growth in annual carbon emissions during the same period if the global society continues business as usual. Emissions must fall between the 450 ppm and 550 ppm lines as shown in figure 11.2, in

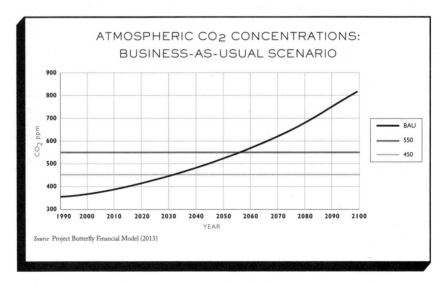

• *fig. 11.2:* Project Butterfly's modeling efforts reveal a constant rise in CO_2 concentration levels as the global economies continue to grow and further rely on carbon-based fuels.

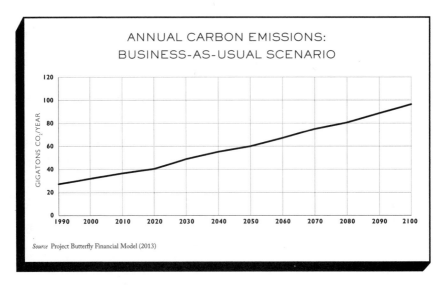

ANNUAL CARBON EMISSIONS:
BUSINESS-AS-USUAL SCENARIO

Source Project Butterfly Financial Model (2013)

✦ *fig. 11.3:* Low-carbon sources and renewable energy sources will experience tremendous growth under the business-as-usual case, but the long-term trend for annual carbon emissions will increase as long as the global economies continue to rely on fossil fuel sources.

order to achieve, respectively, no more than a 3.6 degree Fahrenheit (2 degree Celsius) or 5.4 degree Fahrenheit (3 degree Celsius) increase in global temperatures within the century.

The other critical assumption to highlight is that the rate of annual emissions growth of CO_2 in the business-as-usual scenario parallels the growth in GDP but is actually declining as a percentage of total GDP. In fact, the business-as-usual scenario actually includes a fairly significant decline in the energy intensity per unit of GDP, which is in part why I said previously that it is not the worst-case scenario. As companies continue to advance their technology, their management teams are incentivized to increase efficiency by reducing costs. Over time, companies typically improve costs and performance by continuing along the learning curve. The revolutionary discovery made by the Project Butterfly new business case is that by speeding up these processes, we accelerate the substitution of renewable energy for conventional fuels. It is this phenomenon, as much as any direct benefit from renewable-portfolio-standards policies that dictates a shift in the energy mix, that we want to positively influence.

Furthermore, under the Project Butterfly business-as-usual scenario, the rate of carbon intensity of primary energy (what the suppliers uses) is going down as these producers face new regulations that limit their pollution levels and as they seek out improvements to their own manufacturing processes. However, the rate of carbon intensity of final energy (what the users use) is going up. This macro-trend goes back to our chapter 5 discussions on the return on energy from the amount of energy invested to extract and produce that source. Over time, the energy industry has exploited the easiest-to-access sources of energy, and we are now forced to look toward more and more difficult geographical areas in order to extract an ever-increasing amount of energy to fuel continued economic growth. The recent rush toward unconventional gas and oil from tar sands (discussed in chapters 5 and 6) is an example of this increasing level of carbon intensity. This corresponding relationship between final energy and carbon intensity is likely to continue unless the energy industry dramatically accelerates the substitution of fossil fuels with new renewable energy supplies.

The kind of investments that we make should also be the ones that fare the best in either the business-as-usual scenario or any new business case. The issue is making sure that the investments are cost-competitive at the margin. The difference between business as usual and any new business case is just how big this margin needs to be.

PERSPECTIVE OF THE ENERGY SUPPLIER

The perspective of the supplier in the Project Butterfly business-as-usual scenario will likely see three major trends in the years to come. First of all, electricity from natural gas–fired generation will eventually begin to rise in cost as fuel costs compete with other sources of energy such as oil. This trend will be driven primarily by a continually increasing demand for transportation, by fuel switching from oil to gas, and by declining global resource availability in spite of new drilling technology. The second trend is the declining costs for renewable energy as a result of technological innovation and improvements in distribution and installation. The third trend is the continued growth in electric generation from coal because of its low cost of extraction and relative global abundance.

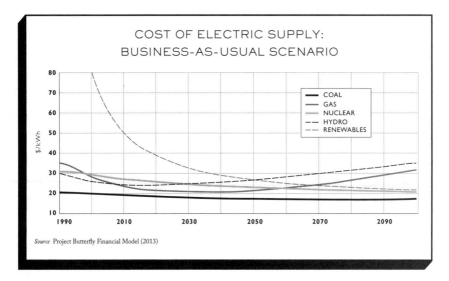

• *fig. 11.4:* Renewable sources of energy are poised to become cost competitive. However, the existing infrastructure surrounding fossil fuels is a very large hurdle to overcome.

Figure 11.4 tells nearly the whole story of why the global community is stuck in the business-as-usual scenario. The market is responding to lower renewable energy costs. However, the continued availability of oil, even at higher costs, and the long-term supply of cheap coal keep the market for both oil and coal flowing. Oil and coal may fail to continue to grow along historical patterns, but their continued growth is likely as long as they remain so difficult to substitute.

The consequence for the supplier is that oil and coal will remain strong in the business-as-usual scenario. So too will the renewable energy business. It is only under a new business scenario where suppliers of coal and oil will lose their competitive edge and where renewable energy will rise to dominance.

PERSPECTIVE OF THE INVESTOR/LENDER

Both the equity investor and the lender are looking for opportunities to place capital. However, the single focus of lenders is to provide capital for all growing industries, whereas the equity investor faces a more dynamic set of circumstances. As I discussed in chapter 7, nuclear energy is challenged, from the lender's perspective, by the scale of the investment requirements and the underlying technological risks. Consequently, lending to nuclear energy enterprises currently requires substantial public guarantees beyond the size of the balance sheets of the utilities supporting them. Coal-fired generation is tried-and-true, but new projects are subject to potential and uncertain regulatory restrictions.

For the lender, renewable energy, on the other hand, is hot. It seems that nearly every major bank has a renewable-energy financing program ready to fund projects that are utility scale and that have long-term supply contracts with access to the grid. Lenders are willing to provide loans to projects that have off-take agreements in excess of the loan terms and that show meaningful and positive IRRs to their equity investors. Moreover, lenders are looking for debt coverage ratios (DCRs) that are improving rather than declining. The consequence is a greater lending appetite for electricity generation from renewable energy sources because unlike conventional energy, they will not incur any future extraordinary expense from a potential carbon tax or a carbon cost from a cap and trade system.

Additionally, the financing of conversions of coal-fired power plants to natural gas is likely to remain a trend. New, independent natural gas plants may have difficulty attracting financing without long-term supply guarantees for their fuel, however. As mentioned in chapter 6, the economics of natural gas power generation are vulnerable to fuel-cost risk. Nevertheless, Project Butterfly's simulations do not reflect a downward trend. Overall, the business-as-usual scenario forecasts strong short-term returns for investors in just about all technology areas. Over the long term (greater than twenty years), however, our model shows only a slowing of investments in natural gas in the business-as-usual scenario as investors begin to realize diminishing returns.

PERSPECTIVE OF THE ENERGY USER

The price of energy is a bottom-line issue for the majority of energy users in today's economy. The demand for low-priced energy will likely continue into the future in spite of rising environmental costs or increased resource depletion. Certainly there are those few who are willing to spend a premium to market rates (commonly called a "green premium") as a means to satisfy other innate interests. Overall, however, the global population will demand the lowest-cost option as a means to guide their life purchases. Considering that nearly 1.1 billion people live on a dollar per day, it would be impossible to expect any kind of green premium from them. Even in the United States, as many Americans juggle their jobs, their children's education, their health care, and their house payments, energy costs are a bottom-line issue.

Because of these bottom-line realities for the energy user, trying to rationalize increasing the price of energy to account for externalities becomes a highly charged public discussion. However, the perspective of the energy user still doesn't change the rationale for fixing a price on carbon emissions to address the need for climate change mitigation because there is still a cost to be paid.

Fortunately, policy makers on a global scale have some "wiggle room" if they can contain changing prices by redirecting subsidies to end users and by stimulating innovation to both reduce costs today and preempt eventual price increases due to resource depletion in the future. The views of the environmental steward and the energy user must therefore be rationalized. Someone will have to pay the piper, so to speak. Still, if it makes intuitive sense for the energy user to bear the additional cost, then it is possible for policy makers to intervene and redirect subsidies to bridge the transitional costs.

There is good news. One of the other surprising findings of my work with Project Butterfly is that our modeling shows global electricity prices declining in the business-as-usual case for the next thirty to forty years in spite of the impact of resource depletion. Even business as usual should mean rising prices for gasoline; this scenario also predicts falling prices for electricity and, in the aggregate, generally declining prices as the energy industry deploys new capital and competition drives down costs. Under the new business case, we expect to see gasoline prices continue to rise; electricity prices, on the other hand, should rise and then fall, again thanks to the deployment of new capital and innovation, as well as to redirected subsidies. However, the basic concept for policy makers is to set carbon prices that will incentivize the promotion of renewable energy and the electrification of transportation, including automobiles, as a means to mitigate the consequences of this shift in the earth's global energy mix. That means addressing the needs of the energy user in the mix.

Energy users should and will be the focus of new policies, as they will experience the greatest impact as an entire class. It is in this regard that the global society must find ways to minimize the negative feedback from the social and economic implications of the new business case, especially as existing subsidies for fossil fuels are eliminated. The Project Butterfly team, after months of review, reluctantly concurred with our modeling experts that redirecting subsidies is the quickest and likely the most efficient means of reducing energy user costs.

THE NEW BUSINESS CASE

The Project Butterfly new business case is the path to reducing total CO_2 concentration levels while still finding areas of alignment among the four stakeholder perspectives. This new business case builds on the Project Butterfly Sustainability Model of achieving a maximum sustainable yield on natural resources while still increasing the total commercial value. Moreover, the new business case offers visibility into whether the global society will be able to achieve a simultaneous benefit to commerce, by evaluating differences in the conditions of the other stakeholders. In this regard, the innovation that the Project Butterfly team is attempting to deliver to the market is not necessarily an optimal recommendation. Rather, it is a methodology for identifying and aligning stakeholder interests.

To create alignment, the issue becomes one of improving the conditions of the supplier as a class by increasing the supplier's net present value (NPV) compared with the NPV under the business-as-usual scenario. The global energy user can and should expect to make an investment in the form of short-term higher costs, but should eventually see long-term costs decline. The lender would like to see improvements in the lending environment to suppliers as a result of improved debt coverage ratios (DCRs). When we aim to accomplish these three tasks while also minimizing the environmental costs, it becomes clear that creating greater energy efficiency is truly the backbone (the beef, not the buns) of any energy policy.

The new business case, therefore, can optimize the financial values, both long- and short-term, for each energy stakeholder while minimizing the continuous buildup of our carbon debt. The path may be the one less traveled, but if the objective is profit maximization, then the issue for policy makers is clarifying the end game to balance competing interests. The transformation of the global energy mix can be reached by evaluating policies that would allow for a return on investment to a particular stakeholder even if that stakeholder has to incur a short-term cost to accommodate the requirements of the steward. The balancing act between value and cost will create in all policy makers a mind-set of being able to agree to a set of strategies that can achieve the desired energy mix.

The Project Butterfly team worked to simulate a new business case by minimizing the number of variables that were needed to reach the stated objectives. We populated the model with the following variables:

» An increase in efficiency of new capital per annum, by promulgating coherent regulatory structures
» A global emissions price per ton of carbon emissions
» Redirected subsidies for new energy projects that are tapping renewable resources

Project Butterfly's new business case emphasizes energy efficiency and, by extension, the efficiency of the deployment of new capital, so that annually we are setting an expected 3 percent increase in efficiency per annum. The model includes a global emissions price of $45 per carbon ton, effective by the end of 2016. Our model continues to assume the capital growth rate starting at 3 percent that would appear in our business-as-usual scenario, but that rate then tails off to 1.5 percent by the end of the century. Furthermore, we have set a global subsidy for renewable energies and hydroelectric power equivalent to $10 per gigajoule (which would create a total of $230 billion by 2020 while reducing subsidies for oil and gas by $1 per gigajoule (a total of $340 billion by 2020). For a further discussion of how we chose the input variables for the new business case and which assumptions they reflect, go to our website: www.projbutterfly.com.

NEW BUSINESS CASE KEY VARIABLES AND ASSUMPTIONS

Expected increase in efficiency of new capital	3% per annum
Global emissions price implemented by 2016	$45 per carbon ton
Global subsidy for renewable energies and hydro	$10 per gigajoule until 2100
Reduction of subsidies for oil and natural gas	$1 per gigajoule until 2100
Capital growth rate	3% (same as business as usual)
Long-term capital growth rate	Trail to 1.5% by end of century (same as business as usual)

Source Project Butterfly

✦ *table 11.1:* Key variable inputs that form the new business case.

The Project Butterfly Financial Model observes conditions in three future years—2020, 2040, and 2060—that represent snapshots of a continuous flow of investments. Other variables that are important to our discussion, as reflected in our new business case and modeling software, are the index of Reducing Emissions from Deforestation and Forest Degradation (REDD), which reflects global efforts to reforest at a rate equal to any deforestation, and the index of other GHG emissions, which reflects non-carbon emissions and an extension of the proposed policies to mitigate GHG emissions from the energy industry.

The concept behind the new business case is that the $45-per-ton price on carbon will put increased pressure on conventional power sources and will increase both the competitiveness of alternatives, including renewable energy, and the efficiency of demand- and supply-side energy. Based on our modeling, the $45-per-ton price point sufficiently accounts for the market impact of externalities of conventional power, but is not such a high price that it leaves existing infrastructure with no purpose. Raising carbon prices to a point where existing infrastructure is stranded would have altered the team's assumptions about the growth of the global economy and would no longer have allowed apples-to-apples comparisons between the underlying principles of business as usual and the Project Butterfly new business case. Rather, our interest is to measure the impact of a carbon price on technology sets or energy types. The rationale for our inputs will be reviewed in depth in the chapters that follow.

When we run the numbers, the results of the model are very encouraging. There have been many nights, though, when the Project Butterfly team has gone home negatively shaken by some of the results. What has inspired us to carry on is this crucial point: Mitigating climate change is not about contrasting the cost of climate change against the cost of mitigation. It is about comparing values and generating new wealth. Putting a price on carbon, redirecting subsidies from fossil fuels, and encouraging regulatory regimes to open their markets and to promote energy efficiency will encourage suppliers and financiers to invest toward rebuilding our global energy system, thus shifting the global energy mix from conventional fuels to new technologies that will reverse the upward trend in the buildup of GHGs.

This is interesting news to the investors of the world, who are afraid that the implementation of setting a cost for hydrocarbons into the economic system will hinder their returns. The Project Butterfly Financial Model shows that carbon pricing actually redirects investments into technologies with a much more promising long-term return for each class of stakeholders—suppliers, investors/lenders, and (eventually) energy users.

RESULTS OF THE NEW BUSINESS CASE

For sure, implementing Project Butterfly's new business case will take some significant political effort, but the return for the four global energy stakeholders—the energy user, the energy supplier, the investor/lender, and the environmental steward—will pay off. Let's review Project Butterfly's new business case and look at the changing conditions for each stakeholder.

In the new business case, the steward sees a substantial reduction in the buildup of GHGs over those noted in the business-as-usual scenario. This reduction is the result of an attempt to minimize resource depletion and keep existing supplies available for future use at more sustainable yields. In essence, a price on carbon hinders the producers' ability to develop and market the relatively limited quantities of fossil fuels as substitutes emerge, and therefore allows the resource to be available for a much longer period of time.

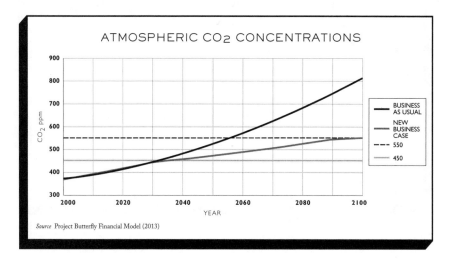

★ *fig. 11.5:* Although atmospheric CO_2 is still increasing, the new business case greatly hinders the rise of CO_2 concentrations.

As figure 11.5 shows, CO_2 emissions are still above the 450 ppm target set by the International Energy Agency (IEA). But there is a nearly 40 percent reduction in emissions, from slightly above 800 ppm (the level reached in the Project Butterfly business-as-usual scenario) to the 550 ppm achieved in the Project Butterfly new business case. With a handful of variables, it becomes clear which path the global community must take in order to begin to reverse the trend line. Figure 11.6 compares annual CO_2 equivalent emissions, which is a measure used to compare the emissions from various greenhouse gases based upon their global warming potential, in both the new business case and the business-as-usual scenario from the years 2000 to 2100. The most immediate observation with regards to the graph is the massive decrease, and almost long-term "flatlining," of the emissions in the new business case. Both graphs illustrate the importance of reducing global CO_2 equivalent emissions right before the year 2020 if we are to avoid surpassing the 550 ppm mark and subsequent global catastrophes.

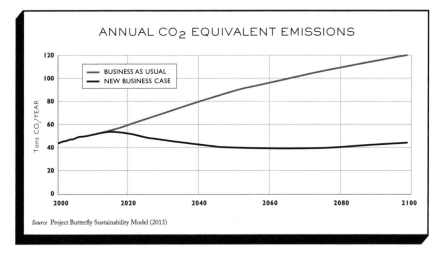

• *fig. 11.6:* Under the new business case, a major adjustment to the annual output of CO_2 will occur around the year 2020 as a result of policy adjustments. Without these policy adjustments, annual carbon emissions are projected to continuously increase through 2100.

The outcome for the energy supplier, in aggregate, is also positive. Project Butterfly's results with regards to the total net investor values (the NPV) are very exciting: The new business case, with its price on carbon and its redirection of subsidies, is the clear path to undertake in terms of protecting the environment. But it is also the path that will result in the largest returns to investors over the time horizon of our modeling (recall that there are three snapshot years: 2020, 2040, and 2060).

There will be casualties, however. The price on carbon and the end of subsidies to the oil and gas industries will harm net returns for oil and gas suppliers in the short term, even though renewable resource investors will realize increasingly positive returns. By 2040, in terms of strong and continuous returns, the new business case will be by far the most ideal scenario for investors, and this trend will continue into 2060 and beyond. Our results show that policies that fix a price on carbon will stimulate innovation in a way that would not be possible within the business-as-usual scenario.

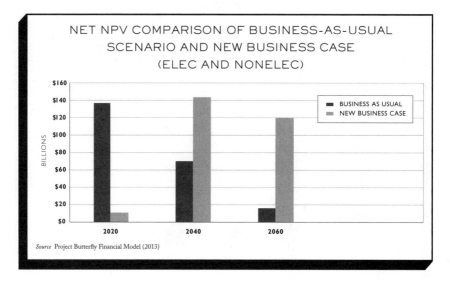

♦ *fig. 11.7:* While the new business case incurs a short-term decline in performance and return, its medium- and long-term performance and return for investors heavily outperforms the business-as-usual scenario.

The energy investor also benefits from the new business case. The new regulatory environment encourages distributed generation-creating opportunities within a more diversified banking system. Instead of big banks funding big projects, we see a move toward smaller-scale implementation that matches supply with demand. As is clear from the graphs comparing the NPV of the business-as-usual scenario and the new business case (see figure 11.7), the new business case can be described as a scenario with a short-term sacrifice, yielding a high degree of medium- and long-term wealth. This graph is the aggregate NPV of both electric sector investors (traditional power plants) and nonelectric sector investors (fuel for vehicles).

The cumulative IRR for each snapshot year (see figure 11.8), which also includes both electric and nonelectric fuel sources, follows a path similar to that of the NPV for each snapshot year. While there is some short-term decrease in the value of the IRRs in the new business case, the overall trend either maintains a strong return or even slightly increases over time. If nothing else, the new business case demonstrates a consistent improvement in the rate of returns, which is sure to please investors.

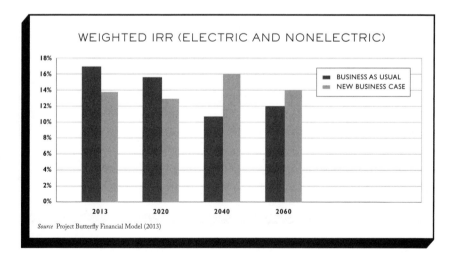

Source Project Butterfly Financial Model (2013)

• *fig. 11.8:* IRRs in the new business case increase marginally by 2060 compared to approximate 5% decrease in IRRs for business as usual.

It is also very important to consider the needs of the lender, as very often it is this stakeholder's ability to leverage a project that generates stronger returns for the equity investors. Without financing, many projects would never meet the required returns, jeopardizing future investments in similar endeavors. Similar to the NPV and IRR results, the new business case with regards to DCRs (see figure 11.9) can be described as a scenario that requires short-term sacrifice but provides long-term benefits. While certain energy types will certainly face a heavy headwind, the majority will be able to show their lending institutions stronger ratios than they would otherwise present.

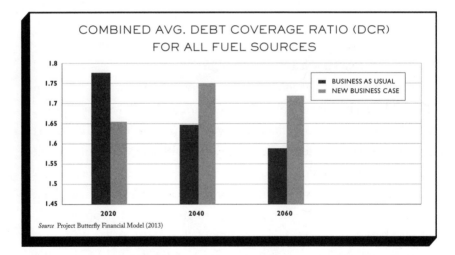

• *fig. 11.9:* Similar to IRR and NPV, the new business case DCR is an important metric that follows a similar "short-term sacrifice, long-term gain" trajectory.

The most intriguing interpretation of our results is an obvious downward trend for NPVs, IRRs, and DCRs under the business-as-usual scenario. The NPVs and DCRs experience a continuous decrease through 2060, and the IRRs experience a decline up until about 2060. Many factors are responsible for these shrinking values, but the following are some of the largest contributors:

Infrastructure lock-in: Our modeling efforts indicate that by the end of the century, if no immediate action is undertaken, coal, oil, and natural gas will continue to dominate the landscape. Countries such as China and India will be responsible for consuming a large degree of these fuels in the coming years, and the infrastructure that will be built (some with lifespans as long as fifty-plus years) will act as a barrier, due to their likely already paid-down debt obligation and low operation costs, to new power-generating entrants that can promise higher returns.

Resource constraints: Riding the coattails of infrastructure lock-in, conventional sources of power, such as oil and natural gas, will face exhaustion well before the end of the century. This "race to the bottom of the barrel" will force companies to locate more and more difficult-to-access resources even as they enjoy ever-diminishing returns. While most certainly there will be companies that can turn a profit in this new environment, the majority will lack the technical knowledge needed to survive.

Turning to the stakeholders, the energy user cuts across demographics—to also include the supplier, the investor/lender, and the steward—so it's fitting that this group benefits in the broadest possible terms. The user sees a renewable energy system fostering greater health and well-being for his or her community and home. National security is enhanced by the generation of homegrown power rather than reliant on foreign supplies to meet domestic needs. Smaller-scale generation leads to greater social empowerment, as schools, hospitals, and businesses seek to self-generate rather than rely on expensive and invasive centralized transmission and distribution systems.

One of the challenges the Project Butterfly team faced when projecting the results of the new business case for the energy user was how best to combat the escalating prices that would accompany the removal of subsidies to traditional power-generating resources and the addition of a cost to the system in the form of a price on carbon. However, once the results were uncovered, we were satisfied to see that the ongoing and significantly lower fuel prices of renewable energies allowed the final energy price to eventually slope downward to a point lower than in the business-as-usual scenario (see figure 11.10).

The way to shorten this time frame, and to compensate for the short-term investments the user will have to make, is to provide direct subsidies for either the suppliers or the users of renewable energy. In Australia, for example, low-income households receive an energy rebate that is funded by the national carbon tax. Similarly, revenues generated either from an allocation of carbon emissions or through a carbon tax can be used to fund a direct subsidy for new investments in renewable energy. Therefore, in order to balance the requirements of the user, the implementation of direct subsidies to end users or to new suppliers is one of the key variables of the Project Butterfly new business case. The more market-focused these subsidies can be, the more powerful their presence can be in the marketplace.

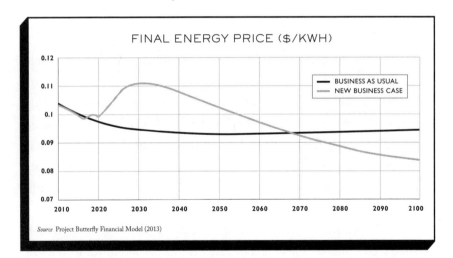

FINAL ENERGY PRICE ($/KWH)

Source Project Butterfly Financial Model (2013)

◆ *fig. 11.10:* Due to a cost imposed on the system and the removal of subsidies for conventional power producers, the new business case sees a temporary spike in the final energy price, but eventually drops below the business-as-usual scenario level when the benefits of low fuel costs for renewable energies become realized.

THE PACE OF COMMERCIALIZATION

Finding the right balance between the key energy stakeholders will have far-reaching implications. Inserting a cost to emitting GHGs will create both cost and value. One of the dynamics that makes it difficult to model any energy system is the increasing pace of commercialization. The acceleration of commercialization both helps and hurts efforts to reduce energy demand as the global society tries to mitigate GHG emissions. It took forty-six years from the time the power line infrastructure was installed until a quarter of the US population received electricity. It took thirty-five years for the telephone to make its way from the inventor's bench to the market. It took sixteen years for a quarter of US citizens to get a PC, and just seven years for most of us to receive Internet access. This increased pace of commercialization can help us deploy new capital with a lower energy and carbon intensity if the appropriate policies are put in place.

However, if policy is not applied, commercialization of energy-intensive goods and services can also increase total emissions. For much of recent history, the idea of profitability has consumed entrepreneurs. New riches can offer a family higher education, housing, and health care. These are very valuable and coveted services in a very competitive world. In order to achieve success using the new business case, however, the entrepreneurial spirit of individuals like Steve Jobs (Apple), John D. Rockefeller (Standard Oil Company), and Warren Buffett (Berkshire Hathaway) must be guided toward innovating reductions in total energy costs and in GHG emissions. Otherwise, the pace of commercialization will drive economic growth to levels that will overwhelm our current supply of energy.

With this concept in mind, Project Butterfly stands by a general thesis: By creating a clear market signal and by using regulatory incentives to stimulate market development, the global society can unlock the power and potential for technological innovation to address climate change. Chapters 12, 13, and 14 will review the potential for the energy industry to respond to a new business case. I will explore the promise that renewable energy, demand-side energy efficiency, and supply-side energy efficiency holds for the economy, the environment, and business, if this market signal were to actually materialize. The key to the success of these approaches is fostering the kind of innovation that is critical to the new business case and showing how it can be profitable. Remember, to create a new business case requires firing the imagination of investors. By showing how suppliers and bankers can make money, you have done your job.

Fostering such change to achieve greater profitability among leading suppliers and technology is possible because to address climate change, much of what is required is simply accelerating a conversion to demand-side and supply-side energy efficiency rather than continuing to subsidize conventional power sources and leaving regulatory structures in place that limit substitutes or the development of alternatives. Otherwise the aforementioned pace of commercialization will also overwhelm our global ecosystem by increasing the energy intensity and carbon content of the global economy.

MAXIMIZING THE OUTCOME FOR ALL STAKEHOLDERS

There is no question in my mind that a consensus in the United States will eventually form around the basic principles outlined in Project Butterfly's new business case, regardless of the politics. States and cities around the country are working together to incorporate best practices to promote sustainability. It is not just a California trend or a Boulder phenomenon. One of the US cities leading the charge toward sustainability is Chicago, Illinois. For example, former Mayor Richard M. Daley led a green roofing program to reduce air-conditioning loads while beautifying the downtown skyline. Retired from politics, Daley is now taking his show on the road, helping to form a network of US cities seeking to adopt sustainability practices. Meanwhile, Hank Paulson, former secretary of the Treasury during the George W. Bush administration, is operating his Paulson Institute out of the University of Chicago, focusing on sharing best practices for urban development between the United States and China. The consensus must start somewhere, and perhaps these individuals have it right—cities may be the best places to start.

Our proposed new business case and the corresponding Project Butterfly Financial Model have the potential to create greater transparency in any international negotiation about climate change and in any domestic initiative to form either a cap and trade system or a carbon tax. By offering a set of distinctions related to the key stakeholders, and by developing the capacity to model the impact on those stakeholders, Project Butterfly has made it possible to form a simple policy to address a complex problem. The simulations run by Project Butterfly suggest that policies can be implemented that will minimize the side effects of making a change to the economics of renewable energy sources and that will maximize the outcome of this change for all stakeholders.

This modeling exercise looks at the global energy mix and the impact of each stakeholder (by class and by energy type) in that energy mix. However, the model was constructed on the fundamental principles that are set in traditional energy project financing, so it may look familiar to those in the energy industry. In fact, using the Project Butterfly methodology, it's possible to look at an individual project or a portfolio of projects—similar to that which an electric utility company might hold. It's also possible to look at the energy mix of a single country, measuring its carbon footprint, the impact on its economy, and the returns to its key stakeholders: the energy user, the energy supplier, the investor/lender, and the environmental steward.

Some people will disagree with the new business case and its results. They will take issue with the assumptions or with the inputs in the model. I am sure some will even think I ought to be tarred and feathered for heresy for suggesting that the market isn't perfect under all conditions. Others will fault me for my faith in the markets. But I ask you to look over the math before you join the naysayers. I invite you to visit www.projbutterfly.com and view the model results in more detail. Discover how you can become a better steward, whether you are the CEO of an energy company, a policy maker, an energy manager of a Fortune 500 company, or an investment banker—or none of the above. Whether you agree or disagree, please post away on the Project Butterfly forum. Your insights could be helpful. Our plan is to continue to refine the model, using it as a stepping-stone to reduce global GHG concentration levels before the tides rise.

Before you make up your mind, however, please keep reading. The next few chapters provide a review of the technologies at the core of mitigating the buildup of GHGs. These are the kinds of suppliers and technology that will benefit under the Project Butterfly new business case—and that we can all invest in.

KEY OBSERVATIONS

The key observations we can make about the Project Butterfly new business case are as follows:

» If the global community does not do more to promote the mitigation of climate change through reducing GHG emissions from existing and future energy infrastructure, the Project Butterfly business-as-usual scenario forecasts the buildup of CO_2 concentration to more than 800 ppm by the end of the twenty-first century—a level that will be catastrophic by any measure.

» The business-as-usual scenario includes current efforts to promote renewable energy and energy efficiency, but with too many carbon sources and insufficient carbon sinks, the burning of fossil fuels will continue to cause dangerous GHG buildups. The new business case acknowledges that more needs to be done.

» The goal of the Project Butterfly new business case is to optimize financial values while minimizing the buildup of global CO_2 concentration levels. To achieve this goal, the Project Butterfly team has run a forecast that assumes that new regulatory structures will be promulgated, to increase the efficiency of new capital; an emissions price will be set, to internalize the environmental cost of GHGs; and subsidies from fossil fuels will be redirected, to spur innovation in alternative energy sources.

» The results of Project Butterfly's simulations are encouraging. The new business case simulation shows a significant reversal in the upward trend of GHGs and an improvement in the financial conditions of each of the four energy stakeholders. Through innovation, this can be just the beginning.

Pioneers take the arrows.
Settlers take the land.
—Amory Lovins

CHAPTER 12

COMING OF AGE: RENEWABLE ENERGY

My wife of more than twenty-five years is a fully engaged mother, an artist extraordinaire, and a PhD candidate. She is no slouch. Years ago, however, when she and I first started to go on walks together, I would get a little frustrated. I wanted us to walk at a pace that might raise our heart rates sufficiently to constitute an aerobic experience. But along the way my wife would inevitably spot a cluster of flowers, a nest in a tree, or an alternative path that required stopping and taking a moment to breathe the fresh air. It took me about twenty years to figure out that it was not her disdain for exercise that dictated the pace of our walks. Rather, for her, our time together was actually much more than just exercise. It was an opportunity to explore the visual world and thus turn our walks into something much more special.

I may never be able to express adequately how very grateful I am for my wife's aesthetic point of view. She has forever influenced how I see the world. I have visited steel plants in Cleveland, Ohio, and I now see their furnaces as foundries and their workers as artists. I have climbed to the top of wind turbines in Lander, Wyoming, and I now see every windmill as a moving sculpture. These experiences have left me awestruck at human ingenuity and industry. The perspective I've gained from my wife has taught me to consider the aesthetics—not just the efficiency—of what society and our economy builds.

I believe that others in the global energy industry could benefit from this novel approach. Perhaps they need to take a walk with my wife.

Discussions around energy are usually mundane, but they can be fairly philosophical at times, too. Does anyone truly care about the underlying energy system that fuels and powers our economy? Why all the fuss about where energy comes from? Many would say, "All anyone cares about is that when you flip the switch, the light comes on." Others would say, "As long as the electric bill is cheap, nothing else matters." But my wife's influence would lead me to believe that the concern of humanity is not about electricity itself, but rather about how very deeply we regard the energy that supports our lives. Humans crave the comforts of the underlying energy services: heat, cooling, light, and interconnection.

The difference between cheap electric power and the quality of the energy service provided may be subtle, perhaps. Cheap electricity doesn't necessarily translate into an improved quality of energy service, nor do inexpensive energy services always translate into a dim room. But the difference is also profound. One perspective is concerned solely with the price of a kilowatt-hour whereas the other also considers the quality of the full energy service and delivery. Reflecting on this issue for years, I have often felt that the difference between these two perspectives may hold the key to whether or not humankind has the potential to live within a sustainable environmental footprint.

Think of it this way: Calculating the price of electricity is simple. You add up the number of kilowatt-hours used and multiply them by the unit cost. However, calculating the true cost of energy services requires a more dynamic set of equations. The cost of energy services accounts for the price of electricity or fuels needed to produce the same levels of heat, cooling, and light, but it must then be adjusted by other factors that may increase or decrease energy usage. Calculating energy services requires the amortization of both those costs and the benefits, which can range from improvements to a building envelope (such as insulating your home) to the upgrade of a lighting system. New insulation can provide greater comfort with a smaller heating load. An upgraded lighting system can increase the lumens per watt or the quality and spectrum of light, and can reduce the total wattage. The impact of these adjustments varies greatly. A single change can either decrease or increase energy usage, demand, and the total cost of the energy service.

Moreover, as I look at the sources that supply our global energy services, I realize that at some level people also care about the safety, health, and beauty of our energy system. From a community perspective, we all care about the quality of life and safety of our neighborhoods. These cares lead communities to act on such issues by placing new transmission lines underground, improving the quality of the air we breathe, and storing waste safely. For example, if a storm or a terrorist attack knocks out the power system, we hope our provider has a backup generator. Because humans care about such things, we must compare the alternatives of one system to another. We must then value the costs and benefits of each.

As I reflect on my many walks with my wife, I realize how much I have learned from her. The aesthetics of our surroundings are not some kind of product from an extracurricular activity. The aesthetics of our surroundings lie at the heart of an industry that is vital to the human condition.

A DIFFERENT KIND OF COMING-OF-AGE STORY

Renewable energy is now part of most urban planning efforts. It has finally come of age. It is one of the most exciting new sources of energy supply, whether or not we consider it as part of the business-as-usual scenario or the new business case. Nonrenewable energy, almost by definition, cannot be part of a global sustainability model. However, the Project Butterfly team has had to confront the issue of whether renewable energy might ever be sufficient to provide a realistic alternative that can be promoted through the new business case to levels sufficient to make a dent in and even redefine the global energy mix.

Keep in mind, however, that renewable energy is not the total solution in the Project Butterfly new business case. This will become clear over the next three chapters. Renewable energy is simply the foundation on which the global community can build a workable solution for our long-term energy future.

Such a bold statement recognizes all the starts and stops in the renewable energy industry's past. It recognizes that over the past four decades the renewable energy industry has experienced times of both prosperity and disappointment, and that it will experience ups and downs again. Indeed there is a certain unique cyclicality to the renewable energy industry. For example, as conventional energy prices surge in response to supply constraints, new investments in renewable energy typically take a leap forward. When conventional energy prices fall due to inevitable recessionary pressures, the development of renewable energy takes a step back. When geopolitics collide with national policy initiatives over depleting resources, government steps back up to the plate for renewable energy and investments in renewable energy take another leap forward. When geopolitical tensions ease, public funding for renewable energy slows. It is part of the very nature of the system that the global community has created. We must both accept it and adjust to it as we navigate our course.

The energy industry has witnessed this cyclicality over the past forty years. Similarly, federal government and industry support for renewable energy has waxed and waned. It is nothing new. For example, on June 20, 1979, President Jimmy Carter installed thirty-two solar collectors on the roof of the White House, and not just for space heating and hot water. The larger intent was to demonstrate to the world the importance of supporting new energy technology in the face of historically high oil prices. By 1986, though, the oil markets had crashed and oil prices with them. President Ronald Reagan slashed national R&D budgets for several renewable energy technologies, cutting tax breaks for the deployment of wind turbines and solar collectors. A few years later, when President Reagan had the solar panels removed from the roof of the White House, it was a symbolic act.[221]

Politics aside, the practice of generating power from windmills, water, and the sun has in fact been with us for centuries. That said, commercial-scale power from renewable energy has only recently become sufficiently advanced to compete head-to-head with conventional energy sources. Large-scale wind and solar projects have become a larger and larger percentage of the overall market in the past few years. Renewable energy, including conventional hydropower, now accounts for 13 percent of total US energy consumption.[222] Industry experts predict that even given current trends, renewable energy will double in capacity to reach approximately 23 percent of total US energy consumption by 2035.[223]

Project Butterfly's forecast, based on our business-as-usual scenario, shows that by 2024, globally, renewable energy will surpass oil as a producer of electricity. By 2045 electricity from renewable energy will represent about half as much as the energy supply from natural gas. Under our business-as-usual scenario, it will take renewable energy until 2070 to eventually surpass natural gas as global supplies of conventional natural gas wane. The problem is that these predictions, while substantive for renewable energy, are still not good enough to meet the conditions required to adequately reduce global GHG levels. The new business case demands a more dramatic acceleration in the development of renewable energy resources.

The new business case simulation run by the Project Butterfly team presents a clear shift in the makeup of our global energy mix. In our model, the renewable energy industry surges forward to become the leading power source in the global energy mix by 2041 and remains the dominant source to the end of the century. The following figures represent the difference between the business-as-usual scenario and Project Butterfly's new business case with regards to renewable energy (including hydropower).

Figure 12.1 shows a dramatic increase in renewable energy in terms of the total percentage of global power generation following the immediate introduction of a $45-per-ton price on carbon, reaching approximately 64 percent of total generation by the end of the twenty-first century. The difference from

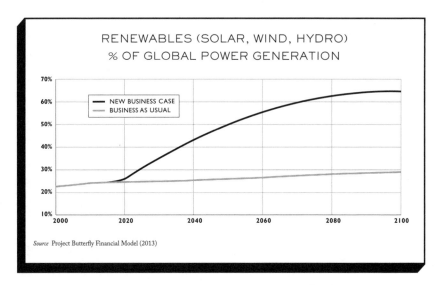

RENEWABLES (SOLAR, WIND, HYDRO)
% OF GLOBAL POWER GENERATION

Source Project Butterfly Financial Model (2013)

• *fig. 12.1:* By 2040, renewables as a percent of total power generation under the new business case break the 40 percent barrier, whereas renewable technologies under the business-as-usual scenario never quite breach this same marker.

the business-as-usual case is startling in spite of renewable energy's natural progression as a competitive alternative to conventional power sources over the same time horizon.

Figure 12.2 makes this observation even more compelling. Renewable energy achieves this higher level of total power generation (as shown in figure 12.1) with proportionally less investment than was necessary in the business-as-usual scenario.

The surprising result begins to reveal the true potential of the new business case: greater delivery of service for less capital investment. It demonstrates the veracity of the claim we made above—that we can indeed address climate change by focusing on the quality of the required energy services rather than simply on the cost of the kilowatt-hour. The Project Butterfly team considered this outcome a "eureka" discovery in our work. We were the settlers coming along after the pioneers. Many had traveled the distance in their global energy and climate modeling, but possibly few had discovered its true significance.

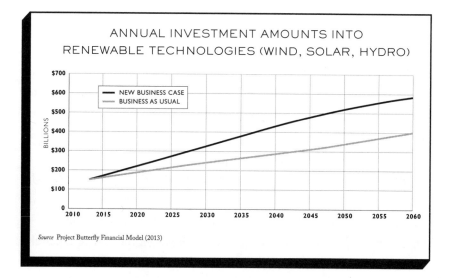

ANNUAL INVESTMENT AMOUNTS INTO
RENEWABLE TECHNOLOGIES (WIND, SOLAR, HYDRO)

Source Project Butterfly Financial Model (2013)

✦ *fig. 12.2:* This figure demonstrates the increased desire of investing in renewable technologies under the new business case as compared to the business-as-usual scenario. Notice that figure 12.1 demonstrates how renewables in the new business case comprise almost 65 percent of the generating capacity in 2100, but the investment amounts in figure 12.2 are only $200 billion between the business-as-usual and the new business case. This difference is the reason why it is so important to start the transition as soon as possible, as the early years in increased investing offer huge payoffs down the line.

RENEWABLE ENERGY
AND A NEW RESILIENCE

The acceleration of renewable energy under the new business case is not a result of just throwing subsidies at a different technology. Such a claim is counter to our analysis and ignores a simple reality: The global renewable energy market is maturing as a viable and highly competitive industry, while massive subsidies are being funneled into conventional fuel supplies and while no price is being set on externalities. The new business case illustrates a changing landscape that puts a price on carbon and subsidizes user costs in order to finance a smooth transition to renewable energy, similar to betting on a winning horse after the starting bell has sounded. For example, deal flow in renewable energy has continued to grow ever since the global economic meltdown of 2008 through 2012 in spite of a number of uncertainties (the poor health of the eurozone, for example). This growth was not stymied by cuts in renewable energy programs in Spain and Italy. Nor did it falter when the US Congress failed to extend existing renewable energy tax credits until the final hours of 2012 (and then was unable to extend them beyond 2014) or when natural gas prices declined due in part to federal subsidies threatening the economics of competing transactions.

In 2011 total global transactions in renewable energy and energy efficiency reached $53 billion, up 40 percent from 2010.[224] In spite of all of these risks, the global renewable energy market is showing a new resilience—a critical attribute of any maturing industry. Moreover, the mix of renewable energy technologies has expanded, from being historically dominated by large hydroelectric projects to being more equally divided among solar, wind, and biomass ventures. For example, in the United States, 79 percent of the $15.3 billion worth of renewable energy deals completed in 2011 consisted of solar and energy efficiency projects.[225]

That same year, financing by large industrial players began to provide further third-party validation of the renewable energy industry. Private equity continued to be a source of funding, but large, prominent companies have been acquiring smaller ones with new and more advanced smart grid, solar panel, and wind technologies. In Europe, even risk-averse pension funds have entered the renewable energy business. In 2011 a Danish insurance group, PensionDanmark, purchased a 50 percent interest in one of Europe's first offshore wind projects.[226] Far from a government-funded R&D project, the investment—by such a large European pension fund—is a testament to renewable energy's arrival on the global scene. The move demonstrates that renewable energy as a power source can rival, scale, and compete with any conventional source of energy.

Starting in 2008 in other countries, such as Brazil, mergers and buyouts among small and medium-size energy companies—including the purchase of my company, Econergy International, by GDF Suez—began creating consolidated renewable energy "powerhouses." These transactions clearly demonstrated that renewable energy no longer meant pilot projects funded by USAID and the World Bank; rather, renewable energy is now of interest to large, international energy companies that are aggressively competing for large-scale renewable energy supply. The renewable energy industry is taking hold as a resilient and viable alternative to conventional power suppliers. The Project Butterfly new business case offers an approach that would build organically on these successes and would eliminate key barriers to further growth, such as removing incentives for conventional power that rely on burning fossil fuels.

LIMITLESS POTENTIAL TO POWER THE PLANET

The new business case relies on a critical assumption that may now seem obvious to all of us: If, as a global community, we are to significantly reduce GHG emissions, we must not only use energy much more efficiently but also substitute some of the energy currently being supplied by fossil fuels with energy sources that have a much lower carbon footprint. For this to happen, it will be crucial to greatly increase the role of renewable energy, especially (but not only) if any increase in nuclear energy generation seems limited, as discussed in chapter 7.

Let us now look at the potential and some of the history of the renewable energy industry. Renewable energy resources are diverse, a fact that perhaps is not generally appreciated. Natural energy resources, such as the wind, sunlight, or heat from below the earth's surface, are transformed by technologies that range from heat engines to mechanical turbines to photovoltaic (PV) panels. All of these technologies can produce energy to power our cars, homes, and businesses. Renewable energy technologies currently at our disposal are, however, at different stages in their evolution; some are mature, some are evolving rapidly, and some are in a nascent stage of development. These technologies and natural resources also vary hugely in terms of their potential capacity and reach. For instance, certain resources, such as the sun, have almost limitless potential to power the entire planet, while others, like geothermal power, are restricted to areas where the resource is active.

This diversity makes it difficult to generalize about renewable energy, but it also is part of the intrigue and challenge of accessing renewable resources. Fortunately, it makes for a diversified portfolio of technology risk, and the potential exists to aggregate different renewable energy technologies into a single solution. However, from the outset it is clear that the range and potential of substituting renewable energy technologies for electricity generation (and building energy use) are much greater than for substituting transport fuels. This will have long-term consequences for the future. For example, it will make electric vehicles central to the debate of creating a viable plan to mitigate climate change. Bottom line: Electrifying our transportation system, rather than using renewable energy to fuel vehicles, would create an alignment of interests among equity investors, suppliers, and lenders for maximizing the potential for renewable energy.

Let's review the five most prominent renewable resources for generating electricity: hydropower, wind, biomass, geothermal, and solar. All five have the physical capacity to completely reshape the global energy mix. Each is experiencing state-of-the-art commercial development with an eye to unleashing its full potential in coming years. The implications are far-reaching.

HYDROPOWER

Hydropower is the granddaddy of renewable energy resources. Water has been harnessed to do mechanical work for more than a millennium—mostly for grinding grain. The largest mill to be found in the Roman Empire was impressive and complex; it had a remarkable estimated shaft power of about 14 kW. Many centuries later, and soon after the inauguration of Edison's Pearl Street power station, a small hydro plant was used to electrify an upstate New York community near Niagara Falls. As various technologies have improved—turbine design, electricity transmission, and dam construction in particular—the largest hydro plants have grown to be ever larger. The largest power generation complexes in the world today are still hydro plants, and several of these wonders have capacities of 10,000 MW or more. Yet hydro facilities can also be very small commercial plants of less than 100 kW, and in fact they range in every size and capacity in between.

In the United States, for example, there are approximately 2,200 hydro-power plants, 1,800 of which are smaller than 30 MW. Amazingly, electricity from hydropower accounts for about 8 percent of the nation's total installed electric-generating capacity of approximately 1,000 GW, or 1 million MW. Hydro capacity and output grew steadily until the early 1970s, as shown in figure 12.3. Since then output has oscillated at around 275 terawatt-hours (TWh), or 275 million megawatt-hours. Total capacity has continued to grow modestly into the 1990s and is now 78 GW, but this growth has mostly involved "super-turbinizing" existing plants, which adds capacity (for peak load, for example) but little output. Figure 12.3 gives an idea of the natural year-to-year variability of hydro flows since the mid-1980s.

Conventional hydro is not generally considered to be a significant

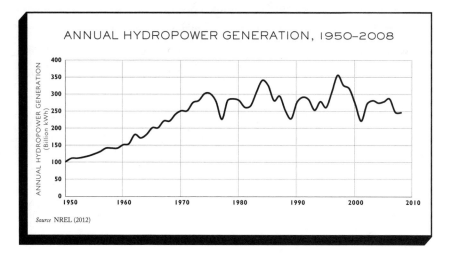

Source NREL (2012)

◆ *fig. 12.3:* Demonstrates how hydropower generation rapidly increased from 1950 to about 1975. However, since then the amount of generation has remained about the same, although it has also been at times volatile.

resource for future expansion in the United States, because most of the large resources have already been tapped. Nevertheless, there is a surprisingly large untapped potential in relatively small hydro plants (50 MW or less). Providing this new capacity is likely to be relatively expensive by the standards of historic hydro projects, but the effort could still be profitable compared with other sources of supply—and thus very profitable compared with conventional energy under Project Butterfly's new business case with its price on carbon.

Many individuals and organizations disagree with the use of hydropower, asserting that it should be withdrawn if it interferes with a nation's many rivers. There is almost as much global activity today dismantling dams (in order to address existing environmental challenges) as there is constructing them. Nevertheless, generating power from existing dams could play a much more significant role in addressing our energy needs than is usually assumed. First, the thousands of dams that do not produce power, which currently act as storage reservoirs for flood control, irrigation, and so on, could be retrofitted with electric turbines. Furthermore, although hydro is considered to be a "mature" technology, this doesn't mean that innovative tapping of this resource has stopped. In fact, new technologies have been developed over the past decade that open significant possibilities for generating electricity from dams that, when they were originally built, did not have viable power generation options. Best of all, electricity from hydropower presents a unique opportunity as the energy industry builds out a smart grid. Hydrological reservoirs can be tapped when they are needed, making it by far the cheapest energy storage in the world.

WIND

Wind has been another source of mechanical energy for more than a millennium, mostly to pump water and to power sailing ships. In fact, the world's first phases of globalization, in the seventeenth through the nineteenth centuries, were born on sailing ships whose technology was constantly improving.

However, by the mid-nineteenth century, sailing's commercial heyday was over because steamships provided cheaper service.

As a source of energy for the working economy, however, wind became restricted to the water-pumping windmills that have dotted rural America, especially in the Great Plains. Until the early 1980s, that is, when state and federal incentives inevitably promoted innovation for a new technology—and birthed a new industry.

In fact, ever since the year 2000, wind energy has been the renewable energy star. Diverse technology improvements since the beginning of the new millennium have driven down costs, and the market for wind energy has taken off as incentives have appeared again through mandated utility portfolio requirements over the last two decades. In the United States, wind capacity soared from about 3 GW in 2000 to 47 GW in 2011 (more than 4 percent of total US capacity). Something similar happened in other parts of the world, and total capacity increased in that same time period by 40 GW—to 238 GW—by 2011.

This decade of expansion stimulated many advances in wind energy technology, including the drive to develop taller towers, longer blades, and more powerful turbines. Typical rotor diameters doubled to 90 meters, and turbine capacity quadrupled. At greater heights, the average wind speed increases significantly, which means the same kilowatt of capacity can produce more kWh. This is important because power output increases by the cube of the wind speed. Thus a 25 percent increase in average wind speed increases output by 95 percent. Similarly, if an average wind speed of 6 meters per second produces 1,000 kWh, a wind speed of 7.5 meters per second produces 1,953 kWh.

However, the development of wind as a new resource has not been a path along a perfect straight line. The sharp increase in demand reversed the long-term decline in cost per kW throughout the 1990s. Basic inputs of materials and labor became more expensive. The shift to taller towers also increased cost per kW, though this tended to be offset by the higher capacity factor of the machines. But since 2011, with the world's economic slowdown, the cost per kW has come down. Modest gains in the development of wind energy are beginning to reemerge, and the industry can likely expect to see more of the same over the next several decades.

In fact, the biggest improvements in wind energy are expected to show up not in further reductions in the cost per kW but in the capacity factor of each unit. Whereas historically plants have had capacity factors oscillating around 32 percent, the norm is expected to approach 40 percent in the future. This implies an increase from 2,800 kWh to 3,500 kWh of installed capacity, a 25 percent improvement in a given wind turbine's total production.

Location is part of the key to unlocking these additional benefits and technologies, and efforts to identify the best locations are also improving. Wind is less site-specific than is hydropower, but wind potential is much higher than average in certain regions. The best terrestrial wind resources are located in a broad region of the Great Plains, where wind can travel over long distances virtually unimpeded. Construction of wind turbines in this region exploded in the early 2000s, and a large percentage of the nation's wind turbines are now located here.

Another point to reflect on is the distribution of the US population. The areas with the best onshore wind potential coincide to a considerable extent with a swath of Midwestern counties that have decreasing populations. In fact, the rural Great Plains has been losing residents for decades, and many communities struggle to maintain basic services. Wind energy represents perhaps the biggest opportunity to stop this "hollowing out" in the Great Plains region. This somewhat indefinable social good is something worth considering when one thinks about the costs and benefits of promoting wind energy.

Other excellent areas with a high degree of wind resources tend to be located offshore. One major advantage of offshore wind farms is that compared with terrestrial farms, they tend to be much closer to coastal centers of demand, requiring less long-distance transmission capacity. The expansion of transmission corridors presents a huge problem, mostly because of difficulties with licensing and disagreements about how to allocate the costs between consumers in different states.

One disadvantage of offshore wind, of course, is expense. Building a kW of offshore capacity in a body of water today is about 75 percent more expensive in the short term than building on land ($3,500/kW versus $2,000/kW). There are as yet no offshore wind farms in the United States, though more than a thousand towers, producing 2 GW of power, have been built in Europe. An interesting domestic option is the Great Lakes, where there are many site opportunities with water depths that are shallower than those off ocean coastal areas. Plus, lakes have fresh water, which is less corrosive to the towers than seawater.

In terms of potential, there is little doubt that high-quality wind sites could produce a very large share of future electricity needs at a generation cost competitive to today's average user costs. The problems, as I will discuss later in this chapter, are the variability of wind and the challenges getting that electricity to market.

BIOMASS

Biomass, such as plant material or agricultural waste, was the largest source of energy for almost all societies until the Industrial Revolution. The burning of wood or manure for heating and cooking was a common practice. Then the growth of large cities and the rapid increase in the demand for energy drove the energy market to coal, which was often cheaper to produce and could be transported much greater distances due to coal's higher energy density.

For example, in the United States during the early nineteenth century, biomass still supplied about 90 percent of the "inanimate energy" (that is, excluding human and animal labor), although coal was gaining a larger presence in some eastern cities. But coal's share had risen to 50 percent of the inanimate energy by the 1880s and to about 75 percent in 1900.[227] As the new century opened, biomass was well on its way to becoming a marginal fuel. The outcome was a favorable consequence of the dramatic drop in the burning of wood fuel. Since the nineteenth century large swaths of deforestation have now grown back, demonstrating how a resource can be renewable even if it has become finite, as nature's ability to regenerate is restricted.

The cost of biomass energy to the supplier and energy user is often uncertain, because supplies can be erratic. For biomass to increase its share of the world's generating capacity in modern times, the most obvious way forward is to locate new plants next to where residues and wastes become concentrated. As is often the case in these concentrated areas, however, the volume of material is not quite sufficient to warrant the construction of large biomass plants and still finance the transmission costs to get the power to market. Consider municipal solid waste, which is one of the largest concentrated sources of residues. In theory, even allowing for a slight increase in recycling could translate into generating as much as 12 GW of base-load power to meet minimum demand (about 80 TWh) by 2050. Using greater biomass for power production will require greater resource planning, which is under way in certain regions where wind and solar may not be as readily available.

For example, a recent review by the National Renewable Energy Laboratory (NREL) estimates that between 90 GW and 100 GW of biomass-fired power (approximately 10 percent of today's total installed capacity in the United States) would be necessary in order to achieve a level of 80 percent electricity generation from renewables by 2050 in the United States.[228] (Of this, between 15 and 20 percent would be "co-fired" with coal, which requires much lower capital costs and is marginally more efficient.) Moreover, unlike wind and solar energy, biomass-derived electricity would provide base-load capacity: "firm" power that would be constant day and night. One advantage of this resource is availability: Substantial biomass is available in certain regions of the United States that have no other high-quality renewable resources to substitute for fossil fuels, as shown in figure 12.4. (The potential for hydropower, not pictured here, is more geographically distributed, but major expansion of hydro resources is usually excluded from any calculation.) This geographical fit between biomass resources and centers of energy demand would lessen the need for more transmission capacity.

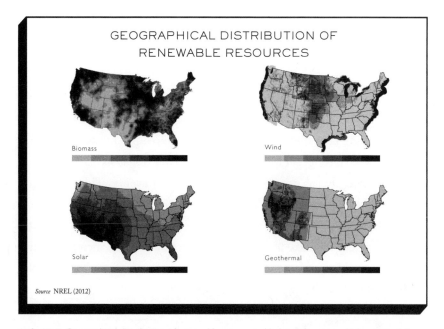

GEOGRAPHICAL DISTRIBUTION OF
RENEWABLE RESOURCES

Biomass

Wind

Solar

Geothermal

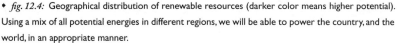

Source NREL (2012)

• *fig. 12.4:* Geographical distribution of renewable resources (darker color means higher potential). Using a mix of all potential energies in different regions, we will be able to power the country, and the world, in an appropriate manner.

Up to now, I have not mentioned one of the largest elephants in the room when considering biomass. The most prominent form of biomass energy is the production of liquid fuels for transport. Despite the pervasive nature of the debate over ethanol, it is generally agreed that using corn to produce ethanol is inherently a very limited option for large-scale, widespread use. Supplying the world's growing food needs is already a daunting challenge. Diverting a significant share of a key crop to produce fuel is simply not sustainable. For example, even if the entire US corn crop were used for fuel, it would substitute for only about 15 percent of the country's gasoline consumption.

If liquid fuel is to be produced from biomass, that source must be ligno-cellulose (a combination of lignin and cellulose that strengthens woody plant cells) or something more exotic, like algae. Unfortunately, no breakthrough in either of these approaches is yet in sight, but if lignocellulose were to become a viable feedstock for liquid fuels, then the question would be whether it makes more technical and economic sense to use biomass to generate fuel or to generate electricity. For example, would a ton of lignocellulose drive a car further when converted to liquid fuel or when used indirectly to power electric vehicles?

The world's largest energy companies and start-up ventures are working to make these "next-generation" fuels viable. Additional R&D is required, but clear market signals promoting a switch from conventional fuels to alternatives would further attract additional risk capital to drive innovation and commercial-scale operations. For example, clear signals of the United States' ability to produce biomass-to-electricity generation through increased petroleum taxes would stimulate innovation and allow an integration of technologies to meet NREL's 80 percent by 2050 objective.

GEOTHERMAL

Geothermal energy is one of the earliest examples of any renewable energy source. As far back as ten thousand years ago, Paleo-Indians used pools and springs of hot water created through heat and pressure from underneath the earth's crust to cleanse themselves, cook their food, and even provide peaceful respite. As anyone who has ever visited a natural hot springs can tell you, these places—often considered sacred ritual sites—impart a strong sense of wonder.

However, only within the past one hundred years has industry been able to harness the power of these waters to provide electricity. The first recorded geothermal power plant went into operation in 1921, when John D. Grant was able to harness enough electricity to power a small resort in northern California. Unfortunately for Grant, the rapid development of other sources of power, such as petroleum-fueled generators, killed the economic competitiveness of his technology. The geothermal industry as a whole had to take a seat on the sidelines for many years thereafter. But then in 1960, the first large-scale geothermal electricity-generating plant began operation near the

Mayacamas Mountains north of San Francisco. This new plant encouraged the development of others in the United States as well as in other geothermal-rich regions of the world that neighbor tectonic breaches that permit the release of heat from the earth's core.

In the United States today, there are about sixty-nine generating facilities in operation,[229] with 2.4 GW of effective capacity and producing 15 TWh of power.[230] This makes the United States the largest geothermal producer in the world, though in some small countries the relative role of geothermal is much larger. For example, 30 percent of total electric capacity in Iceland,[231] and 13 percent in New Zealand, is generated from geothermal energy, compared with 0.3 percent of total capacity in the United States, because of the much higher thermal gradient[232] and the relatively higher resource temperatures in those countries.

The basic principles behind geothermal technology are very simple. The core of the earth radiates heat outward toward the crust. As this heat moves farther away from the core, it warms rocks and deep pockets of water. In essence, the earth's crust acts as a thick insulating blanket, and the heat underneath is efficiently released only when pierced by volcanic activity or artificially through drilling. Geological formations that contain water—called "hydrothermal fields"—can be exploited with existing technology. To be economically viable as an electricity-generating resource, these hydrothermal fields must contain water at temperatures of at least 230 degrees Fahrenheit (110 degrees Celsius). The potential for this kind of geothermal resource in the United States is limited: about 9.07 GW in identified fields and a 5 percent probability that up to a total of 16.5 GW could be used for generating purposes.[233] This is less than 1.5 percent of current US installed capacity, though the share of generation output is bigger since geothermal operates at base load and has high-capacity factors if the right geological conditions are met.

However, much larger geothermal resources exist and may someday be exploited, though the necessary technologies have not yet fully advanced. One additional source is geopressurized fields; another is hot brine, which comes up with oil and gas production. The greatest potential of all exists in high-temperature, impermeable rock formations that are within two to four miles of the surface. These formations would need to be fractured to allow the extraction of heat similar in approach to fracturing for natural gas. The potential capacity in this case could be very large—perhaps as much as 500 GW in the western United States, or roughly half of US existing installed capacity today. The cost to the end user could potentially be very attractive.

SOLAR

Solar energy is the most abundant and widely distributed of all of the renewable energy resources. In theory, it could supply all of the world's energy needs many times over. Unfortunately, the variability and other negative characteristics of solar energy have made it the most expensive of all the renewable resources to convert into useful energy services on a large scale. But technological innovation over the last several years is making huge progress in reducing costs.

Generally, the energy industry treats intelligent building design (also known as "bioclimatic architecture"), which exploits natural lighting and minimizes thermal loads via "passive solar energy," as a kind of energy efficiency. Direct solar energy, however, adds functionality to intelligent building design. The most widespread application of direct solar energy today is for heating water.

Water at 110 degrees Fahrenheit (43.3 degrees Celsius)—roughly the temperature of the cooling water exiting a thermal power station—is, in thermodynamic terms, relatively "low-quality" energy. But a significant share of the world's residential energy use goes into producing such low temperatures, since that is all people need for most chores and daily activities, such as washing clothes, doing the dishes, or taking a bath. Solar collectors can be quite efficient in converting solar radiation into heat, with values between 50 and 70 percent of the incident radiation. In higher latitudes, however, the resource is least available when one needs it most—that is, in the winter. In order to avoid oversized systems with capabilities that are unnecessary during most of the year, the majority of solar water heating comes with a fuel or electrical backup. Critical to sound economics and to environmental efforts is optimizing the size of solar water-heating systems while minimizing the conventional backup.

Of broader significance for solar energy is the steady decline in the cost of producing electricity from the sun's light, especially with photovoltaic technologies, as shown in figure 12.5. The price of the modules at the heart of the solar energy system has roughly followed a 20 percent learning curve for decades. In plain English, this means that with every doubling of world cumulative sales (which in effect translates to installed world capacity), the cost of PVs has fallen by 20 percent. In 2000 the average module price was more than $9 per Wp (or "peak Watt"—when the module is operating at full capacity). By early 2012, the cost dropped to less than $1, which in terms of an energy bill translates into lower energy user costs. No other energy supply

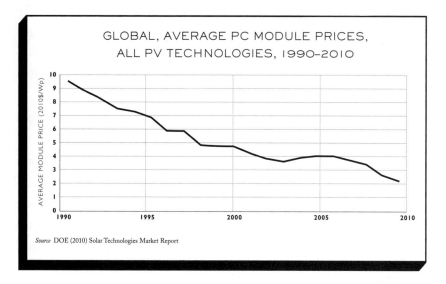

GLOBAL, AVERAGE PC MODULE PRICES, ALL PV TECHNOLOGIES, 1990–2010

Source DOE (2010) Solar Technologies Market Report

♦ *fig. 12.5:* Man has been able to convert solar power into usable electricity for the better part of a century, but over the past several decades the technology has exploded with massive price cuts.

technology has even come close to achieving this trend of cost reduction on a sustained basis.

The fundamental reason for solar energy's extraordinary performance may be inherent in the technology: The roots of photovoltaics are in the semiconductor industry, which has shared the decline in costs from lower circuitry and higher production runs, not in mechanical or conventional electrical engineering. In any case, there is something extraordinarily elegant about a PV system, with the shimmering dark surface of the module and no moving parts.

From now on, however, progress in cost reduction will be increasingly influenced by improvements in project components outside the basic PV module. Until recently, the module dominated the installed cost of a PV system, but now the balance of plant (BOP)—the remaining systems, components, and structures that comprise a complete solar power plant—has taken the spotlight. The average cost of all PV systems installed in the United States in the last quarter of 2011 was about \$4/Wp. For residential systems, the cost was a bit over \$6.[234] There is a lag between bulk sales of modules and actual installation. Nevertheless, it is becoming clear that reducing the cost of BOP is now a challenge that is at least as important as continuing to reduce the cost of the module.

However, as the market grows, the incentives and means to reduce BOP should also improve. In 2011 the installed capacity of PVs increased worldwide by 30 GW, to 70 GW. In the United States, capacity has reached 4 GW. Solar energy is beginning to achieve market scale, which facilitates the expansion of installers with lower margins and attracts capital to invest in innovations for key "ancillary equipment" such as inverters (which transform DC current into AC). For example, the price reduction of modules in the past couple of years has happened so fast that the practices for installation in the "rooftop market" as opposed to ground-based solar farms may not have had time to catch up and create new optimizations.

The modularity of PV technology reinforces the geography of the basic solar resource. Sunshine is everywhere. This makes photovoltaics the ultimate "distributed generation" energy. There is little need to transmit renewable electricity over long distances.

Many people—including me—find photovoltaics very attractive. Yet even in the groundbreaking NREL study of how to achieve an 80 percent share of renewable energy sources of the US electricity supply, its role is projected to be very modest. Meanwhile, the role of solar thermal power plants or concentrated solar power (CSP) is projected to be much larger. The existing capacity of CSP plants in the United States is currently 5 percent that of photovoltaics, and CSP appears to offer less potential for cost reduction. But CSP potential is expected to show significant progress because of its unique characteristics to hold onto energy after the loss of direct radiation; in order to obtain high temperatures, the plants must concentrate the light onto a single tower that can retain the energy. The benefit of CSP plants is that they can be designed to incorporate increasing amounts of thermal storage (up to six hours) so their hour-to-hour output is less variable than other forms of solar energy. That means that solar plants can continue to produce power during the night. Another advantage of CSP plants is that they must be relatively large in scale. This means that CSP has significant potential where

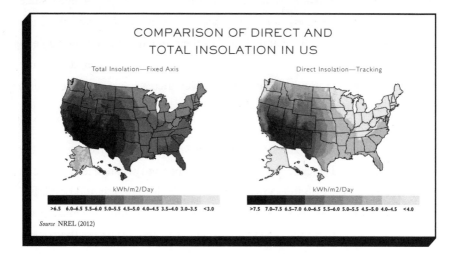

• *fig. 12.6:* The southwestern United States, with its relatively low cloud cover rates, is the most ideal location for most types of solar technologies.

the largest concentrations of sunshine are allowed to penetrate the atmosphere. In the United States, as figure 12.6 shows, this means that the desert regions of the Southwest show the greatest potential to produce quality energy from solar sources. Whichever technology offers the greater advantages, innovations in solar energy continue to be a main attraction for the energy industry.

THE VARIABILITY OF RENEWABLE ENERGY

The world's current electrical grid is not accustomed to dealing with variability. The variability of power supply and the dependency on the location of resources are the most substantive criticisms of a policy backing full-scale deployment of renewable energy.

LOCATION, LOCATION, LOCATION

The most important characteristic of an energy resource is where it is found, and in general, renewable resources are limited to quite specific areas. The situation is similar to that of oil and conventional gas, or even shale gas and coal, whose fields appear as specks on a map. However, the high energy density of conventional fuels makes them much more transportable—especially oil, since it is a liquid. Natural gas has taken longer to become an international commodity, but with an ever-increasing network of trunk pipelines and advances in liquefied natural gas (LNG), it is now becoming a global commodity.

The situation is very different with electricity generation from renewable energy resources. Typically, power must be generated where the resource is found, and transmission lines are costly and difficult to permit and build. For renewable energy to work at a sufficient scale, the energy industry must innovate ways to accentuate the benefits of renewable energy sources. The trick is making the best use of locations that are rich with resources and connecting them to where there is demand. For example, hydro potential is extremely site specific. Only specific sites on specific rivers provide enough flow and storage capacity to be viable for hydropower. Similarly, conventional geothermal plants must be located above localized hydrothermal fields where the resource is typically abundant.

Land areas with exploitable wind resources are often quite small, with the exception of the wide swaths of windy areas in the Great Plains. Even so, wind power plants must be located in these areas in order to extract that potential. It is also important to remember, as mentioned previously, that the energy potential from wind increases with the cube of the wind speed. About 10 percent of the US land area has average wind speeds of at least 7.5 meters/second, while about 50 percent has a wind speed of less than 5.5 m/s. The same plant in the high-wind area will produce at least 155 percent more power than in the area with lower-speed winds. Consequently, natural incentives to concentrate capacity in specific regions are strong.

Biomass plants also must be close to the source, because the fuel is bulky and expensive to transport. In the case of concentrated residues, the biomass plant will almost always be located where the residues are produced. Dispersed residues will be found mostly in regions with prominent agricultural or forestry sectors (for instance, the Corn Belt). In this latter case, efficiency in gathering resources will be critical.

The least geographically concentrated resource is solar radiation. Almost 15 percent of the territory of the contiguous lower 48 states—the Southwest desert region—has very high average insolation, above 6 kWh/m2/year. Yet almost 65 percent of the country's area has insolation between 4.5 and 6 kWh/m2/year. The gradient of attractiveness between the most commercially viable areas and the merely average or mediocre regions is not nearly as steep as with wind power. For example, the difference in insolation between Los Angeles, considered a sunny city, and Boston, in the Frost Belt, is only 17 percent. The difference in performance between such locations will be even less pronounced, because high temperatures (characteristic of places with the highest insolation) actually reduce the efficiency of PV systems.

The regionalization of renewables almost certainly means a substantial increase in the need for interregional transmission of electric power. While fossil fuel and nuclear plants can be built relatively close to demand centers even when their fuel is brought from afar, renewable energy plants must be built where there is a match between the resource and the delivery of the electricity to market. Reflecting this fact, the largest long-distance transmission interconnections in the world have been generally associated with hydropower. Churchill Falls, a generating station in Labrador, Newfoundland (Canada), supplies much of the power for New England and New York State. The Pacific Intertie transmission line links the Northwest's hydro to California's market.

How much more regional interconnection will be needed if renewable energy is to be implemented on a broad scale? The answer depends on the particular mix of renewable and fossil fuel capacity that emerges over the coming decades. Extensive development of wind resources in the sparsely populated Great Plains is likely to require more interconnection capacity than will offshore wind nearer to demand centers. An emphasis on building

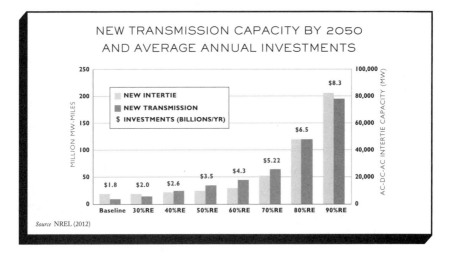

Source NREL (2012)

• *fig. 12.7:* Due to the distributed nature of renewable energy, increasing amounts of renewable energy (RE) powering the world will also require a large amount of new capital to be dispersed to the construction of new transmission capabilities.

central stations for solar power will increase the need for transmission, while a proliferation of distributed PV rooftop systems or increased generation from biomass would require less infrastructure. Figure 12.7 shows NREL's estimates of changes in transmission needs (including interregional interties, displayed in narrow, lighter bars) as renewables' share of generation increases.

The existing total transmission capacity in the contiguous United States is estimated at 150 million to 200 million megawatt-miles (MW-miles.) The new transmission capacity in MW-miles, shown in the figure, includes transmission interconnection capacity needed for renewable energy. Demands for new transmission capacity are much greater in the figure's 80 percent and 90 percent scenarios, but lie within the recent historical range for total investor-owned utility transmission expenditures in the United States ($2 billion/year to $9 billion/year, from 1995 through 2008).

RAMPING UP AND DOWN

Location and transmission issues aside, another factor that will influence transmission needs is the variability of new supplies of renewable energy and the approaches taken to deal with it. As I have noted, not all renewable resources imply variable generation. Both biomass and geothermal tend to operate on base load. Wind and solar are variable, however, and a potentially dramatic increase in the role of either raises legitimate questions as to how to incorporate them into an electric grid that must provide continuously reliable power.

When considering the challenge of variability, it is important to distinguish between different scales of time. Output may vary over very short time periods, like seconds or minutes, or over longer periods, like months, seasons, or years. Most discussion focuses on relatively short-term variations that can have a more unpredictable impact on both the operation of the grid and the dispatch of capacity. However, the energy industry usually uses the following operational categories (shown here with their requirements) to mitigate the impact of variability:

» Load regulation: Reaction times of a few seconds to minutes

» Load following: Reaction times of about ten minutes to a few hours

» Plant scheduling: Fluctuations anticipated up to twenty-four hours in advance

» Unit commitment: Fluctuations anticipated a day or more in advance

In addition, the ability to quickly "ramp" output up and down is crucial for dealing with load regulation. Renewable energy suppliers can implement several strategies to deal with variability. The first is to build a power plant capable of handling variations in demand, such as for biomass and CSP. Grid operators have always had to contend with varying demand and with occasional unplanned outages when, for some reason, a chunk of generating capacity is suddenly lost. Having variable power plants adds a new element to this scenario. As a result, energy suppliers must determine the amount of remaining generating capacity that needs to be ramped up or down to meet variable requirements.

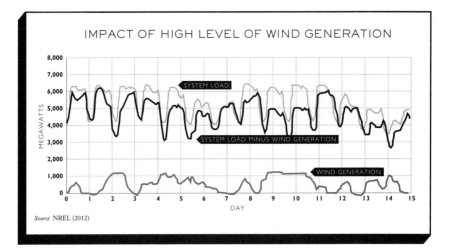

• *fig. 12.8:* In this depiction of the hourly load shapes with and without wind generation, the top gray line represents the system load with wind generation in the mix. With the addition of the wind, the system experiences less dramatic shocks and overall greater power.

Figure 12.8 illustrates the impact of wind on a hypothetical power supplier. The lighter curve represents the system load including wind generation. The darker curve shows the system load without wind generation. While variable power sources such as wind can be a great benefit to the power system, figure 12.8 demonstrates the need to have backup power.

Energy industry experts generally expect that as wind and solar energy become a larger percentage of the global energy mix, suppliers of renewable energy will need to develop additional rapid ramping capability, a second strategy for handling the variability of a renewable power supply. Much of the generation capacity today is not well suited for this reality. For example, coal and nuclear plants are relatively slow to react beyond a small range. However, simple gas turbines are more flexible and can start up in ten minutes if necessary. The best conventional technology for ramping is hydroelectric energy using reserves, where valves can simply be opened or shut.

Adapting to the increasing share of variable supply from renewables will require technology innovations and changes in grid operators' criteria regarding what to dispatch and when. The criteria currently in place were developed based on a grid supplied mostly by fossil fuel thermal plants and involving various assumptions that would no longer fit with new and emerging conditions. However, this is where the electricity grid can benefit from modern technologies through automation and smart metering.

Increasing the flexibility of existing thermal generation capacity would be another obvious strategy for handling resource variability (see chapter 14 for a full description of supply-side energy efficiency strategies). This suggestion fits the Project Butterfly new business case for smarter grid applications and investments in supply-side efficiency. Increasing the flexibility of existing thermal generation capacity will enable greater levels of adoption of renewable energy resources. If market price signals, which value this flexibility, were clear, manufacturers of automation technology would doubtless respond. There are already marked differences in the flexibility of otherwise similar plants, such as combined-cycle natural gas plants that can more easily integrate into a total utility solution.

The remaining strategy would be to also enhance the ability of the grid operator to quickly reduce consumer demand for a short time only. This capability for "demand response" is one of the prime objectives as suppliers gradually introduce the smart grid and smart meters as part of demand-side energy efficiency (a subject I will discuss in detail in chapter 13). Demand response is expected not only to flatten peaks of energy user demand but also to react to rapid shifts in supply or demand. In these moments of fluctuation, the ability to shift instantaneously by as little as 1 to 2 percent of user demand, for even a few minutes, can greatly simplify the supply-side response.

MAKING BIG MONEY IN ENERGY STORAGE

There is potential to unlock significant innovation in the power market by expanding energy storage capacity, so suppliers can store electricity when relatively low-cost supply exceeds demand and inject it back into the grid when the cost of marginal supply is high. The 2012 analysis by NREL (proposing how to increase renewable energy to an 80 percent share of power generation by 2050) made an attempt to estimate how much additional storage might be needed and what technologies might provide it. Altogether, to provide solar energy economically, suppliers would require approximately 80 to 100 GW of new storage capacity. Including existing storage and the thermal storage in CSP plants, total storage would be equivalent to about 16 to 17 percent of average daily consumption. To explore this possibility, NREL assumed some additional pumped hydro but emphasized two new sets of technologies: batteries and, especially, compressed air. The jury is still out, but the potential for significant innovation in energy storage may be the next phase for making big money in the energy business.

LOOKING TO THE PAST FOR GUIDANCE

When the future is unknown, we would be wise to look to the past for guidance. Renewable energy has been with us since the beginning. Hot water coming out of the ground is nothing new. Christopher Columbus sailed to the Americas five centuries ago, but using wind to power ships is several millennia older than that. It is appropriate, therefore, that as we reach for a global sustainability model, we utilize the vast technological know-how we have developed over the past two hundred, one hundred, and even ten years to capture it. The global society can exploit this know-how to create technology like the smart grid, which will optimize resource usage and energy storage—an issue I will explore in more detail in the next chapter.

As pioneers in renewable energy, we face a number of issues when it comes to harnessing these resources. Yet if we are willing to take the arrows, we will also reap the rewards.

KEY OBSERVATIONS

The key observations about the potential of renewable resources are as follows:

» Hydro, wind, solar, geothermal, and biomass can be integrated into a dynamic system to meet the majority of our global energy needs. If the United States can find a pathway forward, as indicated by the 2012 NREL study, then the development of a similar plan for the global energy industry ought to be possible.

» Variable availability of renewable energy resources is a big challenge that imposes some costs, but the full deployment of renewable energy remains a viable means to dramatically decrease annual emissions of GHGs and thus global concentration levels of CO_2.

» Sound energy policy and market innovation can work together to shift the energy mix, especially if competition is opened up to let new technologies (such as demand-side and supply-side energy efficiencies) compete.

What the caterpillar calls the end of the world, the master calls a butterfly.
—*Richard Bach*

CHAPTER 13

One of the oddest moments in my business career came when I was CEO of Highland Energy. The venture capital–backed energy company had designed a comprehensive energy efficiency project for a church-affiliated hospital outside of Fort Worth, Texas. The principal measure we were proposing was the construction of a large icemaker that would freeze water overnight and provide chilled water to cool the hospital's air during the day. The electricity to make the ice would be tapped at night, when the lights were off and idling power plant generators had little cooling load to meet. During peak hours, when other facilities were craving power to meet the demands of air-conditioning loads, the hospital's cooling efforts would require no more electricity than the wattage to run a few fans over the ice. The hospital would benefit by avoiding higher daytime utility rates. The utility would benefit from reduced demand during its peak hours of operation.

My company had negotiated a contract that detailed the total investment amount and our share of the benefits. Len Rozek, the senior project manager, had told me the night before that I could expect to find a signed contract on my desk when I came into the office in the morning. However, when I arrived, Len was already at his desk and had consumed half the coffee pot. He promptly informed me that we had not received the signed copy as expected and that he had received a phone message from the hospital's CFO. Len had been waiting for me before returning the CFO's call.

Len and I discussed what possible issues might still be open. Did the hospital want to further negotiate the terms of the deal? Or had they uncovered a mechanical issue? We knew of no plausible reason for the delay. I wished Len good luck, and he picked up the phone to call the CFO. A few minutes later Len came into my office with his eyes wide open and his jaw nearly on the floor. "The CFO has a final question he wants to ask us," he said. "If God ever makes energy free, does the hospital still have to pay?"

After a moment of disbelief over the question, we found ourselves in a slight panic. Certainly this was a matter we had not considered when we were drafting the agreement. So we pulled out our copy of the proposed agreement and looked at the clause regarding payment obligations. Payment was subject to a simple calculation: namely, the difference between the price of electricity during the day and the price of electricity during the night, multiplied by the number of kilowatt-hours expended to make the ice. We reasoned that since any number multiplied by zero is zero, we concluded the following: "If God makes energy free, then the hospital will not have to pay." Len went back to his office and called the hospital's CFO to inform him of our finding. We had a signed copy of the contract by that afternoon.

Demand-side efficiency in the energy industry may be the closest equivalent to the biblical world in which cleanliness is next to godliness. Demand-side efficiency is certainly the moral equivalent of keeping your house in order. In a practical world, demand-side energy efficiency is maximizing the greatest value from any investment while minimizing total costs. It has the added benefit of directly reducing GHG emissions by eliminating the need for the power generation that produces those emissions.

FEEDING THE 51 PERCENT

It is commonly known that the United States has less than 5 percent of the world's population and yet consumes close to 25 percent of the world's energy resources.[235] How, then, will the planet feed eight billion and then nine billion people by midcentury? How can we support even half that growth? Moreover, try to imagine the impact on our world's resources if a simple majority of the global population were living in accordance with the US standard of living. How can even 51 percent of our global population live a lifestyle similar to that of the average US household without blasting through the earth's natural resources, as current trends indicate will happen? The impact would be staggering.

In fact, simple math says that feeding 51 percent of the world's population living at the same standard as in the United States would require more than 250 percent of the world's current annual consumption. Obviously, raising the standard of living of the world's population to such a level would threaten the already stretched sustainability of the planet. Reports of the United States reducing its carbon intensity per each dollar of GDP is a good thing, certainly. But as we look at this kind of global growth, not just in population but in the compounding nature of increased GDP per person, we quickly come to the conclusion that such a scenario will require every nation to radically reduce both its energy intensity per capita and the carbon content of each unit of energy. This is the only route that will allow us to indeed raise the level of the world's standard of living while avoiding both greater conflict over our global resources and an even higher rate of growth in GHG emissions.

When we evaluate the rise in energy demand and the available resources the world has to draw from, it becomes clear that wondering how to support the enhanced lifestyle of a growing population is not a theoretical consideration. The rapid development of nations such as China and India is transforming the standard of living of hundreds of millions of people every year. For the first time in history, it is possible to forecast that within a few decades, the majority of the Chinese population will live in relative comfort, the way the relatively small middle class in China lives now. This forecast, of course, is dependent on the persistence of current trends, keeping in mind that there is always the potential for a collapse to the international system that might make the 2008 Great Recession look like a minor disturbance. In fact, such a collapse might even be prompted by a global economy that is simply unable to acquire the natural resources to sustain these higher levels of economic activity.

The solution to managing population growth and resource depletion may therefore start with making a global declaration that shakes up the world similar to how the US Declaration of Independence did more than two hundred years ago. Shifting energy from one source to another is not necessarily the whole answer. The real solution may be as basic as declaring, "More is not always better." Our raised standard of living affords us many opportunities, yet many times at a very high cost. The current incarnation of the "American Dream" has long surpassed earlier versions, such as in the 1930s when politicians wanted to promise that there would be a chicken in every pot and a car in every garage. While the United States has still not achieved this dream in reality, our nation has produced the greatest wealth in the world. But we have also built a culture that values saturation over satisfaction. Switching to a different, more conservative value—to "more is not always better"—would lead us to the pursuit of energy efficiency, similar to the pursuit of happiness as promised in the Declaration of Independence. Perhaps this approach can provide us the very foundation required for a new business case—not just for the United States, but for the world.

If bringing 51 percent of the world's population up to the US standard of living equates to consuming more than 250 percent of the world's current annual consumption, then we need to raise the red flag now. Not just about rising CO_2 levels, but about a world that simply must shift its values before it's too late. Can we really make a major change that fosters economic growth but radically slashes the energy and carbon intensity of every new dollar in our global economy? Is it idealistic to think that we could ever redefine our sensibilities so drastically? It might be. But if such a solution is at all possible, then the pathway forward is clear.

I argue that it *is* possible and that the solution is, quite frankly, simple.

THE PURSUIT OF ENERGY EFFICIENCY

How far can energy efficiency take us, and how quickly can we get there? Before I can answer this two-part question, I have to acknowledge that there is some dissension about whether or not demand-side energy efficiency is really and truly part of the solution. Dissenters argue that the pursuit of energy efficiency will not decrease demand but rather will cause new opportunities for consumption and thereby increase the global demand for energy. These dissenters claim that as efficiency improvements drive down the cost of energy services, they create new markets by lowering the price point of entry, enabling people to use more of a given service to meet an endless potential for new applications. They say the result is more energy use, not less.

There is history to back up their argument. I have even found myself making this argument on more than one occasion. One such example of this phenomenon was when electric motors replaced pulley systems driven by steam engines in factories. As motors became more plentiful and the costs dropped, the market found more and more applications for their use. The lower costs for higher-efficiency motors only created greater demand.

Proponents of energy efficiency argue the opposite. They acknowledge that energy efficiency prompts more applications of the same product, but they believe focusing on the elasticity of new demand as prices drop misses the much larger point: Efficiency is the path of moving from the consumption of commodities to the consumption of services that *dematerializes* the economy. The service supplier, compared with the commodity broker, is more focused on maximizing customer satisfaction or on maximizing total value by minimizing resource consumption. Moreover, service suppliers can price their services in accordance to the value created rather than through competitive selection. For example, the service provider can offer a long-term contract that expresses the provider's "take" as a percentage of the net benefit; meanwhile, the commodity salesperson would maximize his or her take by selling as much stuff as possible. Energy efficiency is about doing more with less. It repositions the actual commodity in terms of the value it is creating. As the demand-side dissenters claim, energy efficiency will indeed open new markets as commodity prices fall. But it will also drive down both energy intensity and carbon content—the exact phenomenon that the Project Butterfly team seeks.

We know that energy efficiency leads to reductions in energy intensity. So, therefore, the debate is whether investing in energy efficiency leads to reductions in final energy demand or causes large "rebounds" in energy demand. The concept of a *rebound* is at the base of the dissenter's claim—that energy efficiency leads to greater demand in response to cost reductions for the same level of service.

Project Butterfly has researched the issue and found independent data that refutes the rebound hypothesis by suggesting that rebounds from the end user are small and decreasing, and that rebounds at the economy level are trivial and actually produce a net positive effect.[236] The research is interesting because evaluating the impact of a single cause and effect is difficult. By looking globally at the energy efficiency improvements of new capital over time, you see how even the smallest net positive effect compounds year over year and, given a constant level of economic growth, reduces final energy requirements. Project Butterfly's new business case and modeling work support this idea. Our studies show that year-over-year improvements in energy efficiency lead to dramatic reductions in the future capital required to sustain the same level of economic growth.

Moreover, demand-side energy efficiency is based on the concept that waste is a design flaw rather than a necessary by-product of economic activity. When we deplete our natural resources, we set the boundary for growth, because too much consumption will forever diminish our natural reservoir's capacity to regenerate. One of the clearest examples is a lake or a bay that is threatened by overfishing. Efficiency is part of the path to finding the balance between optimal levels of fishing and exceeding the maximum yield (discussed in chapter 9). Finding energy efficiency opportunities is similar to optimizing a value that is constrained by a resource or flow, without depleting the flow. The result is profit maximization over time.

Looking globally, however, the first order of business is to apply more energy-efficient technologies to improve the carrying capacity of our planet. To do this, we as a global society must redefine how we relate to our energy system. The other option, of course, is to decrease the population of our planet. The reality is, this latter approach would be particularly difficult to achieve, at least without global war or famine. Considering how to maximize the yield of the earth's natural resources through a restraint is likely a much more helpful approach to reducing final energy demand. Energy efficiency then provides the fundamental base for optimization and the pathway to sustainable value creation—in other words, the Project Butterfly new business case.

THOSE WHO HELP THEMSELVES

If the human race continues to operate under the business-as-usual scenario, our global economy may run afoul and may never be able to deviate from the unfavorable course outlined in part II. The global energy mix will change some from its present configuration, but its direction may resemble more of a shifting of tides, influenced by marginal improvements in the cost of energy supply, rather than a tidal change. Instead, if we change our perspective on energy to more closely resemble the perspective described in part III, then we are far more likely to drastically reduce resource use, even with more people living at a higher standard of living. The path to getting there may be building incentives into the economy for reducing GHGs and moving decisively to reduce final energy demand, taking bolder actions to change the current conditions for how we conduct business. Incentives to increase demand-side energy efficiency will act as a de facto mandate to CFOs and energy managers, compelling them to work together to reduce costs and increase value. Such a change may seem gargantuan in nature. But each initiative will mean a small but essential adjustment in our economic DNA that will lead us to realize big gains. Hoping that God intercedes, or even that the gods on Mount Olympus step in, may be a necessary ingredient to the entire equation. But I rather like my grandmother's advice: "God helps those who help themselves."

Therefore I advocate encouraging the global society to do what it must do. We should encourage energy suppliers to incorporate the externalities caused by power generation and to change the rules of engagement between supplier and user in order to give energy users full access to alternatives, *including reducing their energy load.* Small changes will scale to provide a massive solution to climate change—and demand-side energy efficiency is part of this rapid and required industrial innovation, too.

Let's step away from the minutia of the debate over energy efficiency. The big-picture question is this: How do we organize humankind to behave in a way that will allow us to live comfortably on our resource-rich planet with eight and then nine billion inhabitants, all while avoiding famine and nuclear war? Reflect for a moment on the scale of what will be needed. Such an effort, I suspect, will require every form of capital employed since the 1930s, when we struck the New Deal. The global society will need the assistance and full cooperation of national regulatory bodies, including the environmental regulators of every country (such as the US EPA) and all of the international financial institutions (such as the International Monetary Fund, the World Bank, and the World Trade Organization) that have helped lift our global economy to its current level since World War II. I suspect that it will also take the full participation of nearly every public company and every small, medium, and large private company, along with the individuals who run them, to rethink how they do business. Reorganizing our perspective will also require every individual to make difficult personal decisions about how they and their families eat and live. What makes the change even more daunting is that it will require people to make these changes in every nook and cranny of the planet.

The question then becomes, how can we create a simple solution that will affect the greater global society while engaging nearly everyone on the earth? The answer is investing in demand-side energy efficiency in order to reduce energy loads. In other words, the global community needs to develop the kind of thinking that made a hospital want to make ice at night in order to cool things down at a lower cost during the day.

CARBON INTENSITY METRICS

When we are looking at our global energy mix, one of the easiest ways to track the progress of demand-side efficiency measures is with a carbon intensity metric: a measure of the amount of CO_2 that is released with the operation of any kind of facility or complex. The energy user can range from a home to a large data center to a hospital to an automobile manufacturer. By now it should come as no surprise that a facility operating within the new business case burns less CO_2 for every unit of energy consumed. But just *how much* less is burned? The answer is truly surprising.

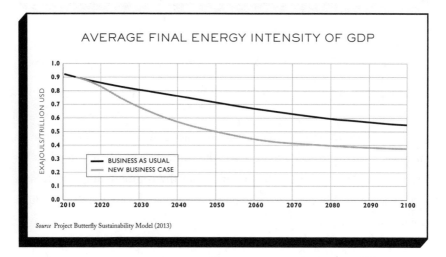

AVERAGE FINAL ENERGY INTENSITY OF GDP

Source Project Butterfly Sustainability Model (2013)

• *fig. 13.1:* As more and more emphasis is placed on demand-side energy efficiency measures in the business-as-usual case, the amount of carbon dioxide for every trillion US dollars (USD) rapidly decreases.

Figure 13.1 demonstrates the carbon intensity of global GDP for a given year. While the trend in the business-as-usual scenario is a steady decline in the amount of CO_2 that is used for every $1 trillion generated, the new business case uses less than half of that amount. The reason for this large difference derives primarily from the implementation of demand-side efficiency measures early on in the simulation. CO_2 savings from these efforts

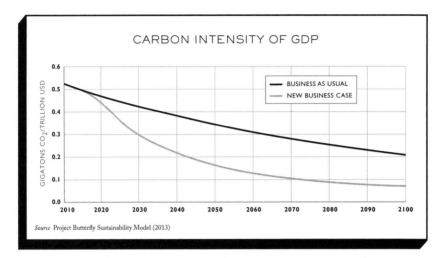

CARBON INTENSITY OF GDP

Source Project Butterfly Sustainability Model (2013)

• *fig. 13.2:* Largely due to more emphasis on demand-side energy efficiency measures, the new business case is able to use less energy to create the same amount of wealth—or in this case, GDP. Because these energy efficiency measures have such a large impact, more effort needs to be given to implementing these types of technologies.

can accumulate to have a large impact on the final outcome. We choose to make these demand-side changes for the same reason we tell our kids to begin saving early on: The effect is similar to the compounding nature of a savings account. Simple measures taken immediately can result in a much larger end figure.

While a lower level of carbon for every unit of global GDP generated is great for the environment, a lower average final energy intensity of global GDP (see figure 13.2) as a result of energy efficiency is even better. The reason is that lower average energy intensity means fewer resources will be needed to supply the same amount of energy. This is good for the environment, good for reducing the global community's dependency on nonrenewable resources, and good for long-term profitability.

Figure 13.3 is an illuminating graph demonstrating the importance of demand-side energy efficiency measures. The most obvious point for both the business-as-usual scenario and the new business case is an upward trend in the amount of required energy to meet final demand. Rising demand in final

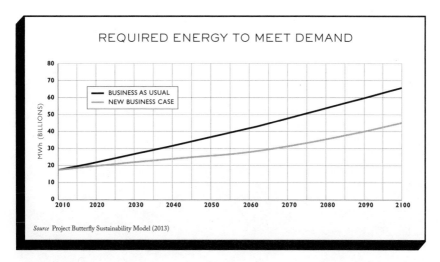

REQUIRED ENERGY TO MEET DEMAND

Source Project Butterfly Sustainability Model (2013)

• *fig. 13.3:* While the global GDP grows at the same rate in both simulations, the new business case requires less energy and produces less environmental pollution.

energy is driven by a growing global population and a larger percentage of the current population gaining access to energy. However, because the new business case shows substantially less required energy than the business-as-usual scenario in spite of an increasing population base, less energy is being produced, which in turn means that less carbon is being released into our atmosphere. Thus the final energy intensity is lower than it would be in the business-as-usual scenario. In both of these scenarios, global GDP grows at the same rate. The difference is in the way the energy is produced in order to generate the same level of GDP vis-à-vis GHG emissions.

SPARKING INDUSTRY

Opportunities in energy efficiency are not new. Increasing the efficiency of energy conversions has been at the heart of many of the technical innovations that have sparked the world's industries since the dawn of the Industrial Revolution (see text box).

Lighting provides a dramatic example of the impact of efficiency improvements on the human way of life as technologies evolve. There have

FROM STEAM TO INTERNAL COMBUSTION

English ironmonger Thomas Newcomen commercialized the first steam engine in 1712 in a business operation financed by a close precursor to today's venture capitalist.[237] He invented the Newcomen engine in order to pump water from the floor of the mines near his home in Devon, England. These mines would often flood with water, limiting the depth at which minerals could be found. The conversion of energy from coal into useful work to pump water from coal mines was about 0.3 percent—a dangerous process akin to a human-activated fire engine. Newcomen invented a piston that used chemical energy to rock the fulcrum that pumped the water, significantly improving safety and the efficiency and depth of the mining operation.

The next major energy-efficient innovation was in 1775, when James Watt teamed up with Matthew Boulton to introduce a new condenser to their steam engine that maximized the efficiency of the steam used to pressurize the cylinder. The condenser would provide a crucial enhancement, increasing the efficiency of steam engines by 2 percent (about seven times the efficiency of the original machine). James Watt enabled the critical step that took the steam engine from a niche machinery to revolutionary technology. Subsequent improvements to the Watt/Boulton engine would have huge impacts over the next 150 years, leading to efficiencies of 12 percent in piston engines by the late nineteenth century and another 18 percent by 1915. These radical advances in the efficiency of engines reduced costs, increased outputs, and propelled the global economy through the post–Industrial Revolution.

More efficient internal combustion engines eventually replaced steam piston engines. But whereas steam piston engines are now found mostly in museums, steam turbines still dominate electricity generation. In 1920 the best turbogenerators were almost 20 percent efficient. In 1960 the best plants were approaching 40 percent efficiency. Today, at full load, the best plants have reached 48 percent efficiency and higher.

been four waves of technological development in lighting, the fourth of which is just starting (see figure 13.4). From antiquity until about 1800, the technology or efficiency of lighting changed very little in terms of how many candles were used or how daylight was maximized into living spaces. At the turn of the nineteenth century, artificial light was a luxury powered by animal and vegetable oils and was used sparingly. For every watt (W) of fuel consumed, about 0.06 lumens (a measurement of candlelight equivalent) was produced.

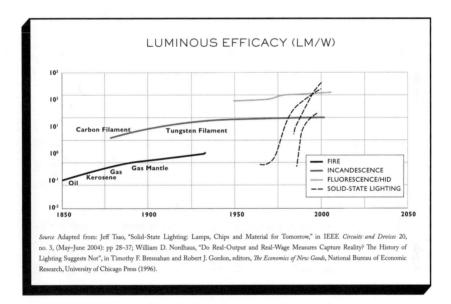

LUMINOUS EFFICACY (LM/W)

Source Adapted from: Jeff Tsao, "Solid-State Lighting: Lamps, Chips and Material for Tomorrow," in IEEE *Circuits and Devices* 20, no. 3, (May–June 2004): pp 28–37; William D. Nordhaus, "Do Real-Output and Real-Wage Measures Capture Reality? The History of Lighting Suggests Not", in Timothy F. Bresnahan and Robert J. Gordon, editors, *The Economics of New Goods*, National Bureau of Economic Research, University of Chicago Press (1996).

♦ *fig. 13.4:* The historical trend of innovations in lighting has displayed tremendous increases in efficacy.

The efficiency of lighting from oils (including the new "rock oil," or kerosene) improved gradually, and by 1875 it had perhaps even doubled with the most advanced lamps. Meanwhile, starting around 1820, "town gas"—a commercialized fuel from the distillation of coal—was provided to light the world's larger cities. These first public systems were slightly more efficient than oil lamps (0.08 lumens/W of fuel). The efficiency of these new lighting systems increased rapidly, however, and by the late nineteenth century had reached 0.6 lumens/W, an eightfold increase in energy efficiency. But a whole new technology had entered the scene by then, based on a new energy form: electricity.

In 1883 Thomas Edison introduced the first commercial package to sell light from electricity. The selling point was not price (about $4/kWh in current dollars) but convenience and, above all, safety; gas lamps posed the omnipresent danger of fire. Edison's first carbon fiber incandescent lamps produced 2.6 lumens/W of electricity. Subsequent improvements increased output to 6.5 lumens/W by 1910. Ten years later, a new type of incandescent lamp that used tungsten fibers was sweeping the market; it had an output of 11.8 lumens/W.

Within a period of sixty years, the efficiency of converting energy into light increased about a hundredfold. Of course, the new technology depended on converting fuels into electricity, which reduced the efficiency improvement fivefold. Still, the gain was at least twentyfold, and the steam engines used to generate electricity were also improving their efficiency every year. Another advantage was that the new technologies used relatively cheap fuels, whereas lamps had required relatively costly liquid fuels, like sperm whale oil.

The shift to electric lighting was only the beginning of a new series of innovations. By the mid-twentieth century, fluorescent lighting (still at 11.8 lumens) had become widespread. By the early 1990s, compact fluorescent lamps had an output of about 70 lumens/W. Fluorescent lighting began to penetrate the traditional market of incandescent lamps. Today a whole new technology is entering the market. LEDs offer the next generation of higher efficiency, including a precision control of lighting, which tends to reduce perceived lighting needs, thus cutting back on waste.

A TREND TOWARD IMPROVEMENT

Clearly, the discussion of increasing energy efficiency is not about reversing historical trends. It is not about throwing us back to the Stone Age. Energy efficiency is about reinforcing historical trends. Increasing the efficiency of a vast range of energy transformations has been a key characteristic of the past three hundred years of industry. New technologies are being continuously developed, as we have seen with the continuous invention of lighting technology and with the ongoing switch to renewable energy sources. It is just a matter of how long it takes to accept this move forward and how much resistance to innovation is built into the system.

I will give you a couple more examples. We are surrounded by household efficiency improvements. The modern US refrigerator uses two-thirds less electricity than a 1970s model. It costs less and has many more features. For decades, boilers and new air conditioner condensers have improved their efficiency at rates of 3 to 5 percent a year. In the 1990s, many US households retrofitted their homes with double- and triple-pane windows to reduce heat loss and employed E-glass technology to reflect heat away from or into the home, depending on the season. The next generation of windows offers printable liquid crystal coating to absorb the amount of energy that passes through them. This new breed of "smart" windows allows more of the sun's rays in during the winter and reflects more heat out in the summer.

New forms of insulation have been used throughout commercial and residential buildings in order to substantially improve the thermal resistance of houses and other buildings. Most residences constructed in the 1980s and 1990s used a fluffy pink insulation built into the walls and crawl spaces to add a buffer of air that limits heat or cooling loss. Today contractors spray thermal barrier gels with superinsulating properties into tight spaces at a fraction of the cost of just a few decades ago. The gels minimize unwanted airflow, making homes more comfortable and substantially reducing heat and cooling losses.

In industrial facilities, replacing equipment such as pumps, fans, blowers, turbines, and propellers with more efficient technologies can produce massive electricity savings. For example, rotors are now being replaced with technologies that are spiral-shaped to improve fluid movement. This new shape can achieve dramatic savings by reducing resistance and maximizing flow.

Many of the other products consumers purchase are embodied with substantial energy intensity due to the construction materials and the cost of transporting inputs and products to market. Some basic materials are very energy intensive: metals, plastics, cement, glass, paper. The technologies that produce these materials are relatively mature, so additional and large efficiency gains are not often possible. Even so, there is a record of steady improvement in sectors such as the steel industry, as shown in figure 13.5. Note not only the improvement over time but also the differential or substantial gaps between regions of the world that deploy greater efficiency.

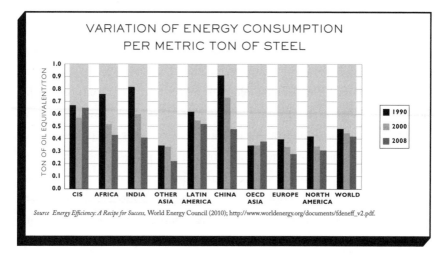

VARIATION OF ENERGY CONSUMPTION
PER METRIC TON OF STEEL

Source *Energy Efficiency: A Recipe for Success,* World Energy Council (2010); http://www.worldenergy.org/documents/fdeneff_v2.pdf.

♦ *fig. 13.5:* Some regions see substantial energy being saved in the manufacturing of steel today as compared to levels seen in 2000 or 1990.

REDUCE, REUSE, RECYCLE

Reduce, reuse, recycle. Children in the United States are taught this slogan as part of their duty to ease global warming and to improve energy efficiency. However, as adults, we rarely incorporate these methods into our business-as-usual mind-set. Reducing, reusing, recycling, and even repairing can induce a powerful shift toward lower costs, including energy costs, and can improve productivity and drive profitability in businesses. Some of the biggest gains to be made with energy-intensive materials are through reductions in the weight needed in given products, such as steel in automobiles. Major efficiency gains also can be made through measures to reuse and recycle materials. Steel from recycled scrap requires one-quarter the energy of steel produced from iron ore, which results in a dramatically reduced carbon footprint. In fact, the steel industry captures more than half of its waste. As other industries follow suit, energy use and CO_2 levels can drop significantly.

As a consequence, changing the way we think about waste can mean dramatic changes in the health of the planet. For example, in 2009 concerned citizens of Yampa Valley, Colorado, started a zero waste initiative within the Steamboat Springs ski area.[238] Three years later, the area's waste had been reduced by more than 70 percent and was on target to achieve the goal of eliminating 100 percent of waste by 2014.[239] This impressive change was made possible by the cooperation of local industries, the community, and local government. The local tourist industry agreed to shift container purchases to 100 percent recyclable or compostable material, while the garbage service and community members began an aggressive composting and recycling program. Shifting from landfill waste to alternatives like composting has been proven to reduce GHGs.[240] Whereas landfills create an environment favorable to methane-producing, anaerobic decomposition, growth from composting has the opposite effect, absorbing CO_2.

In the process of shifting from a wasteful society to a sustainable one, the world community will fundamentally change its perspective. This will create opportunities to do more than just achieve environmental and energy sustainability—it will also present changes to society itself. Given this general context for future energy demand, our business-as-usual scenario still forecasts a steady decrease in the energy intensity of the economy. For example, the Energy Information Adminstration's reference case in its *Annual Energy Outlook* published in 2010 projected a 40 percent decline in total US energy consumption per unit of GDP by 2035, including a 32 percent reduction in electricity. This decline in "energy intensity" partly reflects the expectation of a reduced share of manufacturing in the US economy, but it is mostly attributable to gradual improvements in the performance of various types of equipment. This projected decline follows a similar decline of 40 percent in the intensity of energy use between 1980 and 2008.

Deeper reductions in the energy and carbon intensity of electricity are possible and will be needed to meet the requirements of the Project Butterfly new business case. As Craig Sieben, the Chicago-based CEO of Sieben Energy Associates, says, "We have been telling clients the same message for more than twenty years: They can save 30 percent of their energy bills today, even if they did a major upgrade within the last decade." These cuts can be achieved through a combination of currently available technologies and future innovations that are "in the pipeline."

The potential for a large increase in the share of renewable energy for electricity generation by 2050[241] (which I pointed out in chapter 12) suggests that the intensity of electricity use (kWh/GDP) could fall as much as 66 percent by that year compared to 2008 levels. This level of reduction will not be easy to achieve. It will require clear signals to suppliers and consumers of goods and services, heightened awareness on their part of the benefits and possibilities of not only energy efficiency but also renewable energy, and measures (such as financing) that facilitate translating awareness into action. The benefits, however, will also be substantial, even without considering the reduction in CO_2 emissions. The cost of energy services will be reduced, which will enhance economic competitiveness. Bottom line: Energy supply is much more capital intensive than most economic activity. Saving energy does not require large capital expenditures. However, it is labor intensive, employing mechanical and electrical contractors to change out energy systems.[242] The consequence is greater employment per dollar of investment to save energy rather than the employment that results from making new energy.

The commercial potential for demand-side energy efficiency will continue to increase across a broad front, beyond the gains already achieved. One big reason to expect this trend is the strong interrelationship between energy use and the information technology revolution that is already well under way (and that shows no sign of stopping). Information technology is transforming products, services, and entire supply chains as a kilowatt travels from the power plant to your front door. Improved cost controls are possible by simply turning off devices that are not being used, enabling consumers to see the impact of management and operating performance in real time. Widespread availability of information unleashes commercial potential by motivating the consumer to switch over to new and better-performing materials (often made possible by new R&D). These new products are made available in faster-than-ever times to market.

CAPTURING LOST POTENTIAL

None of this is easy. Energy efficiency requires creativity and the engagement of our brightest minds. Demand-side energy efficiency will be one of the most promising businesses for the next few decades regardless of whether the global society enters into a new business case. My point is just that the new business case reinforces what is already happening, as required to meet the needs of the environmental steward. The relatively short timeline from concept to design to implementation and finally to results makes demand-side energy efficiency the first consideration for any group looking to reduce costs or to restrict sources of GHGs. Whether you are a climate negotiator, a utility regulator, an energy manager, an end user, or an entrepreneur looking to find low-hanging fruit, demand-side efficiency will probably provide the highest-yield returns because it is not just about switching fuels. It is about eliminating their unnecessary use.

The intellectual challenge surrounding energy efficiency, then, flows from the necessity of looking at the whole system and addressing each of its fundamental layers. If we see waste simply as a by-product of poor design, energy efficiency is the way to capture lost potential and redirect it. Implementing renewable energy sources can go a long way toward reducing losses in the systems that surround electricity generation, as discussed in chapter 12. But by integrating supply-side and demand-side energy efficiency, we can start to distribute and transmit the energy being produced even as we reduce peak loading, thus avoiding unnecessary new investments by flattening out the demand curve.

The question before us, however, is how to promote radical efficiency improvements through creating market signals that reduce energy resource use and mitigate climate change. The approaches vary widely between major segments of energy users. In transport, users range from individuals in their private cars to large corporations running railways, airlines, and truck and maritime fleets. In industry, there are huge differences between big firms in energy-intensive sectors, such as steel, cement, and chemicals, and the large number of lighter industries, where energy is a smaller share of total costs. For example, energy efficiency for buildings range from making private homes smarter to retrofitting cooling and heating loads for shopping centers, hospitals, and public and private office buildings.

In some sectors, such as residences and individual transport, minimum efficiency standards and performance rankings of equipment can play a critical role in the success of energy initiatives. Large, energy-intensive industries and transport service companies tend to use their own in-house expertise. These industries may need incentives to make efficiency a priority. In fact, a key to unlocking the potential for efficiency gains seems to be a strong energy-efficiency-services industry.

ENERGY EFFICIENCY AS A CLIMATE-CHANGE TOOL

Some argue that in spite of energy efficiency's clear benefits to businesses, demand-side efficiency as a climate mitigation tool must be able to scale at a meaningful level to address global warming. In other words, if it takes each of us to change a lightbulb to make a meaningful change, then relying on energy efficiency requires too many of us.

The Project Butterfly team has reached a very different assessment from the conclusion these critics have reached. We are proposing a comprehensive plan that includes new power generation. But underlying the fundamentals of the plan is demand-side efficiency. In fact, the view of the Project Butterfly team is that demand-side energy efficiency is the most rapid and scalable technology of all the possible mitigation strategies because it puts the power of the solution in everyone's hands.

Why? Energy efficiency breeds energy efficiency. Lower-wattage lightbulbs that render higher lumen output and a greater spectrum of light create less heat, and less heat means less air-conditioning. The cycle of efficiency continues to feed itself. Similarly, superinsulating a home not only makes it less drafty and more comfortable but also lightens both the heating and the cooling loads. Or consider a consumer's choice of vehicle: Smaller cars require smaller engines. Smaller engines require less fuel. Less fuel means a lighter car that uses less steel, which preserves natural resources, too.

Nevertheless, many consumers find it difficult to imagine how, say, a single family's purchase of incandescent lightbulb might make a difference. The energy reduction from one purchase, they argue, is infinitesimal compared with the big changes required to address climate change. My answer is this: Imagine a continuous improvement in the efficiency of new capital, accelerating at an additional 2 to 3 percent a year across the global economy, and compare the impact of such an improvement with the business-as-usual scenario over fifty or one hundred years. Then imagine working on both sides of the equation: improving the efficiency of energy supply and also the efficiency of new lighting, cooling, and heating systems for buildings and of motors, fans, and boilers for industry. The global investment required to produce the same amount of electricity would decline, as would the requirements on the demand side to meet or exceed the same level of service. What's more, the financial capital that otherwise would have been deployed to build conventional energy supplies can be redirected to more productive uses and redeployed toward creating greater value.

The potential impact of demand-side energy efficiency on the climate change calculation is far-reaching—that is, if the global society can incentivize its use. As annual improvements in global efficiency compound over fifty years, the world economy would experience a substantial decrease not only in energy intensity per dollar of GDP, but also in the amount of final energy required to sustain the same level of economic growth and prosperity.

Energy efficiency measures are small in nature and by design, but they are solutions that can be put into the hands of millions of people, if not billions, to implement. Changing a lightbulb from an incandescent to a compact fluorescent, or to an LED, is the first step in a long process. Small changes can then add up quickly.

As one of my favorite CFOs has said to me, "If you watch your pennies, your dollars will watch themselves."

KEY OBSERVATIONS

The key observations from this chapter about the realities of demand-side efficiency are as follows:

» Demand-side energy efficiency is based on the idea that waste is a design flaw. By finding the balance between sustainable use and resource depletion, both energy users and suppliers can maximize total value of the resources at hand.

» Implementing demand-side energy efficiency requires comparing energy investments to core investments by using IRR and NPV calculations. Enabling businesses to evaluate energy efficiency options will require greater education and support of third-party energy services companies.

» Energy efficiency places value on producing satisfaction by minimizing consumption, especially resource use. Shifting to an economy that values energy efficiency will lead to greater services and less focus on commodity pricing. The result is a highly productive but dematerialized economy that will directly reduce GHG emissions and lower the concentration of atmospheric CO_2.

Forget distinctions. Leap into the boundless and make it your home!
—*Chuang Tzu*

CHAPTER 14

I'm no Charles Dickens, but I do have a tale of two cities to tell. These two unique cities are my favorite in the world to visit. Beijing, China, and Rio de Janeiro, Brazil—world-class cities with world-class problems. They stand in deep contrast to each other regarding how they make use of their limited resources and how they build efficiency into their energy supply. Their tale will help illustrate key differences in two approaches to energy.

As the capital city of the People's Republic of China, with a population in excess of twenty million, Beijing is the country's political, cultural, and educational center. It is important to get a sense of scale: The city is approximately 100 miles wide and 110 miles long, and it is growing in nearly every direction. Both ancient and modern, Beijing houses the Forbidden City, where emperors reigned for centuries, and is also full of large commercial centers and high-rise office complexes that by any standard are impressive architectural achievements. Coal-fired power plants throughout Beijing power the city and support its nearly continuous growth, electrifying its ever-expanding urban neighborhoods and all its commerce and industry. Beijing's homes have coal-fired stoves used for both heating and cooking meals. Its streets bustle with constant traffic.

Not surprisingly, Beijing's air quality is among the worst in the world. You can be within twenty, even ten miles of the Taihang Mountains and still it is often impossible to see even a faint outline of these mountains due to the smog and dust. You know this is the haze of pollution and not the overcast fog of a rainy day, when the sky above is blue. In the winter, when you first arrive in the city, the smell of burnt coal stings your nose. Nevertheless, you cannot help but be awestruck by Beijing's robust economy. The city is still one of the best places in all of China to shop and trade, just as it has always been, back to the days of its imperial roots.

Growing its urban areas has been at the heart of the Chinese economic strategy, and Beijing has served as one of its primary models. Individuals in China are nearly ten times more productive in contributing to the nation's economy when they move from their rural setting into a major metropolitan area like Beijing. To meet the social demands of China's swelling cities, mayors are encouraged to sell the land at their cities' perimeters to developers. Home buyers in these new developments become taxpayers. New tax revenues are then used to build new roads, bridges, power plants, and transmission lines to service each city's growing population and attract even more businesses and factories into the cities. The urbanization of China's largest cities, such as Beijing, is at the heart of what is driving new energy demand in the industrializing world.

Rio de Janeiro, Brazil's second-largest city, with more than six million inhabitants, does not have the luxury of building outward indefinitely. The city is nearly completely surrounded by long, sandy white beaches facing the Atlantic Ocean or majestic mountains shooting straight out of the water toward the sky. In fact, thanks to the combination of rich culture and the grandness of its physical landscape, UNESCO has recently granted Rio the distinction of being a World Heritage site. The hills of Rio are covered in shantytowns, or *favelas,* that provide a colorful backdrop and make it one of the most beautiful cities I have ever seen. Some might be surprised to hear this description, but the unique blend of colors and panoramic views would make the underlying real estate worth a fortune if you could transplant the city landscape into any part of the industrialized word. Plus, from nearly anywhere in the city, you can look up and see one of the world's most famous statues: Cristo Redentor, or Christ the Redeemer. This makes the entire city almost a temple unto itself.

Rio is exceptional for many reasons beyond its grandeur and natural beauty. While it is neither the capital of Brazil nor its financial center, Rio, like Beijing, is the country's cultural center. São Paulo, to the south, serves as the country's commercial center. São Paulo is the city where money is made from the trade of the nation's principle goods. But Rio is the city where Brazilians and international tourists flock to spend their cash. Some of the city's world renown is the result of the city government's extraordinary effort to ensure that its beaches are pristine every morning and accessible to everyone—rich and poor alike—all day long. These beaches are an essential part of Rio's renewable resources—just a small illustration of the value it places on its natural surroundings.

The natural beauty of Rio is also enhanced by the other ways the city deploys its resources and capital. The city government invests in educational facilities, and as a result Rio serves as a home to many universities and institutes. The city is alive with exotic food, Carnival celebrations, and music and dancing—especially samba and bossa nova. Rio's varied culture comes from its mix of indigenous people, European settlers, and African descendants—a heritage that has coalesced into a single culture with its own dialect, known as *Carioca*.

Rio and the daily life of its residents are powered much like the rest of Brazil. Electricity is transmitted from the vast hydrological reservoirs built to the north, along the tributaries of the Amazon River. Hydropower provides a reliable source of power that is both clean and free of fuel charges. But relying on the transmission of power from afar has meant that Rio is subject to frequent brownouts and occasional blackouts. Drought conditions can leave the hydro reserves stressed, affecting the entire country and its demand on this natural resource. City officials respond by trying to isolate Rio into a power island, limiting transmission by tapping both a large nearby hydropower plant and a dedicated nuclear power station to deliver the power it needs.

Whether in Beijing or in Rio, residents take ownership of their city and value the aesthetic nature of its many assets. Beijing city officials are aware of the air quality problem and are converting their coal-fired plants to natural gas in order to reduce polluting emissions. Officials in Rio, aware that the city needs more power, have chosen to adjust the pricing of utility rates in order to encourage users to turn off electric appliances during peak periods of energy demand and, if possible, to avoid increasing the amount of power generation required to serve the city. Time-of-day pricing is a national policy in Brazil, but only high-voltage consumers are able to participate. Rio city officials are pushing to give low-voltage consumers the choice of opting in to time-of-day pricing, with new smart meters. The governments of both cities are exploring ways to use their energy assets as a means to preserve capital for their respective communities beyond just powering commerce.

By choosing to look at the overall affordability of their energy services rather than simply the cost of the kilowatt-hour, the cities of both Rio and Beijing are assessing the full cost of services, including environmental impacts on the quality of life of their citizens. If energy services serve a population's energy needs and work to make habitats stronger, healthier, and wealthier, then that population is very likely creating a system of permanent sustainability. The city planners of both Beijing and Rio have begun to find their pathway forward.

No doubt, Beijing and Rio are on different trajectories as they seek to build upon their natural assets. Nonetheless, their city planners are working to find new ways to change their energy systems and to build in greater sustainability. The next step in improving supply-side efficiency for these modern day cities—as for communities around the globe—is to add in costs where costs are due.

EFFICIENCY LEADS TO EFFICIENCY

Just as success builds on success, efficiency leads to greater total efficiency. This is true for both demand-side and supply-side efficiency. As renewable energy becomes a larger percentage of the global energy mix (as I outlined in chapter 13), both the conversion and the resulting energy mix must be optimized to breed efficiency and reduce the carbon content of each unit of energy. The global community therefore needs to get the most out of the fuel we use—our "supply"—regardless of whether it is finite or renewable. To accomplish this, innovation must be seen as the pathway forward, just as it was for demand-side efficiency.

Supply-side efficiency means yielding the same level of output while expending less energy, regardless of whether the task is going from mechanical energy to electric energy (turning a turbine to generate electricity) or from chemical energy to mechanical energy (firing a piston to spin a tire on an auto). Supply-side efficiency improvements often naturally stem from the necessity to produce a higher yield from the same level of energy or resources. Simply put, supply-side efficiency is the result of the supplier working to conserve resources (such as fuel) while also becoming more competitive. These natural and businesslike motivations open up opportunities for growth and create greater profitability. In this light, supply-side efficiency also finds its way squarely into the Project Butterfly new business case.

Figure 14.1 is an output from the Project Butterfly modeling work that most effectively demonstrates the power of supply-side energy efficiency measures. The graph presents a macro-picture that demonstrates the impact and importance of internalizing an externality such as GHG emissions and reveals how this cost translates into greater supply-side innovation. As you can see, the business-as-usual scenario has a slightly upward trending line in the carbon intensity of final energy. This trending line can be attributed to the fact that emerging economies such as China and India will be primarily powering their society with power from fossil fuel sources, including conventional coal, even though their use of renewable energy will grow. While renewable sources of energy under the business-as-usual scenario gain a larger and larger share of overall generation, the high carbon intensity of coal, combined with relatively little emphasis on supply-side efficiency, will cause the overall carbon intensity of final energy to increase to the end of this century.

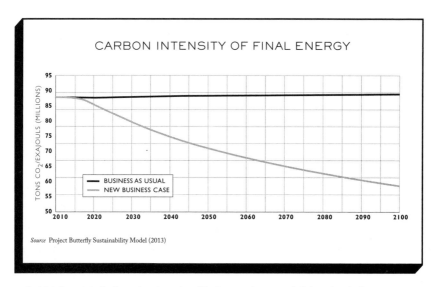

• *fig. 14.1:* Interestingly, the carbon intensity of final energy increases slightly under the business-as-usual case. This can be attributed to the increasing dependency upon fossil fuels in such countries as China and India.

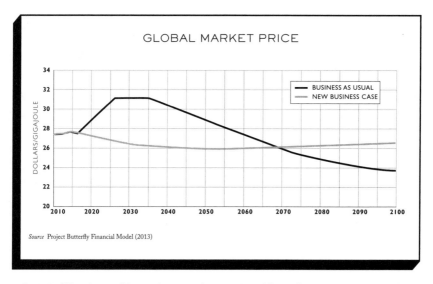

• *fig. 14.2:* Although several factors determine the trajectory of the market price curve, supply-side efficiency measures greatly aid in bringing down the final price the consumer pays.

On the other hand, by applying a cost of $45 per ton of carbon, the Project Butterfly new business case realizes a quick and consistent decrease in the carbon intensity of final energy over the forecasted time horizon. A significant level of planning and monitoring will certainly be necessary to achieve these levels of reduction. The good news is that much of the technology needed to make these changes, such as computerized automation to optimize fuel efficiency and hours of operation, already exists. It needs only to be spurred and incentivized through the right market signals.

Therefore, one of the intended results of creating market signals for implementing supply-side efficiency measures is the eventual decrease that will result in the final cost to the energy user, an effect that is displayed in figure 14.2. While short-term costs are almost a guarantee with supply-side efficiency measures (think of upgrading a power plant or installing a new boiler), so, too, are eventual price savings once the new equipment goes into operation and the costs are amortized. The graphical shape in this figure is important because the similar pattern—short-term cost and long-term benefit—can be applied to just about any energy efficiency operation. The essential feature of any program to increase supply-side efficiency is the eventual cost savings that make up for the initial burden.

THE SMART GRID AND SUPPLY-SIDE EFFICIENCY

The pathway to alleviate the risks associated with dependency on conventional fuels is the rapid development of a smarter electrical grid. Public and private investments into smart grid technologies are a critical part of both the business-as-usual scenario and Project Butterfly's new business case as the energy industry struggles to cost-effectively meet demand, because the smart grid makes better use of our existing energy infrastructure. The development of a smart grid also presents the most interesting outcomes for yet-to-be-discovered innovation that can lead to rapid reductions in energy use and in the carbon intensity of final energy. Currently, an aging electrical infrastructure, an uncompetitive power market, and an extremely centralized means of transmission dominate the US and global energy landscape. Over the next forty years, the US electric power sector could require investments of as much as $3.5 trillion just to replace its aging infrastructure.[243] When we look globally, the size of the problem only becomes greater. An investment in smart grid technologies eases the transition.

For example, with regard to the relatively uncompetitive nature of the US power market, about 70 percent of all customers are served by utilities, which are regulated by state public utility commissions.[244] This means it is up to the elected or appointed state regulators to fairly distribute the costs and benefits between customers and shareholders, while simultaneously maintaining oversight on the utilities' investment activities. Within this system, the themes of reliability and consistency have dominated the energy industry, while operating efficiency and revenue growth, which are normally themes actively present in a free market system, have taken a seat on the sidelines. These same sets of circumstances apply to the global energy market.

Finally, inherent dangers exist within the complex and highly interconnected electric power grid if it is well maintained and part of any transition plan. Just as the financial crisis of 2008 spread quickly around the globe and caught many individuals and nations off guard, large regions and even entire nations can feel the effects of brownouts or blackouts. A move toward a more distributed and smart electric grid is crucial to any effort to mitigate these risks.

For example, in July 2012, India experienced a two-day blackout that left six hundred million people without power. About half the country was literally operating in the dark. Market analysts immediately drew India's economic ambitions into question. The concern was over whether India's inefficient power sector would be able to electrify the country's long-term growth. The *Washington Post* reported that the collapse of India's electric grid led to the largest power blackout in global history.[245]

The state of the electric sector in the United States is not that much of an improvement over India's. One has only to recall the large August 14,

2003, blackout that affected more than fifty million people over nine thousand square miles from Toronto to New York City, closed thirteen airports, and caused economic losses (as estimated by public officials) of between $4.5 billion and $8.2 billion. All this was the result of a few power lines in Ohio, which were being fed by a poorly maintained nuclear plant, falling into some branches.[246] On top of this, cyberattacks, very similar to the 2010 Stuxnet worm that targeted Iran's uranium enrichment plants, are a growing concern to global security agencies. Though seemingly rare, these instances demonstrate the far-reaching effects of power grid failure and the susceptibility of a highly interconnected grid. They also demonstrate the need for a change. Developing a smart grid is a way to add value for the energy user and to reduce costs to the energy supplier.

According to the EIA, demand for electricity in the United States is projected to increase at a 1 percent annual growth rate to the year 2035.[247] While the demand for power is no longer increasing as rapidly as it once was, new energy sources will be as important as ever in meeting the demands of the energy user. More than 70 percent of existing US coal plants are more than thirty years old, and 33 percent of them are more than forty years old.[248] The American Society of Civil Engineers released a 2011 report stating that the current electrical grid will ultimately break down by 2020 unless a staggering $673 billion is invested for repairs and replacements.[249] This aging infrastructure, and the lack of a coherent plan to modernize it, is especially alarming when we take into account the actions that other nations are taking. China, for example, already has plans to install three hundred million smart meters to dispatch power by 2015 and will also invest $47 billion over the next five years to improve its energy infrastructure.[250] While China is gearing up for the next generation of electrical grids, the United States appears to be pushing this issue to the back burner. The question that emerges is how to most effectively update existing energy infrastructure?

Traditional coal plants, for the most part, have already experienced their heyday, and next-generation coal plants equipped with carbon capture and sequestration technology (CCS) face their own hurdles without any ability to capture a benefit from reducing emissions. For many individuals, meeting the needs of our growing hunger for power without making dramatic changes to the energy system that has served us so well in the past is an idea that doesn't make any sense. To me, investing in the CCS movement makes sense because it enables existing infrastructure to continue earning a return. Trying to model CCS specifically was beyond the scope of Project Butterfly, but there are still a few observations we can readily make.

For utility planners, reliability of the system is what ultimately matters. Just as a diversified stock portfolio produces less volatile and more predictable returns, so, too, would an electrical grid realize these benefits when being powered by many power plants working together. The more highly integrated grid, coupled with the vast amount of available information technology, can allow customers to have more choices about when they purchase their power and for how much. For instance, digital displays empower customers to decide whether they want to run the dishwasher now or wait for a better time when demand, and therefore the price of electricity, is lower.

Significant investment in smart grid technologies would have a triple effect in making these potential benefits a reality, as follows:

1. Reduce the cost of new supply by decreasing the impact of variable supply.
2. Send a strong market signal to consumers about making their own investments in smart grid technologies to gain the benefits of reduced load and costs.
3. Increase the reliability of the electric system as a result of equipment upgrades and reduced maintenance requirements.

This is not just wishful thinking. Technologies are being implemented as we speak that achieve these benefits throughout the world. Portugal drastically increased its reliance on renewable energy from 17 percent in 2005 to a remarkable 45 percent in 2010, and that nation's infrastructure investments in improved transmission are what made this possible.[251] Denmark currently obtains more than 25 percent of its electricity from wind power. Denmark's goal is for 35 percent of its energy to come from renewable sources by 2035— and for 100 percent, including heating, industrial activity, and transportation, by 2050.[252] While there are distinct differences between the United States and nations like Portugal and Denmark, the fact remains that large-scale adoption of smart grid technologies is possible as a means to transition to an energy mix more reliant on renewable energy.

What follows is a broad overview of changes that must be made in our existing power infrastructure to realize the potential for supply-side efficiency and to obtain minimally the results present in the simulation underlying the Project Butterfly new business case. Some aspects of my recommendations may surprise you. These recommendations are certainly outside of conventional thinking within the environmental community. The Project Butterfly new business case is offering a business view with an eye toward environmental stewardship. The concept is simple and the approach is pragmatic. The objective is to use the marketplace and the drive toward greater profitability in order to complete the necessary transition to a sustainable global energy mix.

COAL AND SUPPLY-SIDE EFFICIENCY

Let's continue our investigation of supply-side efficiency measures by focusing on the largest supply of fossil fuels: coal. The largest single percentage of the world's power supply mix today comes from coal-fired power generation. Although coal-fired power plants are the worst of GHG emissions offenders because of the high carbon content of their fuel, simply shutting them down is neither practical nor politically feasible, in spite of claims by US power producers that it is the only response to "Obama's War on Coal." But closing coal-fired plants may not be necessary, even considering our current carbon load. Keep in mind, building wind farms to replace aging coal-fired power plants will likely take decades. Considering the need to transition to a renewable energy economy over time, the easiest and most reachable target may be to increase the efficiency of coal-fired power generation by reducing the CO_2 content.

There is even new coal technology that can enhance supply-side efficiency and reduce emissions. This technology can and should be immediately deployed in addition to building wind farms and other renewable sources of energy if investment in energy efficiency upgrades provide competitive returns. Why, then, hasn't this already been done? Why isn't this new, more efficient technology being employed to reduce GHGs and increase profitability from coal-fired power plants? The answer is because the rules that govern the operation of these plants lack appropriate regulatory structures and price signals required to incorporate new technology and processes. It is far easier to do nothing. For the risk averse, it is also difficult to justify new investments that, so the argument goes, may or may not increase efficiency or ever afford the right to cost recovery. In the business-as-usual regulatory environment, there is simply too much uncertainty regarding investment recovery from nearly any investment in coal generation, regardless of its environmental or financial benefits.

Moreover, the IEA *World Energy Outlook* estimates that 1.4 gigatons of CO_2e (carbon dioxide–equivalent) emissions can be avoided by replacing existing coal plants (those older than twenty years) with new coal plants. Without the appropriate regulatory environment, however, it is difficult for a utility or power plant owner to justify making infrastructure improvements that would cost hundreds of millions of dollars per plant. Complicating this resistance to upgrading is the fact that because of its environmental costs and the failure to develop a clear operating path to a cleaner version, coal as a fuel source is constantly on the chopping block. Power plant owners have reason to fear that even new or upgraded coal-fired power plants could be closed in an instant as a response to new environmental regulations or legislative initiatives as long as the rules remain unclear. Even if Governor Mitt Romney had won the 2012 presidential election, a new, more coal-friendly administration would have given a power plant owner only four to eight years of reprieve for an asset that can last thirty, forty, or even fifty years. In contrast, sufficient incentives need to be implemented to spur investments in new technology that can increase the thermal efficiency of existing infrastructure and thus substantially reduce the carbon intensity of final energy.

To some, this lack of regulatory certainty may be a surprising twist to the issue. But that is the situation in which we still find ourselves today in the United States, where coal-fired power plant owners are discouraged from upgrading or modernizing their plants to ensure greater supply-side efficiency. For example, the EPA issued new rules for coal-fired power plants in December 2012 to comply with the Clean Air Act. But rather than cooperate with the EPA to create a regulatory environment that works, pro-coal business associations and legislative efforts have continued to try to gut these programs every step of the way. This is an unfortunate side effect of a democracy that may be too heavily influenced by corporate lobbyists. It ruins the possibility of realizing a considerable reduction in emissions simply by setting the right regulatory policy—one that sends a strong signal that burning carbon and producing GHGs has a cost.

I am suggesting that if the goal is to decrease final energy and to reduce carbon intensity, coal-fired plants do not necessarily have to be shut down. Instead, regulators can incentivize power plant owners to modernize their coal fleets by issuing new permits for cleaner-burning coal plants or by extending existing permits in exchange for replacing or upgrading old power plants with new ones that run more efficiently. A streamlined permitting process can be a way for regulators and power plant owners to negotiate investments into upgrades that would produce immediate environmental and financial benefits. China has already eyed the benefits of such a policy and is using carbon intensity as a key measurement to make its economy more efficient. In fact, in January 2013, China announced that it had already reduced its carbon intensity 3.5 percent against its 2011-to-2015 goal of reducing the carbon intensity of its economy by 17 percent.[253]

To be clear, the coal industry will face sizable hardships under the new business case. Project Butterfly's modeling efforts reveal that by the year 2070 coal's global output in terms of megawatt hours (MWh) will decrease to nearly half of what it is at present. So a half century down the road, only those operators with the ability to implement state-of-the-art sequestration and efficiency technologies will be left operating. Environmentalists may argue that this decline is too slow a process, but to me it seems realistic. Power plant owners can be part of the solution if given the right incentives. One aspect of this modernization involves achieving greater supply-side efficiency via what is known as "clean coal."

CLEAN COAL

There are new designs for more efficient coal-fired power plants that can and should be deployed to dramatically decrease the amount of CO_2 emitted from the same unit of energy generated by coal combustion. New technology can clean up the emissions of existing coal-fired power plants by reducing not only CO_2, for example, but also mercury—by either consuming or sequestering the resultant emissions. All together these designs and technologies constitute what is typically referred to by the power industry as *clean coal.* These efficiency improvements make sense as a transitional technology along the way to a renewable and sustainable electric power system.

The bottom line is this: To make new investments, changes to the existing poor regulatory environment are necessary to reassure power plant owners and encourage them to invest in clean coal technologies. Suppliers need assurances that future regulations will not prohibit them from receiving a return on the invested capital required to retrofit existing plants and/or to implement efficiency requirements for new power plants. The situation can be incredibly complex and lethargic. A power plant owner anticipating regulation and a future incentive to clean up operations will actually wait for the program to be put in place rather than be an early mover. Regulations can be stringent or even costly, but they don't need to be. Rather, it is imperative that regulations be clear and decisive so the power plant owner can reliably respond. It is not the presence of regulations but rather the absence of clear regulations that creates the most market damage.

One way for regulators to create a clear market signal is to offer incentives to power plant owners by allowing accelerated depreciation for new investments in energy efficiency. For example, recovering waste heat from power plants to produce additional electricity reduces the rate of emissions per level of output by expanding output volume for the same level of energy. Recovering waste heat also represents an opportunity to generate extra profits for the owner: In many older power plants, up to 60 percent of the heat produced by the combustion process is lost, but converting this waste heat to useful energy can have a major impact on a power plant's total efficiency. Even if the excess heat cannot be used to generate additional electricity, it can be used for drying coal (reducing its moisture content) on-site. Drier coal burns more efficiently, which in turn improves a plant's overall thermal efficiency. These upgrades to operations require capital, however, and before committing to implementation, plant owners need to be satisfied that they will have sufficient operating time to recover their capital and generate a return. A clear regulatory policy will alleviate their concerns.

Moreover, in new coal-fired power plants, supercritical, ultra-supercritical, and integrated coal gasification combined cycle (IGCC) technologies can all be employed to reduce GHG emissions and to improve overall efficiency.[254] For example, the IGCC process reduces sulfur, mercury, and GHGs by turning coal into a synthetic gas. It's cleaner because the impurities are removed before the gas is combusted. This method results in improved efficiency over conventional coal-fired power generation because the combustion exhaust is passed to a heat recovery steam boiler to produce electricity. The resulting synthetic gas can then be repurposed for transportation and chemical processes. This approach creates a solution not only for electricity generation but also for meeting demand for industrial fuels.[255]

Thermal efficiency for most subcritical power plants hovers around 37 percent. New supercritical or ultra-supercritical power plants operate at much higher operational efficiency, providing lower fuel consumption and therefore lower CO_2 emissions per unit of output. State-of-the art supercritical steam-generation plants operate at a net efficiency of greater than 40 percent.

Ultra-supercritical power plants can do even better, approaching 45 percent. New steel technologies enable these newer power plants to reach higher temperatures, which reduce total emissions and increase energy output for the same level of energy input.

BARRIERS TO DEPLOYMENT

Despite all of the benefits these clean(er) coal technologies provide, there are substantial barriers to their deployment. First of all, because power plant managers are isolated from conventional procurement procedures, these managers lack the training that internal initiatives or third-party suppliers could provide. The older engineers—those who either built the system or were trained by the original builders and operators—are retiring or are being hired away by consulting firms to retain industry knowledge. Younger engineers are often lost when it comes to managing these aging power plants, which lack the automation that is intuitive to the younger generation. No amount of college or armed services training can prepare new engineers for the wide variety of patchwork components that are present in older power plants. Second, dissemination of the know-how associated with implementing new, clean coal technologies requires interaction among third-party technology vendors, utility owners, and plant managers. And third, installation of these technologies involves high up-front costs that would not be recovered if the plant were to be shut down prematurely.

Although these barriers are not insignificant, simply employing "best practices" and installing power plant computer automation can dramatically increase output and decrease emissions, including a power plant's GHG footprint. Yet for all the theoretical benefits, both financial and environmental, the situation on the ground is that existing coal-fired power plants can continue to burn coal for years without paying environmental costs if the business-as-usual regulatory environment is allowed to persist. You just throw the coal into a furnace and it burns. The lack of any visible, immediately discernible environmental costs is part of the problem. There is inadequate incentive for change, and very few experienced engineers are even available to do any non-mandated best practice or environmental work toward upgrading these power plants' operations. It is just too easy to let sleeping dogs lie.

Nevertheless, the situation is dire. Without mandates, power plant owners have no incentive to make capital expenditures that would offer a sizable difference. In a utility-regulated market, the power company estimates its costs and the regulator sets the rates for cost recovery. The only responsibility of the power plant owner is to keep the plant operating, not to make it clean burning. Without a commitment from the public utility commission or other governmental authority for cost recovery, investments in supply-side efficiency don't necessarily enter into the equation because reduced costs may not actually increase a utility's profitability. The absence of a culture that enables the application of new technologies means that the world's coal plants will continue to operate with a business-as-usual mentality until the regulators demand different results, including implementation of best practices or improved cost competiveness.

What is the solution to this challenge? How can industry and government do more to encourage supply-side efficiency? By changing the principles of incentives so they encourage training and empower power plant operators to cut costs (including environmental costs) and to maximize profitability rather than simply reporting costs to justify utility rates, or even by exposing power plant owners to open competition, the energy industry could make great strides in reducing the global community's carbon footprint.

BEST PRACTICES FOR SUPPLY-SIDE EFFICIENCY

So, what are these "best practices" that can help improve power plant efficiency? Some are complex, but most are simply common sense (see figure 14.3). The cornerstone of power plant efficiency is diligence. For example, keep the equipment clean and well functioning. Turn it off when it is not being used.

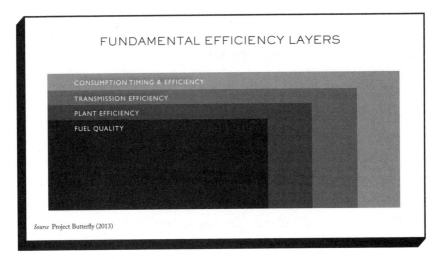

FUNDAMENTAL EFFICIENCY LAYERS

CONSUMPTION TIMING & EFFICIENCY
TRANSMISSION EFFICIENCY
PLANT EFFICIENCY
FUEL QUALITY

Source Project Butterfly (2013)

♦ *fig. 14.3:* Electrical efficiency is interconnected but begins with fuel quality.

The US Department of Energy (DOE) highlights technical feasibility and efficiency ranges for common coal-fired power plants (see table 14.1). While not all of these improvements are possible at every power plant, the average power plant could gain, at a minimum, an estimated 1 to 2 percent efficiency increase *for each improvement*.[256] Keep in mind that efficiency increases are additive—even a half-point efficiency increase can yield significant GHG reduction and hundreds of thousands of dollars in fuel cost savings.

However, simply improving the efficiency of fossil fuel–powered generation is not enough. The energy industry must address the fundamentals. At the core of the efficiency solution is fuel quality. Some fuels have a higher calorie content than others; higher-quality coal, coupled with efficient combustion, results in a higher proportion of energy output. This means that less fuel is consumed to produce the required electricity, thereby reducing GHG emissions, as illustrated in figure 14.4.[257] So, upgrading from lower-quality coals should be the first step.

But first, it is imperative for regulators and suppliers to differentiate between high-quality and low-quality coal. The IEA uses two basic categories of coal, based on geologic rock type: hard (anthracite, coking, bituminous, and

POWER PLANT EFFICIENCY IMPROVEMENTS

Power Plant Improvements	Efficiency Increase (percent)
Air preheaters (optimize)	0.16 to 1.5
Ash removal system (replace)	0.1
Boiler (increase air heater surface)	2.1
Combustion system (optimize)	0.15 to 0.84
Condenser (optimize)	0.7 to 2.4
Cooling system performance (upgrade)	0.2 to 1
Feedwater heaters (optimize)	0.2 to 2.0
Flue gas moisture recovery	0.3 to 0.65
Flue gas heat recovery	0.3 to 1.5
Coal drying (installation)	0.1 to 1.7
Process controls (installation/improvement)	0.2 to 2.0
Reduction of slag and furnace fouling (magnesium hydroxide injection)	0.4
Sootblower optimization	0.1 to 0.65
Steam leaks (reduce)	1.1
Steam turbine (refurbish)	0.84 to 2.6

Source Department of Energy/National Energy Technology Laboratory

◆ *table 14.1:* There are many ways to increase power plant efficiency. Above are technologies listing efficiency increase by percentage.

sub-bituminous) and brown (lignite and peat). Hard coal is more desirable because it is a higher-grade coal.

All coals in those two basic categories are not the same, however. Coal is also categorized by its calorific value (kcal/kg), the percentage of moisture, and the degree of volatile matter or, conversely, the ash content. Contaminants such as mercury are also an important variable to consider. Higher-moisture coals burn less efficiently, and coal with higher ash content causes excess slag and disposal problems.

When you hear estimates of large deposits of coal, enough to run the global electric system for hundreds of years, it is the low-quality coal supplies

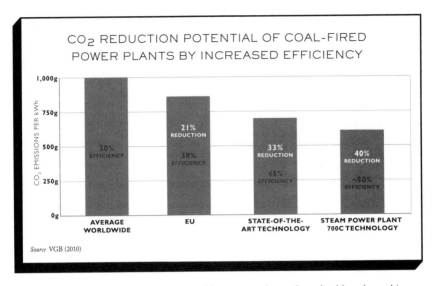

CO₂ REDUCTION POTENTIAL OF COAL-FIRED POWER PLANTS BY INCREASED EFFICIENCY

Source VGB (2010)

• *fig. 14.4:* This graph depicts the reductions in CO₂ emissions that can be realized. In order to drive this trend, better technologies must be implemented and regulations must be enforced.

that proponents are positing. These remain abundant, whereas the high-quality coals are dwindling. Under the business-as-usual scenario, as high-quality coal resources become increasingly scarce, lower-grade deposits will meet the demand for coal. If the energy industry is going to burn coal, we need to modify the quality of these low-quality deposits in order to avoid the corresponding negative environmental consequences. By upgrading the composition of coal, the energy industry can mitigate environmental consequences and begin to move toward the Project Butterfly new business case.

Figure 14.5 shows some interesting results comparing the thermal efficiency of coal-fired power plants in various countries. For example, note the increased efficiency of Japan's and Germany's coal facilities relative to that of India's and China's facilities. The reasons for the gaps in efficiency vary, but may include average age of the facility, investment rates in new technological improvements, and the quality of fuel supply.

In part, my analysis comes from personal experience with upgrading coal. I spent two years as the CEO of Denver-based Evergreen Energy, a

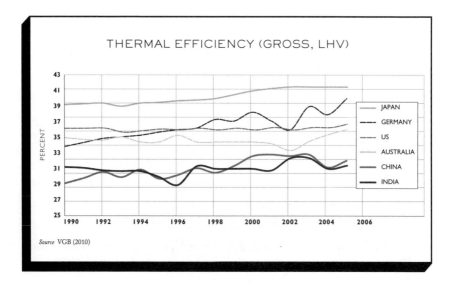

+ *fig. 14.5:* While the trend toward fulfilling the potential for efficiency improvement in hard coal-fired plants is certainly improving, large reductions in global CO_2 can be realized by increasing the use of high-quality coal and by upgrading low-quality coal.

NYSE Arca–traded company, trying to market a patented coal upgrading process—a technological advancement twenty-five years in the making. The core concept of the upgrading process was to improve the quality of coal by pretreating it prior to combustion. The methodology mimicked natural processes, using pressure to uplift the British thermal units (Btus) of low-grade coal, which reduced the moisture content and contaminants. The resulting fuel burned more efficiently. It promised to turn vast stores of low-quality coal into something that would be gentler on the environment.

Unfortunately, Evergreen Energy's coal upgrading technology was a market solution before its time. The company received exceptional support from the capital markets, but the price spread between low-quality and high-quality coal continued to fluctuate in accordance with market demand. The difference was never big enough or sustained long enough to hedge the spread. Without receiving a premium for reducing the emissions content—a premium that some form of regulatory or legislative enforcement could have easily provided—Evergreen couldn't get its proposed upgrading facilities to pencil out as merchant facilities. The price of a ton of coal didn't provide an environmental premium. The Btu improvement alone wasn't enough. Moreover, the company couldn't secure long-term supply agreements from coal-fired power plant owners, who were reluctant to move in a new direction without greater certainty from the regulatory environment. Einstein had it right. The problem can't be solved until a change in consciousness occurs.

In my experience with Evergreen, power plant owners hesitated to enter into long-term take-or-pay agreements for coal supply. Nor did they agree to operate a coal upgrading plant at their own facility using their waste heat to improve the economics of the Evergreen Energy process. Bottom line: Power plant owners were risk averse to the long-term commitments required to construct a new capital project without regulatory assurances, fearing that any changes to their system might disrupt their process and short-term profitability. They simply couldn't make an economically sound decision that looked beyond the next year or two.

In the early 2000s, coal upgrading began to show the potential to make a profound impact on the efficiency of coal-fired generation, but efforts to upgrade have taken a backseat because regulators failed to accommodate the fundamental changes required to mitigate environmental costs.

THROUGHOUT THE WORLD

The issue of what to do with our coal-fired power plants is a serious one, and it is not just a US problem. In the United States, approximately 8.5 percent of all coal-fired generating capacity is set to retire over the next five years, which will leave a very large gap to be filled.[258] Throughout the world, however, approximately half of the coal-fired fleets have been in service for more than twenty-five years. Few of these aging plants have had any kind of major retrofits. Often the automation and control systems, while adequate to ensure reliability in their day-to-day operations, need upgrading if plant owners and managers are to control fuel costs and improve overall operations and maintenance.

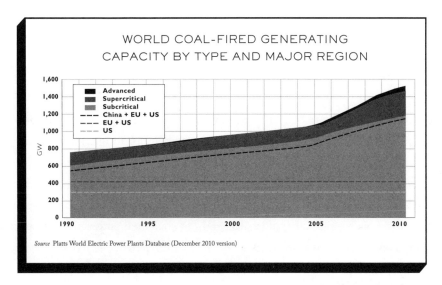

* *fig. 14.6:* In the past several decades, China has been the country most responsible for the increased global consumption of coal. While this has been a blessing for China's economy, the dependency on low-grade coal has made the environmental problems associated with the burning of coal that much worse.

According to the IEA's 2011 *World Energy Outlook,* approximately 75 percent of global coal-fired power plants are in subcritical condition, meaning they operate with lower thermal efficiency than supercritical, ultra-supercritical, and IGCC plants. Figure 14.6 paints an accurate picture of the world's current portfolio of coal assets and reveals that the vast majority of coal-fired power plants are powered using subcritical sources of fuel. Moving to more advanced technologies would substantially add to generation capacity and significantly reduce GHG emissions for the same level of power output.

The kind of energy policies that might provide strong enough price signals to stimulate innovation in the coal industry include:

» Strengthening efficiency and CO_2 abatement requirements (such as performance standards for existing and new plants)
» Strengthening programs to develop both domestic and international financing mechanisms for existing plant retrofits and new plant construction

» Creating trading standards for emissions credits, such as allowing power plants to trade Kyoto-like credits associated with investments in coal burning efficiency.

For the latter policy to be effective, such credits would need to be valid for a long period of time, perhaps decades, to allow power plant operators to fully capture the environmental benefits. Other policies may need to be eliminated, including the New Source Performance Standards (NSPS) issued by the EPA. The NSPS limit the modifications that can be made in a plant. These limitations were originally put in place to limit coal-fired power plant expansion in anticipation of stricter environmental controls being issued. However, these kinds of policies need to be realigned with the immediate objectives—greater efficiency and fewer GHG emissions—in order to make sense in the context of a coherent and clear energy policy.

Moreover, if we in the United States are to make a commitment to mitigating climate change, politicians and lobbyist groups must stop meddling with regulation by using appeals to the Supreme Court as a way to stonewall energy policy. In September 2011, in response to congressional pressure, the Obama administration announced that it was withdrawing several of the EPA's new power plant rules and regulations for further review. These rules had been issued to meet the EPA's obligation (under the Clean Air Act) to mitigate GHG emissions. Many of them would have been useful. The Tailoring Rule, for example, would have forced power plant owners to review their plant operations, report their emissions, and deploy best available control technology—including energy-efficient technologies, computer automation of process controls to manage heat rate and to reduce cooling costs, and changes in fuel types to optimize fuel mix—in order to qualify for a permit to operate. These changes alone, according to the DOE, had the potential to increase efficiency by up to 2 percent. A power plant owner would not only be providing reliable power but would also be responsible for minimizing costs to the user and negative environmental impacts.

As an industry veteran who wants to see innovation in the power industry,

I feel it makes sense to require utilities to deploy best available technologies and to publicly report on their efforts and results as part of their permitting process. In fact, as an executive who has tried—sometimes successfully and sometimes unsuccessfully—to sell third-party energy efficiency services into the electric industry, I see the measure as a way to promote new technology and share knowledge of what works within the power industry. Such efforts would only help the energy industry develop a road map for achieving a rapid decline in GHG emissions and improving operational performance for large power suppliers.

If you accept that energy supply will be a regulated market no matter what circumstances arise, you probably agree that good regulations add teeth to strong market signals. Think of what would happen if a power plant in the United States failed to get its permit renewed. The market would perceive the failure of regulators to issue a new permit as a "pricing signal," which would push other power plant owners toward the deployment of best available technologies. For example, instituting baseline measurements across the industry would prompt power plant owners to recognize the cost-benefit of upgrading or improving a coal fleet rather than shutting it down. In the absence of clear standards, a utility may decide to just shut down an aging plant rather than make plant upgrades. Remember, power companies are extremely risk-averse and do not like negative publicity. And there's not much use for a decommissioned power plant—try putting one in your municipal dump. The lack of external regulations, combined with vague internal policies and corporate decisions, encourages the business-as-usual scenario, which leads the energy industry to believe that doing nothing is the only option. But by now it should be clear that a better option is available.

NUCLEAR ENERGY AND SUPPLY-SIDE EFFICIENCY

In the debate over nuclear energy, proponents of natural gas often try to characterize nuclear energy as being uncompetitive with power fueled by natural

411

gas (see chapter 7). The comparison is unfair. The largest costs incurred during the development of a new nuclear power plant are in the construction process, whereas it costs much less to build a natural gas–fired power plant or even an equivalent wind farm. However, the difference that makes nuclear power potentially competitive is that for natural gas–fired generation, fuel equals about 82 percent of total operating costs, while in the case of nuclear energy, fuel costs equal about 10 percent of total operating costs.[259] The other benefit of nuclear energy is that, once a plant is built, it is a stable source of power.

Other opponents advance a different argument, claiming that nuclear energy is just too costly independant of alternatives. It takes years to get a new nuclear power plant online. Meanwhile, solar and wind facilities can be brought online within a year or two from permit to commissioning. Moreover, nuclear energy can be a national security risk, potentially creating untold costs and concerns ranging from the disposal of nuclear waste to the threat of nuclear proliferation (also discussed in chapter 7).

Supporters of nuclear energy respond to criticism by arguing that security alliances and monitoring can be used to virtually eliminate the possibility of nations acquiring nuclear weapons capability and that construction can be standardized to reduce costs. Supporters also say that while there is the potential danger of a nuclear disaster, such as the world witnessed in 2011 in Japan, these accidents have been minimal compared to the benefit that can be derived from a healthy nuclear industry. Such risks can be further mitigated by ensuring the employment of best practices and by working to ensure quality controls.

Just like all power sources, nuclear energy has its benefits and its drawbacks. It has evolved to become the perfect example of a power source under scrutiny: Potential investors have differing views on whether or not the lifetime operation of the plant can be profitable, beneficial overall for the planet, or good for business. However, as a technology that positively changes the carbon content of the global energy mix, nuclear energy appears to meet the guidelines of Project Butterfly's new business case. If certain additional measures are taken, it does.

These measures for the nuclear energy industry may be very simple and may even be consistent with the other recommendations that define the new business case proposed by the Project Butterfly team. Internalizing pollution costs will foster a more equitable market in which each energy source, including nuclear energy, can compete fairly based on all of its measurable costs and benefits. Making nuclear energy feasible might come down to nothing more than adding a fairly simple feature: Let nuclear energy compete by giving it full credit for its low carbon benefits, if it is willing to internalize its disaster risk and waste costs without shedding them onto the public through federal government support. The internalization of disaster risk can be achieved by applying an insurance premium per megawatt hour in order to build up a disaster relief fund in the event of a major accident or terrorist attack. The fact that nuclear plants generate considerable power means that even a fairly

GROWTH OF A NUCLEAR DISASTER
RELIEF FUND WITH DIFFERENT PREMIUMS

Premium per MWh generated by nuclear plants	$3.00	$4.00	$5.00	$7.00
Level of insurance fund in 2020 (billion $)	$16.9	$22.6	$28.2	$39.5
Level of insurance fund in 2030 (billion $)	$41.2	$54.9	$68.6	$96.0
Level of insurance fund in 2040 (billion $)	$65.4	$87.2	$108.9	$152.5
Cost of insurance premium per total MWh (2010)	$0.61	$0.81	$1.02	$1.42

Source Department of Energy/National Energy Technology Laboratory

◆ *table 14.2:* The table assumes that the payment of premiums starts at the beginning of 2014 and that nuclear generation is maintained at the 2010 level of 807 TWh/year.

modest premium could soon produce a fund with considerable reserve capital. Table 14.2 summarizes a simplified calculation to illustrate the magnitude and cost of establishing a nuclear disaster relief fund.

For example, a premium of $4 per MWh of electricity generated by nuclear power plants would result in accumulated payments to the fund of $22 billion by 2020 and $55 billion by 2030, if payments were to begin in 2015. The values for outlying years shown (2030 and 2040) are probably somewhat high, because nuclear capacity is likely to fall as plants are retired and because few new ones are scheduled to be built within the next ten to fifteen years. The impact of the premium on the average cost of power would be small. In the example given, the cost would be only $0.81/MWh (.08¢/kWh)—less than one-tenth of a penny—based on the market share of nuclear power in 2010. If the nuclear energy industry were to grow, the cost would likely fall as management improves the efficiency of its capital deployment.

The Price-Anderson Act, which provided suppliers of nuclear energy back in the 1970s with federal guarantees, was conceived at a time when civilian nuclear power barely existed. There was no possibility then of rapidly accumulating a credible fund for disaster relief based on premiums. But that assumption has been obsolete for the past three decades. It is now possible to take advantage of the opportunity to create a more market-based insurance approach. Such an approach would make nuclear energy fit as part of the Project Butterfly new business case.[260]

Monetizing and internalizing the *real* costs of the risk of accidents may shift preferences of investors, suppliers, and users away from nuclear energy, but they may also force the necessary innovation to bring nuclear energy out of the realm of science fiction and into a reality where capital markets can do their magic. Taking this path may be a tough pill to swallow, but it can open up the energy industry to the potential of real solutions to resource depletion and climate change.

ENCOURAGING ENERGY EFFICIENCY

Making the changes to outdated power plants and to the low-quality coal deposits that fuel them will require the formation and articulation of a sound energy policy. Encouraging energy efficiency—especially supply-side efficiency—needs to be the first priority. Building incentives for energy efficiency investments must start by internalizing the cost for burning fuels that generate GHGs and by allowing the power plant owner to trade any credits generated through capital investment to reduce GHG emissions. This simple two-step process will also produce a price signal that drives power plant owners to seek out efficiency improvements that will allow them to meet compliance requirements. Where things go from there is anybody's guess.

The great thing about innovation is finding what you don't expect to see. New information technologies are changing the way small and big companies alike are doing business and can improve operations within power plants. In fact, there is every reason to believe that new technologies can improve supply-side efficiency in a single coal-fired power plant. Demanding that power plant managers install best available technology, or changing the regulations to guarantee a power plant's operations in exchange for energy efficiency investments, can produce more reductions in GHG emissions than a dozen wind farms offsetting natural gas–fired power generation. In fact, upgrading coal-fired power plants can be part of the conversion to renewable energy by providing ramp-up capacity that helps smooth out the variable load from wind and solar energy. Aging coal facilities will require upgrades before they can provide this service to the overall grid, but this type of overhaul is a logical place to start and probably more environmentally friendly than simply letting existing coal facilities go to waste.

Eventually, coal-fired power plants will become relics; that is a certainty. In the meantime, though, adopting a favorable regulatory environment that encourages new investments with the goal of increasing efficiency and decreasing CO_2 intensity can drastically reduce the GHG footprint of the global energy industry. However make no mistake—that change won't happen without clear direction from regulators and their utilities through market signals such as a carbon tax. The direction can be as simple as allowing power plant owners to capture profits through reducing costs that also decrease power plant emissions. Such an approach is a win-win, and I can assure you: The market will respond. Third-party companies will bring to the marketplace innovative and environmentally friendly technologies that, without regulatory reform and incentives, would otherwise never get adopted.

Cities like Rio and Beijing are seeking solutions. The solutions are out there, and there are ways to encourage the market to find them. The energy industry is stuck in its ways, but it defaults to inaction because it *can,* not because it *wants* to. The force of inertia is preventing climate action from taking place. Luckily, though it is not a quick fix, it is an easy fix.

WORLD ENERGY USE FOR THE REST OF THE CENTURY

Fossil fuels have been the primary source of the world's energy for more than a century, but their supreme rule will eventually come to an end. True, it will likely take more than a hundred years for the global energy system to deplete the world's coal deposits, even under the business-as-usual scenario. In the meantime, the emergence of economies such as those in China, Brazil, India, and some of their satellite economies are placing enormous pressure on the capacity of traditional fossil fuel sources to meet growing demand. If no new policies are adopted by the major polluting countries, global fossil fuel demand will increase by as much as 80 percent by 2050. The global rate of GHG emissions will spiral out of control, and there will be no way to stay under the 550 ppm level set by the Project Butterfly new business case as the minimum requirement (let alone the 450 ppm benchmark targeted by the IEA). Currently, emissions from fossil fuel power generation are responsible for approximately 45 percent of energy-related CO_2 emissions.[261] Given expected industry growth under the business-as-usual case, this figure will rise dramatically unless two things happen: (1) The global community agrees to place a price on GHG emissions that will curtail the growth of traditional coal-fired generation, and (2) government and industry players make efforts to dramatically improve both demand- and supply-side efficiency and capture emissions before they are released into the atmosphere.

Meanwhile, renewable energy is surging in the marketplace. Energy efficiency investments are also growing rapidly. However, renewable energy and energy efficiency are not growing fast enough to actually replace fossil fuels in accordance to the projections and the requirements imposed by Project Butterfly. Something more is needed—and that something is fixing a price on carbon, not mandating alternatives, so that there is a clear market signal for all to see.

KEY OBSERVATIONS

The key observations from this chapter about the encouraging prospects of supply-side efficiency are as follows:

» Supply-side efficiency is a result of yielding the same (or a higher) level of output while using the same level of resources and/or expending less energy.

» The single largest percentage of our global power supply mix comes from coal-fired power generation. Building wind farms to replace coal-fired plants will take decades, but in the meantime it is possible to increase the supply-side energy efficiency and decrease the carbon intensity of the world's existing fleet of coal-fired plants. This option is the lowest-hanging fruit—a real opportunity to reduce global GHG emissions in the short term.

» Regulations that reward new capital investments in existing infrastructure can help put a price on GHG emissions and help the market meet energy demand as long as the supplier employs best practices to reduce energy content and carbon intensity.

» Technologies that can clean up GHG emissions from coal-fired power generation do exist. These technologies improve the thermal efficiency of coal-fired generation and can include actual sequestering of GHGs, specifically CO_2.

» The key to unlocking the potential for dramatic GHG reductions is internalizing the cost of emissions while opening the door to new technologies, such as nuclear power, and incentivizing power plant owners to act in their own self-interests and reduce their own costs.

PART IV

. . .

RECOMMENDATIONS

I know not with what weapons World War III will be fought, but World War IV will be fought with sticks and stones.

—Albert Einstein

CHAPTER 15

CROSSING THE ROAD: CREATING A SUSTAINABLE FUTURE

When I was young, my mother instructed me to look twice before crossing the road. "First you look to your left," she would say. "If you are in London, England, you would look first to your right. But in Des Moines, Iowa, you look first to your left and *then* to your right." She would finish by saying, "After you look both ways to make sure the road is clear, you cross the street." So I have always looked twice. Sometimes I even look three times. It seemed like good advice to me.

Later in my life, I came to an even deeper understanding of my mother's words of wisdom. I have learned that if, as you are crossing the road, you freeze like a deer at the sight of an approaching set of headlights, you will find yourself stranded between your natural fight-or-flight instincts. And you will get hit. This has led me to understand a second lesson: Once you have made the decision to cross the road, cross it. That is to say, if you have stepped into the intersection, having already looked to your left and right, don't stop midstride—go ahead and follow through on your decision. If you proceed to engage in a philosophical argument with your colleagues while standing in the road, you may find yourself missing your opportunity to cross—or worse yet, being struck down without ever knowing what hit you.

The overwhelming majority of climate researchers—between 97 and 98 percent, in fact—believe that climate change is under way because of human activity.[262] By recognizing this staggering consensus, the global community has, in essence, looked to the left. By reviewing the data ourselves (as in chapters 2, 3, and 4), we have looked to the right. Now it is time to cross the road. The climate scientists who have alerted the global community to climate change have also asked us to take action. To do otherwise would leave us stranded—either on the curb, absentmindedly watching traffic, or worse, standing defenseless in the middle of the road.

REEXAMINING THE KYOTO PROTOCOL

As the global community considers its next move toward climate action, it is important to recall that this is not the first time we've stood curbside and wondered how to get across. Let's now reexamine, from the perspective of Project Butterfly, the first binding international agreement on the development of clean technology: the Kyoto Protocol.

Because of Kyoto, governments and corporations alike are taking actions to address climate change. These efforts cannot be dismissed lightly. The prime examples of government action are, of course, related to the international efforts to form the UNFCCC back in 1992 and the Kyoto Protocol back in 1997. The UNFCCC set global and individual country targets to reduce GHGs below 1990 levels. The Kyoto Protocol, in turn, made these targets mandatory for industrialized countries such as the United States, Russia, member countries of the European Union, Great Britain, and Australia, and voluntary for emerging and nonindustrialized nations such as India, Brazil, and China.

The industrialized nations that signed and ratified the agreement agreed to reduce their emissions or to buy credits from others to meet their targets. The nonindustrialized nations that signed the Kyoto Protocol agreed to work toward their emissions targets by developing clean energy in cooperation with other parties to the agreement without having to accept any firm targets. Regardless of the structure, the reach of the Kyoto process transcended national government action and galvanized independent energy suppliers, energy users, international banks, and municipal and statewide programs to reduce global GHG emissions. As a result, these suppliers and bankers financed and built thousands of renewable energy projects under the Kyoto Protocol. They crossed the road.

However, if we are to judge these initiatives relative to their targets, then the efforts taken under the Kyoto Protocol are failing to meet the requirements of the Project Butterfly new business case. In fact, these attempts are failing to meet the very objective that the UNFCCC and Kyoto initially set out to accomplish in the 1990s: to reverse the buildup of CO_2 by reducing the rate of emissions to below 1990 levels. As the Project Butterfly business-as-usual scenario shows, rather than CO_2 concentration levels decreasing, they will more than double by the end of the twenty-first century. The Kyoto Protocol is failing to deepen the commitments already made by key individual nations and, as a result, it is failing to become a working international agreement. It is just not producing big enough results.

Why?

As we look at the Kyoto Protocol from the perspective of Project Butterfly the answer emerges quickly: Leadership is missing. Instead of rallying around the cause of averting catastrophic climate change, and focusing on opportunities for economic and social development, climate negotiators have allowed themselves to be bogged down by bureaucratic details and disagreements over who will pay the cost of mitigation. Those who must take decisive action to mitigate climate change are standing in the middle of the road, arguing about how to get across. Behind this inaction is a strategic flaw in the entire approach taken by climate negotiators.

The flaw is this: The Kyoto Protocol relies on a "rationing" system between nations that ultimately encourages participants to betray it. Each party tries to negotiate the largest ration of carbon emissions in order to hoard its right to fossil fuel consumption. Then, when the agreement no longer suits national interest, the individual country acts in ways that undermine the agreement by either openly ignoring it or backing away from its commitments.

The negotiating formula for Kyoto has been similar to the Nuclear

Non-Proliferation Treaty, discussed in chapter 7. The containment of nuclear weapons technology relied on Cold War politics in which third-world countries participated in a "world order" that received encouragements in the form of subsidized goods and services from first- and second-world countries. For example, the United States would send financial aid and military support to its allies in key regions, while the Soviet Union would do the same to expand its global reach. It was easy for countries to join the NPT—until they were compromised by their desire to develop nuclear weapons. Under Kyoto, Canada is a good example of the strategic flaw. It first ratified the agreement and later rejected it when the country's emissions rose beyond its Kyoto commitments.

Alternatively, the Project Butterfly methodology implies that a different approach should be taken between nations in a more competitive and open world. If we apply the principles underlying the Project Butterfly methodology, we can begin to isolate the unique interests of the parties and then try to form agreements that align the key stakeholders' interests. If we recognize that solutions can be found where an alignment between key global stakeholders is possible, climate negotiators will be in a much better position to negotiate a more meaningful agreement (or set of agreements) that could lead to direct action between energy suppliers and users.

REVEALING DIVIDED CAMPS

The Project Butterfly methodology is an analysis that breaks down the unique interests of each stakeholder in a transparent way and then searches for solutions that align each interest. By evaluating the disagreements over the Kyoto Protocol that fully revealed themselves in the wake of the 2008 Great Recession, perhaps we can learn where it is possible to align interests. These disagreements flared up for the whole world to see at a key event, the Conference of the Parties meeting in Copenhagen in December 2009. The parties in attendance disagreed on several core issues that had always plagued the negotiations of the Kyoto Protocol. But this time, when the parties were seeking to extend the agreement and to make the measures mandatory, the disagreements became too big to ignore.

In fact, the meeting in Copenhagen revealed for the first time that there was more disagreement over the UNFCCC and the Kyoto Protocol than there was consensus. Negotiations to extend the Kyoto Protocol came to an impasse, and the negotiating teams that represented their respective countries essentially fell into, as Project Butterfly understands it, three deeply divided camps. Each of these camps have remained at odds with one another ever since. No reconciliation is in sight.

CAMP I

The Project Butterfly team has identified the first camp, "Camp I," as being composed of the richer industrialized countries, including the United States and most of the nations of the European Union. These nations faced the most severe criticism from the public media for their failure to bridge a new agreement in Copenhagen and replace the expiring Kyoto Protocol. The Kyoto Protocol, negotiated in 1997, had called for a new agreement before the December 2012 expiration date. An extension of the agreement was essential to keep the capital markets engaged in carbon trading, which was an underlying principle of Kyoto. Climate negotiators from Camp I feared that failure to bridge the differences might throw global efforts to mitigate climate change back decades. In spite of their interest in reaching a new agreement, Camp I nations stood their ground and took the heat.

Nevertheless, the position of Camp I was very clear: Industrialized nations were willing to enter into a new agreement subject to similar commitments by all parties. In essence, the United States and industrialized Europe did not want to cap their GHG emissions if other nations from the largest emerging economies—such as China, India, and Brazil—remained free from a mandatory cap on their own emissions. According to Camp I, a replacement agreement would therefore have to be binding on all parties in order to be acceptable to any one party within the Camp I nations.

The other aspect to the Camp I position was that any limitations placed on industrialized nations must not cut into current consumption levels. Fairly divided emissions targets meant that the current level of each nation's emissions is grandfathered in as part of any baseline calculation. Early on in climate negotiations President George H. W. Bush (Bush 41) recognized the danger of limitations on US growth when he declared, while attending the 1992 Rio Earth Summit, "The American way of life is not negotiable." The concern from the very onset of the UNFCCC was that efforts to reduce GHG emissions must be voluntary to avoid a potential situation in which an existing country would be incurring penalties for economic growth.

Camp I negotiators feared the financial disruption that would inevitably follow from any agreement to cap their GHG emissions, if indeed they were to ever exceed their own caps. The industrialized nations of the United States and Europe relied heavily on built-in capital that was highly dependent on continued growth and consumption of fossil fuels, including natural gas. If the United States and Europe entered into an agreement that set mandatory caps and then exceeded them, these nations would require a large sum of capital not only to replace existing infrastructure with lower-emissions-level technology, but also to pay penalties. The financial consequences of paying penalties while simultaneously covering the cost of replacing infrastructure would be, in the eyes of Camp I climate negotiators, even more unimaginable than the worst consequences of climate change.

The consequences would be so severe, in fact, that any agreement that tried to tie down industrialized nations to a binding reduction target would be dead upon arrival. For a large industrialized nation that entered into such an agreement, the consequence would be so untenable that it would force the nation to default on its Kyoto commitments, similar to Canada's withdrawal from Kyoto as a response to rising emissions in its province of Alberta. The circumstances would likely be the same for an emerging economy, but the size and prospect for an industrialized nation would be staggering. Any nation with its eyes wide open would not agree to any meaningful mandate with real financial consequences. According to Camp I climate negotiators, commitments would therefore need to be limited to voluntary action.

Both presidents Bill Clinton and George W. Bush (Bush 43), and their respective climate negotiators, weren't quite as blunt during their tenure as Bush 41 had been. However, they still made it clear that the United States would not shoulder restrictive limits that were not applied to all other nations. Otherwise, such a position, they believed, would have been politically unworkable. Critics would claim that such an agreement would put the United States and other industrialized nations at a clear disadvantage, in a position where they would no longer be able to hold on to their global leadership.

The other objection from Camp I climate negotiators was over the role of the UN as the convener of the UNFCCC, the parent agreement to the Kyoto Protocol. The role of the UN created inherent discord because some circles within Camp I saw any international agreement that placed the UN as arbiter as threatening the nation-state system and each nation's basic sovereignty. These nations did not want the UN to have the authority to set standards for carbon accounting and trade and to require sovereign nations to comply. An international agreement under the UN's direction to manage GHG emissions was like an arrow to the heart of the hydrocarbon-based economy in those nations, threatening both the largest energy suppliers and the users of oil, coal, and natural gas.

Camp I's position was clear for all to see. Both national and corporate suppliers whose revenues are highly dependent on oil, coal, and natural gas would have a lot to lose if the Kyoto Protocol radically shifted the world's energy mix toward renewable resources. Suppliers of oil, coal, and natural gas would be negatively affected by sudden reductions in demand and possibly by increased regulatory costs. Only a few visionaries within Camp I could see how this stakeholder class might profit from the development of alternatives and renewable substitutes by converting their own service offerings. Those with faith in such a possibility weren't blind to the entrenched interests of the large oil companies that own the full supply chain—starting with their offshore drilling operations and stretching all the way to their retail gas stations. However, in looking toward a replacement for the Kyoto Protocol, Camp I negotiators wanted to give oil, coal, and natural gas companies the opportunity to fold into the international process.

CAMP II

"Camp II" nations, on the surface, appeared to be diametrically opposed to the position of Camp I. Camp II represented the nations from the emerging economies, such as India, Brazil, and China, that were willing to build new renewable energy systems to reduce their carbon intensity. Camp II nations were unwilling, however, to enter into any kind of limitation on their total CO_2 emissions. In Copenhagen, Camp II nations wanted to see cuts to the industrialized nations' GHG emissions—but did not want any kind of caps or limitations imposed on their own GHG emission levels. The logic behind their position was that emissions per capita in emerging economies were already substantially below those of the industrialized economies. They wanted time to "catch up."

The concern of Camp II nations was backed up by observations that in emerging economies, the average rates of economic growth were well above global GDP and therefore it would be too expensive to limit or cap their emissions growth rate. They would have to either substantially improve the efficiency of new capital or invest in massive clean energy programs—all without assurances of support from the industrialized nations. The consequence of such an agreement would be untenable if emerging economies found themselves paying penalties and without the cash or financial support to invest in actual mitigation. Their worst nightmare was the prospect of an international agreement that would lock in the right of industrialized nations to continue to dominate global markets.

The view of Camp II negotiators was colored by an increasingly progressive view of the world. In fact, Camp II's position was similar in many respects to the culture of the 1960s generation in North America and Europe, which rejected the status quo and demanded greater economic and social democracy. In the eyes of Camp II negotiators, the Kyoto Protocol was, or needed to be, part of a greater economic and social democracy. However, the prevailing perspective on the issues surrounding climate change was very different. The 1960s generation, of which I would consider myself a young member, had already been through the "revolution of consumption." After growing up in a period of economic prosperity, much of my generation chose to reject commercial pursuits—only to later embrace them. But it is harder to renounce something that you haven't yet experienced. This is the case for much of the world, and especially for those living in an emerging economy. Citizens of Camp II nations, the Indian mother and the Brazilian businessman alike, may want the social and economic democracy promised by the Kyoto Protocol, but they also believe that they have every right to develop the way citizens of the United States and the industrialized nations of Europe have.

In fact, the view of Camp II is steeped in anticolonialism. The discourse in many emerging economies renders views on climate change in some ways more consistent with the view of evangelists in the United States, who see the mitigation of climate change as potentially counter to God's desires or to preparing for the Second Coming. Some evangelists see the use of the earth's natural gifts as their right and even their duty. The anticolonialist view (that of "the new left") is colored by the history and conditions experienced by these nations. It emphasizes that industrialized nations were the ones that created the climate change problem in the first place through rapid industrialization and economic greed. Therefore the rich world is responsible for most of the GHGs in our atmosphere, the thinking goes, and it will take years for the emerging economies to contribute their fair share of atmospheric pollution. Emerging, or poor, economies therefore feel they have the right to pollute without constraints as they grow, just as the industrialized world did.

The perspective of Camp II nations has also been adopted by certain populist politicians, who like to characterize climate negotiations as part of a continued colonialist policy of rich countries to keep poor countries poor. These populist politicians may see climate change as a real threat, but they want the industrialized nations to take responsibility for it and to leave them out of it.

For example, President Evo Morales of Bolivia showed up to the 2009 Copenhagen conference in his country's native dress to serve as a spokesman and leader of his people. In the aftermath of Copenhagen, President Morales said:

This is why Bolivia will not accept an agreement reached between the world's biggest polluters that is based on the exclusion of the very countries, communities, and peoples who will suffer most from the consequences of climate change. In fact, some scientists tell us that the Copenhagen Accord could lead to temperature increases that would threaten much of humanity. This is why I said in Copenhagen that if governments could not come to an agreement because of self-interest or ideology, it is time for the people to decide.[263]

This position is very revealing, and it illustrates the Camp II perspective. President Morales could have sought the help of international investors when he was first elected into office, building renewable energy systems, working with others to mitigate climate change, and creating economic opportunity in even a poor Latin American country.[264] Bolivia is rich with mineral and energy resources. It enjoys unique biodiversity and enormous hydrological reserves that President Morales could have used to sustainably build out his country's energy resources and also provide services to its neighbor, energy-starved Chile. To top it off, Bolivia also has the lion's share of the world's low-cost reserves of lithium, the basic resource for high-performance batteries, as a bargaining chip. Evo Morales had it within his grasp to enter into profitable investment agreements and to end more than one hundred years of conflict with Chile by sharing Bolivia's resources. Instead, his populist ideology drove his administration to nationalize Bolivia's energy industry rather than to encourage foreign capital to invest in new technologies and supplies.

Though it can be criticized, the perspective of Camp II—that it is the responsibility of the industrialized nations to address climate change—is not without merit. Put yourself in the shoes of the working people from emerging economies. They want to consume the luxury goods that their new wealth can afford. Their leaders want them to consume more, too, so that their economies can grow and attract new capital. In places like Brazil, India, and China, people are experiencing the pleasure of having their first car, their first air conditioner, or more meat in their diets. These are the benefits that follow the exploitation of natural resources. The only question is whether the global society overseeing shared natural resources will create a sustainable balance between supply and use by successfully transitioning to a global energy mix resembling the new business case as outlined by Project Butterfly.

CAMP III

The nations in the third group, "Camp III," are the ones most likely to suffer from rising global temperatures in the near term. Within this group, island nations lead the pack and want to inspire the entire world to act. These are the countries that are likely to lose significant landmass to rising sea levels. The other nations represented in Camp III include many of the African and Pacific countries in the low-latitude regions that are likely to experience significant drought and damage to their agricultural industries. Crop yields in some African countries, for example, could fall by up to 50 percent by 2020.[265] Meanwhile, water runoff from the Himalayan glaciers may at first increase as ice melts and then come to a dramatic stop.

The position of Camp III is equally clear and pragmatic from its point of view. Camp III nations want the nations of Camps I and II to stop the bickering and enter into a definitive agreement. They want Camp I and Camp II nations to take dramatic and immediate action to reduce their CO_2 levels.

They want global targets and hard commitments set by all nations, and they are willing to participate themselves.

The politics of Camp III couldn't be further afield from those of Camps I and II. It is hard *not* to sympathize with Camp III nations, because their fate might already be sealed. Their canoe may have already gone over the falls. Even under our new business case, island nations will be the first countries to suffer the full consequences of climate change—namely, rising sea levels as CO_2 concentration levels top 450 ppm, as they will inevitably do. Moreover, many of these islands are highly dependent on oil as their primary energy source—so much so that many are still producing electricity from oil-fired power plants built in the 1950s and 1960s. No matter what steps are taken, the situation for island nations will be challenging. Many island nations spend up to 30 percent of their GDP on imported oil to supply their energy needs.[266] Island nations have limited access to the international capital that could help them build new or renewable energy infrastructure and become part of any international effort to fully transition to a new energy economy.

The position of Camp III negotiators is bold. They want the world to convert to renewable energy resources, and they would like to start by converting their own economies. They see the value of converting to renewable resources as a means to build economic independence, but they face significant roadblocks. Still, a few island nations are putting their (scarce) money where their mouth is, working to transition their small economies from petroleum dependence to reliance instead on hydro, solar, geothermal, wind, biomass, and other renewable energy resources—even coconut oil. For example, island nations in Africa, the Caribbean, the Indian Ocean, and the Pacific are working collaboratively to improve their energy efficiency and develop clean power sources. Islands like Tonga in the Pacific have already become energy independent, while others are working on a plan to do the same by 2020.[267] Small island nations within Camp III are demonstrating their willingness and ability to participate in a global solution to climate change.

The position of the island nations relative to reaching an international climate agreement has been that any international target for CO_2 concentration levels should be below 350 ppm. They reject any notion of a 450 ppm target that other nations are proposing. Camp III negotiators, backed by scientific evidence, believe that the lower level of CO_2 concentration would keep global temperatures at a level where island nations would likely survive. Further, these island nations want mandatory international targets to be firm and binding on all nations. Otherwise, in the common view among representatives of those island nations, targets are meaningless.

PROJECT BUTTERFLY RECOMMENDATIONS

On the surface, the conflicts between the signatories of the Kyoto Protocol make it appear as if the world's nations are pitted against one another in perpetuity and competing over natural resources. Each camp has a different set of special interests, and negotiations look like a zero-sum game. The truth is a bit obscured, however. The fact is, there is a general consensus among the different camps on the urgency of addressing climate change, and each one of these camps embodies many of the concerns of the energy supplier, investor, and energy user when they are evaluating market opportunities.

Nonetheless, these three camps are clearly at odds with one another. The Kyoto Protocol is a system that is simply not working. Meetings and discussions among the parties to the agreement continue because there is consensus about the impact of climate change, but the terms and conditions of a meaningful and comprehensive agreement must be modified to create alignment among the different camps.

STOP TRYING TO RATION

Project Butterfly's first recommendation is to stop attempting to ration GHG emissions.

Generally, climate negotiators view an international agreement as imperative. They pitch examples of independent action that nations take with respect to their own efforts to switch to renewable energy resources. These individual efforts are usually expressed as a summary of progress or as part of each nation's individual report card. Each nation's report serves up a little healthy competition between countries on how they are doing. However, what is missing for climate negotiators is not the pomp and circumstance associated with any single effort to mitigate climate change. It is the application of both a "carrot" and a "stick" as these negotiators work to form international agreements. Clearly articulated carrots and sticks are missing because climate negotiators feel that they have enough of a challenge just trying to herd the members of each unique camp into a single agreement.

SEEK MULTIPLE AGREEMENTS

Project Butterfly's second recommendation is to stop trying to bring all countries into one agreement.

The Project Butterfly team believes that both a carrot and a stick must be proffered when negotiating any kind of business transaction, especially if that transaction is an international agreement between nations. This belief is based on the premise that for any agreement to hold when the inevitable challenges crop up, especially when an agreement lasts for years and conditions inevitably change, there must be a positive consequence for living up to the agreement. Likewise, there must be a negative one for failing to live up to it. Climate negotiators are clear about the threats of both climate change and energy resource depletion—the "sticks." The challenge is identifying incentives that can be used as "carrots" and working them into an agreement. In a comprehensive, "all-in" transaction, the carrots are not always obvious and may not be the same for all parties. The carrots are therefore far more elusive.

Breaking down climate negotiations into individual agreements between individual parties, rather than forcing all nations to participate in a single agreement, would change the situation and allow negotiators to identify the carrots. The Project Butterfly team maintains that there is a single carrot that ties all these agreements together and offers the *opportunity for innovation.*

Its value is already perceptible, and its solutions are ubiquitous, though the *application* of any solution is almost always unique. That carrot is simply the message that a global economy increasingly run on renewable energy *can* liberate each nation from the conundrum presented by an economy run on finite fossil fuel resources, especially oil. But for the individualized carrots to be identifiable, the benefits need to be tangible and direct to each party.

Everyone around the negotiating table needs to recognize the carrot dangling before them and disregard whatever entrenched interests might exist in order to reach out and grab the true prize. In this way, climate change presents an existential issue for climate negotiators, but it also connects the global community to an opportunity for rapid technological and social innovation.

The situation between the three negotiating camps transforms when we start looking at one-off negotiations aimed at reducing GHGs. Those who perceive the obvious opportunity must take a stand and assert that inaction associated with business as usual is unacceptable. It may be true that you can lead a horse to water and that you cannot force him to drink. However, it's also true that you can leave the horse behind. The human race is confronting a challenge that threatens its very existence. In this case, there is merit in responding to inaction with indignation. There should be no tolerance for any one party to hold all other parties hostage. Why not let those nations that want to align their interests with others in forming new international agreements do so? In fact, they should be encouraged to do so outside the context of the Kyoto Protocol.

INCENTIVIZE TRADE AGREEMENTS

Project Butterfly's third recommendation is to incentivize trade agreements.

The world's renewable energy pioneers have already created an affirmative signal by deploying utility-scale wind farms and solar plants throughout the United States and Europe and into emerging economies within Latin America and parts of Asia. These pioneers have demonstrated to capital markets that the transition from finite energy sources to renewable resources is technically feasible, not some impossible dream. Bringing the costs down for renewable energy is the carrot. For the scale to fully tip in favor of our continued survival and prosperity, this trend must continue and the technology behind it must be moved into new markets. Forming international agreements to transfer new technology into new markets is therefore the way to move forward.

As of now, however, the global community may still not have all the technologies, the necessary institutional support, and the social dynamics needed to carry out the transition to a sustainable economy built on renewable energy and energy efficiency. Project Butterfly's review suggests that such technologies are available, but to actually deliver the goods, a little faith in the capital markets is required. International efforts must be designed to amplify the commitment among groups of nations to move forward with a renewable energy revolution in order to boost and even accelerate the transition to a new global energy mix. Otherwise it will be a case of too little, too late. The Project Butterfly team suggests that to accelerate the transition, a new commitment by like-minded nations is the missing piece of the puzzle.

Every negotiator, every climate change activist, every individual who benefits from the energy grid can express indignation over inaction in the face of real possibility—and real need. Every one of these individuals can demand that all forms of capital suppliers, all technology providers, and all energy-related institutions organize themselves to act. Camps I, II, and III must bridge their differences and keep their eyes on the prize in order to effectively shift the energy mix. When like-minded nations work together, the solution may be far simpler than a single comprehensive agreement relying on targets and dates.

Rather than nations negotiating caps on one another, the focus should be on *creating the right kind of incentives between nations.* The focus should be on *breaking down barriers that limit rapid innovations.* The focus *should not be* on trying to create a rationing system that has to work for everyone.

TAX, CAP, AND TRADE

Project Butterfly's fourth recommendation is to employ best practices by agreeing to tax, cap, and trade.

The key to successful negotiations of any international agreement to reduce GHG emissions is to apply best practices when they are called for. Taxing emissions and setting up a cap and trade system are the two methods for internalizing the estimated environmental costs of GHG emissions, as I have discussed throughout. Both methods have been presumed to work. Each of the two methods has clear costs and benefits. However, both a tax directly on carbon emissions (based on an excise of CO_2 equivalents) and a cap and trade system can be independent of any kind of international agreement. So it is important as we look at the Kyoto Protocol that we not throw out the baby with the bathwater.

Internationally, cap and trade systems have been emphasized far more than carbon taxes. As I have discussed, the Kyoto Protocol set caps on some countries and was designed to permit trading between signatories. The European Trading System (ETS) is a more classic cap and trade system. Under the ETS, all participants are subject to caps. The credits are traded directly, without the intermediation of governments. The Waxman-Kerry bill, which passed in the US House but died in the Senate in 2010, is another prominent example of a proposed cap and trade system. Beyond these, there are many examples of voluntary cap and trade systems in place (many of them in the United States), while a number of developing nations are considering mandatory cap and trade systems for specific sectors.[268]

The setting of a cap creates a price. The price of a unit of traded allowance, generally called a "carbon credit," depends on how restrictive the cap is compared with current levels of emissions. The logic behind trading is that some energy users will have lower costs of compliance than others. Those with low costs of compliance can trade some of their allowance to those with higher costs. As a consequence, cap and trade stimulates market suppliers and energy users to find sets of solutions with the lowest cost to attain the overall target reduction in emissions.

Compared to a carbon tax, a cap and trade system has some distinct advantages as a stimulus to innovation. One of the advantages is being able to quickly prioritize the value of offsets that would reduce a particular power plant's potential penalty cost. Rather than trigger the penalty, the power plant operator will first evaluate internal efforts to produce energy efficiency and then, as a last resort, seek to purchase carbon credits to reduce the plant's liability.

However, a cap and trade system also suffers from several disadvantages that must be addressed. First, no one has figured out how to apply a cap and trade system in certain important energy-consuming sectors. Road transport, which is responsible for a large and increasing share of GHG emissions, is one of these sectors. The residential sector and wide swaths of the commercial sector (especially smaller businesses) present similar problems. In each of these cases, there are far too many individual energy users to practically participate in a cap and trade system.

The second problem with cap and trade is the difficulty in setting the right level for the cap. The target reduction from the emissions baseline should be realistically achievable: neither overambitious (too large a reduction) nor too easy (too small a reduction). Setting these "Goldilocks" values requires, at a minimum, very detailed information about energy use in the market and about economic, technical, and institutional factors that may alter energy use in the near- and medium-term future.

The third problem with a cap and trade system is that setting a cap is complicated when trading between industries is allowed. Demand for credits in one industry can affect the prices in another.

The difficulties in setting the Goldilocks value for the cap compound rapidly as the reach and diversity of the economic sectors expand and the time frame extends further into the future. For example, it is impossible to predict how fast some innovative measures can be adopted and how soon their effects will register. This presents a huge problem for setting credible caps at the national level with a time horizon of one or two decades—as was done by the Kyoto Protocol.

Another concern with cap and trade is the extent to which foundational agreements underlying the market are actually enforced. What are the consequences if the commitments are not met by any one nation? A single country has a reasonable chance of imposing and enforcing credible sanctions under domestic cap and trade systems for particular sectors, whereas in the case of an international cap and trade agreement, it is difficult to establish a credible sanction. Even so, some of the schemes being proposed now are voluntary, which further complicates trading between markets. For example, credits generated under a mandatory system are likely to have greater value than credits generated under a voluntary system. Under a voluntary system, there will probably be more sellers than buyers, limiting the value of trade.

FOCUS ON A CARBON TAX

Project Butterfly's fifth recommendation is to focus on a carbon tax.

Globally, there are few examples of a carbon tax system, though some countries have introduced the concept.[269] The widespread view is that carbon taxes are kind of a "third rail," politically speaking—an unpopular, even untouchable option. Part of the resistance to a carbon tax in the United States is that critics assume it will simply add to the existing tax base. Nevertheless, most economists believe that a carbon tax is much less distorting than most other taxes are and that it could be part of a fiscal reform without necessarily raising overall tax revenues (a situation often referred to as "revenue neutral"). As a result, interest in the use of a carbon tax is growing, particularly as the shortcomings of a global cap and trade regime have become more apparent.

Directly taxing carbon will promote innovation as both the energy supplier and the user respond to the change in relative prices of different energy resources. If the carbon tax tips the scale, the energy user will naturally seek the lower-carbon option. The supplier will in turn react and seek ways to reduce not only the cost but also the carbon content of the source of supply. Meanwhile, a tax also makes it easier for governments to establish, and commit to, the cost of a defined climate change policy. Taxing authorities can then examine the results and evaluate changes in policy over time to see if they are producing the desired market behavior and to ensure that adequate revenues are being generated to cover costs.

Compared with a cap and trade system, a carbon tax provides a financial spur that is likely to cost less per dollar of public revenue. Why? Largely because the revenues from a cap and trade system go to the market players, while those of the carbon tax go directly to the government. Some of the government's carbon tax revenues may be directed to programs that support innovation and adoption of new technologies, though admittedly the impact of these programs will depend heavily on their efficacy. Under a cap and trade system, however, for an equivalent price per ton of carbon, the volume of total activity will be much higher and thus result in greater innovation. Changes in relative prices of energy will create a direct stimulus to private-sector innovation. Thus one might expect a similar impact on potential innovation for an equivalent price.

Under the cap and trade system, public authorities receive revenues based on emission allowances actually sold to emitters,[270] whereas a carbon tax is applied much more uniformly to all carbon emitters. Given the same price of carbon, the flow of payments or revenue to public authorities is substantially larger with a carbon tax, so taxing carbon first makes more economic sense.

RECOGNIZE THAT A CARBON TAX ENCOURAGES TRADE

Project Butterfly's sixth recommendation is to recognize that taxes are part of life.

Using taxes to solve climate change is a double whammy: a solution no one likes to solve a problem no one likes. For most of the world, however, paying taxes means driving on safe roads, sending children to decent schools, and enjoying a national defense. We need these things to make a healthy lifestyle possible. Likewise, we may need to pollute to run industry or to keep our homes warm. The thrust of the Project Butterfly argument is simply that whoever is responsible for the pollution should pay for it. The concept of paying a tax to pollute makes sense. It meets a certain reasonableness criteria.

Moreover, a carbon tax is a mechanism that each nation can clearly enforce. Indeed, a carbon tax would be a relatively simple tax to collect compared with many other types of taxes. The price of carbon is set by the tax and is signaled to *all* sectors in the economy of that country. Variations in supply and demand in particular sectors may be less intense at the same carbon price than with a cap and trade system. The act of implementing a tax would also be a clear signal of intent by a government that it means to take on additional measures to reduce the nation's carbon debt.

Finally, a carbon tax is less distorting on wealth creation and employment than are income taxes or payroll taxes. To the extent that a carbon tax is offset by tax reductions elsewhere in an economy, it can be used to reduce the level of more distorting taxes, thereby contributing to faster economic growth. In other words, *tax what you burn, not what you earn.* In fact, the characteristics of a carbon tax might be increasingly attractive as governments throughout the world try to resolve their fiscal dilemmas. Taxes on income limit innovation by reducing capital in the hands of all corporations, whereas taxes on burning natural resources can spur innovation through trade.

For political reasons, it is unlikely that a carbon tax would initially be set at a level that fully covers all of the environmental externalities of carbon emissions—a value which, in any case, is quite uncertain. However, such a tax could be increased gradually over time as its impact is assessed and the favorable effect on a nation's tax structure becomes evident.

The Project Butterfly's global modeling in part III suggests a price on carbon of $45 per ton. However, there is general agreement that significant shifts in the supply mix may begin to occur with even a low carbon price of $10 per ton of CO_2 equivalent. This seems like a powerful initial level for a carbon tax. Table 15.1 summarizes the impact of three different levels of tax. With the tax at $10 per ton of CO_2, the increase in the average price of electricity and gasoline to consumers is quite modest (5.8 percent

IMPACT OF CARBON TAX ON THE COST OF
SOME FUELS AND ELECTRICITY IN THE UNITED STATES

Carbon tax ($/ton CO_2)	$10.00	$15.00	$20.00
Additional cost of gasoline ($/gal)	$0.086	$0.130	$0.173
Additional natural gas ($/MMBtu)	$0.530	$0.795	$1.060
% increase in 2010 natural gas price (Henry Hub)	12.1%	18.2%	24.2%
Additional cost of coal ($/MMBtu)	$0.950	$1.425	$1.900
% increase in 2010 coal price (delivered average)	39.8%	59.7%	9.6%
Additional cost of average MWh—2010 ($/MWh)	$5.72	$8.58	$11.44
Additional cost of MWh from coal (average)—2010 ($/MWh)	$9.98	$14.97	$19.96
Additional cost of average MWh—2010 (% consumer cost)	5.8%	8.7%	11.6%
Additional cost of average MWh—2010 (% generation cost)	9.2%	13.8%	18.4%
Total revenue ($ million)	$56,350	$84,525	$112,700

Source Project Butterfly (2013)

♦ *table 15.1:* Calculations based on the EIA's early version of the 2012 Annual Outlook. Data for 2010.

for electricity and 2.2 percent for gasoline at $4/gallon). At the same time, the impact on coal prices and on the cost of electricity generated from coal is substantial. Such a price suggests that a tax at this level could have a significant impact on pricing of conventional electricity generation. While creating only a small change in the overall cost of electricity to consumers, a carbon tax could begin to encourage marketplace competition and to finally tip the scale toward greater use of renewable resources.

IMPOSE A BORDER ADJUSTMENT TAX

Project Butterfly's seventh recommendation is to impose a tax on those nations that have not internalized the cost of their GHG emissions.

The Project Butterfly recommendations are bound to be criticized by some as unrealistic. The chief complaint will be that anything that increases the cost of energy hurts the economy. Some will argue that a carbon tax will weaken the competitive nature of a nation. Some might even say, using an argument that mirrors the discussion in chapter 5, that enforcing an environmental tax would be tantamount to committing economic suicide in a competitive world. However, as the Project Butterfly Financial Model revealed in chapter 11, placing a global tax on carbon does not necessarily change the cost of energy. In fact, the theoretical $45-per-ton price on carbon reduced final energy demand and improved the economic conditions of all classes of stakeholders over time. In other words, the internalization of GHG emissions' environmental costs encouraged stakeholders to innovate and engage more deeply in the market, not to drop out or cower in the face of some void left by fossil fuels.

Nevertheless, a tax of $45 or even of $10 per ton would have a negative impact on the competitiveness of certain sectors of the economy. If the businesses within these industries are unable to innovate, and if trade rivals in other nations do not also internalize these costs, then it would be reasonable and fair to apply a Border Adjustment Tax (BAT) to compensate for the cost difference in goods imported from trade rivals. The level of the BAT would be based on an analysis of embodied carbon emissions in the products of the importing country. That is, the value of the tax would vary from product to product, depending on the carbon emissions each product represents. Grouping products into categories with approximately the same level of embodied carbon emissions would simplify things.

Fortunately, the World Trade Organization (WTO) already accepts the principle of a BAT of this sort.[271] The BAT would address concerns about the potential negative effects of a carbon tax on the domestic economy that might occur when other nations achieve a market advantage. It is less clear whether the inverse would be acceptable: an equivalent subsidy on embodied carbon emissions in products exported to those countries that do not internalize GHG emission costs to the same extent. Even less clear is whether that approach would be desirable, since this subsidy would actually provide a disincentive for those countries to internalize costs. However, given the wider international context of climate change mitigation strategies, this concern seems to trump any possible benefit of such a subsidy to exporters.

Because the BAT would largely attenuate the negative impact of the carbon tax on the competitiveness of key trade sectors, countries that choose to adopt these taxes would be freer to select their own initial tax levels. The endless quandary of Kyoto-like negotiations dissolves in an instant. There is no need to achieve a universal agreement on either taxes or the level of reduction. If a BAT is applied by enough nations that import enough goods, it will encourage other nations to reconsider their own approach vis-à-vis a carbon tax. The initial club of nations working together through trade agreements eventually will expand as a result of continued alignments of interests. And, given the efficiency of carbon taxes from an economic and fiscal perspective, nations with higher carbon taxes may find themselves better off over time— more advanced technologically and also benefiting from greater trade and economic growth.

COMPLEMENT A TAX WITH A CAP

Project Butterfly's eighth recommendation is to combine whatever works.

The carbon tax can work. It has clear benefits, as the Project Butterfly Financial Model has shown and as I have reviewed in the previous sections. However, a tax doesn't have to work alone. While the cap and trade and carbon tax systems are usually treated as mutually exclusive approaches, both can be applied within the same market. In fact, the two systems can be complementary.

It would be possible, and it could be very desirable, to combine a nationwide carbon tax with a cap and trade system just for particular sectors, shaping the programs to achieve desired characteristics. Sectors such as electric power and some energy-intensive industries, like urban solid waste, are reasonable candidates for a cap and trade system. The prices resulting from these sector caps could also be used as parameters in calculating the BAT, which would eliminate most of the competitive disadvantage in trade sectors sensitive to energy costs.

Of all the sectors, the electric power sector presents probably the most interesting possibility for a cap and trade system. The sector is a very large carbon emitter—often the largest, as in the United States. Furthermore, the electric power sector includes a relatively small number of companies, making it easier to ensure approval and compliance, and there is only one product: electricity. The world's electric power sectors are already largely regulated, and the public domain offers a huge amount of information on which to base estimates for a cap.

There are also many ways to reduce emissions per kWh of power produced in the electricity sector, through efficiency or through substituting renewable energy into the mix, as chapters 12, 13, and 14 reviewed extensively. This wide range of options (and, in the United States, the diversity of conditions under which generators operate) provides fertile terrain for the application of a cap and trade system that would complement a carbon tax system.

Moreover, electricity is a pervasive energy vector throughout the world economy. Greater certainty as to how the CO_2/kWh ratio will evolve in the medium-term future will be helpful for consumers and equipment suppliers in downstream sectors of the economy, such as industry and transport, to plan and implement their own carbon mitigation strategies. The benefit of a complementary cap and tax system will be greater certainty and latitude in meeting policy goals. For example, nowhere is this more essential than in the road transport sector, which consumes a large and growing share of the world's oil and emits a large and growing share of GHGs. At the same time, consumption of electricity in this sector today is minimal. In the United States, the number of electric and plug-in hybrid vehicles on the road today can be counted in the thousands. Yet looking ahead, the possibility of rapidly substituting gasoline and diesel with electricity is one of the key ways to promote industry growth in the electricity sector, while slowing and then reversing the climb of road transport's worldwide oil consumption and GHG emissions.

However, if electric vehicles and plug-in hybrids are to gain traction as "green" alternatives, they must have unambiguously lower CO_2 emissions in order to compete with equivalent fuel-efficient conventional vehicles. In the United States, this could be achieved with relatively modest reductions in the CO_2/kWh ratio. The complementary cap and tax option would maximize the incentives for both sectors of the economy to participate in new infrastructure investments to bridge this transition to the electrification of the road transportation system. The sooner this can be done, the sooner electric vehicles will have a fighting chance to conquer a significant market share of the global transportation vehicle market.

The electrification of the world's transportation system raises both an interesting challenge and an opportunity for the global electric power sector. Most of the measures needed for a more sustainable energy system ultimately involve decreasing energy consumption through greater efficiency. Electric vehicles, however, open up an opportunity to sell more electricity, not less. Favorable incentives for lighter and more efficient electric cars that dramatically reduce fuel costs for consumers would create huge opportunities for the automobile industry.

The switch to electrified transportation would also be very attractive to the managers and owners in the electric power sector. In fact, such innovation might even fire up the imaginations of entrepreneurs and investors worldwide.

PUSH THE UNITED STATES TO LEAD

Project Butterfly's ninth recommendation is that the United States must take a lead role in international climate negotiations.

After several decades of attempting to mitigate climate change through setting international targets (caps) and dates, the global community should be ready for something different. As the world has seen—particularly in the impasse that has blocked a successor to the Kyoto Protocol—setting such national caps is fraught with problems even if nations agree on the principles of how to allocate the necessary global reductions (which they don't). It is time to consider other strategies for international cooperation and to contemplate the role of the United States in that goal. In order to break the global gridlock over climate action, new thinking is needed.

Negotiations should turn toward agreements on specific policy actions through which individual nations can achieve reductions. These policies should include, but not be limited to, carbon taxes and a complementary cap and trade system, which individual nations could set for specific sectors within their economy.

Furthermore, the international community should abandon the notion of requiring all countries to participate in efforts to curb GHGs. Instead the global society should focus first on agreements between like-minded countries to get the ball rolling. These "clubs" would seek to agree on broad policies and on harmonization between club members. Indicative targets would be set in short-term increments against which the performance of the policy actions can be assessed. Membership in the club would be open to more nations as they decide to adhere to the principles of the club.[272] Adherence should not require anything as portentous as signing a formal treaty, but instead should be treated as something closer to signing a trade agreement. These sorts of trade agreements would dramatically increase the concept's viability in many nations.

For example, in the United States, the executive branch is provided with fast-track procedures for negotiating and approving bilateral and multilateral trade agreements. The procedures call for (1) mandatory consideration of the measure once introduced with specific deadlines, (2) no amendments, and (3) a final up or down vote.[273] In contrast, international treaties such as the Kyoto Protocol can sit in committee for years and never reach the floor—the big-picture equivalent to standing in the middle of the road, paralyzed in the path of oncoming traffic.

Moreover, it is neither realistic nor necessary to insist that the policy actions of each club member—or even the mix of actions—be the same. Any agreement between two parties can be a product of an actual negotiation between suppliers, lenders, investors, and energy users. Each nation will have its own priorities and constraints and will likely fall into one or more of these stakeholder classes. Rather than enforcing a single standard, there should be underlying agreement on some core actions and principles—such as the treatment of intellectual property rights and possible mechanisms for cross-border investments and technology transfers—and on the means of harmonizing differences in the policy approaches, such as a BAT to compensate for varying levels of internalized GHG costs. Nations within a free trade area would therefore naturally converge more on internalizing GHG costs.

The approach summarized here differs radically from the path the global community has followed until now. Instead of trying to allocate unenforceable targets (whose costs are unknown at the outset) among all countries in the world, the focus would be on the following:

» Groups of interested countries committing themselves to specific policies with approximate known costs

» Measures to protect those who internalize GHG costs from the exports of those who do not

The strategy should be dynamic and interactive. As time passes and experience is gained, indicative targets and the associated policies can be ratcheted up by individual nations. The important thing is to begin to create momentum today.

The dangers of climate change will become clearer to a broader public with the passage of time. The environmental stewards of the world have already created—and will continue to report on—critical indexes to measure both the impact of climate change and the benefits of climate change mitigation. Experience is also likely to show that significant reductions in emissions not only can be achieved without economic disruption but can also provide stimulus for low-carbon economic growth. Once we get the ball rolling, these two facts should contribute to growing political support for increasingly robust initiatives to mitigate climate change. As I pointed out earlier, consensus about climate change will emerge as the pathway beyond it becomes clearer.

The United States is the only country in the world that still has enough clout to change the rules of the game. This nation demonstrated that it possessed the power to derail the Kyoto process, an episode I reviewed in chapter 3. The United States can exercise the same muscle to set a progressive course going forward. Besides being an essential party to any meaningful agreement, the United States in many ways has the most to lose and the most to win by addressing climate change. I am not saying that the United States has more to lose than, say, the 350,000 residents of the Maldives Islands, an archipelago in the Indian Ocean. The majority of these 1,200 islands lie less than three feet above sea level, so clearly that nation's very survival is at risk. Instead, I am saying that the United States will lose more in financial terms than any other country, not because of its dependency on oil but because of the sheer size of its economy and its dependency on global markets.

Moreover, the United States is the single largest energy user, supplier, investor, and lender of any single nation within our global energy system. For example, the United States has the largest venture capital market for financing the many innovations that are needed to make any climate action proposal a reality. And it still leads internationally as a technological innovator, providing energy supply opportunities for other nations that want cost-effective energy solutions. As such, the United States has the capacity to integrate the different stakeholders and to advocate new international agreements by offering trade partners both carrots and sticks.

According to the Global Innovation Index, if the United States and the European Union were to enter into a trading agreement on energy with any other emerging economy, the United States and Europe would represent eight of the top ten world innovators. In exchange, emerging economies could provide new markets for the industrialized nations that offered the latest energy technologies. The deal on the table is between the energy supplier with proprietary equipment who is looking for new markets, and the energy user (such as the island nation) who is looking for new sources of supply to end its reliance on oil. For example, the emerging economies of industrializing nations can offer technology suppliers enhanced intellectual property protection, which is currently a limiting influence in the development of new technologies.

Eventually the cultural tide will also turn the conversation toward future allocations of each nation's GHG contributions and away from the GHG emissions of the nineteenth and twentieth centuries. By 2025 the emissions in the twenty-first century are projected to be greater than those of the entire twentieth century. The distribution of each nation's relative GHG contributions will have shifted away from the United States and Europe and toward Asia, making null and void the current claims that the industrialized colonizers of the past are responsible for the ongoing climate crisis. The focus of the conversation will shift from a problem that the industrialized world must solve to a problem that the global community must resolve.

DON'T RELY ON UNITED STATES LEADERSHIP

Project Butterfly's tenth recommendation is not to rely on US leadership.

In spite of Project Butterfly's ninth recommendation that the United States should take the lead on climate action, the entire global community must eventually rise up to address climate change. Island nations and many of the lower-latitude nations that have historically pushed for aggressive global reductions will likely fall in line with a multilateral trade approach. Although Europe is intellectually committed to international agreements that support a cap and trade system, EU members can likely be seduced into a new framework for combating GHG emissions. The key to success is getting either India or China, or both, into a pact with the United States and Europe. For these emerging nations and others like them, adhering does not mean committing themselves to caps that, they suspect, may limit their growth potential. It means only accepting concrete actions, including a carbon tax. In fact, India and China (and other emerging economies) face huge challenges of increasing their fiscal base while increasing and changing their social safety net, so the carbon tax may be attractive as a source of government revenue.

The carbon tax allows individual nations to begin reducing carbon emissions without the need for other nations to participate in the same obligations to make it "fair." Adding a cap and trade system can act as a complementary stimulus. Following this strategy, nations entering into bilateral and multilateral agreements will both encourage trade and boost international efforts to eliminate global GHGs. This will create momentum, eventually, that will likely prove compelling to all. Periodic summits will emphasize what innovations each nation has made, how nations have prospered, and what they have learned—rather than focusing on what other nations should do.

KEY OBSERVATIONS

The key observations from this chapter regarding the implications of the Project Butterfly methodology and the recommendations for international agreements that can create a sustainable future are as follows:

» Climate negotiators working to implement a new, Kyoto-like international agreement to reduce GHGs are bogged down by bureaucratic details and disagreements over the cost of climate mitigation. The conversation is missing an important element: indignation over the global community's continued inaction.

» Climate agreements must incorporate both a stick (the irreconcilable cost of severe climate change) and a carrot (the opportunity for innovation and economic growth). To make this happen, negotiators must stop insisting that all nations enter into a single global agreement. Forming international clubs of like-minded trading groups can create new momentum for radically reducing GHG emissions.

» Cap and trade systems and carbon taxes are the two mechanisms for internalizing the cost of pollution and GHG emissions. The ideal approach is employing a complementary cap and tax system that will require carbon users to pay for the privilege and will incentivize innovation of alternative energy sources.

Does the flap of a butterfly's wings in Brazil
set off a tornado in Texas?
—Edward Lorenz, meteorologist and
pioneer of chaos theory

CHAPTER 16

One of my most distinctive early memories of my daughter is from 1992, when Jessie was four years old. I had pulled into my driveway after a long day of work and was just getting out of my car when Jessie ran up to me, chattering away.

"You are born, you grow old, you die," she said matter-of-factly.

"What?" I asked, picking her up and walking her toward the house.

"You are born, you grow old, you die," she repeated. "It's a *circle*, Daddy."

That time, I got it. She was talking about *life and death*.

My four-year-old daughter had realized that someday I would die, that someday her mother would die, and that someday she, too, would die. Jessie had a friend whose grandmother had just died, which explained where all this had come from. My daughter was not troubled by the grandmother's death. Rather, she was pleased with herself for having grasped a simple idea from such a complex mystery.

My memory of this moment is so vivid because Jessie's observation was so innocent and profound, and without fear. We all contemplate life and death, and our conception of death has an impact on how we live. This conception changes and evolves over time as we grow in our understanding and experiences. Our perspective on the circle of life has a way of both separating disparate cultures and bringing us together. But most of us, regardless of our religious or spiritual beliefs, feel the need to think beyond our own lifetime, to consider what each of us will leave behind. If life is a circle, as my daughter suggested so many years ago, then we all need to be aware of what will come back around.

IT'S TIME TO EVOLVE OUR AWARENESS

As the world's global society confronts climate change, it is important to think collectively beyond our own lives and into the future we are creating. We need to evolve our awareness beyond our own individual legacy and think about our homes, our communities, our nation, and our planet. Our level of self-awareness must balance the needs of the many against the needs of the few while at the same time protecting the rights of the single individual— and the rights of future individuals, further along the spiraling circle of life. Specifically, to address climate change, the energy user, the energy supplier, and the investor/lender must also embrace the considerations and concerns of the *environmental steward*—that is, they must step into the steward's shoes knowing that they, too, share the same concern. Nevertheless, the steward is distinct from the three other classes of stakeholders because the steward's function is to advocate for future generations, to look after long-term well-being rather than short-term profit. The supplier and the energy user are conflicted by other priorities and concerns. However, each of us shares the concern of stewardship.

That said, the policy decisions that have been made in the past—both in the United States and on a global level, particularly through the Kyoto process—have led to our current circumstances of inaction. We have failed to mitigate GHG emissions, and we must share the blame for ineffective past and current policies.

The domestic and international energy systems we have built lag behind where they could be if old and new markets were opened up to innovation. Thanks to the inertia that exists in the system and tethers much of the global society to a business-as-usual scenario, the global energy mix is in dramatic need of a retrofit. But by viewing power generation through the lens of finance, defining—and aligning—the interests of the key stakeholder classes, we can create a sustainability model that allows us to build a new, ecologically viable, and even more profitable business case. This new business case can lead to the implementation of renewable energy sources, the success of demand-side efficiency, and the innovation of supply-side efficiency—which together will substitute for conventional fuels while simultaneously creating new wealth and prosperity. Moreover, the right policies can change the forecast in rising CO_2 atmospheric concentration levels by changing the energy mix, thus reversing the rate of growth in global GHG emissions and leading us on a path toward global sustainability and survival.

Nowhere have I suggested that the path will be easy. As the human population grows toward eight billion, we must find common ground and forge a path that makes our lives and lifestyles possible for more inhabitants than it might seem the planet can sustain. The global community must recognize that humans, too, come from nature. We humans must evolve in order to accomplish what needs to be done. If most of us can agree that progress is inevitable, then it is just an issue of how quickly or slowly it will occur. For a dose of reality, look at what's going on from a technology perspective. There is little doubt that the future will be powered by renewable sources of energy. However, the issue at hand is just when that future will arrive. How quickly will we evolve into the new business case that I've outlined? The timing will determine whether or not we are successful. Will change come quickly enough for us to enjoy our success? Or will it come too late, causing us to spiral into extinction?

In his book *On the Origin of Species*, published in 1859, Charles Darwin observed how "natural selection" produces evolution in all species, including humans.[274] Natural selection defines how species interrelate through competition and how they adapt over time to changes in nature in order to survive. If necessary, each species competes aggressively to the detriment of the other. But the human race can't afford that kind of battle when it comes to climate action. Such fierce competition among nations, if left unchecked, will inevitably lead toward the depletion of the world's natural resources—and toward intense conflict to establish control over our most essential and vital sources of energy.

I have asked myself, faced with the possibility of our own extinction, how will humankind evolve, not just biologically but psychologically? How will we respond to the challenges of the future, both socially and economically? Will a sufficient majority of our global society reach a collective awareness regarding the necessity to both adapt to and curtail climate change, and will we manage to do so? If so, will competition just take another form, requiring greater human coordination against a different kind of threat?

Humanity has faced existential threats before. Recent history alone is full of examples of impending war and of people (sometimes as nations) banding together to coordinate a response. The strategic nuclear arms treaties in the early 1990s are good examples of coordination in the face of danger and destruction. They ended a potentially cataclysmic arms race between two nations divided over ideology and have limited the spread of nuclear weapons. The global society has built institutions like the UN, the World Bank, and the International Monetary Fund, respectively, to keep dialogue among nations open during some of our most intense conflicts; to encourage economic development and end poverty in our least industrialized nations; and to build a financial system that keeps any one nation from going bankrupt because of a temporary shortage of funds. In fact, if you look over the seventy years following the end of World War II—as we have in these sixteen chapters—you will see a world increasingly in search of ways to promote business and trade rather than competition and control. As times and our perspectives have changed, the global society has adapted rather than getting lost in perpetual competition.

What we need to do now is adapt and respond to the new circumstances facing the global community. As the popular saying goes, *It is what it is.* But by "adapting to climate change," I do not mean folding our eight billion tents and then pitching them on higher ground to avoid the next flood. I mean choosing to preserve life by coordinating a global response to climate change. I mean accepting that the relationship between humankind and nature is symbiotic, and that for us to survive, we must be sure that our natural surroundings thrive.

Two questions have fascinated philosophers for generations—with good reason. I believe that how we answer them forms our view of the world and our place in it. These questions are simple: *Who are we?* and *Why are we here?* I thought about these questions deeply while working on Project Butterfly. My answers are simple: We are the children of our planet, Earth. And we are here to serve as stewards of our planet—out of an obligation, not a right.

Scientist and author James Lovelock, who in the 1960s was one of the first to detect the buildup of CFCs in our atmosphere and their role in causing an ozone hole, proposed the "Gaia hypothesis," a theory that suggests that the earth is more sentient than not—that it is a single, self-regulating system with an awareness that is interrelated to our own and that we, therefore, are its children.[275] The idea is not a new one. In Greek mythological history, Gaia is the earth goddess. She is the great mother, an archetype that is found in many of the original stories and traditions throughout the world's vast cultural landscape, including the Judeo-Christian tradition. As I used to tell my young children, "We are all made of the same stardust that is billions of years old, connecting us to all things."

Regardless of your beliefs, it is hard to deny that, as humans, we are deeply connected to the earth and to one another. The rivers, lakes, bays, and oceans of the earth's body act much like the blood, veins, and organs of our own. Our bodies will someday return to dust and become part of the earth, serving as nutrients to feed the soil. These are physical facts of science, but they may also give us a sense of peace, knowing that some part of us, even if it is simply the remains of our body, will live on as the planet rejuvenates.

Exploring the connection between our human existence and the planet Earth raises all sorts of spiritual and scientific questions, but I think we can all agree that the earth's biosphere is a living system and that measuring the stability of its climate should be critical in determining whether the planet is in good health. In fact, it may be possible to look well beyond this simple connection. Scientists should establish health indexes to measure the earth's well-being and should use these indexes to educate the global community. Any responsible human being who accepts that too much of the greenhouse effect disturbs the climate should also accept as fact the value of measuring health indexes. If burning the earth's finite natural resources to power human industry contributes to this problem, then ensuring the health of the planet's ecosystem is therefore a logical and critical way to determine how well the system absorbs or rejects the buildup of new carbon as it is introduced by the global energy mix.

Remember, Charles Darwin claimed that our evolution begins with our common descent. The origins of life on our planet date nearly four billion years ago to a single cell. If the relationship between humankind and nature is symbiotic, then by threatening the planet's carrying capacity, we threaten our own existence. If there is potential for a problem, then the right biological response is not to heighten the competition over the world's natural resources but rather to coordinate the use of them and to elevate the importance of measurement and containment. Moreover, so long as society has visibility into the feasibility of renewable alternatives, we *must* seek such an outcome. In this context, the issue is much bigger than competing over limited global resources. The issue is facing a threat to our very existence.

The key to an evolution in our awareness may be as simple as it is essential: As a global community, we must acknowledge that we have a problem and begin each day with a commitment to addressing it. Or perhaps we need not even agree that we have already exceeded the planet's carrying capacity, so long as we recognize that it is possible to change our global energy mix. Such recognition could lead to a collective agreement that eventually the global community will have to move toward a sustainable model for our human economy. This simple adjustment to our collective thinking may be the flutter of the butterfly's wings that eventually changes everything.

IT'S TIME TO EMBRACE
THE NEW BUSINESS CASE

If business as usual is the equivalent of going beyond the point of no return or falling over the edge of the waterfall, then the new business case calls instead for a portage around the falls. To undertake the portage, we must aim our canoe toward the nearest shore. We must use the current to help push us forward as we steer to shore, rather than exhaust ourselves by fighting against the current. Most important, we must not panic. We must simply disembark and pull our canoe out of the water and commence the journey around the falls.

The worldwide renewable energy revolution—the current that will help push us forward—is already well under way. Despite a varied political spectrum of reactions, there is now general agreement within the energy industry that renewable resources are at least part of the solution to making sure enough energy is generated to meet global demand. Such a view is not enough to address the full extent of climate change, but it is enough to let renewable energy begin to compete with conventional approaches. However, to overcome business-as-usual practices and successfully transform the global energy mix to a sustainable system, the suppliers, investors/lenders, and energy users that make up the energy industry must find ways to work together. We must get new technologies into new and old markets alike, and quickly. We must stimulate further innovation. And we must declare that energy inefficiency is a waste, and that waste contributes to our mounting carbon debt. Waste needs to be stored, and we need to pay the cost for storing it.

Moving forward in the pursuit of a global sustainability model requires a new methodology that considers each stakeholder's claims, starting with the environmental steward's, without unduly compromising any other stakeholder class. This system must take into account the supplier's need to feed its earnings engine and the energy user's desire for reliable and affordable energy supplies. The Project Butterfly Sustainability Model and the new business case require that the regulatory system establish appropriate market signals—such as fixing a price on carbon—that allow and even encourage economic agents to innovate and to optimize the value of the world's natural resources. To optimize, decision makers must recognize energy constraints that are defined not by availability and investments but rather by their natural limitation as renewable resources and their capacity to replenish. The Project Butterfly Sustainability Model thus requires a shift in thinking about resources and resource management in accordance with their entire life cycle.

The foundation of Project Butterfly's new business case, as discussed in chapters 9 and 10, rests on the observations that the economics of renewable energy and energy efficiency are improving. At the same time, our finite resources—oil, gas, coal—are becoming more expensive to extract, and their lower quality results in a net energy decrease. This broad description of the energy mix has held up since the oil crises of the 1970s. During that time, many sources of renewable energy have reached market parity with conventional energy, as reviewed in chapter 10. But the issue of climate change makes it imperative to tip the scales in favor of these renewable sources if we are to successfully avoid a dramatic buildup of GHGs beyond tolerable limits. To accomplish this, applying a cost to the externalities of our traditional fuels (that is, to both the emission of GHGs and the depletion of our natural resources) is imperative and, given that fossil fuels create a cost that has to be paid, appropriate. To solve the *tragedy of the free resource*, where self-interested parties deplete a limited shared resource, someone must pay the environmental cost. The Project Butterfly new business case is predicated on the belief that the direct beneficiary of the resource's use, rather than the global community as a whole, should bear that burden

The cost of staying in a losing game is high. It is not just the cost of keeping aircraft carriers in the Persian Gulf to protect the shipping lanes. It is the cost of maintaining direct and indirect subsidies to an oil industry that stifles competition and limits innovation. It is the cost of developing new sources of oil from offshore drilling wells, shale oil drilling in North Dakota, and racing to the Arctic to find new supplies—all while alternatives, both known and unexplored, are denied at least equal treatment for development.

I am inviting us to take a fresh look at a new game that is afoot, a new opportunity that has been seized by a small band of rebels since the 1970s, many of whom are today leading growing energy businesses. Their aim: to stimulate an economy built on both renewable energy and sustainability, and to implement strategies that are additive to our natural resources because they create viable short-, medium-, and long-term solutions. More of the 2008 stimulus bill is not what I am asking for. Instead, I am suggesting that the global society, and for that matter, the entire global community, buy into a new game that incorporates the cost of pollution into the price of competing supplies—a game that gives human creativity, human ingenuity, and the capital markets that support them the best chance to perform.

IT'S TIME TO CAPITALIZE

Natural resources by definition come from nature, and as I claimed back in chapter 8, humans experience wealth through nature and her gifts. Nature itself is invaluable because once it is irreparably damaged, it is virtually irreplaceable. While a resource resides in nature, therefore, it should not be considered as capital or even valued as capital. Instead capital is created by the transfer of both finite and renewable resources *out of nature* and *into public and private ownership*. We define this capital as "wealth" based on the ability of owners to trade the rights to the benefits of these resources. Once this transfer to ownership is complete, resources become actual capital available for trade and valuation between the supplier and user. Moreover, ownership causes other forms of human capital to emerge, which is critical to wealth creation. These other forms of capital are, in fact, required in order to efficiently move into the Project Butterfly new business case.

In business, to *capitalize* means to match your potential revenues with your forecasted costs and then to determine the investment required to execute on your business case. The first step is to evaluate your assets and your liabilities. For the Project Butterfly new business case, that means we must first evaluate (1) the renewable and nonrenewable resources that have already been transferred from our reservoirs into private and public ownership (our assets) and (2) our carbon debt (our liabilities). We must also look externally, to the established institutions that are at our disposal, in order to form the necessary capital. For example, the Project Butterfly Financial Model and the new business case do not exist in a vacuum; they exist within a certain framework. Consider how a new iPhone application has to meet industry-programming protocols and the standards set by parent company Apple. The same is true when inventing a new electric car that runs on solar energy, keeping in mind that an electric car drives down the same road as a gas-guzzler. The existing roads, the gas stations that can be converted into power stations, and the existing transmission lines all become assets in the new business case.

Critical to our discussion, then, is a survey of the different forms of capital that are necessary to build an economy based upon renewable energy in accordance with the Project Butterfly Financial Model. In order to suc-cessfully meet a community's supply requirements and address environmen-tal challenges, it is essential that each form of capital be robust and fully exploited—and following the description of each, you will note my recom-mendations to achieve this end. These forms of capital are limited, but they can be enriched if we can determine a way, collectively and individually, to honor the sustainable approach I have outlined. Project Butterfly proposes that these forms of capital can work together and achieve optimal levels of satisfaction at reduced levels of consumption. If our proposition holds up, then the capacity to build the wealth, the prosperity, and the security that is so vital to our planet may not be as limited as some suggest.

Such a complete reconceptualization of the approach to the problem requires that we abandon the notion of our global markets possessing unlim-ited demand subject to price fluctuations. This old myth places the economy in a perpetual "recession" or "recovery" as the marketplace constantly struggles to find new equilibriums over price. The new economic paradigm, consistent with the Project Butterfly Financial Model, requires that we view the market just as a single user views an exchange with his or her supplier: The market rewards suppliers for producing increased value and user satisfaction while minimizing the consumption of nonrenewable forms of energy. Operating within this concept, the user seeks to avoid saturation and to balance financial performance with an improved aesthetic outcome. Keep in mind that this is not a level of service that only the wealthy can afford. It is a level of service that we all should expect. It is a level of service that flows from simple planning and is applicable to nearly any organization, ranging from large businesses to community organizations.

What follows is that critical survey of the eight types of capital upon which the global community can build a renewable energy economy—and my recommendations for fully exploiting them.

BUILT CAPITAL

Built capital is the basic existing infrastructure that allows the global community to function: our buildings, roads, electricity-generation facilities, water works, and treatment facilities. Such capital is widespread throughout the global economy and allows other businesses to flourish and families to grow and prosper in a stable, growing economy. Built capital requires capital planning; capital planning requires a continuous review of how existing services are meeting the demands of the community. Typically, regions or neighborhoods that are considered "wealthy" are the result of good planning, as opposed to areas of urban sprawl or underserved areas, which are generally the result of poor planning or the complete lack of any planning.

Recommendation: Empower communities involved in urban and public planning to perform carbon inventories—of both sources and sinks—in order to incorporate strategies to reduce their carbon footprint and their resource waste.

INFORMATION AND TECHNOLOGY CAPITAL

Information and technology capital involves intellectual resources and the ways people harness them to create tools, systems, machines, and materials that improve our industries, our communities, and our homes. Educational institutions, including universities and vocational schools, interact with industries and communities to produce higher learning and to generate wealth through the employment of expertise.

Recommendation: Mandate, fund, and disseminate education on best available technologies in order to measure and improve both demand- and supply-side energy efficiency and to develop renewable energy resources. Engage industry leaders in the curriculum.

SOCIAL OR RELATIONSHIP CAPITAL

Social or relationship capital is embodied in the connections between people and the networks they have built. These relationships are critical to the way society organizes itself to successfully create new opportunities. The creation of the Internet and the development of social networking have allowed suppliers to connect with their customers and to cooperate with other suppliers in a way that has vastly improved the services they are able to provide. Higher levels of coordination enhance user satisfaction, with minimal additional energy requirements.

Recommendation: Include, as part of your mission statement and in conversations with members of your network, your commitment to and ideas for achieving GHG reductions.

HUMAN CAPITAL

Human capital, the richest of all forms of capital (yet often the most overlooked), is the capacity of people to learn, invent, and create, thereby making contributions to society at large. Setting strategic objectives for a community is the critical organizing principle that increases capacity on every level within that community. The way to ensure the survival of human capital is by providing security for all members of the community. Rather than asking future generations to solve the problems that current and past generations have created, we must begin work to solve them now. Such a shift in thinking preserves human capital and requires that knowledge be handed down to improve efficiency through reusing, recycling, and renewal.

Recommendation: Fund community and institutional programs (at both the university and the community college levels) to reach young entrepreneurs ready to engage in sustainability-oriented businesses, and provide them with mentors who have experience in running such businesses. Provide sustainability and energy efficiency information to already-established mentoring programs.

INSTITUTIONAL CAPITAL

Institutional capital is the bedrock of a well-functioning community and includes its legal framework, its law enforcement, and its capacity to address issues of justice. Maintaining a society's institutional capital allows businesses to interact in ways that do not cause a tragedy of the commons (or of the free resource) by overusing shared resources and by depleting other forms of capital critical to the success and well-being of the community. Domestically, a strong legal framework allows us to enforce contracts and to rely on long-term payments. Internationally, the UN has provided global institutions for this purpose, such as the IAEA to enforce nuclear agreements between countries and the UNFCCC to combat climate change. Some institutions may require a makeover or renovation, as many of their components were designed to address issues in the aftermath of World War II. The new global challenges require greater democracy and participation by all nations, which makes room for new leadership and new approaches. Once overhauled, these institutions will provide an international setting for nations to reach agreements and maintain standards for trade.

Recommendation: Require, where appropriate, the reporting of GHG emissions to all stakeholders as a compliance measure at all levels of governance.

FINANCIAL CAPITAL

Financial capital is what we normally think of when we think of capital or money. Financial capital is our capacity to loan resources through the banking system to finance projects within the global community.

Recommendation: Mandate federal, state, and municipal lending programs (in a manner similar to housing programs in the past) for the financing of self-generating energy projects and energy efficiency upgrades for homes and businesses. Position these programs to stimulate greater competition in the energy sector in order to garner support.

RISK CAPITAL

Risk capital is the capacity to exchange other forms of securities and to create equity investment around new initiatives, and as such it is distinct and separate from financial capital. Usually such capital is formed in risky situations where the potential reward is substantial and the project lacks sufficient collateral to attract traditional financial capital. The creation of risk capital often requires the combination and coordination of all other forms of capital in a unified mission or business plan.

Recommendation: Incentivize long-term equity investments by reducing long-term capital gains taxes for energy-related investments. This requires expanding the definition of qualified income under the tax code (so that it is at least similar to what is offered to the oil and gas industry) and offering credits that offset carbon emissions in order to satisfy investors.

POLITICAL CAPITAL

Political capital is the ability to exert influence over others or to gather people and communities in support of a particular issue. For example, when a president is elected or reelected, he or she is said to have a certain amount of political capital garnered during the election process. Perhaps the worst mistake a president can make is not spending this capital. If left in the proverbial bank account, pressures will mount and that political capital will deflate, rendering a new president ineffective.

Recommendation: Vote for representatives who include reducing global GHG emissions as part of their platform.

IT'S TIME TO OWN UP

At the heart of the energy issue is how both the nations of the world and the individual energy suppliers and users will *compete and cooperate* with one another. Capital markets, with competition at their core, have already globalized. In order to create sustainable business practices and avert catastrophic global warming, we need new forms of international agreements aimed at preserving the planet's natural resources. To reduce our collective global footprint, each nation needs to enter into its own federal, state, and municipal agreements between government and industry. In order to ensure compliance in a timely manner, these agreements must be action oriented, contain well-defined carrots and sticks, and clarify both benefits and costs to the supplier and energy user.

Such agreements should focus on willing commitments toward a shared goal. These commitments should be structured so that they honor the self-interest of individual nations, states, and municipalities.

IT'S TIME TO TAX

In ancient Rome the first rule of government was a ban on the burning of garbage—and cadavers—within the city walls. Failure to abide by this edict resulted in punishment and fines.[276] The challenge the global community faces today is that our rules about burning cadavers within the city walls have not sufficiently evolved to our present-day conditions, given the complexity of the energy industry and the corresponding fragility of the planet's ecosystem. Furthermore, the "city limits" have now grown well beyond city walls and river levees. The borders we must concern ourselves with today extend from the upper reaches of the earth's thin layer of atmosphere to the bottom of her oceans.

The Romans developed one of civilization's most impressive empires and created some of the greatest cities and states in history. They financed the expansion of their civilization by creating money in order to tax. In fact, it was the Roman government that first established a central authority over the monetary system. The Romans did this by centralizing and controlling the making of silver coins. Over an extended time period, these coins began to trade at values in excess of their "intrinsic" or replacement cost. As a result, the Roman government began to further experiment with ways to extend the value of these currencies, such as placing price controls on goods. These efforts had a minimal impact and were eventually deemed ineffective. Still, civilizations would attempt to achieve such goals again and again throughout the centuries.

To permit the empire to continue expanding, the Roman government next authorized moneylenders to serve as tax collectors. These moneylenders, who previously had been held in contempt by Roman society, formed new positions and gained new status as agents of the government. The Roman government, by creating a common exchange for the determination and extortion of taxes from agricultural producers and consumers, extended its capacity to generate higher tax receipts and revenue. This taxation system effectively formed commodity-trading centers throughout the Roman Empire, such as Pompeii in southern Italy.

This worked for a few centuries while the Roman Empire expanded throughout the Mediterranean region, but once growth stalled, exports started to fall—and so did the empire. Higher tax burdens were placed on producers to make up for the loss of revenues from declining markets. Increased taxation then left producers with little incentive to increase output. The taxation scheme began to bleed the system dry. No longer did it enhance trade through financing both buyer and seller, but rather it overburdened the marginal cost of production.

The global economy today may be suffering to some degree from the same fate as the Mediterranean region when the Roman Empire fell. Growth and inflation are the arguments of today's Keynesian economists—the solutions that they believe will stimulate global economic activity. In accordance with Keynesian thought, by creating inflation in the system, industry is prompted to spend rather than to hoard cash (which loses value unless it is deployed to earn a higher rate of return). Under inflationary pressure, consumers will buy today rather than tomorrow, hoping to preserve the value of their assets. Growth, however, may have its limits as the ecosystem fails to sustain increasing demand.

Still, the failure to adequately tax the burning of our conventional fuel supply may be at the heart of the systemic challenges to reigniting the global economy. Taxing the burning of carbon may be similar to incentivizing citizens not to burn their cadavers within the city limits. Moreover, the burning of conventional fuels has created an existential question much like the overburdening of the marginal cost of production did in the Mediterranean during the collapse of the Roman Empire. It seems we are creating challenges to the system's supply channels, and these challenges limit the ability of suppliers to focus on producing goods and services that maximize satisfaction, with the least amount of consumption. The current taxation system instead *promotes* consumption and resource depletion through its subsidies of fossil fuels.

The situation today calls for a redesign of national taxation systems relative to environmental and energy policies. Only by instituting a system overhaul will we escape the challenges posed by climate change. For example, in the United States, the solution may be to prompt Congress to take up the issue of public budgets in the context of a new energy and climate policy, rather than to try to address budgetary constraints prior to the formation of such policies. The issues of energy and economic policy may be more interlinked than any of us can imagine.

If we tax the extractive industries and use the proceeds to support investments in renewable energy programs, then the benefits will be regenerative for future generations. This arrangement would be an agreement among the energy user, the energy supplier, and the environmental steward to reinvest tax revenues into a substitute prior to running out of resources or burning them to a level that overburdens our atmosphere and oceans. Taxation would encourage the investor/lender to build substitutes and to support the transition, by providing long-term credit and risk capital as needed.

By taxing the burning of our natural resources, we would be internalizing the costs of pollution, forcing both the supplier and the energy user to pay for the right to pollute. Without a tax, public spending to abate the cost of pollution constitutes a burden to society. By avoiding burning a fossil fuel, we can create a tradable "credit" that would allow others to burn fossil fuels as opposed to paying a tax. Such market mechanisms will spur innovation and new investment.

IT'S TIME TO (RE)REGULATE

Changing the global energy mix will result in a dramatic change to the global economy. Building a global economy based on renewably powered generation and energy efficiency must begin by redefining the game. The new game requires modification of the utility system to empower energy users, energy suppliers, and investors/lenders (while considering the needs of environmental stewards) and to invest in new energy generation.

The process starts by acknowledging that the energy industry is already regulated. The game changer is to reset the regulatory environment in a way that promotes energy efficiency and transparency into the energy asset classes, recognizing that a new global energy mix is possible. By taxing the burning of fossil fuels—either at the mouth of the coal mine or at the tailpipe—government will impose the internalization of the costs to the beneficiary of their use. This will level the playing field and allow competitive alternatives to emerge, facilitating the transformation of the system. The result will be a more robust and competitive energy market and a more sustainable world economy.

If the new regulatory environment is a well-designed package of sustainability regulations and incentives, it will help US businesses plan and invest appropriately, allowing them to prioritize their sources of supply and their uses of energy. Such clarity will help suppliers decide what kind of technologies they should invest in—natural gas? renewable energy? nuclear power?—by comparing the costs and benefits of each.

Internationally, nations should focus on the formation of clubs that can initially begin as bilateral trade agreements rather than all-in commitments. Bilateral trade agreements should include the following:

» An aggressive and progressive GHG reduction target, expressed both as an absolute number and as a carbon and energy intensity index. Targets should serve as guideposts, not mandates. Missing a target should trigger a review of the regulatory system, not a review of the targets.

» A clear domestic price signal that is determined by permit auctioning to upstream emitters if a cap and trade system is pursued. Such pricing should help in forming international agreements.

» Considerable flexibility in achieving reduction targets, including carefully regulated offsets, limited traditional fuel development, and development of alternative renewable energy resources. Mandatory programs that are simultaneously flexible allow for the greatest amount of innovation.

» A carbon tax that forces the supplier of hydrocarbon fuels to take full responsibility for resulting emissions. The tax should be applied at the supplier level and suppliers should be allowed to pass the cost on to the user, the beneficiary. Such a clear market signal will stimulate the creation and formation of substitutes.

IT'S TIME TO REDIRECT SUBSIDIES

Ironically, the common criticism of renewable energy is that utility regulators unfairly promote it through favorable feed-in tariffs and tax incentives. They argue that tax credits and rebates often are in excess of earnings that would favor investment in such projects. Few realize that these inducements have been offered as a way to "level the playing field" against relatively inexpensive conventional fuels and their own subsidy structures. Unfortunately, these incentives have cut both ways: They have improved the user economics through lowering capital costs, but they have also promoted the myth that without these incentives, renewable energy technology cannot compete head-to-head against conventional supplies.

This negative assessment of the promotion of solar, wind, and hydropower development is upside-down. Directly taxing the burning of fossil fuels (that is, taxing them right at the coal mine or the oil well) would allow the market to address these fuels' pollution costs and create a present cost to cover the depletion of natural resources. The basis for this taxation is therefore threefold:

» Market pricing for the finite resources that spring out of our natural reservoirs without taxation can be highly inefficient if it leads to depletion and pollution.
» Supplies of such materials are essential for many industries and cannot be easily replaced or substituted with alternatives.
» Without such a tax, the cost of extraction sets the price in the short and intermediate term when supplies are plentiful.

Over the long term, the economy reaches its peak capacity to extract the resource, and only then does the market begin to price in the resource's eventual scarcity. By taxing the natural resource up front, we incorporate the cost of pollution and create an early signal to the market to develop substitutes. This will give renewable energy resources the necessary clear cost advantage.

IT'S TIME TO TRUST

So, what's stopping us from simply accelerating the inevitable by placing a price on pollution and depletion? In my opinion, what's stopping us is an underlying fear that has guided much of the global society's response to any plan for a global energy policy. It is the fear of losing a "way of life": the freedom to choose from all available options, and the wealth required to maintain a level of comfort, consumption, and convenience that we have all gotten used to. We have become accustomed to, supported by, energized by, and addicted to oil, just as we're beholden to the coffee many of us (including yours truly) drink every morning. Some would even say our addictive behavior with respect to oil is more akin to that of a junkie. Are we willing to suffer nearly anything, including self-destruction, to get our next fix?

The fear is compounded by a concern that this way of life—with unrestricted access to oil—can be taken from us at the hand of another, whether it is the dealer who has raised prices or the regulator who has imposed a cost to limit our use. We fear that those who sit on top of the world's declining energy reserves, and those who control their flow, can withhold the goods. This fear is paralyzing, and it is what creates attachment to the business-as-usual scenario.

Our blind desire to keep oil supply lines flowing traps us in an unsustainable oil game. Moreover, because parties with vested interests see the oil game as the *only* game, the global society has focused energy policy on subsidizing the oil industry and on finding new and more remote places to drill, rather than spending an equal level of effort promoting viable alternatives and substitutes. The situation has become so absurd that US oil companies actually get an oil depletion allowance, which permits them to deduct up to 27 percent of their gross income to account for the fact they are depleting their own income-generating potential. So, rather than paying a tax for depleting a natural resource beyond its ability to regenerate, oil companies are being rewarded for depleting natural capital.

In advising that we move beyond the paralyzing fear of losing access to oil, I do not deny that our dependency on oil presents a risk to national security. Rather, I support the concerns about dependency on a scarce resource. But I also want to clarify that there is a system of reliance built into our existing policies, a system that has created this dependency and caused us to operate in response to *fear* rather than with *faith*.

Fear is a normal response to threats. It is what we choose to *do* with our fear that makes the difference. My fear has in part driven me to write this book. I now know that depleting our global supply of finite natural resources and emitting GHGs beyond the carrying capacity of our planet brings consequences. Furthermore, I now know what it will take to save ourselves from a tragic fate. It will take changing our global energy mix. So my fear is that my children will find themselves in a ruined world, not because we lacked the technology to save it, but because we chose not to make the effort. My fear isn't losing a way of life at the hand of another. It is losing a way of life for my children to inherit—*by my own hand.*

The response of the global community needs to be a demand for a new business case that our global society can implement. My recommendation is to engage the capital markets in the solution. My belief is that once the global community has acknowledged the problem, we can trust that the marketplace will provide whatever is needed so long as the appropriate rules are in place. It might be hard to grasp how incorporating a simple tax will have an impact on millions of decisions that will lead to efficiency and innovation—but it will. The global community does not need to address climate change with command-and-control solutions in order to compete with entrenched interests. Rather, what we need is an alignment of interests between the stakeholders—the energy supplier, the investor/lender, the energy user, and the environmental steward—in order to unleash the power of the capital markets.

International and domestic policies that seek to empower our global society to take action toward mitigating climate change will begin to create the necessary alignment. Around the world, communities and individuals want to respond to the call to address climate change. They want to be part of something bigger. Seeing ourselves as part of a planet that is living and breathing does not shake our beliefs in any god. Instead it connects us and reinforces our role as stewards of the planet. It gives us each a place to begin the necessary work. It is this realization that gives us the comfort of knowing change is upon us.

In my mind, the story of the caterpillar continues to unfold. He wants to convince the other caterpillars that it is possible to fly. The others believe that such an idea is foolish—after all, God has given them many legs but no wings. Still, the caterpillar insists it *is* possible. Earthbound as he is, it is unlikely that he has even met or seen a butterfly. But he believes he can fly. That vision and trust come from within.

We all have the ability to dream of being a butterfly. For the visionary or the entrepreneur, the dream merely needs to find its way into a business plan or an elevator pitch. Born from nothing more than diligence, a deep conviction about what is possible, and a business case that fires up the imagination, the dream can become reality.

NOTES

PREFACE

1. Susan R. Espinueva, "Extreme Events and Climate Change Projections for the Philippines: An Opportunity for Collaborative Research," Japan Society for the Promotion of Science website, accessed August 21, 2012, http://jsps-th.org/wp-jsps/wp-content/uploads/2011/02/25.-SRE-extended-abstract-of-JSPS-international.pdf.

2. Elizabeth Hoff, "Philippines Tropical Storm Washi Donor Alert," World Health Organization website, accessed February 8, 2013, http://www.who.int/hac/crises/phl/appeal/donor_alert_philippines_dec2011/en/index.html.

3. Amir Ahmed, "Death Toll from Typhoon Bopha Tops 1,000 in the Philippines," CNN, December 17, 2012, http://www.cnn.com/2012/12/16/world/asia/philippines-typhoon/index.html.

INTRODUCTION

4. B. S. Fisher et al., "Issues Related to Mitigation in the Long-Term Context," in *Climate Change 2007: Mitigation—Contribution of Working Group III to the Fourth Assessment Report of the Intergovernmental Panel on Climate Change,* eds. B. Metz et al. (Cambridge: Cambridge University Press, 2007), 227–30, http://www.ipcc.ch/pdf/assessment-report/ar4/wg3/ar4-wg3-chapter3.pdf.

5. Arnold J. Bloom and David Hassenzahl PhD, "Sea Level Change in the 21st Century," in *Encyclopedia of Earth*, ed. Cutler J. Cleveland (Washington, DC: Environmental Information Coalition, National Council for Science and the Environment), first published December 16, 2010, last revised January 9, 2011, accessed February 23, 2012, http://www.eoearth.org/article/Sea_Level_Change_in_the_21st_Century?topic=54336.

6. Matthew Heberger et al., "Potential Impacts of Increased Coastal Flooding in California Due to Sea-Level Rise," Rep. Springer Science+Business Media, supplement, 109, no. 1 (December 2011): 229–49, http://www.springerlink.com/content/u7415v51x03r4234/fulltext.pdf.

PART I: THE CASE FOR TRANSFORMATION

CHAPTER 1. LOOKING FOR MONEY: CAN CAPITAL MARKETS CREATE SUSTAINABILITY?

7. "Secretary George Shultz—PSA Event on Capitol Hill March 8, 2013," Partnership for a Secure America website, March 8, 2013, http://www.psaonline.org/downloads/Shultz%20March%208th%20Transcript_1.pdf.

8. Econergy was one of the world's leading and largest developers of projects under Article 12, registered with the United Nations' CDM Executive Board as of February 2006. See Econergy's admissions document available at the Isle of Man company's registry, http://www.gov.im/ded/pvi/pvi_fr.html.

9. "Through a public offering and listing on the London Stock Exchange's Alternative Investment Market in April 2005, Trading Emissions PLC raised £135 million in capital." From Trading Emissions company website, accessed February 9, 2012, http://www.tradingemissionsplc.com/index_english.htm.

10. "Company Profile," Trading Emissions PLC website, accessed February 14, 2012, http://www.tradingemissionsplc.com/index_english.htm.

11. "Trade Growth to Slow in 2012 after Strong Deceleration in 2011," World Trade Organization press release, April 12, 2012, accessed September 2, 2012, http://www.wto.org/english/news_e/pres12_e/pr658_e.htm.

12. "General Information Renewable Energy," Federal Ministry for the Environment, Nature Conservation and Nuclear Safety website, August 2012, accessed September 2, 2012, http://www.bmu.de/en/topics/climate-energy/renewable-energy/general-information/.

13. Paul Wander, "Das Energiekonzept der Bundesregierung 2010 und die Energiewende 2011," September 28, 2010, http://www.bmu.de/files/pdfs/allgemein/application/pdf/energiekonzept_bundesregierung.pdf.

14. "Solyndra Cylindrical Module: Benefits of a Cylinder," Solyndra company website, accessed September 2, 2012, http://www.solyndra.com/technology-products/cylindrical-module/.

15. The *levelized cost of energy* is defined as the constant price per unit of energy that causes the investment to break even.

16. Claudia Kemfert and Dorothea Schafer, "Financing the Energy Transition in Times of Financial Market Instability," DIW *Economic Bulletin* 2, no.9 (2012): 3–13.

17. Louise Osborne, "German Renewable Energy Drive Brings Emissions Cuts Success," *Guardian*, November 26, 2012, http://www.guardian.co.uk/environment/2012/nov/26/german-renewable-energy-emission-co2.

CHAPTER 2. DROUGHT, EROSION, AND SWARMS OF INSECTS: "IT'S JUST THE WAY IT IS"

18. "Report of the Ocean Acidification and Oxygen Working Group," SCOR Biological Observatories Workshop, September 2009, http://www.scor-int.org/OBO2009/A&O_Report.pdf.

19. "Human Settlements on the Coast," UN Atlas of the Oceans website, accessed February 26, 2012, http://www.oceansatlas.org/servlet/CDSServlet?status=ND0xODc3JjY9ZW4mMzM9KiYzNz1rb3M~.

20. "Forest Health: Mountain Pine Beetle—Pine Beetle Epidemic from Canada to Mexico," National Park Service website, accessed September 11, 2012, http://www.nps.gov/romo/naturescience/mtn_pine_beetle_background.htm.

21. "Climate Change: Federal Reports on Climate Change Funding Should Be Clearer

and More Complete," GAO-05-461, US Government Accountability Office, August 2005, http://www.gao.gov/new.items/d05461.pdf.

22. Peter Schwartz and Doug Randall, "An Abrupt Climate Change Scenario and Its Implications for United States National Security," Global Business Network, October 2003, http://www.gbn.com/articles/pdfs/Abrupt%20Climate%20Change%20February%202004.pdf.

23. Steve Cole and Leslie McCarthy, "NASA Finds 2011 Ninth-Warmest Year on Record," NASA website, January 19, 2012, accessed October 17, 2012, http://www.nasa.gov/topics/earth/features/2011-temps.html.

24. "Climate Change and African Political Stability (CCAPS)," the Robert S. Strauss Center for International Security and Law, the University of Texas at Austin, website, accessed March 26, 2012, http://ccaps.strausscenter.org/.

25. "Navy Climate Change Roadmap," US Department of the Navy, April 2010, http://www.navy.mil/navydata/documents/CCR.pdf.

26. "Four-Star Admiral Admits What Scares Him Most: Climate Change," Yahoo! News, March 11, 2013, http://news.yahoo.com/four-star-admiral-admits-scares-him-most-climate-193847846.html.

27. Fred Krupp, "A New Climate-Change Consensus," editorial, *Wall Street Journal*, August 7, 2012, US edition, A13.

28. Damian Carrington, "IEA Report Reminds Us Peak Oil Idea Has Gone Up in Flames," *Guardian*, November 16, 2012, http://www.guardian.co.uk/environment/damian-carrington-blog/2012/nov/12/iea-report-peak-oil.

29. "OPEC's crude oil exports represent about 61 percent of the crude oil traded internationally. Therefore, OPEC can have a strong influence on the oil market, especially if it decides to reduce or increase its level of production." From "OPEC Frequently Asked Questions," Organization of the Petroleum Exporting Countries, Public Relations and Information Department, May 2012, http://www.opec.org/opec_web/static_files_project/media/downloads/publications/FAQ.pdf.

30. Maria Van Der Hoeven, *World Energy Outlook 2011* (France: International Energy Agency, 2011).

31. Ibid.

32. Ibid.

33. Bloomberg New Energy Finance, *Global Trends in Renewable Energy Investment 2012,* Frankfurt School of Finance & Management.

CHAPTER 3. FROM THE COLD WAR TO CLIMATE CHANGE: CREATING A LEVEL PLAYING FIELD

34. Colin L. Powell, "Only One Earth," *Our Planet,* UNEP, August 12, 2002, accessed March 1, 2013, http://www.ourplanet.com/imgversn/132/powell.html.

35. *Cap & Trade: Acid Rain Program Results,* US EPA Clean Air Market Program, accessed April 5, 2012, http://www.epa.gov/capandtrade/documents/ctresults.pdf.

36. See *Kyoto Protocol to the United Nations Framework Convention on Climate Change,* accessed December 1, 2011, http://unfccc.int/resource/docs/convkp/kpeng.html. The Kyoto Protocol, a 1997 amendment to the UN Framework Convention on Climate Change, was designed to reduce the impacts of global warming by stabilizing the growth in atmospheric GHG concentrations. The Kyoto Protocol went into effect in February 2005. Participating Annex I (industrialized) countries committed to a GHG emission reduction of 5.2 percent from the 1990 level, through mechanisms including emissions trading, under the Clean Development Mechanism and Joint Implementation (JI). By 2009, more than 187 countries had adopted and ratified the Kyoto Protocol, representing more than 64 percent of the 1990 Annex I emissions. The ultimate goal of Kyoto was to reduce GHG emissions and convert our energy systems to new, clean technology.

37. In 2009 I was CEO of Evergreen Energy, which was engaged with IBM and Foxconn to develop their carbon reporting system to Apple. Apple announced in July 2012 that it would withdraw from its commitment to meet the standards for environmental compliance. See Zach C. Cohen, "Apple Drops Environmental Certification; S.F. Drops Apple," *USA Today,* July 5, 2012, http://content.usatoday.com/communities/technologylive/post/2012/07/apple-san-francisco-epeat/1#.UE6nAGhQaSA.

38. "Annex: Johannesburg Declaration on Sustainable Development," A/CONF.199/20, Chapter 1, Resolution 1, *UN Documents: Gathering a Body of Global Agreements,* September 4, 2012, http://www.un-documents.net/jburgdec.htm.

39. Brad Plumer, "Around the World, Cap-and-Trade Is Still Alive and Kicking," *Washington Post*, June 6, 2012, http://www.washingtonpost.com/blogs/ ezra-klein/post/around-the-world-cap-and-trade-is-still-alive-and-kicking/ 2012/06/05/gJQACSKVGV_blog.html.

40. Lindsay Mayer, "Big Oil, Big Influence," PBS, August 1, 2008, http://www.pbs.org/ now/shows/347/oil-politics.html.

41. "Toxic Shock," *Economist* website, May 26, 2012, accessed February 12, 2013, http:// www.economist.com/node/21555894.

42. "Almanac: Senator James Inhofe (R), Oklahoma," National Journal Group Inc. web- site, accessed March 9, 2013, http://www.nationaljournal.com/almanac/2008/people/ ok/oks1.php.

43. Andrew Freedman, "WSJ Editorial Board Spins Climate Science, Again," *Washington Post*, November 15, 2010, http://voices.washingtonpost.com/ capitalweathergang/2010/11/wsj_editorial_board_continues.html.

44. See Thomas L. Friedman, "Bush Should Look in His Playbook and Find a 'Reverse,'" *Houston Chronicle*, September 21, 2005, http://www.chron.com/opinion/ outlook/article/Friedman-Bush-should-look-in-his-playbook-and-1563918.php. Friedman's writings inspire the imagination. As he points out here, the past is full of lost opportunities, but we can learn from these lost chances and perhaps make some of them future possibilities.

45. In 1997 the Texas Railroad Commission approved two Texas Utility programs to implement wind power and energy efficiency through demand side management. The commission was headed by Pat Wood III. Highland Energy Group, the first company of which I served as chief executive officer, was one of two contractors under the Texas Utilities DSM program.

46. "Wind Energy Facts: Texas," AWEA website, May 2011, accessed October 24, 2012, http://www.awea.org/_cs_upload/learnabout/publications/6418_2.pdf.

47. "100 Things Americans May Not Know about the Bush Administration Record," *The Administration of President George W. Bush, 2001–2009*, White House archives, accessed April 6, 2012, http://georgewbush-whitehouse.archives.gov/infocus/ bushrecord/documents/appendix_acc_for_web.pdf.

48. Barnaby J. Feder, "Economy & Business; Some Businesses Take Initiative to Voluntarily Reduce Emissions," *New York Times,* December 1, 2003, http://www.nytimes.com/2003/12/01/news/economy-business-some-businesses-take-initiative-to-voluntarily-reduce-emissions.html?pagewanted=all.

49. Christine Todd Whitman, *It's My Party Too: The Battle for the Heart of the GOP and the Future of America* (New York: Penguin, 2005). Also Ron Suskind, *The Price of Loyalty: George W. Bush, the White House, and the Education of Paul O'Neill* (New York: Simon & Schuster, 2004).

50. Audrey T. Leath, "DOE Accepting Public Comment on Energy Efficiency, Renewables Policy," *FYI: The AIP Bulletin of Science Policy News,* no. 71, June 8, 2001, American Institute of Physics website, accessed February 12, 2012, http://www.aip.org/fyi/2001/071.html.

51. *National Energy Policy: Report of the National Energy Policy Development Group,* National Energy Policy Development Group, Office of the President of the United States, May 2001, http://www.dtic.mil/cgi-bin/GetTRDoc?AD=ADA392171.

52. Tom Curry, "Cheney's Day Before Supreme Court," MSNBC.com, April 26, 2004, http://www.msnbc.msn.com/id/4830129/ns/politics-tom_curry/t/cheneys-day-supreme-court/.

53. Douglas Jehl and Andrew Revkin, "Bush, in Reversal, Won't Seek Cut in Emissions of Carbon Dioxide," *New York Times,* March 14, 2001, http://www.nytimes.com/2001/03/14/us/bush-in-reversal-won-t-seek-cut-in-emissions-of-carbon-dioxide.html.

54. One example is Mazdar, an experimental city funded by a $200 million venture capital investment in the United Arab Emirates. Launched by the Abu Dhabi leadership in 2006, its mission is to "advance renewable energy and sustainable technologies through education, R&D, investment, and commercialization." For more information, see http://www.masdar.ae/en/masdar/detail/launched-by-the-abu-dhabi-leadership-in-2006-with-the-mission-to-advance-re.

55. Richard B. Cheney and Liz Cheney, *In My Time: A Personal and Political Memoir* (New York: Threshold Editions, 2011), 315.

56. In the spring of 2009 James Schlesinger, former secretary of defense under President Richard Nixon and secretary of energy under President Jimmy Carter, told me

in a private conversation regarding the prospect for carbon trading in the United States that there would be no climate legislation during the first term of the Obama administration.

57. Terry Anderson and Gary D. Libecap, "Cap & Trade: An Inconvenient Tax," *Defining Ideas*, Hoover Institution website, October 30, 2009, accessed October 25, 2012, http://www.hoover.org/publications/defining-ideas/article/5314.

58. Ryan Lizza, "As the World Burns," *New Yorker,* October 27, 2010, http://www.newyorker.com/reporting/2010/10/11/101011fa_fact_lizza.

59. Andy Newman, "Hurricane Sandy vs. Hurricane Katrina," *New York Times,* November 27, 2012, http://cityroom.blogs.nytimes.com/2012/11/27/hurricane-sandy-vs-hurricane-katrina/.

PART II: BUSINESS AS USUAL
CHAPTER 4. FIRES MOVE FAST: CLIMATE CHANGE AND ENERGY INFRASTRUCTURE

60. "Colorado Wildfires: State and Private Lands," Colorado State Forest Service website, accessed August 23, 2012, http://csfs.colostate.edu/pages/documents/WILDFIRES_year_cb_2009.pdf.

61. The Waldo and High Park fires in the summer of 2012 broke this record again.

62. "Floods: Recurrence Intervals and 100-Year Floods," US Geological Survey website, accessed March 19, 2013, http://ga.water.usgs.gov/edu/100yearflood.html. Technically, a hundred-year flood means that there is a 1 percent chance of a major flood with a peak discharge of twelve thousand cubic feet per second in any given year.

63. Christopher Joyce, "In Southwest, Worst-Case Fire Scenario Plays Out," Minnesota Public Radio, August 24, 2012, http://minnesota.publicradio.org/features/npr.php?id=159848194.

64. Joseph Romm, "Desertification: The Next Dust Bowl," *Nature* 478.7370 (2011): 450–51, doi: 10.1038/478450a.

65. Virginie Marchal et al., *OECD Environmental Outlook to 2050*, OECD website, November 2011, http://www.oecd.org/env/climatechange/49082173.pdf.

66. See www.projbutterfly.com.

67. Thomas R. Karl, Jerry M. Melillo, and Thomas C. Peterson, *Global Climate Change Impacts in the United States: US Global Change Research Program* (Cambridge: Cambridge University Press, 2009), http://downloads.globalchange.gov/usimpacts/pdfs/climate-impacts-report.pdf.

68. Lenny Bernstein et al., *IPCC Climate Change 2007 Synthesis Report—Fourth Assessment* (Geneva, Switzerland: IPCC, 2008), 36, http://www.ipcc.ch/pdf/assessment-report/ar4/syr/ar4_syr.pdf.

69. "Greenhouse Effects … Also on Other Planets," European Space Agency, February 14, 2003, last updated June 10, 2003, accessed August 28, 2012, http://sci.esa.int/science-e/www/object/index.cfm?fobjectid=32528.

70. Working Group I, "The Physical Science Basis," section 7.3.1.1, *Fourth Assessment Report of the Intergovernmental Panel on Climate Change*, eds. S. Solomon et al. (Cambridge and New York: Cambridge University Press, 2007), http://www.ipcc.ch/publications_and_data/ar4/wg1/en/ch7s7-3.html.

71. Mixing 840 billion tons of CO_2 into the atmosphere results in a concentration of 394 parts CO_2 for every million parts dry air, i.e., ppm. See http://www.esrl.noaa.gov/gmd/ccgg/trends/.

72. W. F. Ruddiman, *Earth's Climate: Past and Future* (New York: W. H. Freeman & Sons, 2001).

73. Felix Gradstein et al., *A Geologic Time Scale 2004* (Cambridge: Cambridge University Press, 2004).

74. T. A. Boden et al., *Global, Regional, and National Fossil-Fuel CO_2 Emissions,* Carbon Dioxide Information Analysis Center, Oak Ridge National Laboratory, US Department of Energy, 2011, doi: 10.3334/CDIAC/00001_V2011.

75. P. Friedlingstein et al., "Climate-Carbon Cycle Feedback Analysis: Results from the C⁴MIP Model Intercomparison," *Journal of Climate* 19 (2006): 3337–53, http://journals.ametsoc.org/doi/pdf/10.1175/JCLI3800.1.

76. *Working Group I,* "The Physical Science Basis," section 7.1, http://www.ipcc.ch/publications_and_data/ar4/wg1/en/faq-7-1.html.

77. Methane (CH_4) has a global warming potential twenty-three times greater over one hundred years than that of carbon dioxide. Methane is naturally stored in wetlands and produced as part of biological processes, but it is also present in a solid form, called "clathrates," in the oceans and permafrost regions. As permafrost is lost in the tundra and as ocean temperatures change, the methane present as a solid may be released to the atmosphere. See Gavin Schmidt, "Methane: A Scientific Journal from Obscurity to Climate Super-Stardom," NASA Goddard Institute for Space Studies, September 2004, accessed March 2, 2012, http://www.giss.nasa.gov/research/features/200409_methane/.

78. "On Thinner Ice—Melting Glaciers on the Roof of the World," video (7:58), Asia Society website, March 18, 2010, accessed August 31, 2012, http://asiasociety.org/onthinnerice.

89. Dr. Jeff Matthews, "Earth's Attic Is on Fire: Arctic Sea Ice Bottoms Out at a New Record Low," accessed May 12, 2012, http://urdu.wunderground.com/blog/JeffMasters/comment.html?entrynum=2237&page=29.

80. "Key Indicators: Carbon Dioxide Concentration," NASA Global Climate Change website, last updated January 23, 2013, accessed March 3, 2013, http://climate.nasa.gov/key_indicators.

81. Van Der Hoeven, *World Energy Outlook 2011*.

82. USGS and Sidney Draggan, "Abrupt Changes in the Earth's Climate System," in *Encyclopedia of Earth*, ed. Cutler J. Cleveland (Washington, DC: Environmental Information Coalition, National Council for Science and the Environment), first published February 22, 2010, last revised November 2, 2011, accessed January 25, 2012, http://www.eoearth.org/article/Abrupt_Changes_in_the_Earth's_Climate_System?topic=49491.

83. Hugh Turral, *Climate Change, Water, and Food Security*, Food and Agriculture Organization of the United Nations, 2011, http://www.fao.org/docrep/014/i2096e/i2096e.pdf.

84. *Inventory of US Greenhouse Gas Emissions and Sinks: 1990–2010*, Environmental Protection Agency, April 15, 2012, http://www.epa.gov/climatechange/Downloads/ghgemissions/US-GHG-Inventory-2012-Upfront.pdf.

85. Nathanial Gronewold, "One-Quarter of World's Population Lacks Electricity," *Scientific American* website, November 24, 2009, http://www.scientificamerican.com/article.cfm?id=electricity-gap-developing-countries-energy-wood-charcoal.

86. Jonathan Koomey, *Growth in Data Center Electricity Use, 2005 to 2010*, Analytics Press, August 1, 2011, http://www.analyticspress.com/datacenters.html.

87. *An Inefficient Truth*, Global Action Plan, 2007, http://www.it-energy.co.uk/pdf/GAP%20An%20Inefficient%20Truth%20Dec%202007.pdf. This estimate comes from research and advisory company Gartner.

88. Negawatt power is a theoretical unit of power representing an amount of energy (measured in watts) saved. The energy saved is a direct result of energy conservation or increased efficiency.

89. "Frequently Asked Questions," US Department of Energy, Energy Information Administration website, last updated December 6, 2011, accessed August 31, 2012, http://www.eia.gov/tools/faqs/faq.cfm?id=97&t=3.

90. "Form EIA-860 Database, Annual Electric Generator Report," US Department of Energy, Energy Information Administration website, 2005 data set, accessed August 31, 2012, http://www.eia.doe.gov/cneaf/electricity/page/eia860.html.

91. Marc W. Chupka and Gregory Basheda (The Brattle Group), *Rising Utility Construction Costs: Sources and Impacts*, the Edison Foundation, September 2007, http://www.eei.org/ourissues/finance/Documents/Rising_Utility_Construction_Costs.pdf.

CHAPTER 5. VICTIMS AND SURVIVORS: ENERGY ECONOMICS AND PEAK OIL

92. Andrew Scott Cooper, *The Oil Kings: How the US, Iran, and Saudi Arabia Changed the Balance of Power in the Middle East* (New York: Simon & Schuster, 2011). Mohammad Reza Pahlavi, the Shah of Iran from 1941 to 1979, was one of the founders of OPEC.

93. James Griffin, ed., *World Oil Outlook 2010*, Organization of the Petroleum Exporting Countries (OPEC), 82, accessed May 12, 2012, http://www.opec.org/opec_web/static_files_project/media/downloads/publications/woo_2010.pdf.

94. "US Crude Oil Supply and Disposition," US Department of Energy, Energy Information Administration website, accessed March 2, 2012, http://www.eia.gov/dnav/pet/pet_sum_crdsnd_k_a.htm.

95. Lananh Nguyen, "IEA Sees Oil Supply Rising as Demand Growth Slows to 2017," Bloomberg, October 12, 2012, http://www.bloomberg.com/news/2012-10-12/iea-sees-oil-supply-rising-as-demand-growth-slows-to-2017.html.

96. Griffin, *World Oil Outlook 2010*, 60.

97. Judy Trinnaman and Alan Clarke, eds., *2010 Survey of Energy Resources,* World Energy Council, 2010, http://www.worldenergy.org/documents/ser_2010_report_1.pdf.

98. *Testimony to the US House of Representatives Committee on Appropriations Subcommittee on Energy and Water Development—Facing the Challenges of Oil Dependence and Climate Change: What Will It Take?* (testimony of David Greene, Corporate Fellow Engineering Science and Technology Division, Oak Ridge National Laboratory), February 14, 2008, http://cta.ornl.gov/cta/Publications/Reports/Testimony_DrivingDownGasPrices_Greene.pdf.

99. Jörg Friedrichs, "Global Energy Crunch: How Different Parts of the World Would React to a Peak Oil Scenario," *Energy Policy*, Elsevier, April 24, 2010, accessed December 1, 2011, http://www.sciencedirect.com/science/article/pii/S0301421510002843.

100. Stephan Haggard and Marcus Noland, *Famine in North Korea: Markets, Aid, and Reform* (New York: Columbia University Press, 2007).

101. Ibid.

102. Fabian Kesicki, "The Third Oil Price Surge—What's Different This Time?" *Energy Policy,* Elsevier, December 16, 2009, accessed December 1, 2011, http://www.sciencedirect.com/science/article/pii/S0301421509008933.

103. Amory B. Lovins, *Reinventing Fire: Bold Business Solutions for the New Energy Era* (White River Junction, VT: Chelsea Green Publishing, 2011).

104. David Roberts, "Direct Subsidies to Fossil Fuels Are the Tip of the (Melting) Iceberg," *Grist*, October 26, 2011, accessed January 12, 2012, http://www.grist.org/energy-policy/2011-10-26-direct-subsidies-to-fossil-fuels-are-tip-of-melting-iceburg.

105. Ken Wells, "Big Oil's Big in Biofuels," Bloomberg *Businessweek*, May 10, 2012, http://www.businessweek.com/articles/2012-05-10/big-oils-big-in-biofuels.

106. Triggered by the Yom Kippur War in 1973, OPEC leaders (with the exception of Iraq) curtailed United States oil exports and raised the price of oil by 70 percent, ultimately embargoing oil exports to the United States—prompting an energy crisis. The United States eventually negotiated a lift to the embargo when the OPEC leadership realized that gigantic price jumps coupled with reduced oil production would be economically disastrous to the United States and would undermine its ability to thwart communism. The United States and OPEC leaders were both fearful of the spread of communism and worked together to stabilize the Persian Gulf region, especially after the Soviet Union invasion of Afghanistan in 1979. See Jareer Elass and Amy Myers Jaffe, "The History of US Relations with OPEC: Lessons to Policymakers," in *Energy Market Consequences of an Emerging US Carbon Management Policy,* Energy Forum, James A. Baker III Institute for Public Policy, Rice University, September 2010, http://www.bakerinstitute.org/publications/Amy%20Jareer%20U.S.%20Relations%20with %20cover%20secured.pdf.

107. Chris Skrebowski, "ODAC Newsletter," Oil Depletion Analysis Centre website, September 16, 2011, accessed October 29, 2012, http://www.odac-info.org/newsletter/2011/09/16.

108. Lovins, *Reinventing Fire.*

109. Mark Nord, Margaret Andrews, and Steven Carlson, *Household Food Security in the United States, 2008* (Washington, DC: US Department of Agriculture, November 2009), ERS/USDA ERR-83;66.

110. *The State of Food Insecurity in the World 2011: How Does International Price Volatility Affect Domestic Economies and Food Security?* Food and Agriculture Organization of the United Nations, 2011, 42, http://www.fao.org/docrep/014/i2330e/i2330e.pdf.

111. Nord et al., *Household Food Security in the United States.*

112. "Weekly All Countries Spot Price FOB Weighted by Estimated Export Volume (Dollars per Barrel)," US Department of Energy, Energy Information Administration website, accessed December 1, 2010, http://www.eia.gov/petroleum/index.cfm.

113. Sophia Huang and Kuo Huang, *Increased US Imports of Fresh Fruit and Vegetables,* Report no. FTS-328-01 (Washington, DC: US Department of Agriculture, Economic Research Service, 2007), http://www.unitedfresh.org/assets/files/Increased%20U.S.%20FFV%20Imports.pdf.

114. Rich Pirog and Andrew Benjamin, *Checking the Food Odometer: Comparing Food Miles for Local Versus Conventional Produce Sales to Iowa Institutions* (Ames, Iowa: Leopold Center for Sustainable Agriculture, Iowa State University, July 2003), http://www.leopold.iastate.edu/sites/default/files/pubs-and-papers/2003-07-checking-food-odometer-comparing-food-miles-local-versus-conventional-produce-sales-iowa-institution.pdf.

115. Nora Brooks, Anita Regmi, and Alberto Jerardo, *US Food Import Patterns, 1998–2007,* report no. FAU-125 (Washington, DC: US Department of Agriculture, Economic Research Service, 2009), http://www.ers.usda.gov/media/157859/fau125_1_.pdf.

116. United States Department of Agriculture (USDA), "Chapter 2: Profiling Food Consumption in America," *Agriculture Fact Book 2001–2002,* http://www.usda.gov/factbook/chapter2.htm.

117. "Food CPI and Expenditures: Table 7," US Department of Agriculture, Economic Research Service, accessed December 30, 2009, http://www.ers.usda.gov/data-products/food-expenditures.aspx.

118. P. Hanlen and G. McCartney, "Peak Oil: Will It Be Public Health's Greatest Challenge?" *Public Health* 122, no.7 (2008): 647–52.

119. U. R. Sumaila et al., "Fuel Price Increase, Subsidies, Overcapacity, and Resource Sustainability," *ICES Journal of Marine Science* 65 (2008): 832–40.

120. D. Pimentel and M. Giampietro, *Food, Land, Population and the US Economy* (Washington, DC: Carrying Capacity Network, 1994).

121. D. Pimentel et al., "Reducing Energy Inputs in the US Food System," *Human Ecology* 36, no.4 (2008): 459–71.

122. "Muck and Brass," *Economist,* January 20, 2011, http://www.economist.com/node/17959688.

123. "USGS Release: 90 Billion Barrels of Oil and 1,670 Trillion Cubic Feet of Natural Gas Assessed in the Arctic," USGS Newsroom website, July 23, 2008, accessed May 3, 2012, http://www.usgs.gov/newsroom/article.asp?ID=1980.

124. Sandra Petersen, "Eating Habits of Great White Sharks," Helium website, January 16, 2009, accessed October 23, 2012, http://www.helium.com/items/1299506-great-white-shark-feeding-habits.

125. Nate Hagens, "Unconventional Oil: Tar Sands and Shale Oil—EROI on the Web, Part 3 of 6," The Oil Drum: Net Energy website, April 15, 2008, accessed February 14, 2013, www.theoildrum.com/node/3839.

126. Marcia McNutt et al., *Assessment of Flow Rate Estimates for the Deepwater Horizon/Macondo Well Oil Spill,* Flow Rate Technical Group report to the National Incident Command, Interagency Solutions Group, March 10, 2011, US Department of the Interior website, accessed May 9, 2012, http://www.doi.gov/deepwaterhorizon/loader.cfm?csModule=security/getfile&PageID=237763.

127. Reuters, "Gov't Data Shows Tar Sands Emissions to Rise 226 Percent by 2020," *Inside Climate News,* August 10, 2012, www.insideclimatenews.org.

128. Associated Press, "US Gas Demand on Long-Term Decline after Hitting '06 Peak," *Jakarta Globe,* December 21, 2010, http://www.thejakarta globe.com/naturalresources/us-gas-demand-on-long-term-decline-after-hitting -06-peak/412956.

129. Maria Van Der Hoeven, *World Energy Outlook 2012* (France: International Energy Agency, 2012).

130. Ibid.

CHAPTER 6. FINDING A STRAIGHT LINE TO SAFE HARBOR: NATIONAL SECURITY AND ENERGY SUPPLY

131. An example of such favorable treatment of oil and gas over renewable energy includes the special tax treatment under rules governing master limited partnerships. Qualifying income is treated as a return on capital rather than ordinary income under a dividend classification. For further explanation, see http://www.coons.senate.gov/issues/master-limited-partnerships-parity-act.

132. Amory B. Lovins, *Winning the Oil Endgame: Innovation for Profits, Jobs and Security* (Snowmass, CO: Rocky Mountain Institute, 2004), 21.

133. Ibid. As an approximation, according to the US Energy Information Administration, $3.098/gallon average refined-product price times 19.498 mb/d petroleum products supplied yields $929 billion.

134. United States Energy Information Administration, International Energy Statistics website, April 16, 2013, http://www.eia.gov/cfapps/ipdbproject/IEDIndex3 .cfm?tid=5&pid=5&aid=2.

135. Cooper, *Oil Kings*, 151.

136. Neela Banerjee, "US Report: Oil Imports Down, Domestic Production Highest Since 2003," *Los Angeles Times*, March 12, 2012, http://articles.latimes.com/2012/ mar/12/news/la-pn-report-us-oil-imports-down-domestic-production-highest- since-2003-20120311.

137. National Intelligence Council, *Global Trends 2030: Alternative Worlds*, United States Office of the Director of National Intelligence, 2012, http://www.dni.gov/files/doc- uments/GlobalTrends_2030.pdf.

138. "Renewable Energy Posts Strong Growth under Obama Administration," *Solar Industry* website, Zackin Publications Inc., April 2, 2012, accessed May 5, 2012, http://www.solarindustrymag.com/e107_plugins/content/content.php?con- tent.10024#.UR4QmaU4t8E.

139. Justin Doom, "U.S. Carbon Output to Fall to 1970s Levels by 2040: Exxon," Bloomberg, March 13, 2013, http://www.bloomberg.com/news/2013-03-13/ u-s-carbon-output-to-fall-to-1970s-levels-by-2040-exxon.html.

140. For video footage of the Project Rulison test explosion site, see http://www. youtube.com/watch?v=myXswNUQgLs.

141. Lovins, *Reinventing Fire.*

142. "Potential Gas Committee Reports Substantial Increase in Magnitude of US Natural Gas Resource Base," Potential Gas Committee press release, April 27, 2011, http://potentialgas.org/?s=to+1%2C897.8+trillion+cubic+feet+%28Tcf&op. x=34&op.y=15.

143. "What We Do," Potential Gas Committee website, accessed February 24, 2013, http://potentialgas.org/what-we-do-2.

144. "Hydraulic Fracturing Fact Sheet," Chesapeake Energy website, May 2012, http://www.chk.com/media/educational-library/fact-sheets/corporate/hydraulic_fracturing_fact_sheet.pdf.

145. *Annual Energy Outlook 2012: Early Release Overview*, US Department of Energy, Energy Information Administration website, 2012, http://www.eia.gov/todayinenergy/detail.cfm?id=4671.

146. Ibid.

147. "Chrysler and GM Announce Natural Gas-Powered Pickups," Pickens Plan website, March 5, 2012, accessed March 19, 2012, http://www.pickensplan.com/news/2012/03/05/chrsyler-and-gm-announce-natural-gas-powered-pickups/.

148. "Nat Gas Act Is No Boondoggle," Pickens Plan website, February 29, 2012, accessed March 19, 2012, http://www.pickensplan.com/news/2012/03/01/nat-gas-act-is-no-boondoggle/.

149. "Connecticut's Larson Praises AT&T," Pickens Plan website, February 26, 2012, accessed March 19, 2012, http://www.pickensplan.com/news/2012/02/26/connecticuts-larson-praises-att/.

150. "Monthly Natural Gas Gross Production Report," US Department of Energy, Energy Information Administration website, February 2012, http://www.eia.gov/oil_gas/natural_gas/data_publications/eia914/eia914.html.

151. *Drill Here, Sell There, Pay More: The Painful Price of Exporting Natural Gas,* House of Representatives' Committee on Natural Resources, 2012, http://democrats.naturalresources.house.gov/sites/democrats.naturalresources.house.gov/files/2012-03-01__RPT_NGReport.pdf.

152. *Effect of Increased Natural Gas Exports on Domestic Energy Markets,* US Department of Energy, Energy Information Administration website, January 2012, http://www.eia.gov/analysis/requests/fe/pdf/fe_lng.pdf.

153. The *New York Times* reviewed more than thirty thousand pages of documents obtained through open-records requests of state and federal agencies and by visiting

various regional offices that oversee drilling in Pennsylvania. Some of the documents were leaked by state or federal officials. See http://www.nytimes.com/interactive/2011/02/27/us/natural-gas-documents-1.html#document/p1/a9895 for the most significant documents, made available with annotations by the *Times*.

154. "Committee Democrats Release New Report Detailing Hydraulic Fracturing Products," US House of Representatives Committee on Energy and Commerce (Democrats) website, last updated April 16, 2011, accessed March 3, 2013, http://democrats.energycommerce.house.gov/index.php?q=news/committee-democrats-release-new-report-detailing-hydraulic-fracturing-products.

155. Abrahm Lustgarten, "In New Gas Wells, More Drilling Chemicals Remain Underground," *ProPublica* website, December 27, 2009, http://www.propublica.org/article/new-gas-wells-leave-more-chemicals-in-ground-hydraulic-fracturing.

156. Katie Howell, "Energy Industry Reps Greet House Fracking Probe with Shrug," *New York Times*, February 22, 2010, http://www.nytimes.com/gwire/2010/02/22/22greenwire-energy-industry-reps-greet-house-fracking-prob-63352.html.

157. Lustgarten, "In New Gas Wells."

158. For example, see latimes.image2.trb.com/lanews/media/acrobat/2004-10/14647025.pdf for a 2004 letter from an EPA employee, informing Colorado's House and Senate representatives of his doubts regarding the science behind EPA reports on fracking.

159. Lena Groeger, "Federal Rules to Disclose Fracking Chemicals Could Come with Exceptions," *ProPublica* website, February 16, 2012, http://www.propublica.org/article/federal-rules-to-disclose-fracking-chemicals-could-come-with-exceptions.

160. See note 23.

161. Mark Niquette, "Ohio Quakes Linked to Drilling-Disposal Well, Report Says," Bloomberg, March 9, 2012, http://www.bloomberg.com/news/2012-03-09/ohio-quakes-probably-caused-by-drilling-fluid-well-report-says.html.

162. "Methane vs. CO_2 Global Warming Potential," Methane and Carbon Dioxide Global Warming Potential website, April 13, 2012, accessed February 12, 2013, http://www.global-warming-forecasts.com/methane-carbon-dioxide.php.

163. Robert W. Howarth, Renee Santoro, and Anthony Ingraffea, "Methane and the Greenhouse-Gas Footprint of Natural Gas from Shale Formations—A Letter," *Climatic Change* 160 (2011): 679–90, doi: 10.1007/s10584-011-0061-5.

164. Robert W. Howarth, Renee Santoro, and Anthony Ingraffea, "Venting and Leaking of Methane from Shale Gas Development: Response to Cathles et al.," *Climatic Change* 113 (2012): 537–49, doi: 10.1007/s10584-012-0401-0.

165. Jiang Mohan et al., *Life Cycle Greenhouse Gas Emissions of Marcellus Shale Gas,* IOP Science, August 5, 2011. http://iopscience.iop.org/1748-9326/6/3/034014/pdf/1748-9326_6_3_034014.pdf.

166. Timothy J. Skone, *Life Cycle Greenhouse Gas Analysis of Natural Gas Extraction & Delivery in the United States,* National Energy Technology Laboratory, May 12, 2011, http://cce.cornell.edu/EnergyClimateChange/NaturalGasDev/Documents/PDFs/SKONE_NG_LC_GHG_Profile_Cornell_12MAY11_Final.pdf.

167. Arthur E. Berman, "US Shale Gas: A Different Perspective on Future Supply and Price," *Bulletin of the South Texas Geological Society* 52, no.6 (February 2012): 19–44.

CHAPTER 7. DEATH STARS AND DOOMSDAY MACHINES: NUCLEAR ENERGY AND SCIENCE FICTION

168. See *Small Is Beautiful* by E.F. Schumacher (London: Blond and Briggs, 1973). His seminal work on energy and agricultural practices spurred a revolution on both sides of the Atlantic. Schumacher criticized energy from nuclear power on the basis that it provided a negative energy value and left an environmental nightmare in its place. Schumacher served on the National Coal Board in the United Kingdom.

169. Obi-Wan Kenobi (Alec Guinness) speaks these lines in *Star Wars Episode IV: A New Hope* when he explains that "the Force is what gives a Jedi his power."

170. Toni Johnson, "Global Uranium Supply and Demand," Council on Foreign Relations, January 14, 2010, accessed February 15, 2012, http://www.cfr.org/energy/global-uranium-supply-demand/p14705.

171. Van Der Hoeven, *World Energy Outlook 2011.*

172. "The Dream That Failed," *Economist,* Special Report on Nuclear Energy, March 10, 2012, http://www.economist.com/node/21549098.

173. "Thinking Small: Mini Nuclear Reactors," *Economist,* December 9, 2010, http://www.economist.com/node/17647651?story_id17647651&fsrc=rss.

174. "The Dream That Failed," *Economist.*

175. Albert Einstein, personal communication to F. D. Roosevelt, August 2, 1939, http://media.nara.gov/Public_Vaults/00762_.pdf.

176. Finn Aaserud, "Niels Bohr's Mission for an 'Open World,'" in *The Global and the Local: The History of Science and the Cultural Integration of Europe,* proceedings of the 2nd International Conference of the European Society for the History of Science (Cracow, Poland, September 6–9, 2006), ed. M. Kokowski. Chapter 25, Symposium R-17, "Politically Active Scientists in the 20th Century," http://www.2iceshs.cyfronet.pl/2ICESHS_Proceedings/Chapter_25/R-17_Aaserud.pdf.

177. The treaty entered into force in March 1970, signed by the United States, the Soviet Union, and the United Kingdom. Spearheaded by the International Atomic Energy Agency (IAEA), it called for an end to proliferation as a response to the nuclear arms race of the Cold War. However, it also encouraged the advancement of nuclear research, technology, and usage for "peaceful purposes." See International Atomic Energy Agency, "Treaty on the Non-Proliferation of Nuclear Weapons," INFCIRC/140, April 22, 1970, http://www.iaea.org/Publications/Documents/Infcircs/Others/infcirc140.pdf.

178. Mohammed Haddad and Ben Piven, "Interactive: World Nuclear Club," Al Jazeera website, May 24, 2012, http://www.aljazeera.com/indepth/interactive/2012/05/201252416836407993.html.

179. "Background Notes: India," US Department of State website, last updated December 21, 2012, accessed March 15, 2012, http://www.state.gov/r/pa/ei/bgn/3454.htm.

180. "Background Notes: Pakistan," US Department of State website, last updated August 10, 2012, accessed March 15, 2012, http://www.state.gov/r/pa/ei/bgn/3453.htm.

181. "China, Pakistan, and the Bomb: The Declassified File on US Policy, 1977–1997," the National Security Archive, ed. William Burr, last updated March 5, 2004,

accessed March 15, 2012, http://www.gwu.edu/~nsarchiv/NSAEBB/NSAEBB114/ index.htm.

182. "The Development and Proliferation of Nuclear Weapons," Nobel Prize website, accessed March 15, 2012, http://www.nobelprize.org/educational/peace/nuclear_ weapons/readmore.html.

183. Randy Kreider, "Iran Officially Opens First Nuclear Power Plant," The Blotter: ABC News, September 12, 2011, http://abcnews.go.com/Blotter/ iran-officially-opens-nuclear-plant/story?id=14503010.

184. "Background Notes: North Korea," US Department of State website, last updated December 17, 2012, accessed March 15, 2012, http://www.state.gov/r/pa/ei/ bgn/2792.htm.

185. Charles Galton Darwin, *The Next Million Years* (Garden City, New York: Doubleday & Company, 1953).

186. "ORNL: The First 50 Years (1943–1993)," Oak Ridge National Laboratory Review website, accessed March 25, 2012, http://www.ornl.gov/info/ornlreview/rev25-34/ features.shtml.

187. Light water reactors and other burners like the CANada Deuterium Uranium (CANDU) reactor can also breed some plutonium, but much less, so the recovery of energy goes from the 0.7 percent of U-235 in uranium ore to a slightly higher value. These and many other types of reactors are being used today. See *Nuclear Energy Today,* Nuclear Energy Agency Organisation for Economic Co-operation and Development, 2005, http://www.oecdnea.org/pub/nuclearenergytoday/net/ nuclear_energy_today.pdf.

188. *Thorium Fuel Cycle—Potential Benefits and Challenges,* International Atomic Energy Agency, IAEA-TECDOC-1450, May 2005, http://www-pub.iaea.org/mtcd/ publications/pdf/te_1450_web.pdf.

189. See Duncan Clark, "China Enters Race to Develop Nuclear Energy from Thorium," *Guardian*, February 16, 2011, http://www.guardian.co.uk/environment/ blog/2011/feb/16/china-nuclear-thorium. The Canadians developed the CANDU heavy-water reactor with a somewhat higher breeding ration than light-water reactors (LWRs), but from a proliferation point of view it is even more questionable. The Molten-Salt Reactor Experiment (MSRE) was, in ORNL director Alvin

Weinberg's opinion, ORNL's greatest technical achievement. He called it their "dark horse." Molten-salt breeder reactors are once again on the forefront of current nuclear development, and China is leading the way.

190. John G. Fuller, "We Almost Lost Detroit," *Reader's Digest Press* (New York: Thomas Y. Crowell Company, 1975), http://wsrl.org/pdfs/detroit.pdf.

191. Chester I. Barnard et al., "The Acheson-Lilienthal Report," from *A Report on the International Control of Atomic Energy,* prepared for the Secretary of State's Committee on Atomic Energy, March 16, 1946, http://www.learnworld.com/ZNW/LWText.Acheson-Lilienthal.html#text.

192. "Additional Information Concerning Underground Nuclear Weapon Test of Reactor-Grade Plutonium: DOE Facts," US Department of Energy website, accessed March 28, 2012, http://permanent.access.gpo.gov/websites/osti.gov/www.osti.gov/html/osti/opennet/document/press/pc29.html.

193. In a fit of vainglory and retribution, the Joint Committee for Atomic Energy (JCAE) also changed the name of Oak Ridge National Laboratory to "Chet Hollifield National Laboratory," in honor of the chairman of the JCAE at the time. The name of the lab was soon reinstated due to the insistence of the overwhelming majority of the employees.

194. Vladimir Efimenko, Francis A. O'Hara, and Hans-Juergen Laue, "World Status of Fast Reactor Development," from "Advanced Nuclear Power Systems" in *IAEA Bulletin* 26, no. 4, International Atomic Energy Agency, http://www.iaea.org/Publications/Magazines/Bulletin/Bull264/26404781117.pdf.

195. David Dinsmore Comey, "The Fire at the Brown's Ferry Nuclear Power Plant," from *Not Man Apart* (California: Friends of the Earth, 1976), http://www.ccnr.org/browns_ferry.html.

196. United Nations Framework Convention on Climate Change, *Kyoto Protocol to the United Nations Framework Convention on Climate Change* (1998), accessed March 7, 2013, http://unfccc.int/resource/docs/convkp/kpeng.pdf.

197. CDM technologies are defined broadly under the Clean Development Mechanism (Article 12 of the Kyoto Protocol) as those that advance sustainable development while ultimately lowering emissions. In the article's ambiguity and the subsequent wide range of what qualifies as a CDM technology, advocates of nuclear power

have hailed it as a CDM technology because of its very minimal emissions output, despite its numerous environmental and social costs that are not present in renewable sources. See UNFCCC, *Report of the Conference of the Parties Serving as the Meeting of the Parties to the Kyoto Protocol,* 2005, http://unfccc.int/resource/docs/2005/cmp1/eng/08a01.pdf.

198. "Energy Department Takes First Step to Spur US Manufacturing of Small Modular Nuclear Reactors," US Department of Energy press release, January 20, 2012, http://www.doe.gov/articles/energy-department-takes-first-step-spur-us-manufacturing-small-modular-nuclear-reactors.

199. "Nuclear Power in Russia," World Nuclear Association website, 2011, last updated January 30, 2013, accessed December 21, 2011, http://www.world-nuclear.org/info/inf45.html.

200. A 2006 study by the United Kingdom Parliamentary Office of Science and Technology found nuclear power in the UK to have a carbon footprint of approximately $5gCO_2eq/kWh$ electricity produced. Conventional coal using combustion yielded a footprint in excess of $1,000gCO_2eq/kWh$. See Parliamentary Office of Science and Technology, "Carbon Footprint of Electricity Generation," *Postnote* no. 268 (October 2006), http://www.parliament.uk/documents/post/postpn268.pdf.

PART III: THE NEW BUSINESS CASE

CHAPTER 8. FISHING AT A NUCLEAR POWER PLANT: CREATING A SUSTAINABILITY MODEL

201. Owned by Constellation Energy, the Calvert Cliffs Nuclear Power Plant in Lusby, Maryland, produces 850 megawatts of power and is a popular site for anglers due to the offtake of warm water from its cooling operations.

202. For more information about the Chesapeake Bay Foundation's mission and vision, see http://www.cbf.org/about-cbf/our-mission.

203. "Reducing Nitrogen Pollution," Chesapeake Bay Program website, accessed November 2, 2012, http://www.chesapeakebay.net/indicators/indicator/reducing_nitrogen_pollution.

204. "Video from the Executive Council Meeting," Chesapeake Bay Program website, November 4, 2008, accessed April 7, 2012, http://www.chesapeakebay.net/blog/2008/11.

205. Nancy Stoner, *Testimony of Nancy Stoner, Acting Assistant Administrator,* US Environmental Protection Agency website, December 14, 2011, http://www.epa.gov/ocir/hearings/testimony/112_2011_2012/stoner_121411.pdf.

206. "The Economic Argument for Cleaning Up the Chesapeake Bay and Its Rivers," Chesapeake Bay Foundation website, May 2012, http://www.cbf.org/economicreport.

207. Garrett Hardin, "The Tragedy of the Commons," *Science* 162, no. 3859 (1968): 1243–48.

208. Schumacher, *Small Is Beautiful.*

209. Paul Hawken, Amory B. Lovins, and L. Hunter Lovins, *Natural Capitalism: Creating the Next Industrial Revolution* (Boston: Little, Brown and Company, 2000).

210. "Chesapeake Bay Foundation," Chesapeake Bay Foundation website, accessed February 24, 2012, http://www.cbf.org/page.aspx?pid=433.

CHAPTER 9. BUILDING A BONFIRE:
A PATH TO SUSTAINABILITY

211. For more information about Bhutan's gross national happiness index, see http://www.grossnationalhappiness.com/.

212. C. W. Clark, *Mathematical Bioeconomics: The Optimal Management of Renewable Resources,* 2nd ed. (New York: John Wiley and Sons, 1990).

CHAPTER 10. COMPETING WITH EXXON: DEFINING OUR METHODOLOGY

213. AgSTAR, "Renewable Portfolio Standards," AgSTAR / US Environmental Protection Agency website, September 27, 2012, accessed November 15, 2012, http://www.epa.gov/agstar/tools/funding/renewable.html.

214. Van Der Hoeven, World Energy Outlook 2012.

215. Van Der Hoeven, World Energy Outlook 2011.

216. "Atmospheric CO_2 for December 2012," CO2Now website, accessed November 15, 2012, http://co2now.org/.

217. Alok Jha, "Copenhagen Climate Summit: Five Possible Scenarios for Our Future Climate," *Guardian*, December 18, 2009, http://www.guardian.co.uk/environment/2009/dec/18/copenhagen-five-climate-scenarios.

218. Van Der Hoeven, *World Energy Outlook 2011*.

CHAPTER 11. PULLING US OUT OF THE QUAGMIRE: THE NEW BUSINESS MODEL

219. International Monetary Fund, *World Economic Outlook Report,* January 23, 2013, http://www.imf.org/external/pubs/ft/weo/2012/02/weodata/index.aspx or http://www.imf.org/external/pubs/ft/weo/2013/update/01/pdf/0113.pdf.

220. "Total Midyear World Population, 1950–2050," Negative Population Growth website, accessed November 15, 2012, http://www.npg.org/facts/world_pop_year.htm.

CHAPTER 12. COMING OF AGE: RENEWABLE ENERGY

221. David Biello, "Where Did the Carter White House's Solar Panels Go?" *Scientific American,* August 6, 2010, http://www.scientificamerican.com/article.cfm?id=carter-white-house-solar-panel-array.

222. "Electricity Explained: Electricity in the United States," US Department of Energy, Energy Information Administration website, last updated February 7, 2013, accessed March 21, 2003, http://www.eia.gov/energyexplained/index.cfm?page=electricity_in_the_united_states.

223. *Annual Energy Outlook 2012: Early Release Overview*, US Department of Energy, Energy Information Administration, 2012, http://www.eia.gov/todayinenergy/detail.cfm?id=4671.

224. Nina Chestney, "Renewable Energy Deals Hit Record High in 2011: Report," Reuters US edition, January 29, 2012, http://www.reuters.com/article/2012/01/30/us-renewables-deals-idUSTRE80T00F20120130.

225. Ibid.

226. "Claus Stampe, chief investment officer of PensionDanmark, says green energy infrastructure is becoming an attractive asset in an era of low fixed income returns and volatile equity markets." See Andrew Ward, "Danish Pensions Invest in Giant Offshore Wind Farm," *Financial Times*, April 3, 2011, http://www.ft.com/intl/cms/s/0/7740d04c-5c9c-11e0-ab7c-00144feab49a.html#axzz2LYznGQoo.

227. Steven Skye, "19th Century Energy Challenges," the Neversink Valley Museum of History and Innovation website, 2005, accessed February 21, 2012, http://www.neversinkmuseum.org/19th%20century%t20energy%20final.html.

228. *Renewables Electricity Futures Study*, volume 2, National Renewable Energy Laboratory, Golden, Colorado, 2013.

229. "A History of Geothermal Energy in the United States," Geothermal Technologies Office, US Department of Energy, February 2, 2011, http://www1.eere.energy.gov/geothermal/history.html.

230. Michael Kanellos, "Will We Strike Gold in Geothermal?" Greentech Media website, June 10, 2011, http://www.greentechmedia.com/articles/read/will-we-strike-gold-in-geothermal/.

231. "Impact on Iceland," Orka Energy website, February 21, 2013, http://www.orkaenergy.com/geothermal-energy/impact-on-iceland/.

232. National Renewable Energy Laboratory, *2009 Renewable Energy Data Book*, US Department of Energy, 2010, http://www.nrel.gov/docs/fy10osti/48178.pdf.

233. James W. Hendley II, *Assessment of Moderate- and High-Temperature Geothermal Resources of the United States*, US Geological Service, 2008, http://pubs.usgs.gov/fs/2008/3082/pdf/fs2008-3082.pdf.

234. *US Solar Market Insight Report*, December 11, 2012, http://www.slideshare.net/

SEIA/us-solar-market-insight-report-q1-2012. The capacity factor of PV systems is typically about 20 percent.

CHAPTER 13. WHAT IF GOD MAKES ENERGY FREE? DEMAND-SIDE EFFICIENCY

235. *State of the World 2011: Innovations that Nourish the Planet,* World Watch Institute, 2011, http://www.worldwatch.org/node/810#4.

236. David B. Goldstein, Sierra Martinez, and Robin Roy, "Are There Rebound Effects from Energy Efficiency? An Analysis of Empirical Data, Internal Consistency, and Solutions," *Electricity Policy* website, 2011, http://www.electricitypolicy.com/Rebound-5-4-2011-final2.pdf.

237. Robert Allen, *The British Industrial Revolution in Global Perspective* (Cambridge: Cambridge University Press, 2009).

238. "Zero Waste," Yampa Valley Sustainability Council website, accessed February 4, 2012, http://www.yvsc.org/programs-projects/zerowaste/.

239. Reynolds Wolf, "Turning Leftovers into Soil," CNN, February 12, 2012, http://www.cnn.com/video/standard.html#/video/us/2012/02/13/eco-wolf-zero-waste.cnn.

240. R. W. Beck, Sally Brown, and Matthew Cotton, *Life Cycle Assessment and Economic Analysis of Organic Waste Management and Greenhouse Gas Reduction Options,* RTI International, June 2009, http://www.calrecycle.ca.gov/climate/Organics/LifeCycle/Reports/June2009/Report.pdf.

241. *Renewables Electricity Futures Study,* volumes 1–4, National Renewable Energy Laboratory, Golden, Colorado, 2012, http://www.nrel.gov/analysis/re_futures/.

242. H. Geller, J. DeCicco, and J. A. Laitner, *Energy Efficiency and Job Creation,* ACEEE Research Report ED922, 1992, http://aceee.org/research-report/ed922.

CHAPTER 14. A TALE OF TWO CITIES: SUPPLY-SIDE EFFICIENCY

243. Lovins, *Reinventing Fire.* According to Lovins, this is the "RMI analysis of the estimated undiscounted capital investment in the US electricity system during 2010–2050 in the *Maintain* case."

244. "Coal-Fired Power Plants (CFPPs): Supercritical and Ultra Supercritical Boilers," National Energy Technology Laboratory (NETL), accessed April 2, 2013, http://www.netl.doe.gov/technologies/coalpower/cfpp/technologies/supercritical_utltr_boilers.html.

245. Simon Denyer and Rama Lakshmi, "India Blackout, on Second Day, Leaves 600 Million Without Power," *Washington Post,* August 1, 2012, http://www.washingtonpost.com/world/asia_pacific/huge-blackout-fuels-doubts-about-indias-economic-ambitions/2012/08/01/gJQA7j1LMX_story.html.

246. *The Economic Impacts of the August 2003 Blackout,* Electricity Consumers Resource Council (ELCON), February 9, 2004, accessed February 15, 2013, http://www.elcon.org/Documents/EconomicImpactsOfAugust2003Blackout.pdf.

247. "27 Gigawatts of Coal-Fired Capacity to Retire over Next Five Years," US Energy Information Administration, July 27, 2012, accessed April 4, 2013, http://www.eia.gov/todayinenergy/detail.cfm?id=7290.

248. Dan Eggers and Jon Wolff, "Growth from Subtraction: Impact of EPA Rules on Power Markets," Credit Suisse website, September 30, 2010, accessed February 15, 2013, http://macarthurenergy.com/yahoo_site_admin/assets/docs/Credit_Suisse_-_Coal_Plant_Closures_From_Regulation.320125508.pdf.

249. Economic Development Research Group, *Failure to Act: The Economic Impact of Current Investment Trends in Electricity Infrastructure* (Reston, Virginia: American Society of Civil Engineers, 2011).

250. Andy Bae, "China's Smart Grid Spearhead," Pike Research website, April 26, 2012, accessed February 15, 2013, http://www.pikeresearch.com/blog/china%E2%80%99s-smart-grid-spearhead.

251. Elisabeth Rosenthal, "Portugal Gives Itself a Clean-Energy Makeover," *New York Times,* August 9, 2010.

252. Peter Asmus, "Denmark Aims for 100 Percent Renewables by 2050," Pike Research, April 3, 2012, accessed February 15, 2013, http://www.pikeresearch.com/blog/denmark-aims-for-100-renewables-by-2050.

253. Wan Xu and David Stanway, "China's Carbon Intensity Falls Over 3.5 Percent in 2012: Official," Thomson Reuters, January 10, 2013,

accessed April 2, 2013, http://www.reuters.com/article/2013/01/10/
us-china-carbon-intensity-idUSBRE909OI220130110.

254. "Coal-Fired Power Plants (CFPPs): Supercritical and Ultra Supercritical Boilers,"
NETL website.

255. The primary differences between the three types of pulverized coal boilers are the operating temperatures and pressures. Subcritical plants operate below the critical point of
water (647.096 K and 22.064 MPa). Supercritical and ultra-supercritical plants operate
above the critical point. As the pressures and temperatures increase, so does the operating efficiency. Subcritical plants operate at about 37 percent, supercriticals are at about
40 percent, and ultra-supercriticals are in the 42-to-45-percent range.

An integrated gasification combined cycle (IGCC) is a technology that
turns coal into gas—synthesis gas (syngas). It then removes impurities from the
coal gas before it is combusted and attempts to turn any pollutants into reusable
by-products. This results in lower emissions of sulfur dioxide, particulates, and mercury. Excess heat from the primary combustion and generation is then passed to
a steam cycle, similar to a combined cycle gas turbine. This also results in improved
efficiency compared to the process used with conventional pulverized coal.

256. US Department of Energy / National Energy Technology Laboratory, *Reducing CO₂
Emissions by Improving the Efficiency of the Existing Coal-Fired Power Plant Fleet*,
DOE/NETL-2008/1329, July 23, 2008, http://www.netl.doe.gov/energy-analyses/
pubs/CFPP%20Efficiency-FINAL.pdf.

257. Keith Burnard and Sankar Bhattacarya, *Power Generation from Coal: Ongoing
Developments and Outlook*, IEA, 2011, http://www.iea.org/papers/2011/power_
generation_from_coal.pdf.

258. "27 Gigawatts of Coal-Fired Capacity to Retire over Next Five Years," US Department of Energy, Energy Information Administration website, July 27, 2012,
accessed August 22, 2012, http://www.eia.gov/todayinenergy/detail.cfm?id=7290.

259. Jason Morgan, "Operating Costs of a Nuclear Power Plant," *Nuclear Fissionary*
website, March 15, 2010, accessed November 9, 2012, http://nuclearfissionary.
com/2010/03/15/operating-costs-of-a-nuclear-power-plant/.

260. There are, of course, many issues that would need to be addressed, such as how to
manage the fund to ensure the necessary liquidity, and whether there should be

differences in the premium based on reactor type and operational record. The objective here is simply to put the idea on the table.

261. *Technology Action Plan: High-Efficiency, Low-Emissions Coal,* report to the Major Economies Forum on Energy and Climate, prepared by India and Japan in consultation with MEF Partners, Eldis website, December 2009, http://moef.nic.in/ downloads/public-information/mef%20helec%20tap%2014dec2009.pdf.

PART IV: RECOMMENDATIONS
CHAPTER 15. CROSSING THE ROAD: CREATING A SUSTAINABLE FUTURE

262. William R. Anderegg et al., *Expert Credibility in Climate Change,* PNAS website, December 22, 2009, accessed February 25, 2013, http://www.pnas.org/ content/107/27/12107.full.

263. Evo Morales, "Combating Climate Change—Lessons from the World's Indigenous Peoples," *Los Angeles Times,* April 23, 2010, http://articles.latimes.com/2010/ apr/23/opinion/la-oew-0423-morales-20100423.

264. My personal experience in Bolivia stems from Econergy's controlling ownership in a 147-megawatt hydro facility there, back in 2007 and 2008.

265. "Climate Change: Adaptation Critical as Global Warming Accelerates," from "Ten Stories the World Should Hear More About" series, United Nations website, 2008, accessed September 2, 2012, http://www.un.org/en/events/tenstories/08/ climatechange.shtml.

266. Linda Hutchinson-Jafar, "Small Island States Seek to End Dependence on Imported Oil," AlertNet website, May 28, 2012, accessed September 2, 2012, http://www.trust.org/alertnet/news/small-island-states-seek-to-end-dependence-on-imported-oil.

267. Partnership for Sustainable Development, *100% Renewable Energy Islands,* Global Energy Network Institute website, April 15, 2004, accessed September 2, 2012, http://www.geni.org/globalenergy/library/articles-renewable-energy-transmission/ small-island-nations.shtml.

268. Matthew Carr and Catherine Airlie, "Fourteen Programs Show CO_2 Trade Taking Off: World Bank," Bloomberg website, June 1, 2012, http://www.bloomberg.com/news/2012-06-01/fourteen-programs-show-co2-trade-taking-off-world-bank.html.

269. Marianne Hedin, "US Bucks the Tide on Carbon Taxes," Navigant Research, October 31, 2012, accessed November 13, 2012, http://www.navigantresearch.com/blog/u-s-bucks-the-tide-on-carbon-taxes.

270. In principle, it is possible for governments to sell the original allowances with the market, then trade some of the allowances at a premium to this baseline price. Revenue from the sale of the original allowances is virtually indistinguishable from a carbon tax, and the impacts on the market actors are nearly identical. The possibility of selling the original allowances was considered for the European Trading System (ETS), but was discarded. To my knowledge, there is no case in which the original allowances of a cap and trade mechanism were sold.

271. The World Trade Organization and the United Nations Environment Programme, *Trade and Climate Change,* 2009, WTO website, http://www.wto.org/english/res_e/booksp_e/trade_climate_change_e.pdf.

272. For a more detailed discussion of the deficiencies of the Kyoto Protocol and its underlying premises, and for the reasons for the two main proposals here—concentrating on negotiating actions (not targets) and on mobilizing via clubs—see the excellent book by David Victor, *Global Warming Gridlock,* published by Cambridge University Press in 2011.

273. Vladimir Pregelj, *Trade Agreements: Procedure for Congressional Approval and Implementation,* Congressional Research Service, Library of Congress, 2005, http://www.policyarchive.org/handle/10207/bitstreams/1791.pdf.

CHAPTER 16. YOU ARE BORN, YOU GROW OLD, YOU DIE: FINAL REFLECTIONS AND RECOMMENDATIONS

274. Charles Darwin, *On the Origin of Species* (United Kingdom: John Murray, 1859).

275. James Lovelock, *Scientists on Gaia* (Cambridge, Massachusetts: MIT Press, 1991).

276. The Twelve Tables of ancient Rome outlined the basic rules for the city. Copies of these rules are all that exist today, but consistent through all of the variations

is Rule X, which specifies that disposal of corpses (and in some versions, rubbish) within the city was strictly forbidden and was a punishable offense. Future edicts were more specific on garbage and corpse disposal, and warnings were erected at city boundaries.

GLOSSARY

Atomic Energy Commission (AEC)—A US government agency established to foster and control the peacetime development of atomic science and technology.

balance of plant (BOP)—The supporting and/or auxiliary components (systems and structures) of a complete power plant.

barrels per day (b/d)—A measure of oil output represented by the number of barrels produced in a single day.

Btus (British thermal units)—The amount of heat required to raise the temperature of one pound of liquid water by 1 degree Fahrenheit.

business as usual—The attachment to the normal course of business with respect to the global energy supply.

calorific value (kcal/kg)—The calories or thermal units contained in a substance and released when the substance is burned.

cap and trade—A market-based approach used to control pollution by providing economic incentives for reducing emissions.

carbon capture and storage/sequestration (CCS)—The process of capturing carbon and depositing it in a location where it will not enter the atmosphere.

carbon credits—A permit that allows an organization to produce a certain level of carbon emissions that can be traded in a carbon market.

carbon footprint—The amount of carbon dioxide emitted into the atmosphere by the activities of an individual, a company, or a country.

CH_4 (methane)—A chemical compound that is the primary component of natural gas. It is a potent greenhouse gas.

clean development mechanism (CDM)—As defined in Article 12 of the Kyoto Protocol, CDM allows a country with an emission-reduction or emission-limitation commitment under the protocol (an Annex I Party) to implement an emission-reduction project in developing countries. Such projects can earn saleable certified emission reduction (CER) credits, each equivalent to one tonne of CO_2, which can be counted toward meeting Kyoto targets.

climate change—A long-term change in the earth's climate.

CO_2e (carbon dioxide equivalent)—A quantity that describes the amount of CO_2 that would have the same global warming potential when measured over a specified timescale.

combined heat and power (CHP)/cogeneration—The use of a heat engine to simultaneously generate both electricity and useful heat.

concentrated solar power (CSP)—The use of lenses or mirrors to focus a large area of sunlight onto a small area that will subsequently generate electricity.

Earth Summit—A major United Nations conference held in Rio de Janeiro from June 3 to June 14, 1992, that consisted of 255 governments and 144 heads of state.

energy return on investment (EROI)—A ratio of the amount of usable energy acquired from a particular energy resource to the amount of energy expended to obtain that energy resource.

feedback loops—In environmental terms, a circular trend that can either accelerate or decelerate something. For example, a positive feedback loop can take the form of the ocean evaporating faster, which leads to more water vapor in the atmosphere, which leads to more warming, which evaporates more water.

finite resource—A resource that is formed at a rate much, much slower than its rate of consumption, making it (for all practical purposes) nonrenewable.

fracturing (hydraulic)—The propagation of fractures in a rock layer by pressurized fluid in the attempt to free up the hydrocarbons in the rock.

global community—The people or nations of the world, considered as being closely connected by modern telecommunications.

global energy mix—The sum of all the world's power-producing objects.

global society—The broad range of institutions that operate between the private market and global governments.

global sustainability—A social agreement regarding the allocation and use of our natural reservoirs when natural resources are transferred out of nature and into public or private ownership.

global warming—The increase in the temperature of the earth's atmosphere that causes corresponding changes in climate.

greenhouse gases (GHGs)—A gas that contributes to the greenhouse effect by absorbing infrared radiation. Some of these gases occur in nature (such as water vapor, carbon dioxide, methane, and nitrous oxide), while others are exclusively human-made (such as gases used for aerosols).

GW (gigawatts)—A unit of power equal to one billion watts.

horizontal drilling—Also known as "directional drilling." The practice of drilling nonvertical wells for the purpose of greater resource accessibility and lower drilling platform costs.

integrated coal gasification combined cycle (IGCC)—A technology that turns coal and other carbon-based fuels into gas and then removes impurities before the gas is combusted.

Intergovernmental Panel on Climate Change (IPCC)—A leading international body that focuses on the assessment of climate change.

International Atomic Energy Agency (IAEA)—Established in July 1957, an international organization that seeks to promote the peaceful use of nuclear energy.

International Energy Agency (IEA)—An autonomous organization that works to ensure reliable, affordable, and clean energy for its twenty-eight member countries and beyond.

kWh (kilowatt-hour)—A unit of energy equal to the work done to power 1,000 watts operating for one hour.

Kyoto Protocol—An amendment to the United Nations international treaty on global warming in which participating nations committed to reducing their emissions of carbon dioxide.

liquefied natural gas (LNG)—Natural gas (predominately methane) that has been converted temporarily to liquid form for ease of transport.

liquid metal fast breeder reactor (LMFBR)—An advanced type of nuclear reactor in which the primary coolant is a liquid metal. The advantages include a greater degree of safety, because the reactor does not need to be kept under pressure, and a much higher power density (thanks to the use of liquid metal) than with traditional coolants.

low-carbon technologies—Emerging technologies that aim to deliver minimal or zero carbon emissions.

million barrels per day (mb/d)—The amount of oil that a country or organization is able to produce in a given day.

molten salt reactor (MSR)—A class of nuclear fission reactors in which the primary coolant is a molten salt mixture. The advantage of MSRs is that they run at higher temperatures than water-cooled reactors do and therefore allow for higher thermodynamic efficiency, while staying at low vapor pressure.

MW-miles (megawatt-miles)—The ability to transmit a megawatt of power over the distance of one mile.

National Resource Defense Counsel (NRDC)—An environmental action group of 1.3 million members and online activists working with federal and state environmental and other agencies, US Congress and state legislatures, and the courts to reduce global warming, limit pollution, promote energy efficiency, and conserve natural resources.

natural reservoirs—An aspect of the biosphere that harbors necessary ingredients for life. The atmosphere and the ocean are examples of large natural reservoirs.

negawatt—A theoretical unit of power that represents an amount of energy saved.

new business case—A commitment to creating global sustainability with regard to the management of our shared natural resources.

nuclear fission—A reaction in which a heavy nucleus splits spontaneously or on impact with another particle, releasing energy.

O_3 (ozone)—A colorless, odorless gas that comprises three oxygen atoms. It is found naturally in the earth's stratosphere, where it absorbs the ultraviolet component of incoming solar radiation that could be harmful to life on this planet.

Oak Ridge National Laboratory (ORNL)—A multiprogramming science and technology laboratory with a mission to deliver scientific discoveries and technical breakthroughs that will accelerate the development of solutions in clean energy and global security.

Organization of the Petroleum Exporting Countries (OPEC)—An international body formed in 1961 to administer common policy for the sale of petroleum by its members: Algeria, Indonesia, Iran, Iraq, Kuwait, Libya, Nigeria, Qatar, Saudi Arabia, the United Arab Emirates, and Venezuela.

overnight cost—The present value cost that would have to be paid as a lump sum up front to completely pay for a construction project.

Peak Oil—The point in time when the maximum rate of petroleum extraction is met.

photovoltaic (PV)—A device that uses solar output or electromagnetic radiation to generate power.

Potential Gas Committee (PGC)—An organization with a mission to train geoscientists and engineers for the preparation and dissemination of biennial assessments of the technically recoverable natural gas resource base of the United States.

ppm (parts per million)—A way to denote relative proportions in measured quantities. Carbon dioxide in the atmosphere is commonly referred to by its concentration in proportion to other molecules.

Project Butterfly methodology—An analysis that breaks down the unique interests of each stakeholder in a transparent way and then searches for solutions that align each interest.

Reducing Emissions from Deforestation and Forest Degradation (REDD)—A set of steps designed to use market and financial incentives in order to reduce the emissions of greenhouse gases from deforestation and forest degradation.

renewable electricity credits (RECs)—A representation of the property rights to the environmental, social, and other nonpower qualities of renewable electricity generation. Can be sold separately from the underlying physical electricity associated with a renewable-based generation source.

renewable energy—Energy that comes from natural resources such as sunlight, wind, rain, tides, biomass, and geothermal heat.

renewable portfolio standard (RPS)—A state regulation that requires the increased production of energy by electricity suppliers from renewable energy sources.

renewable resource—A source of energy that can be replenished naturally with the reasonable passage of time.

system dynamics—An approach to understanding the behavior of complex systems over time. It deals with internal feedback loops and time delays.

take-or-pay provisions—A method of ensuring that a transaction occurs, by obligating one party to either take delivery of goods or pay a specified amount.

Tennessee Valley Authority (TVA)—A corporation owned by the US government that provides electricity for nine million people in parts of several southeastern states.

total maximum daily load (TMDL)—A regulatory term in the US Clean Water Act, describing a value of the maximum amount of a pollutant that a body of water can receive while still meeting water quality standards.

TWh (terawatt-hour)—A unit of electrical energy equal to that achieved by 1 terawatt acting for one hour.

unconventional energy—A source of energy that is presently (or within the recent past) not utilized on a large scale but is a promising source of energy in the future. Examples include shale gas/oil, tidal energy, and geothermal energy.

United Nations (UN)—An international organization of countries whose goal is to promote international peace, set up in 1945 as a successor to the League of Nations.

UN Framework Convention on Climate Change (UNFCCC)—An international environmental treaty negotiated at the United Nations Conference on Environment and Development. The objective is to promote the "stabilization of greenhouse gas concentrations in the atmosphere at a level that would prevent dangerous anthropogenic interference with the climate systems."

US Global Change Research Program (USGCRP)—An interagency group tasked with coordinating and integrating federal research on changes in the global environment.

World Trade Organization (WTO)—A rules-based, member-driven organization whose member governments make all decisions and whose rules are the outcome of negotiations among members.

Wp (peak Watt)—A measure of the nominal power of a photovoltaic solar energy device under laboratory illumination conditions.

ABOUT THE AUTHOR

 Tom Stoner is a veteran energy entrepreneur whose interest in energy and sustainability began while he was a student at Hampshire College in Amherst, Massachusetts, and continued through his graduate studies at the London School of Economics. Upon graduating from LSE, rather than getting a conventional job in the aftermath of the 1987 stock market crash, Mr. Stoner joined a handful of entrepreneurs and business visionaries to found the Social Venture Network. He served as its first acting director and later as a member of the board of directors. In the 1990s he built the first independent national energy services company, garnering venture capital to finance energy efficiency upgrades for large energy users coast to coast and then successfully selling the company to a publicly traded utility holding company in 1997.

Following the signing of the Kyoto Protocol that same year, Mr. Stoner became the CEO of a second energy company, which in 2006 was one of world's largest independent developers of carbon credits under the Kyoto Protocol. He took the company public on the London Stock Exchange's Alternative Investment Market in 2006. After selling his company to GDF

Suez in 2008, Mr. Stoner then tried to navigate the waters of the "clean coal" industry by joining a NYSE-traded company as its new CEO.

After more than twenty-five years of experience in the alternative energy industries, Mr. Stoner felt it was time to speak out about mitigating climate change, by creating Project Butterfly and writing *Small Change, Big Gains: Reflections of an Energy Entrepreneur.*